Seishun Academy
Tennis Festival '03

About Takeshi Konomi

Takeshi Konomi exploded onto the manga scene with the incredible **THE PRINCE OF TENNIS**. His refined art style and sleek character designs proved popular with **Weekly Shonen Jump** readers, and **THE PRINCE OF TENNIS** became the number one sports manga in Japan almost overnight. Its cast of fascinating male tennis players attracted legions of female readers even though it was originally intended to be a boys' comic. The manga continues to be a success in Japan and has inspired a hit anime series, as well as several video games and mountains of merchandise.

**THE PRINCE OF TENNIS
VOL. 19
The SHONEN JUMP Manga Edition**

**STORY AND ART BY
TAKESHI KONOMI**

Translation/Joe Yamazaki
Consultant/Michelle Pangilinan
Touch-up Art & Lettering/Vanessa Satone
Design/Sam Elzway
Editor/Joel Enos

Editor in Chief, Books/Alvin Lu
Editor in Chief, Magazines/Marc Weidenbaum
VP of Publishing Licensing/Rika Inouye
VP of Sales/Gonzalo Ferreyra
Sr. VP of Marketing/Liza Coppola
Publisher/Hyoe Narita

Printed in the U.S.A.

Published by VIZ Media, LLC
P.O. Box 77010
San Francisco, CA 94107

SHONEN JUMP Manga Edition
10 9 8 7 6 5 4 3 2
First printing, May 2007
Second printing, July 2007

www.viz.com

PARENTAL ADVISORY
THE PRINCE OF TENNIS
is rated A and is suitable
for readers of all ages.
ratings.viz.com

THE WORLD'S
MOST POPULAR MANGA

www.shonenjump.com

SHONEN JUMP Manga

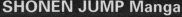

VOL. 19

Tezuka's Departure

Story & Art by

Takeshi Konomi

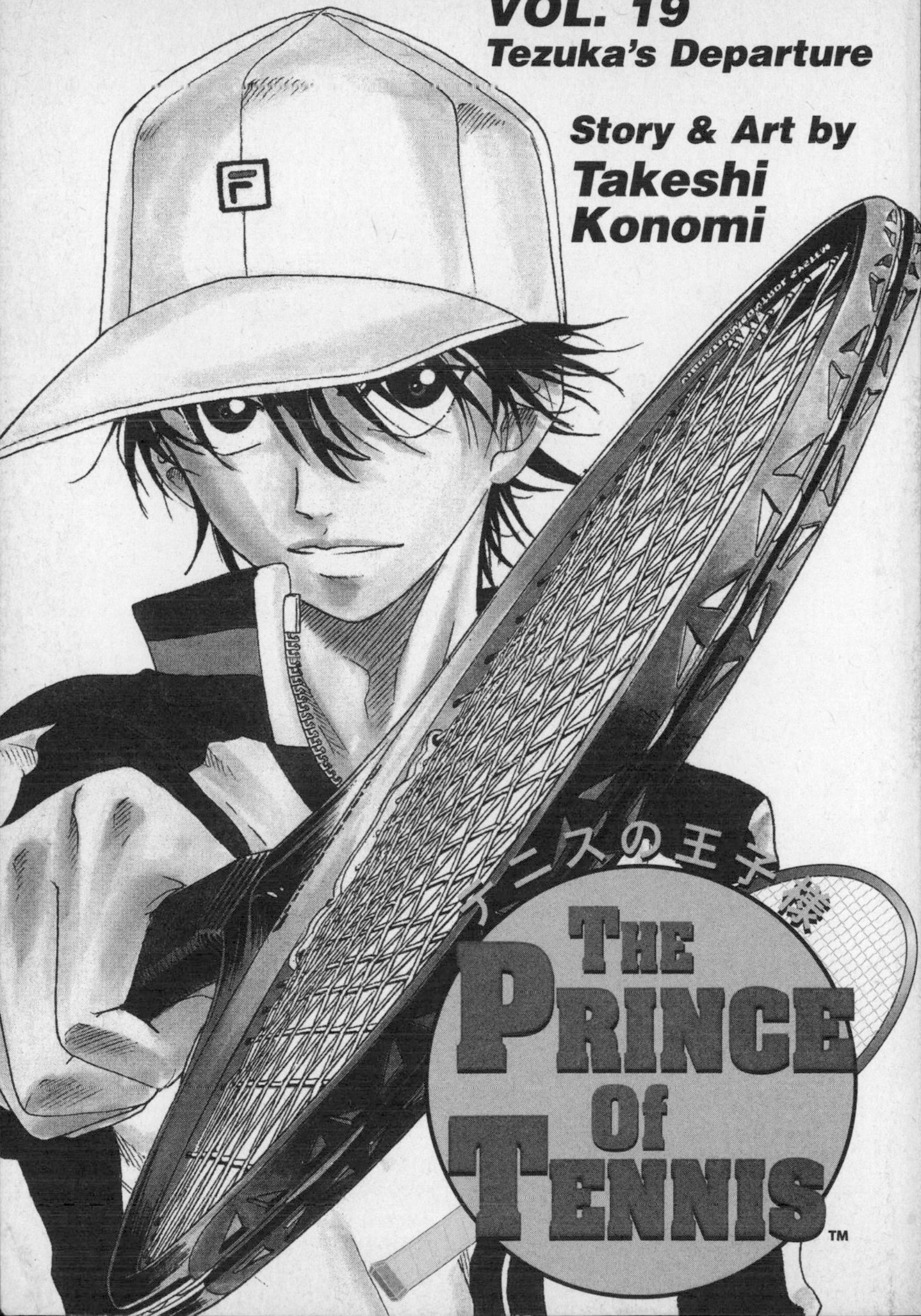
テニスの王子様
THE PRINCE OF TENNIS™

ENNIS CLUB

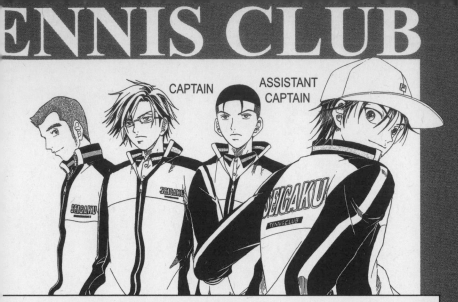

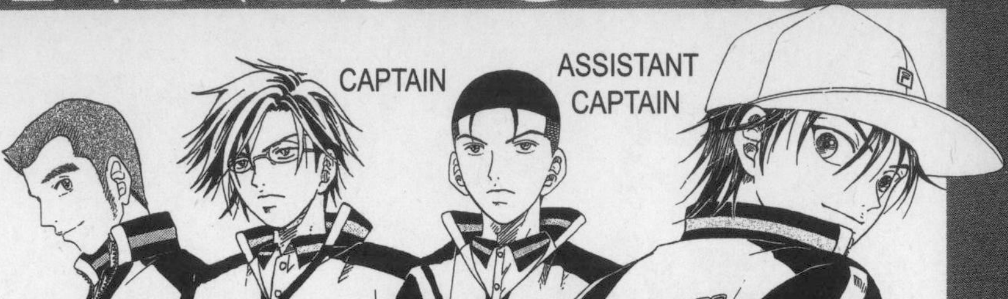
CAPTAIN
ASSISTANT CAPTAIN
SEIGAKU
SEIGAKU
SEIGAKU
SEIGAKU
TENNIS CLUB

• TAKASHI KAWAMURA • KUNIMITSU TEZUKA • SHUICHIRO OISHI • RYOMA ECHIZEN •

STORY &

Seishun Academy student Ryoma Echizen is a tennis prodigy, with wins in four consecutive U.S. Junior tournaments under his belt. Then he became a starter as a 7th grader and led his team to the District Preliminaries! Despite a few mishaps, Seishun won the District Prelims and City Tournament, and even earned a ticket to the Kanto Tournament.

Now, the Kanto Tournament is underway. Seishun's first round opponent is last year's Nationals runner-up — Hyotei Academy! Neither forges a victory even after five matches, so a sixth match between two reserve players is set!

Seishun fields Ryoma, while Hyotei sends Wakashi Hiyoshi, rumored to be the next Hyotei team captain. In the end, Ryoma prevails in the battle between the next-generation players! Ryoma defeats Wakashi in an overwhelmingly tense match, and Seishun advances to the second round!

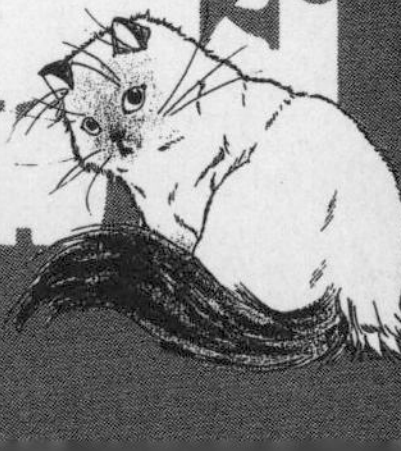

HARACTERS

SEIGAKU T

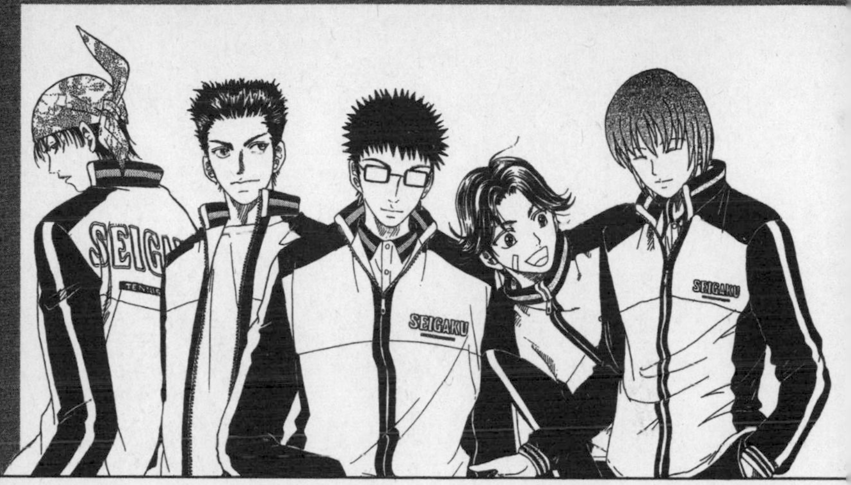

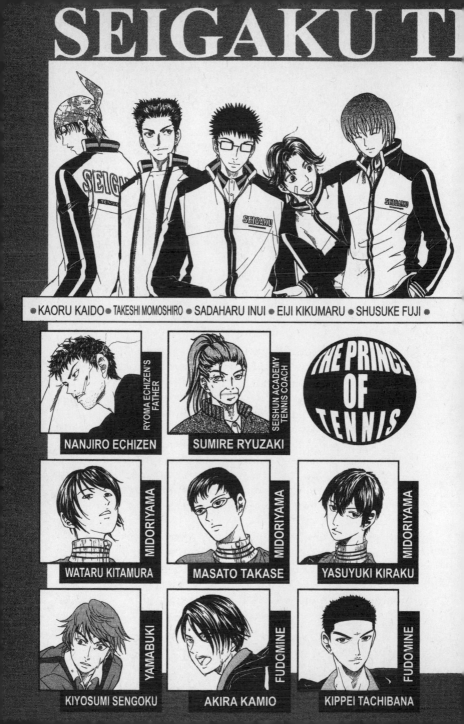

• KAORU KAIDO • TAKESHI MOMOSHIRO • SADAHARU INUI • EIJI KIKUMARU • SHUSUKE FUJI •

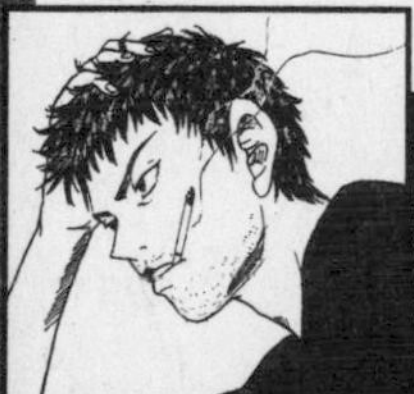

RYOMA ECHIZEN'S FATHER
NANJIRO ECHIZEN

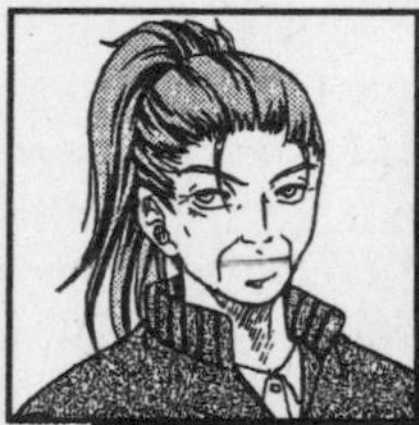

SEISHUN ACADEMY TENNIS COACH
SUMIRE RYUZAKI

THE PRINCE OF TENNIS

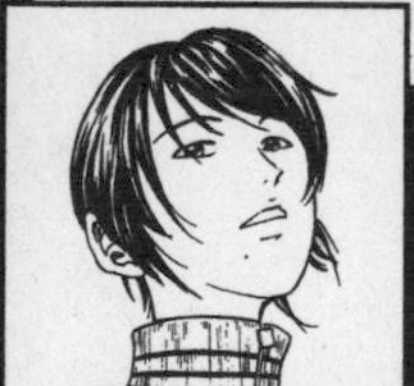

MIDORIYAMA
WATARU KITAMURA

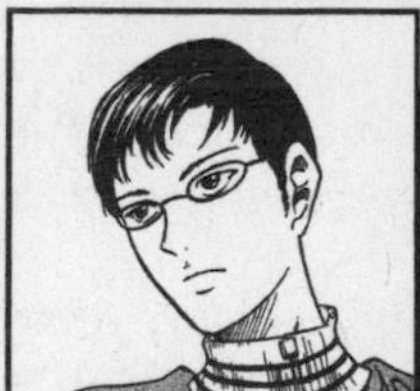

MIDORIYAMA
MASATO TAKASE

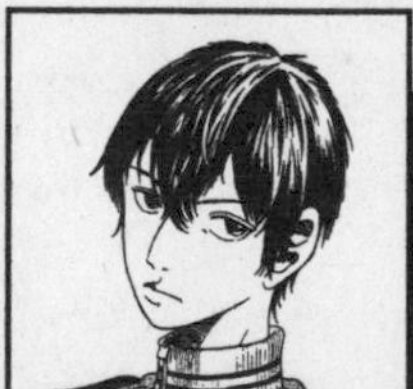

MIDORIYAMA
YASUYUKI KIRAKU

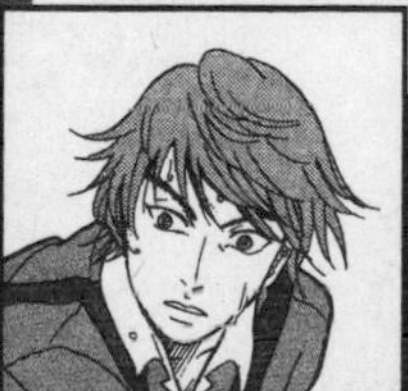

YAMABUKI
KIYOSUMI SENGOKU

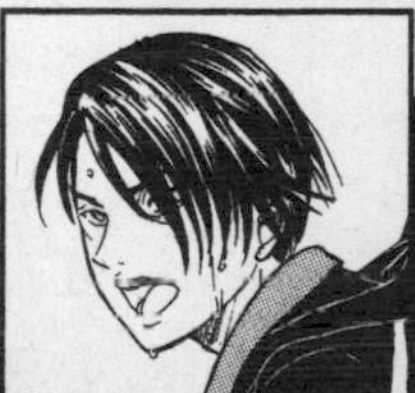

FUDOMINE
AKIRA KAMIO

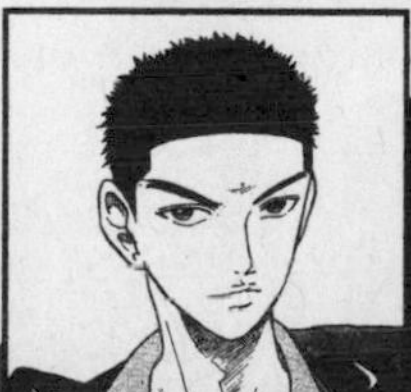

FUDOMINE
KIPPEI TACHIBANA

CONTENTS

Vol.19
Tezuka's Departure

Genius 159: The Prince of Bowling		7
Genius 160: Tezuka's Departure		27
Genius 161: Oishi's New Regime		47
Genius 162: Saitama Midoriyama's Ability		65
Genius 163: Tenacity		85
Genius 164: Everybody's Battles		105
Genius 165: Just a Kid		127
Genius 166: Feel the Rhythm…		147
Genius 167: Sengoku vs. Kamio		166

GENIUS 159: THE PRINCE OF BOWLING

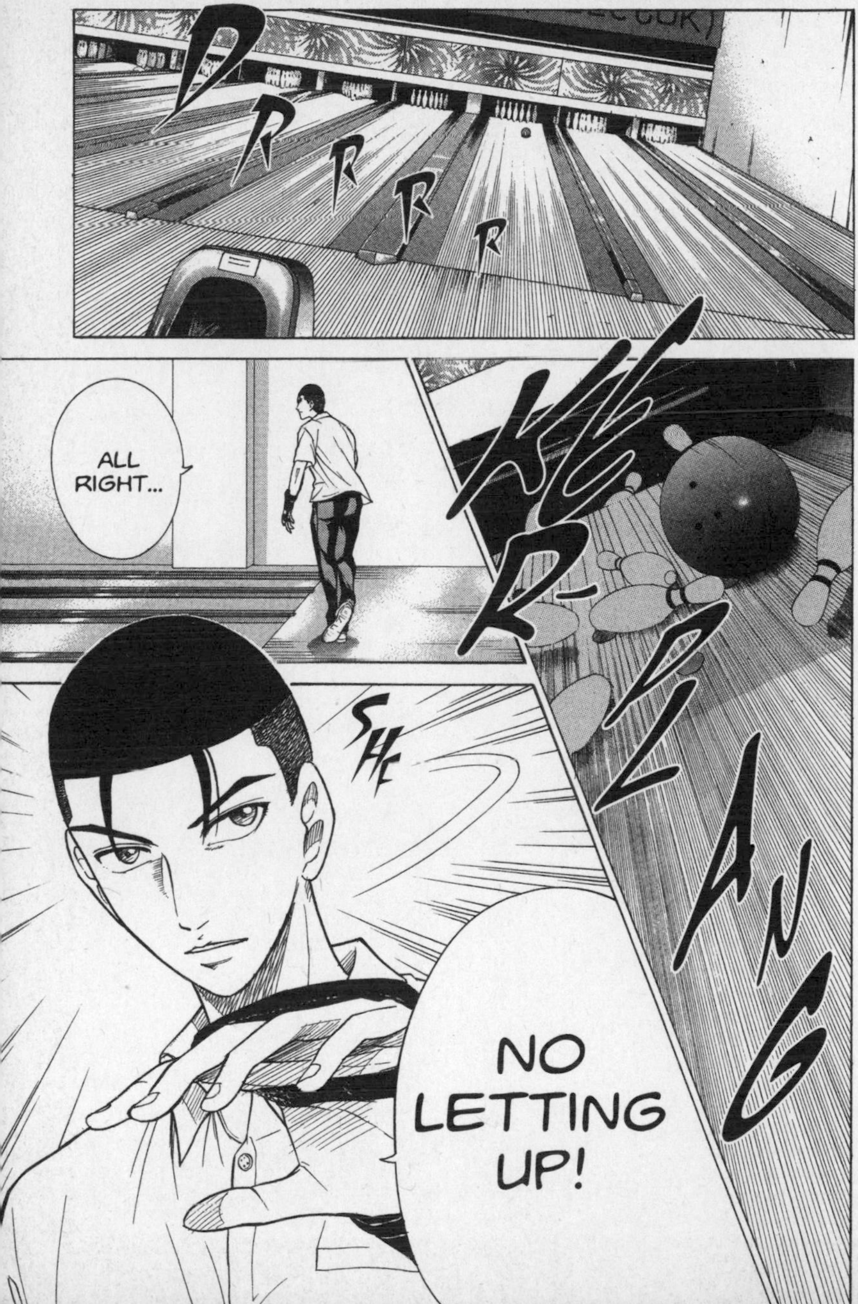
DRRRRR
ALL RIGHT...
NO LETTING UP!

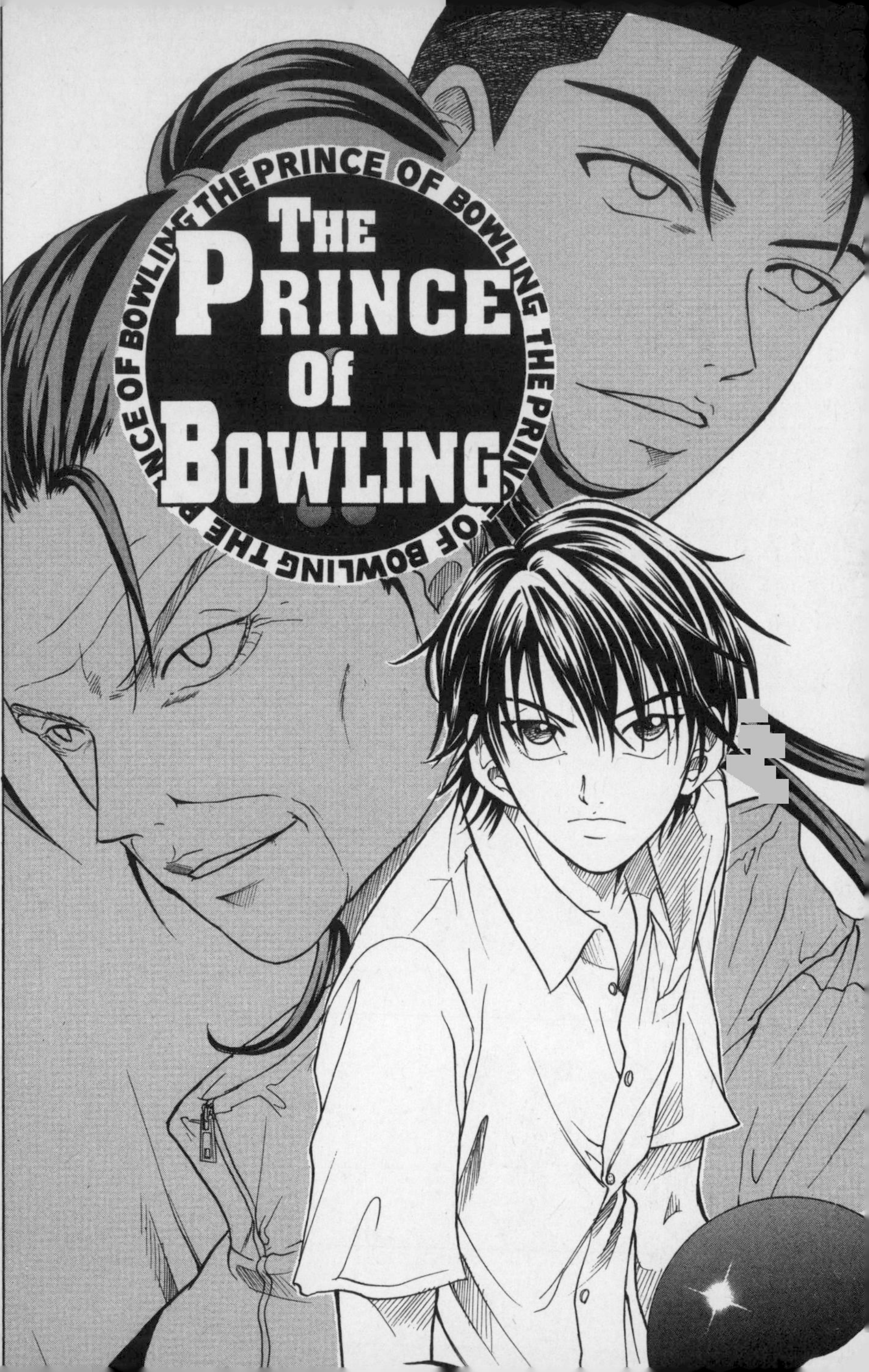
THE PRINCE OF BOWLING THE PRINCE OF BOWLING THE PRINCE OF BOWLING THE PRINCE OF BOWLING
THE PRINCE OF BOWLING

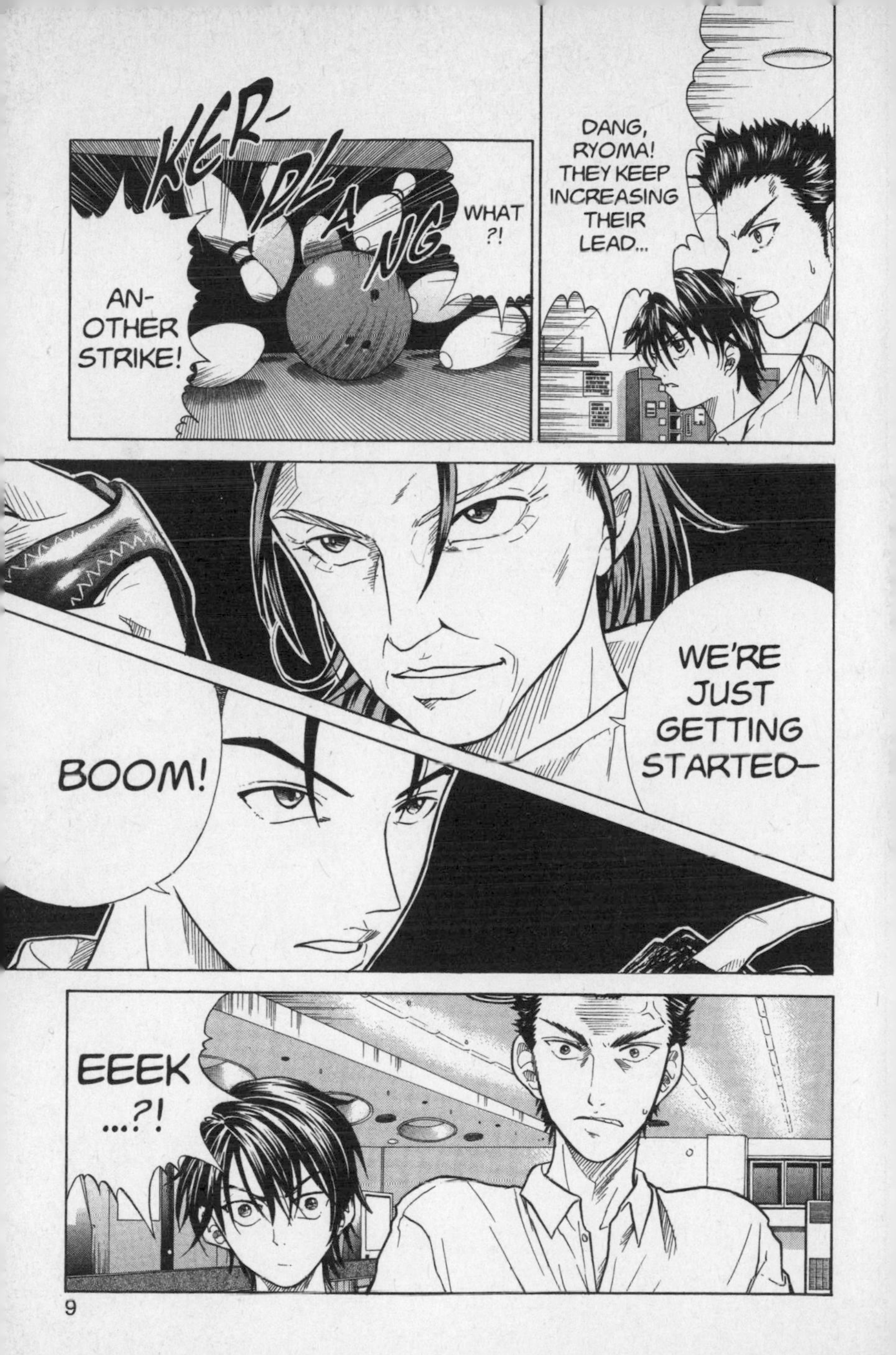
DANG, RYOMA! THEY KEEP INCREASING THEIR LEAD...
WHAT ?!
KER-PLANG
AN-OTHER STRIKE!
WE'RE JUST GETTING STARTED—
BOOM!
EEEK ...?!

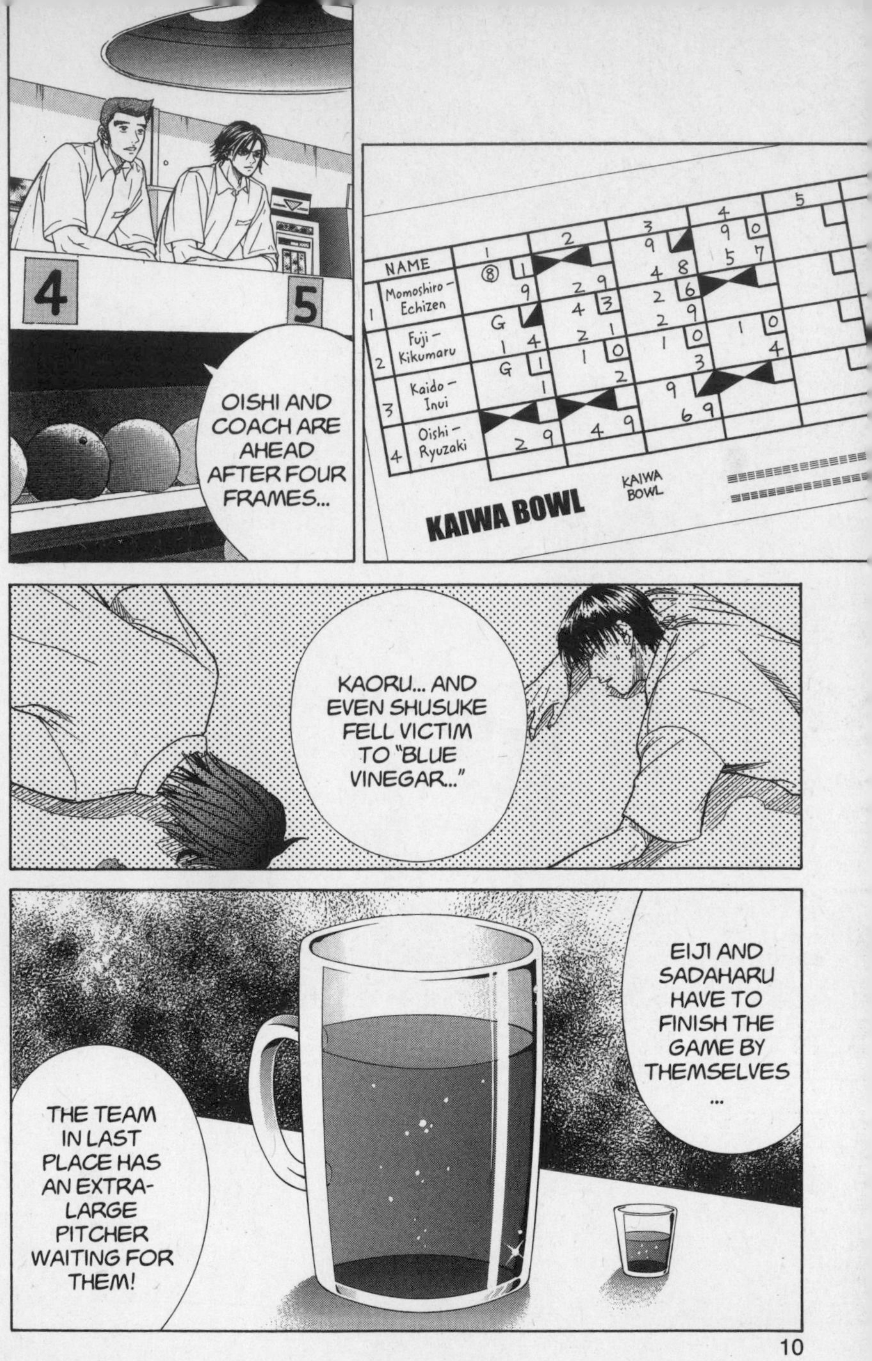
NAME
Momoshiro-Echizen
Fuji-Kikumaru
Kaido-Inui
Oishi-Ryuzaki
KAIWA BOWL
KAIWA BOWL
OISHI AND COACH ARE AHEAD AFTER FOUR FRAMES...
KAORU... AND EVEN SHUSUKE FELL VICTIM TO "BLUE VINEGAR..."
EIJI AND SADAHARU HAVE TO FINISH THE GAME BY THEMSELVES...
THE TEAM IN LAST PLACE HAS AN EXTRA-LARGE PITCHER WAITING FOR THEM!

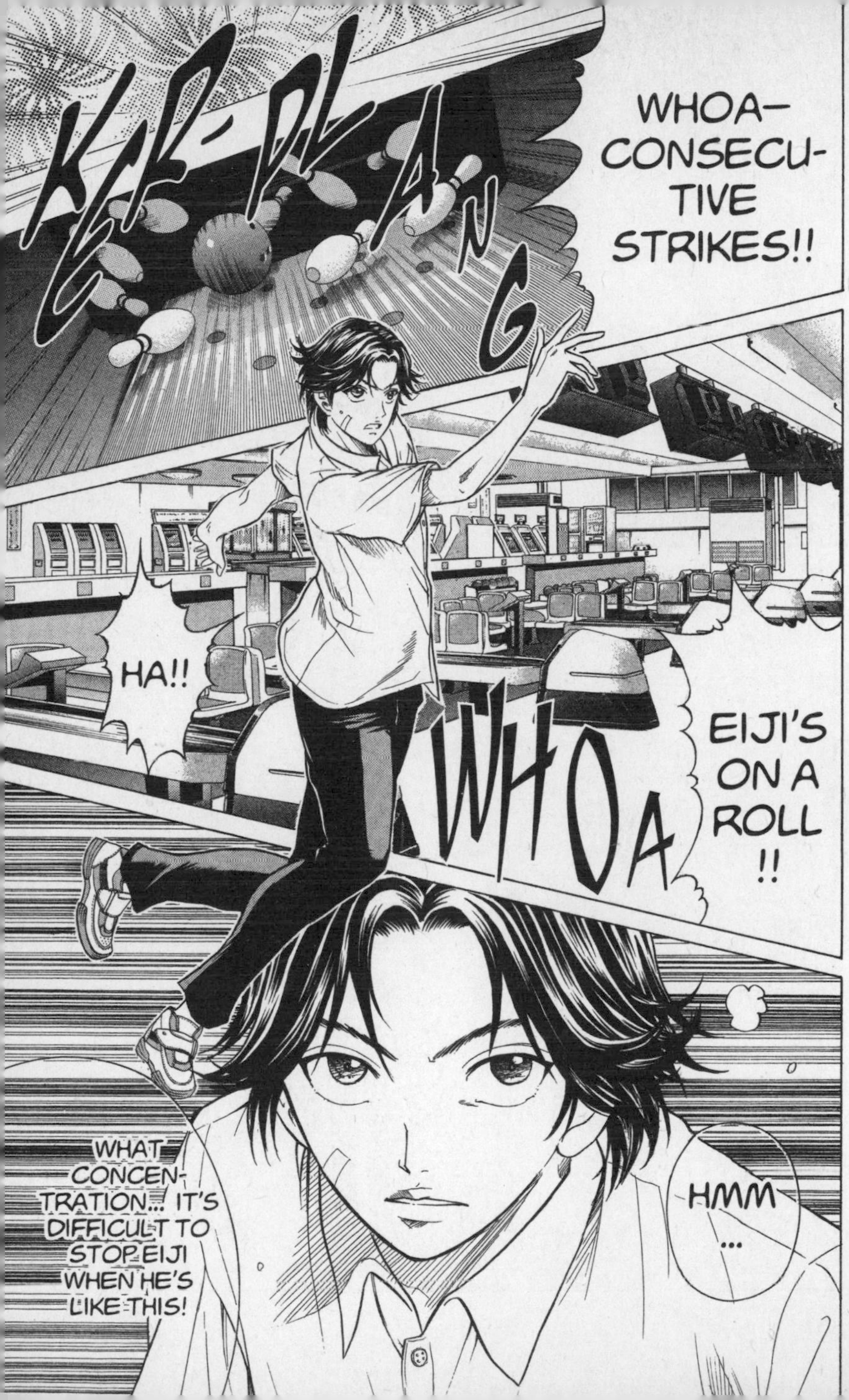
KER-PLANG
WHOA—CONSECUTIVE STRIKES!!
EIJI'S ON A ROLL!!
WHOA
HA!!
HMM...
WHAT CONCENTRATION... IT'S DIFFICULT TO STOP EIJI WHEN HE'S LIKE THIS!

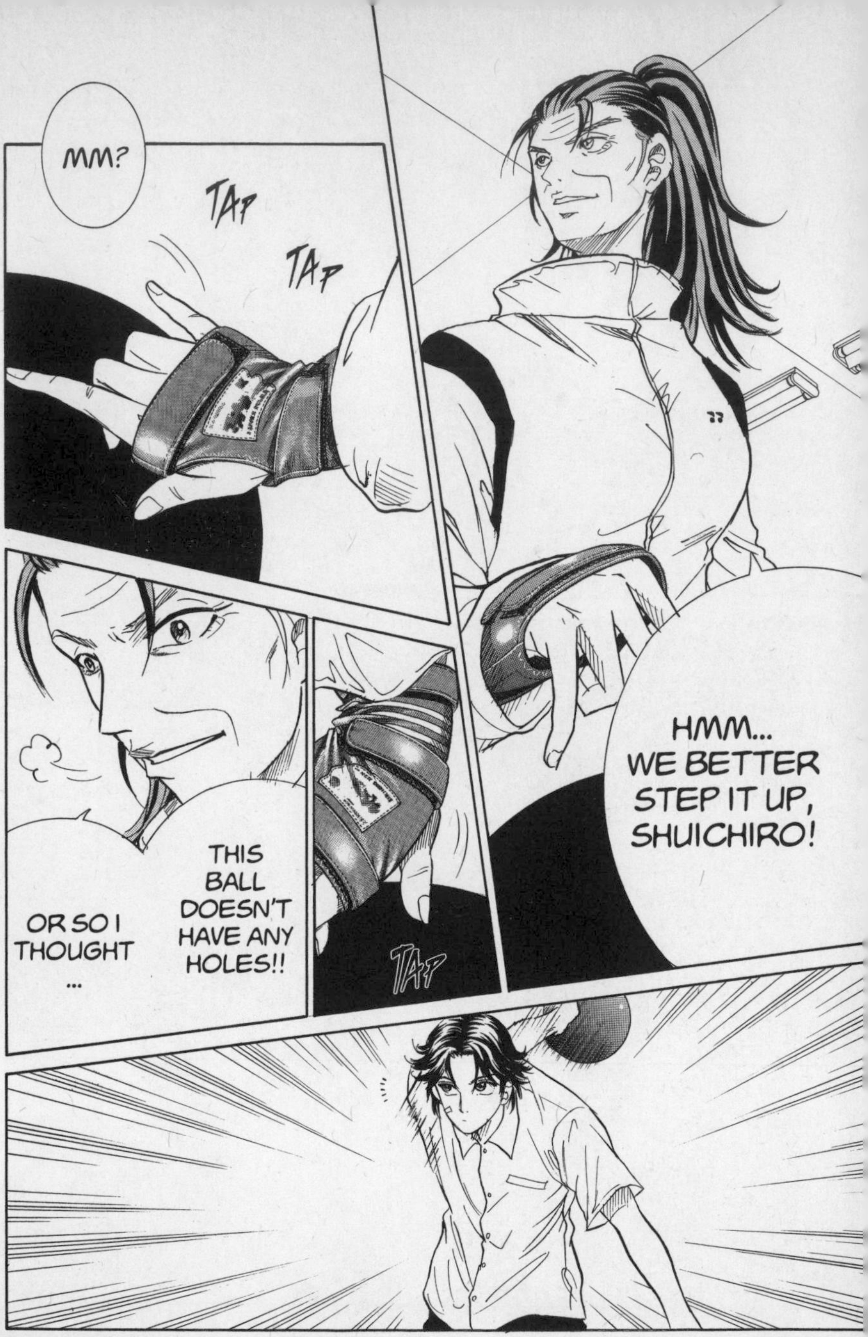
MM?
TAP
TAP
THIS BALL DOESN'T HAVE ANY HOLES!!
TAP
OR SO I THOUGHT ...
HMM... WE BETTER STEP IT UP, SHUICHIRO!

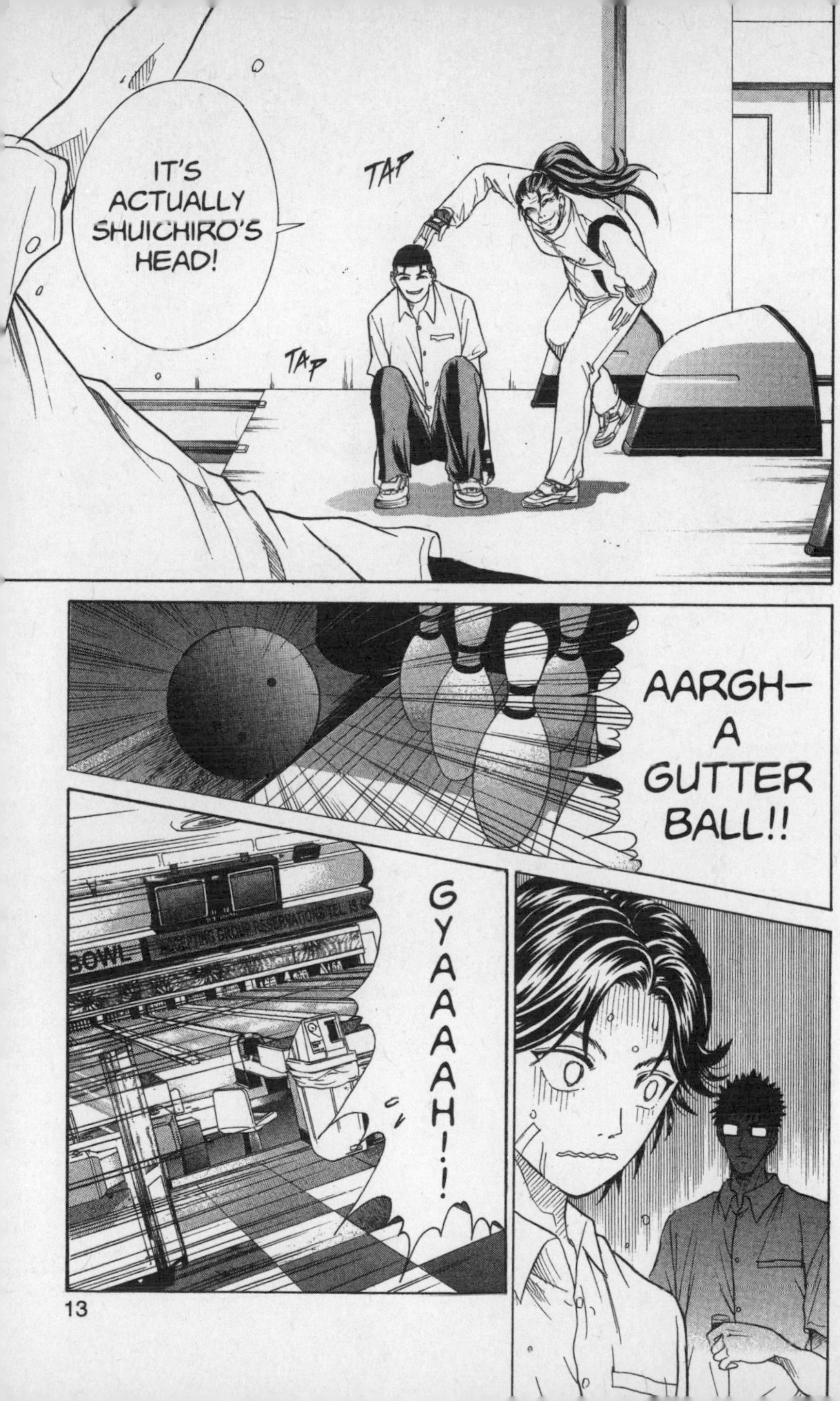
IT'S ACTUALLY SHUICHIRO'S HEAD!
TAP
TAP
AARGH— A GUTTER BALL!!
GYAAAAAH!!
BOWL

READ THIS WAY

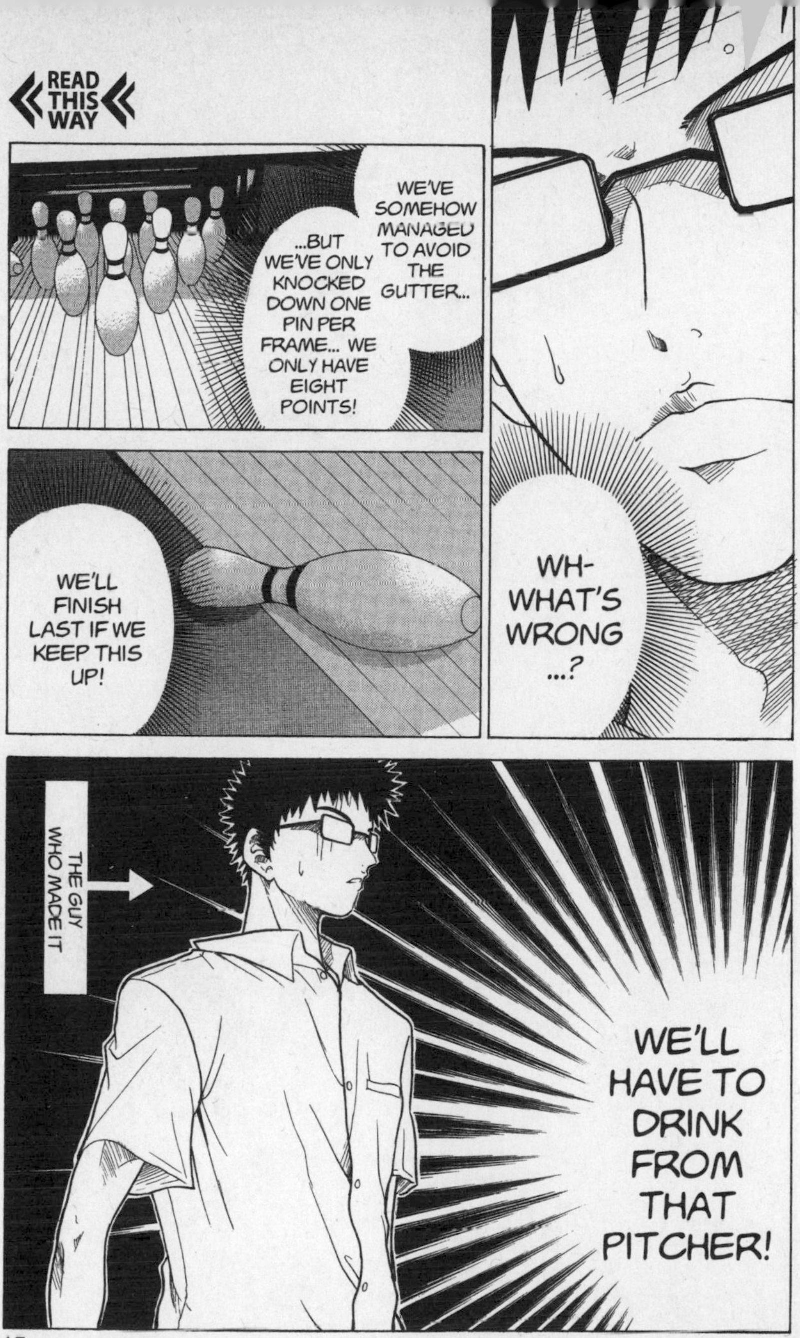
WH- WHAT'S WRONG ...?
WE'VE SOMEHOW MANAGED TO AVOID THE GUTTER...
...BUT WE'VE ONLY KNOCKED DOWN ONE PIN PER FRAME... WE ONLY HAVE EIGHT POINTS!
WE'LL FINISH LAST IF WE KEEP THIS UP!
WE'LL HAVE TO DRINK FROM THAT PITCHER!
THE GUY WHO MADE IT

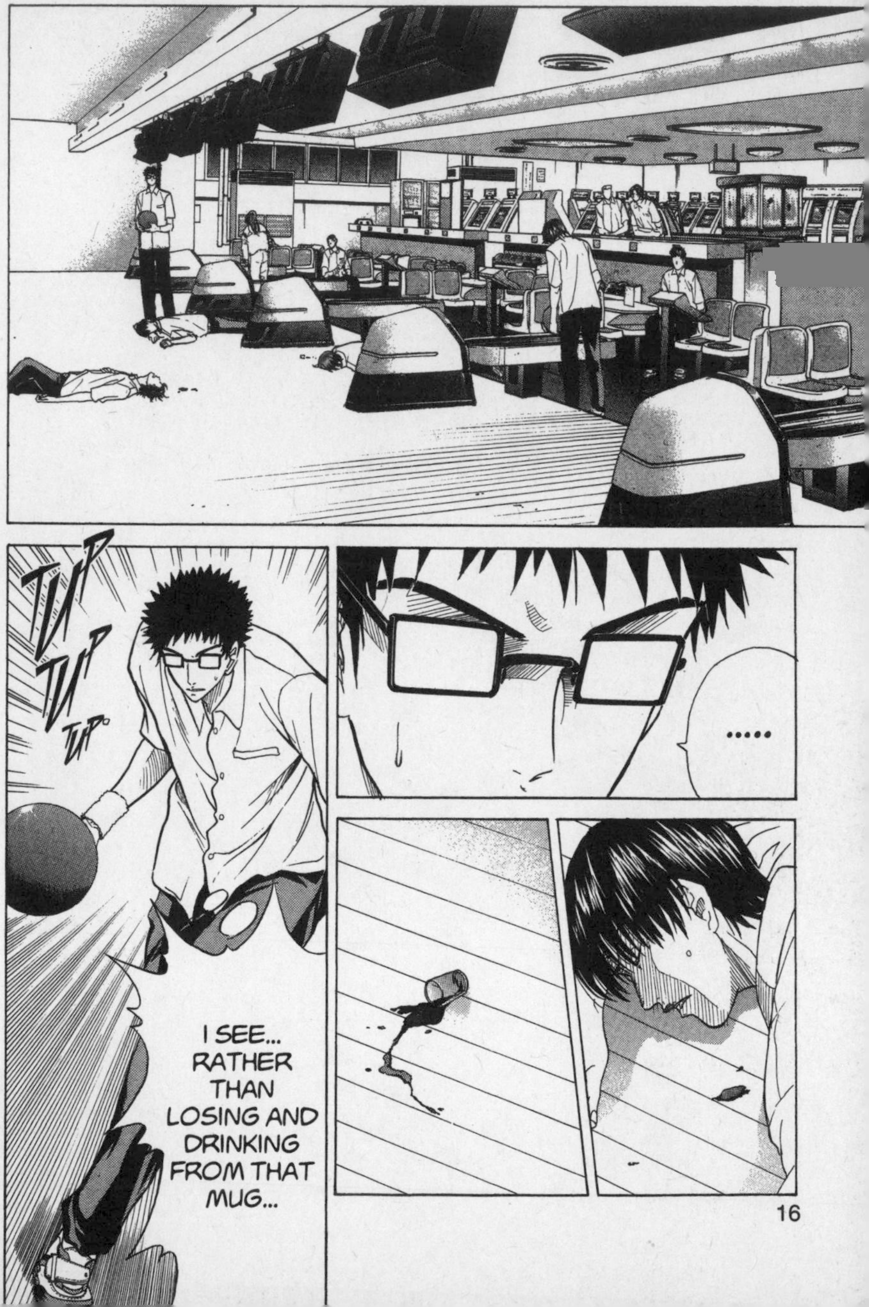
.....
TUP TUP TUP
I SEE... RATHER THAN LOSING AND DRINKING FROM THAT MUG...

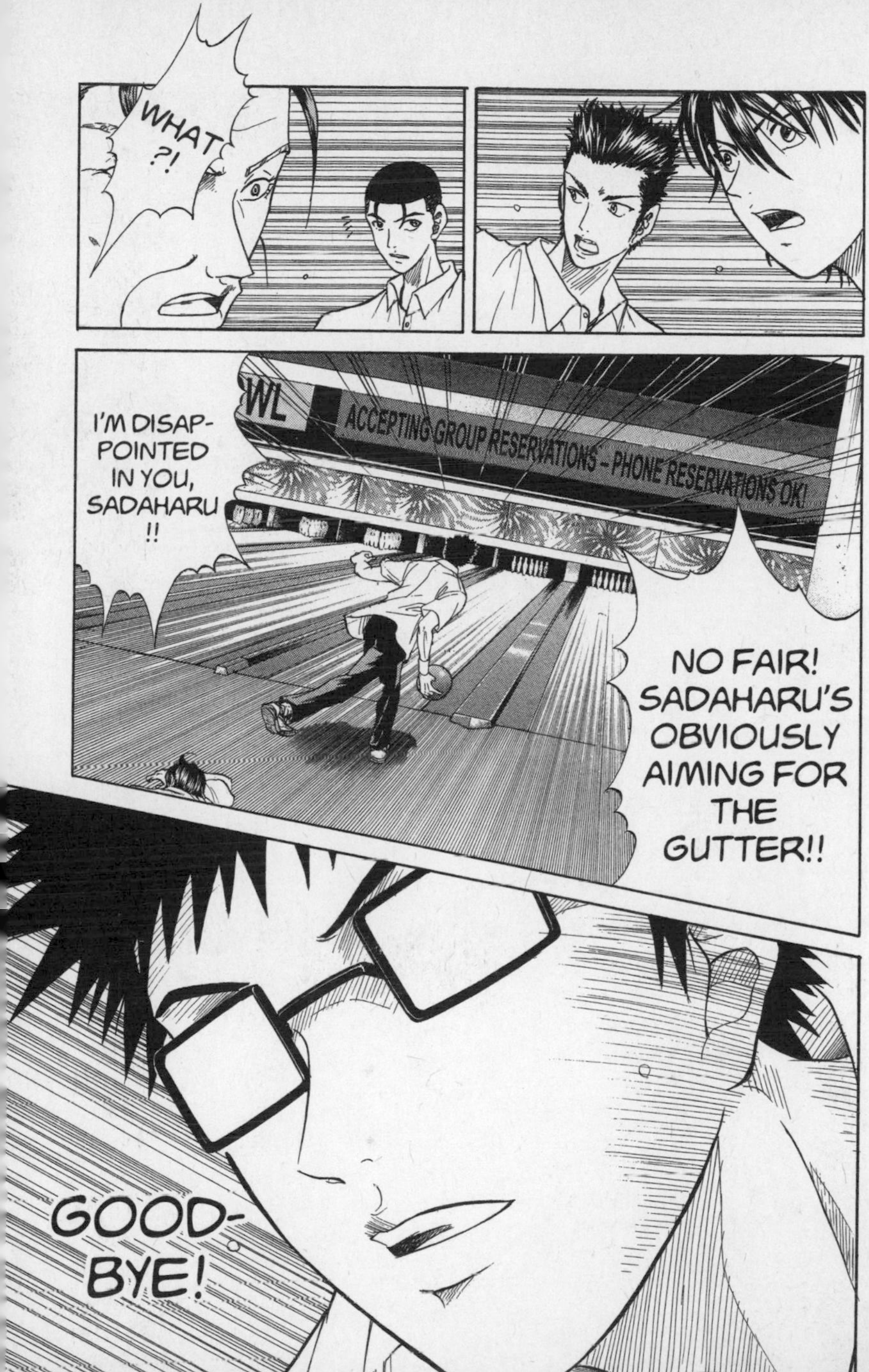
WHAT ?!
WL
ACCEPTING GROUP RESERVATIONS – PHONE RESERVATIONS OK!
NO FAIR! SADAHARU'S OBVIOUSLY AIMING FOR THE GUTTER!!
I'M DISAP-POINTED IN YOU, SADAHARU !!
GOOD-BYE!

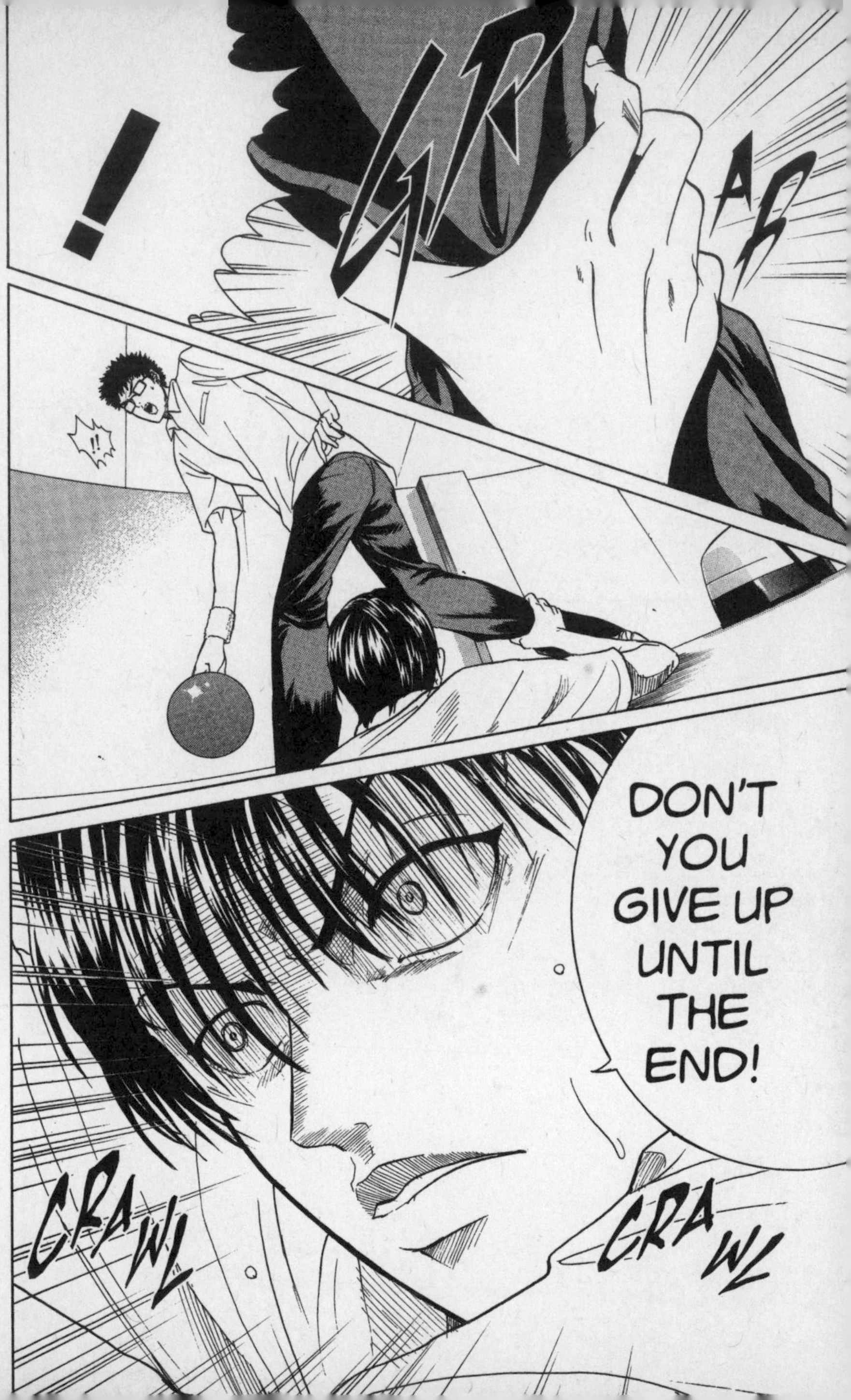
GRAB
!
!!
DON'T YOU GIVE UP UNTIL THE END!
CRAWL
CRAWL

READ THIS WAY

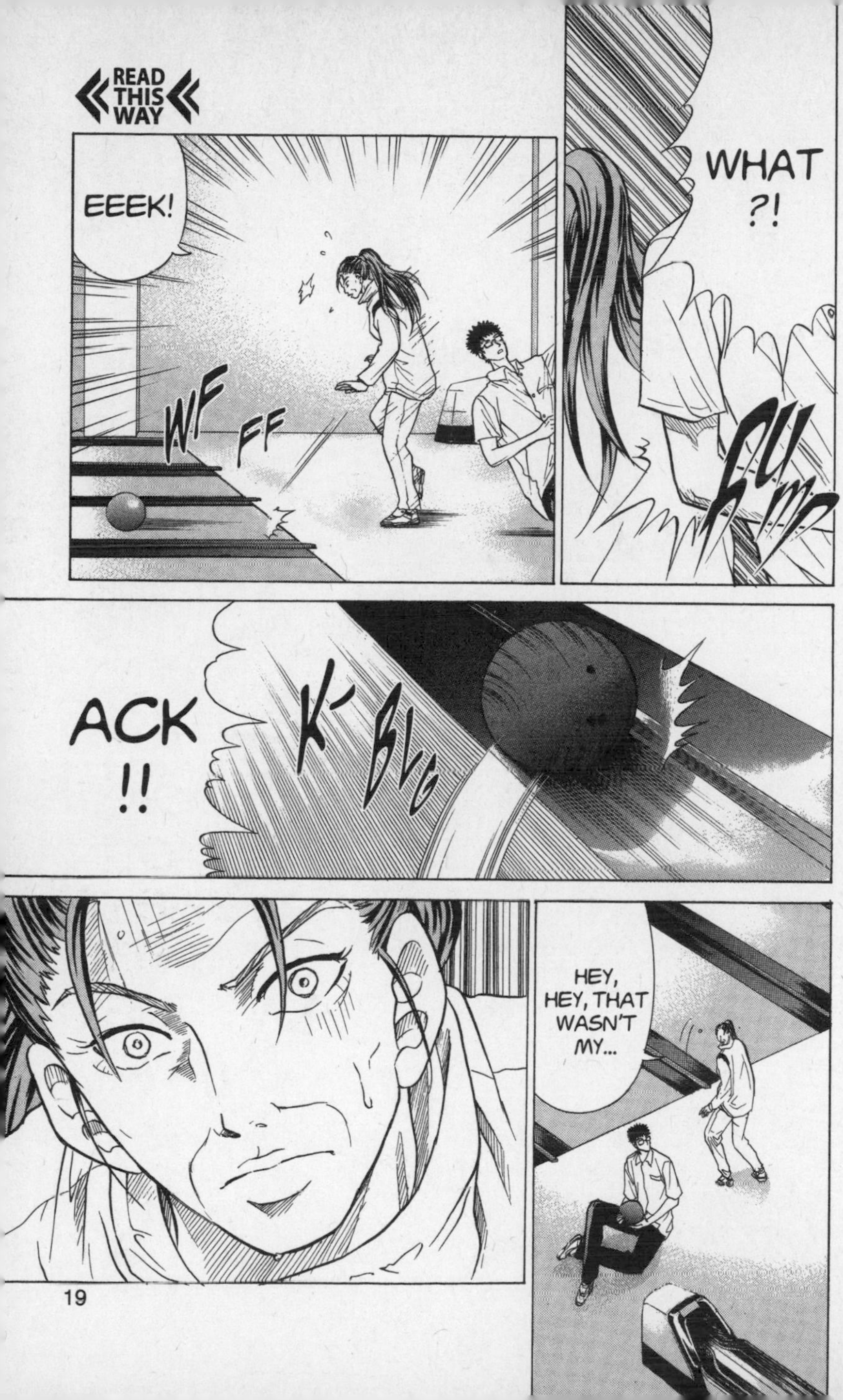
WHAT ?!
EEEK!
WFFF
ACK !!
HEY, HEY, THAT WASN'T MY...

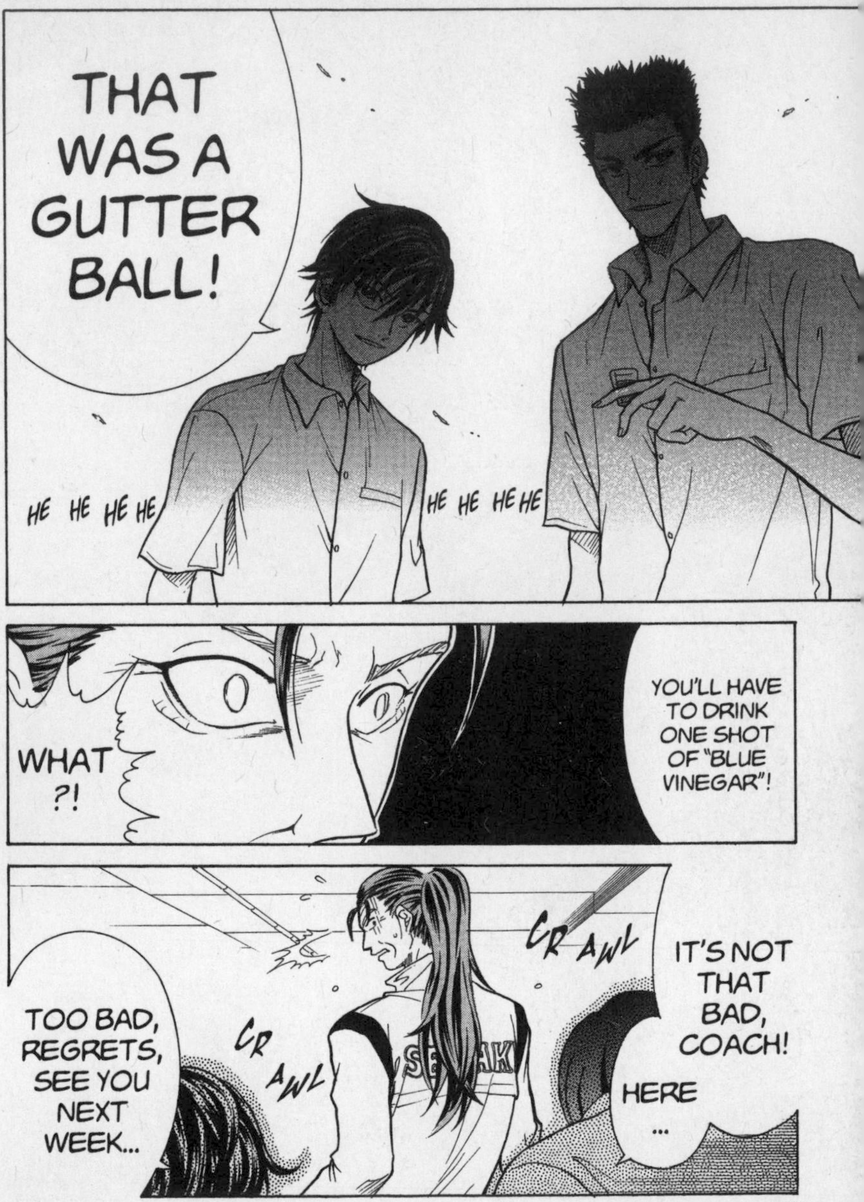
THAT WAS A GUTTER BALL!
HE HE HE HE
HE HE HE HE
YOU'LL HAVE TO DRINK ONE SHOT OF "BLUE VINEGAR"!
WHAT ?!
IT'S NOT THAT BAD, COACH!
CRAWL
HERE ...
TOO BAD, REGRETS, SEE YOU NEXT WEEK...
CRAWL

READ THIS WAY

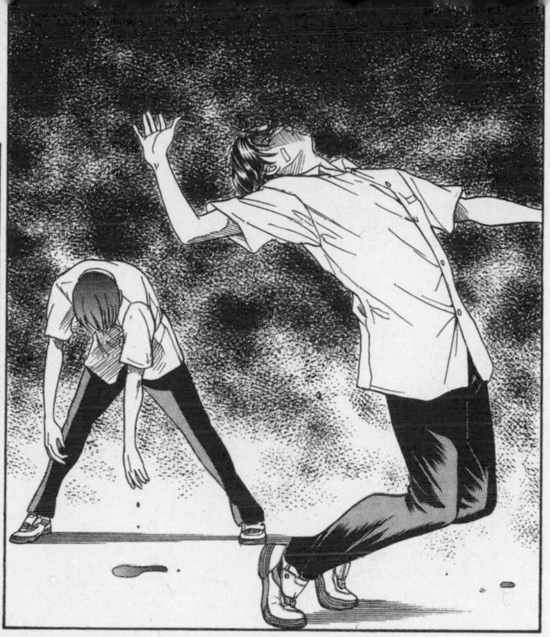

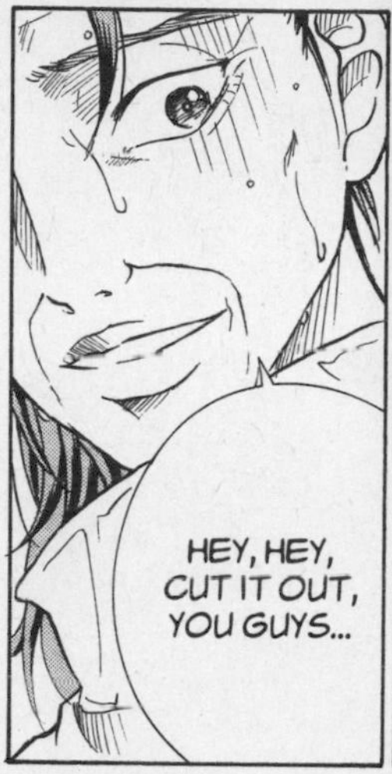
HEY, HEY, CUT IT OUT, YOU GUYS...

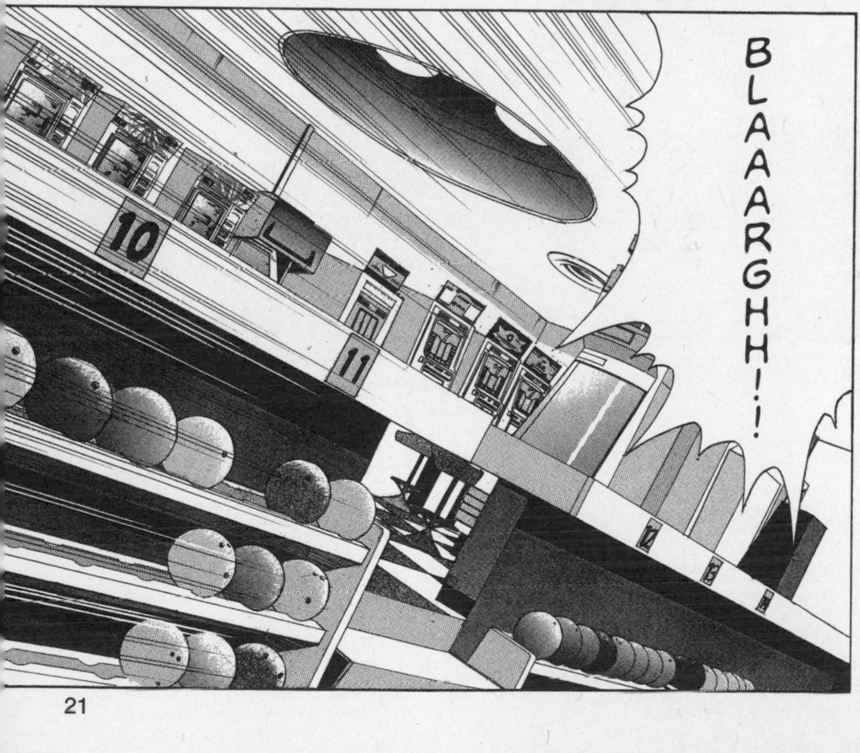
BLAAARGH!!

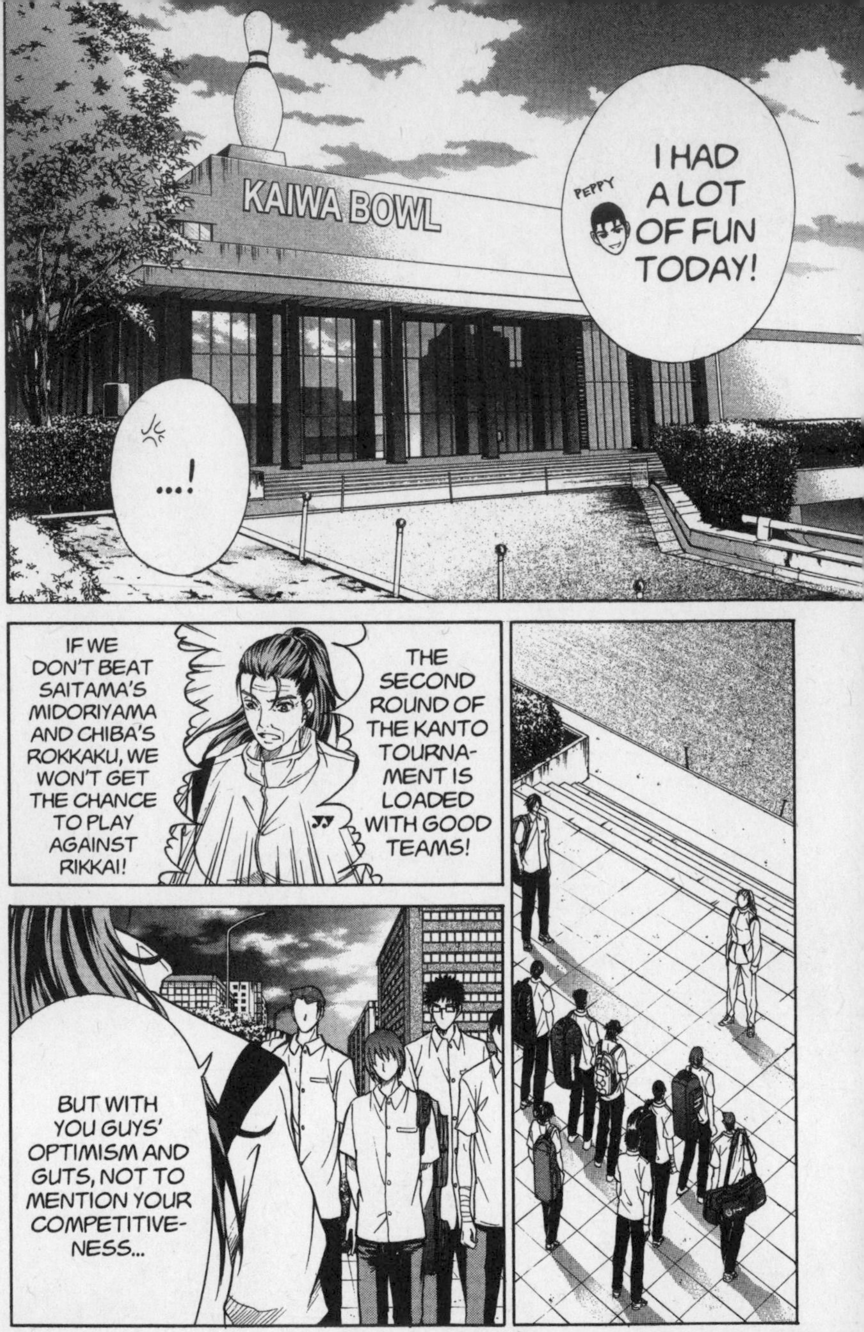
KAIWA BOWL
PEPPY
I HAD A LOT OF FUN TODAY!
...!
THE SECOND ROUND OF THE KANTO TOURNAMENT IS LOADED WITH GOOD TEAMS!
IF WE DON'T BEAT SAITAMA'S MIDORIYAMA AND CHIBA'S ROKKAKU, WE WON'T GET THE CHANCE TO PLAY AGAINST RIKKAI!
BUT WITH YOU GUYS' OPTIMISM AND GUTS, NOT TO MENTION YOUR COMPETITIVENESS...

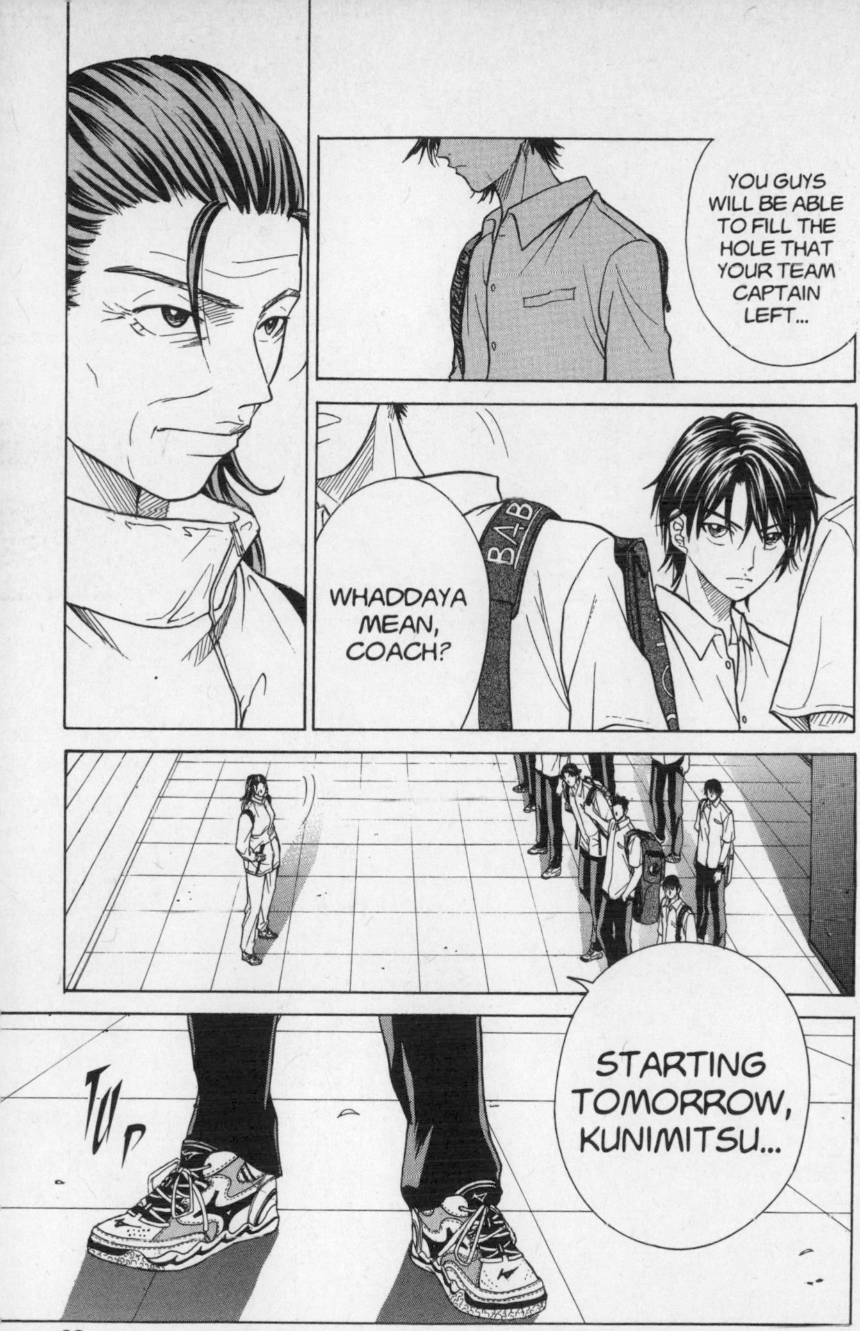
YOU GUYS WILL BE ABLE TO FILL THE HOLE THAT YOUR TEAM CAPTAIN LEFT...
WHADDAYA MEAN, COACH?
STARTING TOMORROW, KUNIMITSU...
TUP

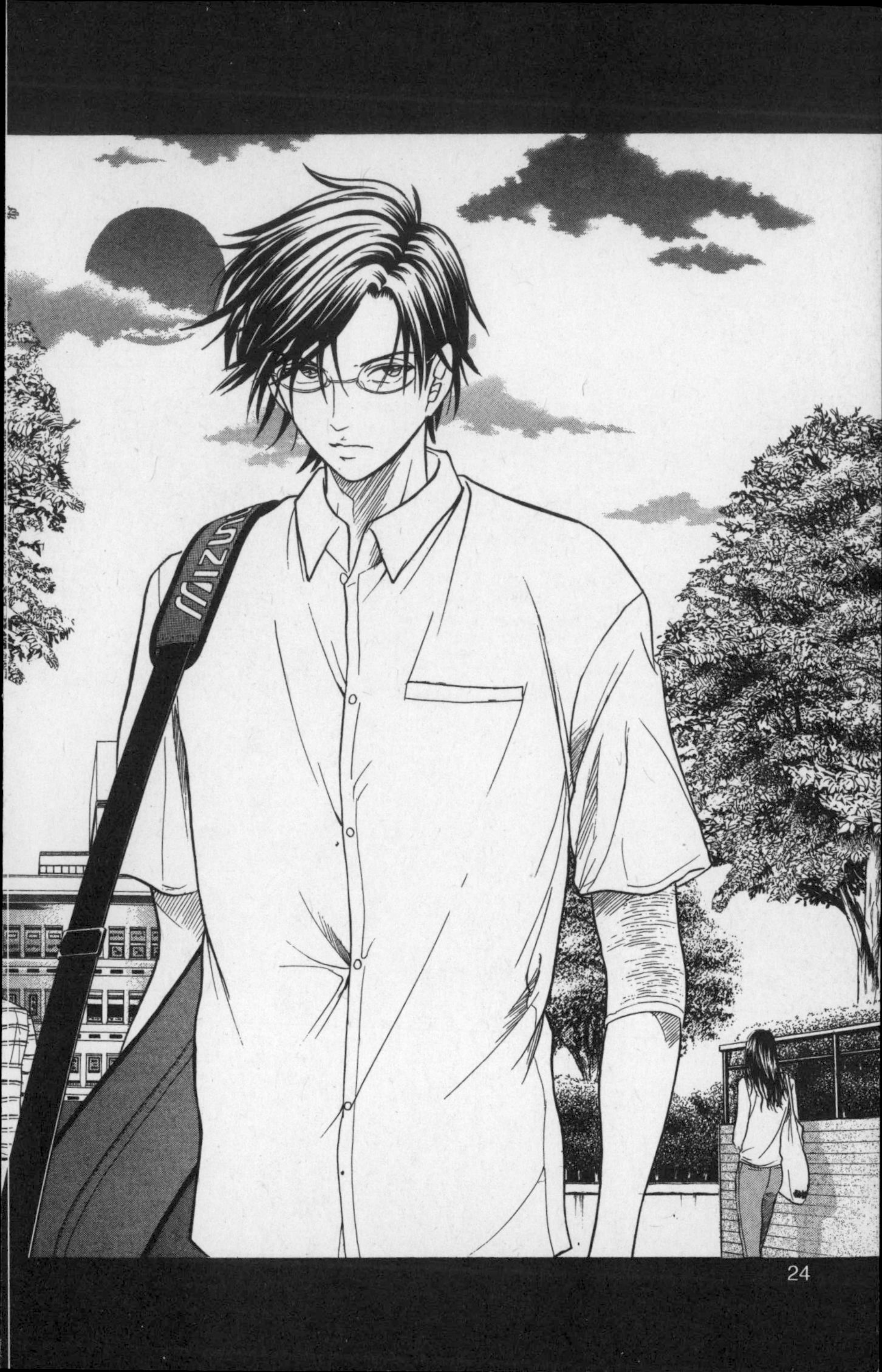

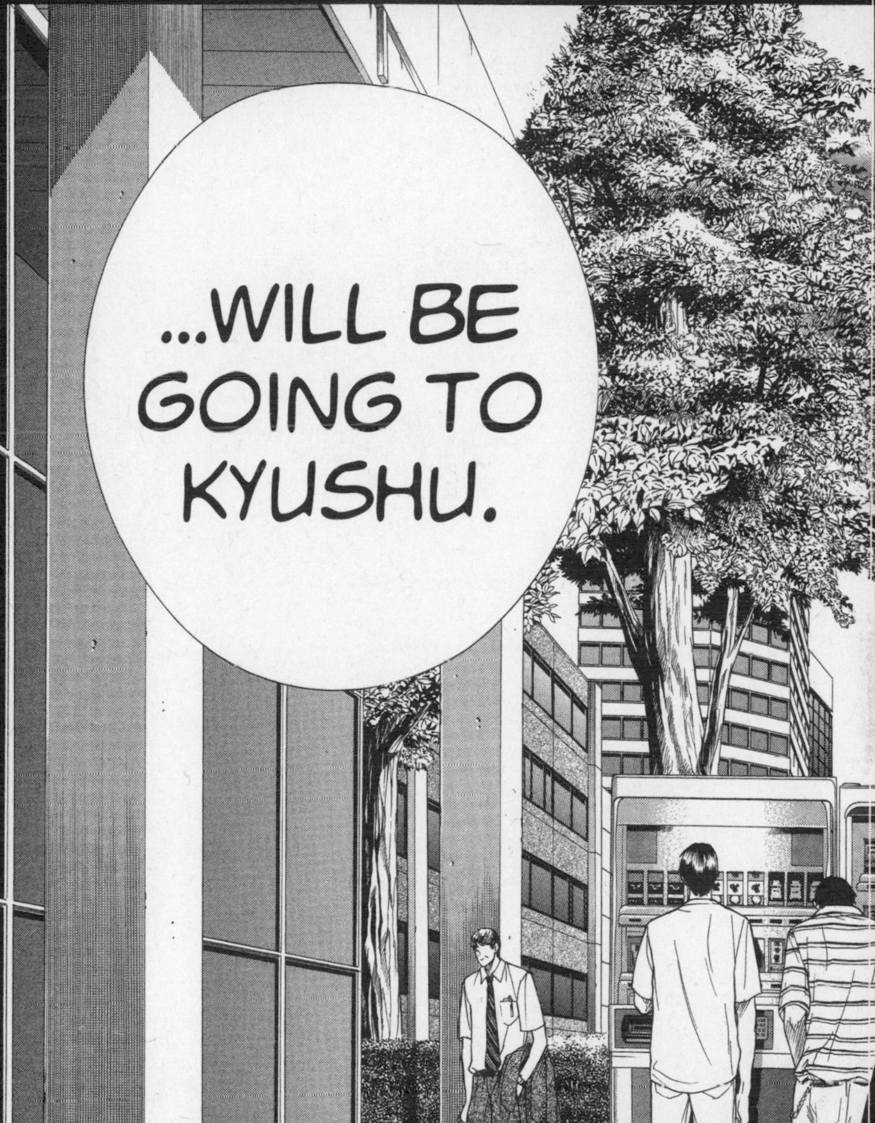
...WILL BE GOING TO KYUSHU.

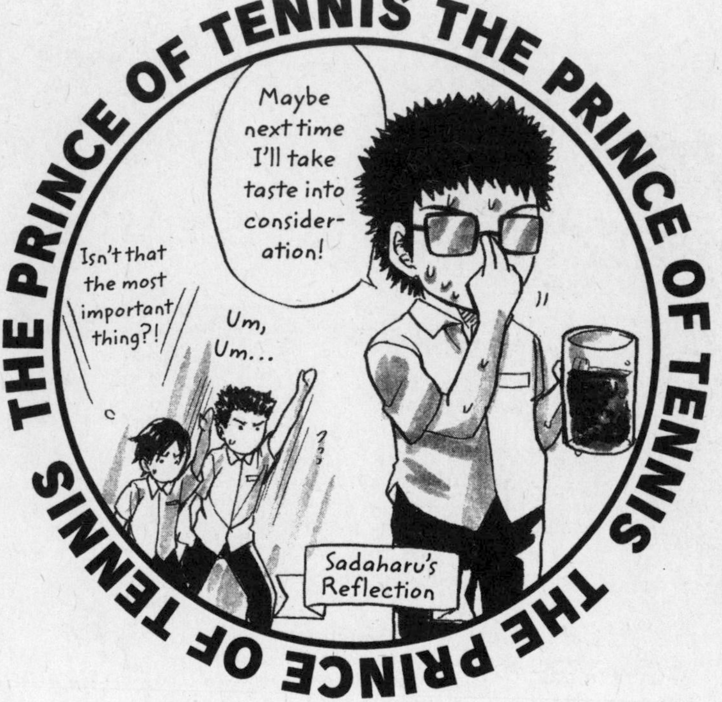
THE PRINCE OF TENNIS THE PRINCE OF TENNIS THE PRINCE OF TENNIS
Maybe next time I'll take taste into consider-ation!
Isn't that the most important thing?!
Um, Um...
Sadaharu's Reflection

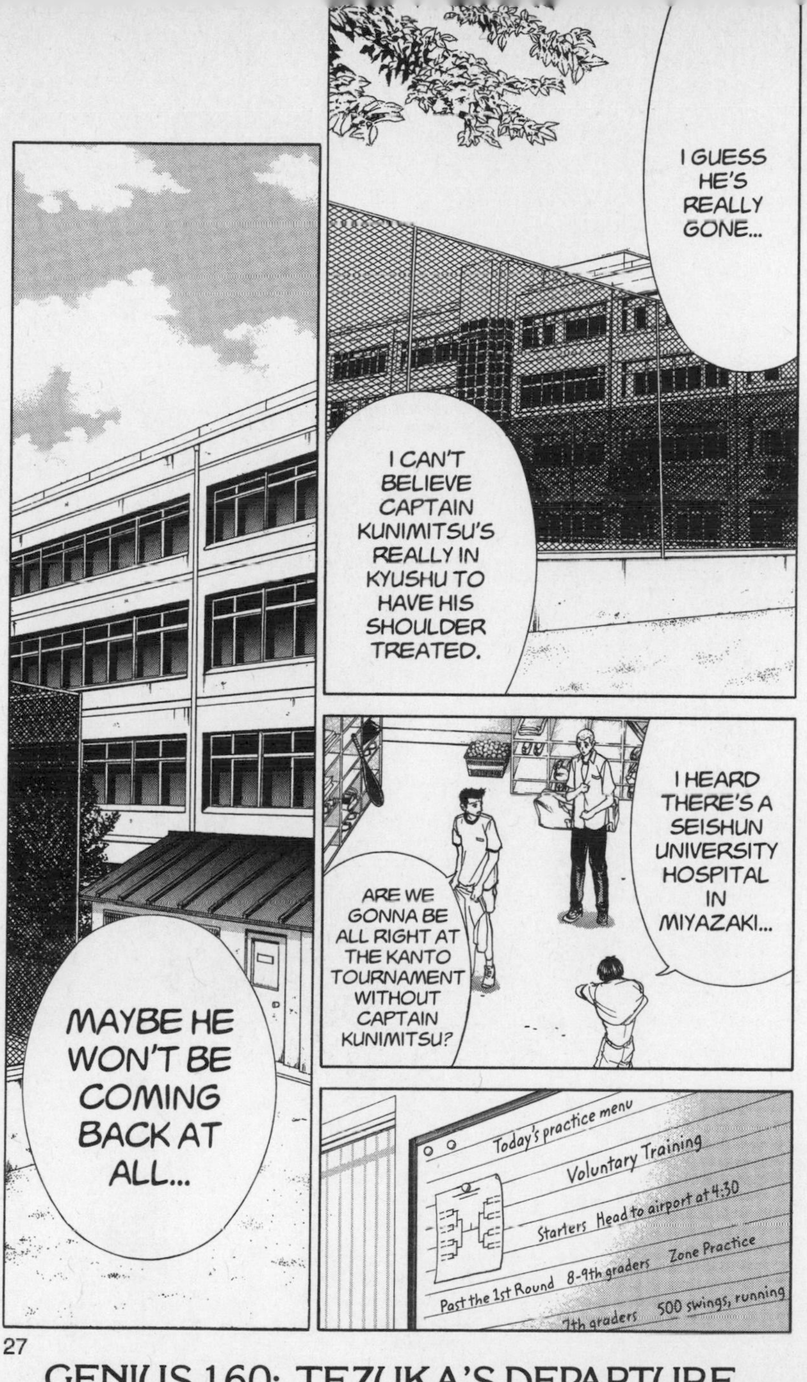
I GUESS HE'S REALLY GONE...
I CAN'T BELIEVE CAPTAIN KUNIMITSU'S REALLY IN KYUSHU TO HAVE HIS SHOULDER TREATED.
I HEARD THERE'S A SEISHUN UNIVERSITY HOSPITAL IN MIYAZAKI...
ARE WE GONNA BE ALL RIGHT AT THE KANTO TOURNAMENT WITHOUT CAPTAIN KUNIMITSU?
Today's practice menu
Voluntary Training
Starters Head to airport at 4:30
Past the 1st Round 8-9th graders Zone Practice
7th graders 500 swings, running
MAYBE HE WON'T BE COMING BACK AT ALL...

GENIUS 160: TEZUKA'S DEPARTURE

GENIUS 160: TEZUKA'S DEPARTURE

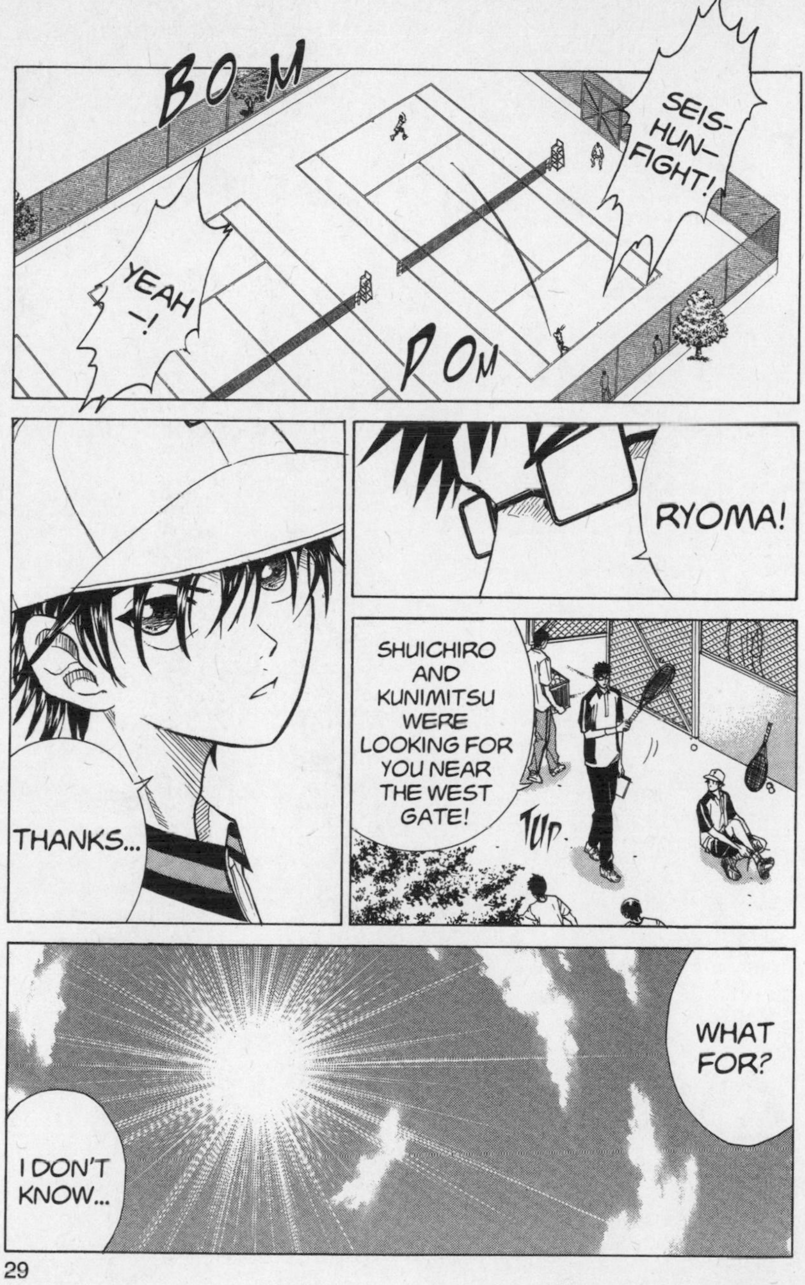
SEIS-HUN-FIGHT!
BOM
YEAH—!
POM
RYOMA!
SHUICHIRO AND KUNIMITSU WERE LOOKING FOR YOU NEAR THE WEST GATE!
TUP
THANKS...
WHAT FOR?
I DON'T KNOW...

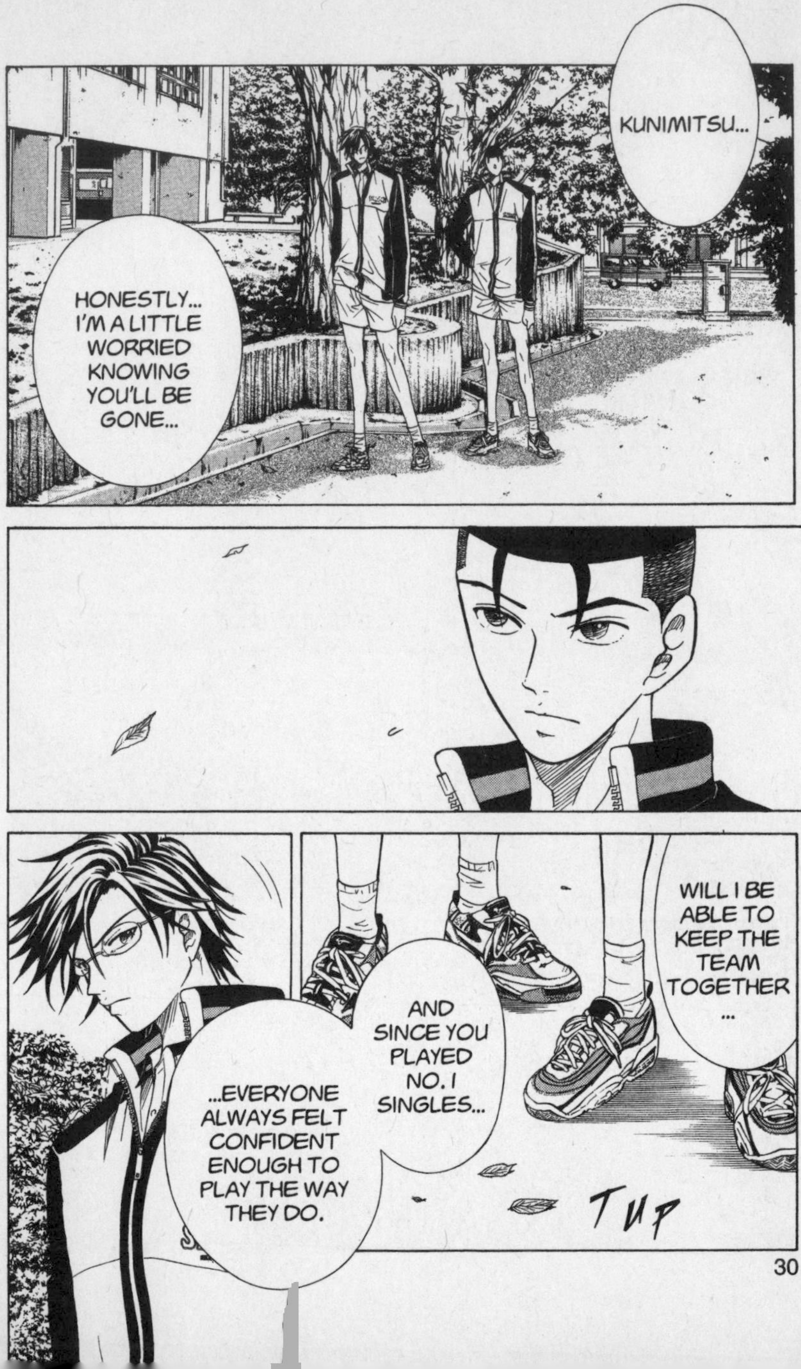
KUNIMITSU...
HONESTLY... I'M A LITTLE WORRIED KNOWING YOU'LL BE GONE...
WILL I BE ABLE TO KEEP THE TEAM TOGETHER ...
AND SINCE YOU PLAYED NO. 1 SINGLES...
TUP
...EVERYONE ALWAYS FELT CONFIDENT ENOUGH TO PLAY THE WAY THEY DO.

READ THIS WAY

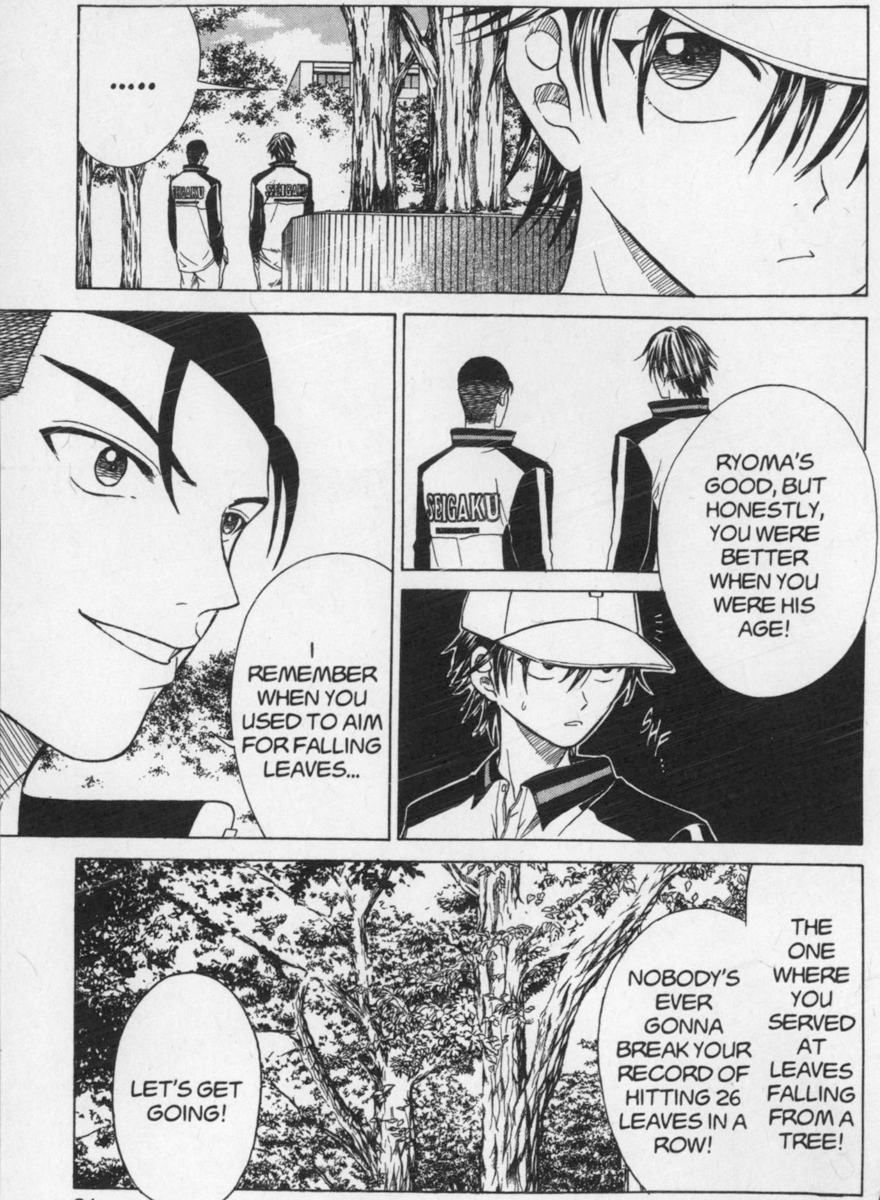

.....
RYOMA'S GOOD, BUT HONESTLY, YOU WERE BETTER WHEN YOU WERE HIS AGE!
SHF
I REMEMBER WHEN YOU USED TO AIM FOR FALLING LEAVES...
THE ONE WHERE YOU SERVED AT LEAVES FALLING FROM A TREE!
NOBODY'S EVER GONNA BREAK YOUR RECORD OF HITTING 26 LEAVES IN A ROW!
LET'S GET GOING!

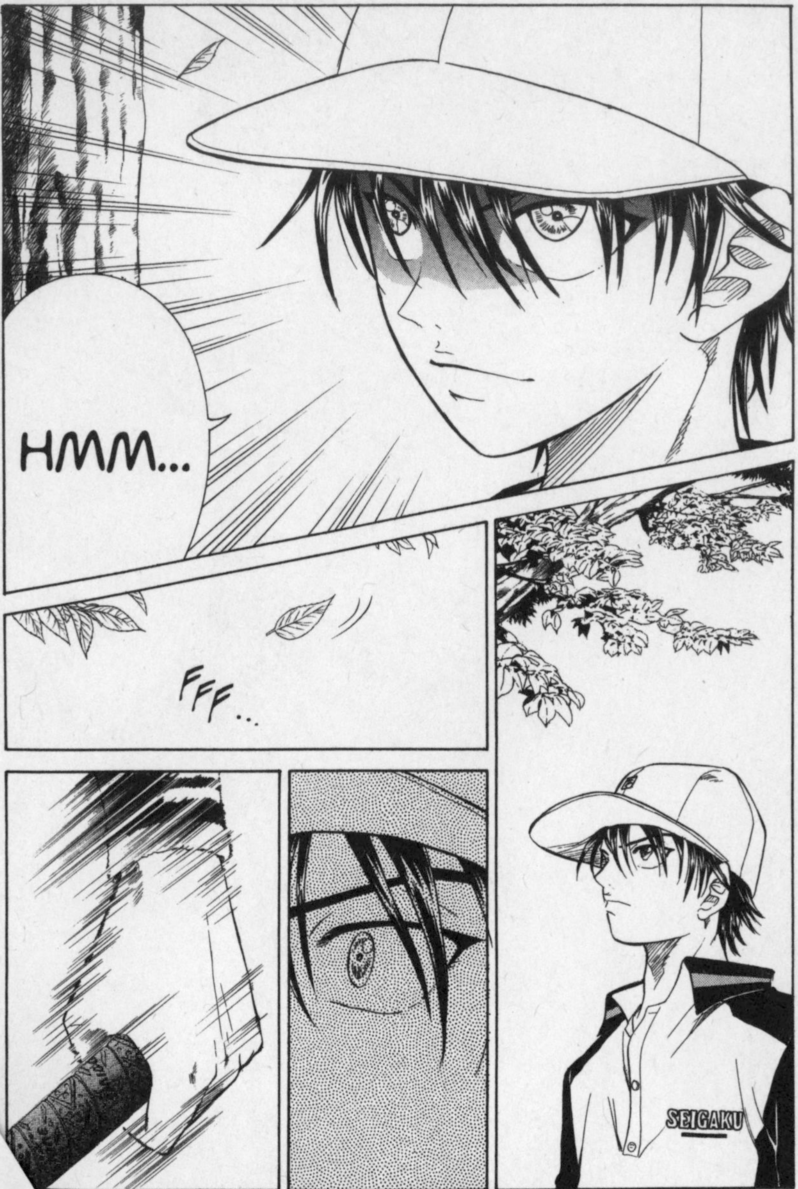
HMM...
FFF...
SEIGAKU

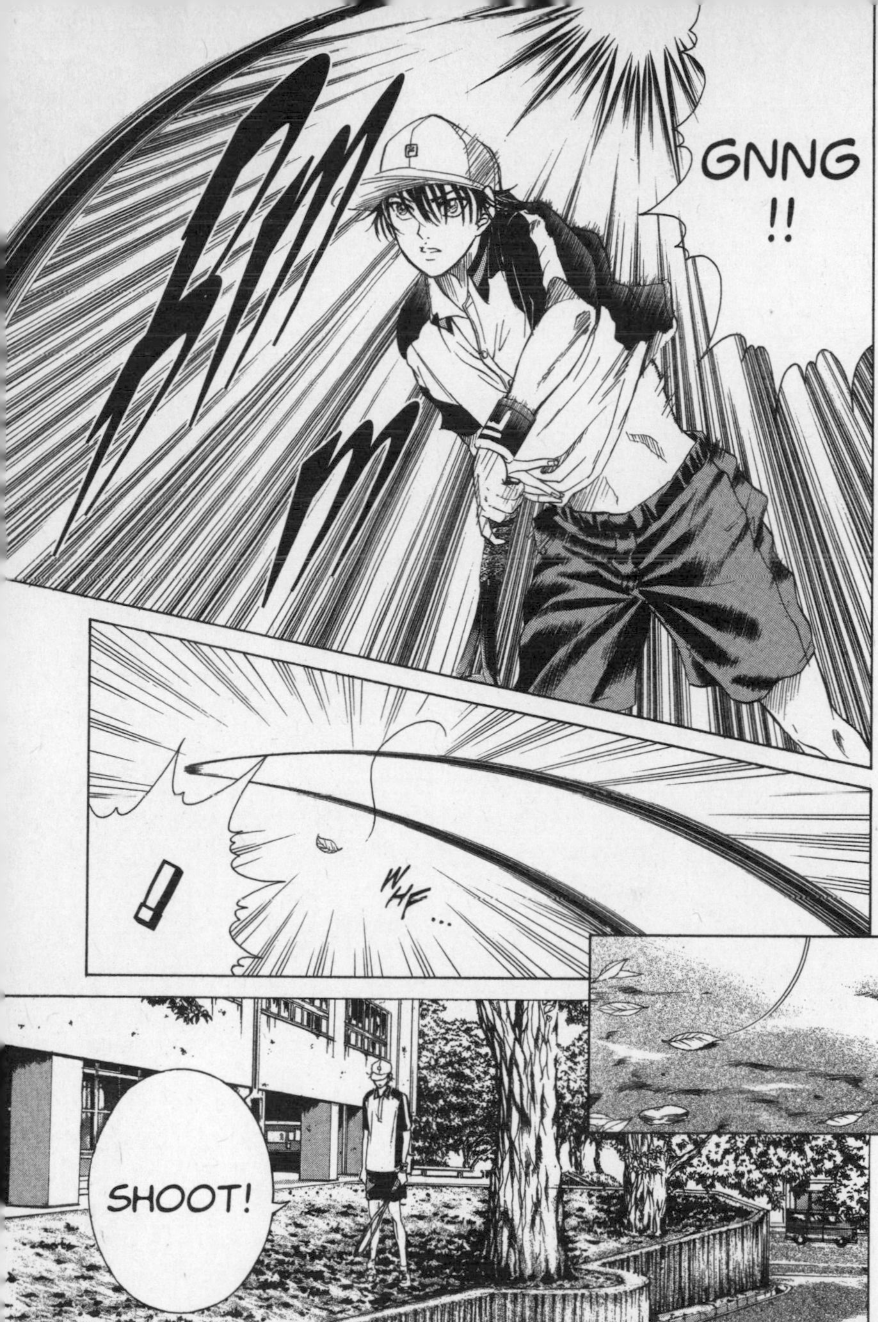
GNNG !!
!
WHF...
SHOOT!

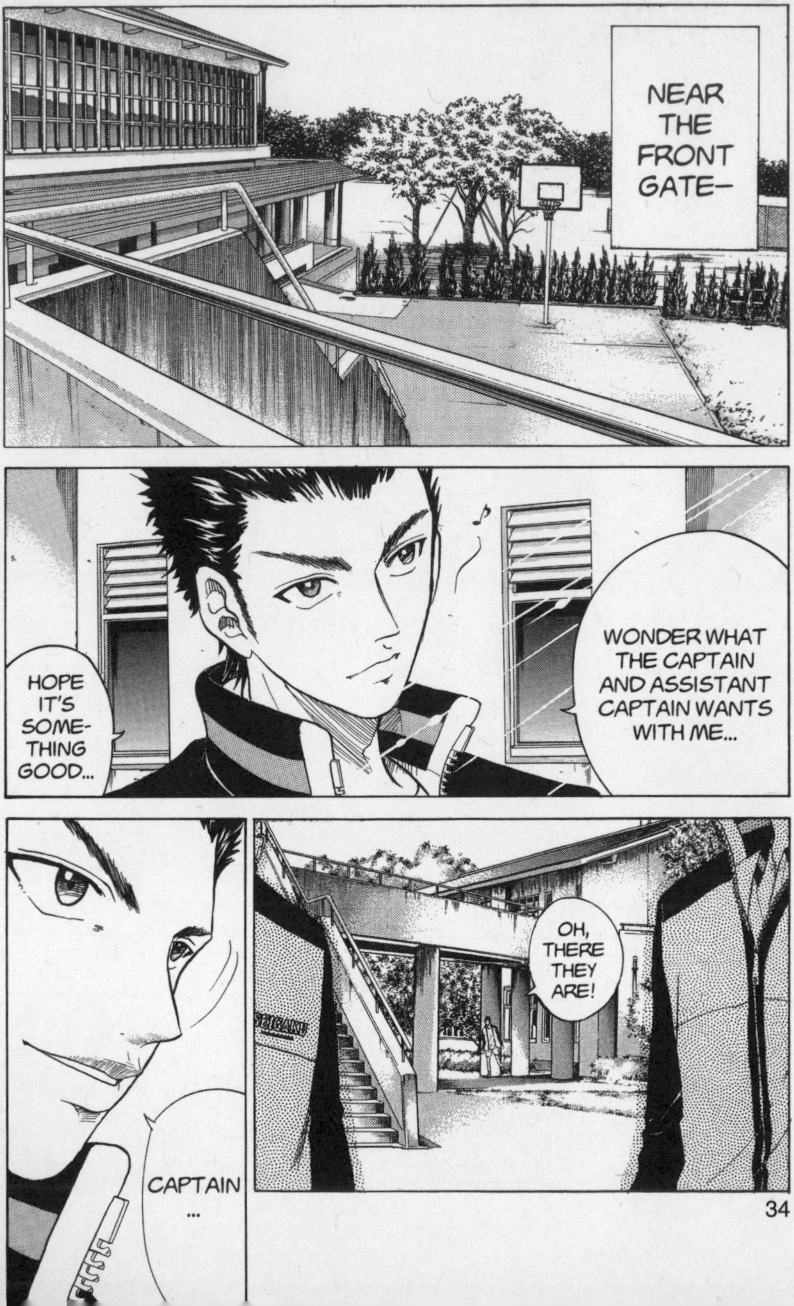
NEAR THE FRONT GATE—
WONDER WHAT THE CAPTAIN AND ASSISTANT CAPTAIN WANTS WITH ME...
HOPE IT'S SOME-THING GOOD...
OH, THERE THEY ARE!
SEIGAKU
CAPTAIN ...

READ THIS WAY

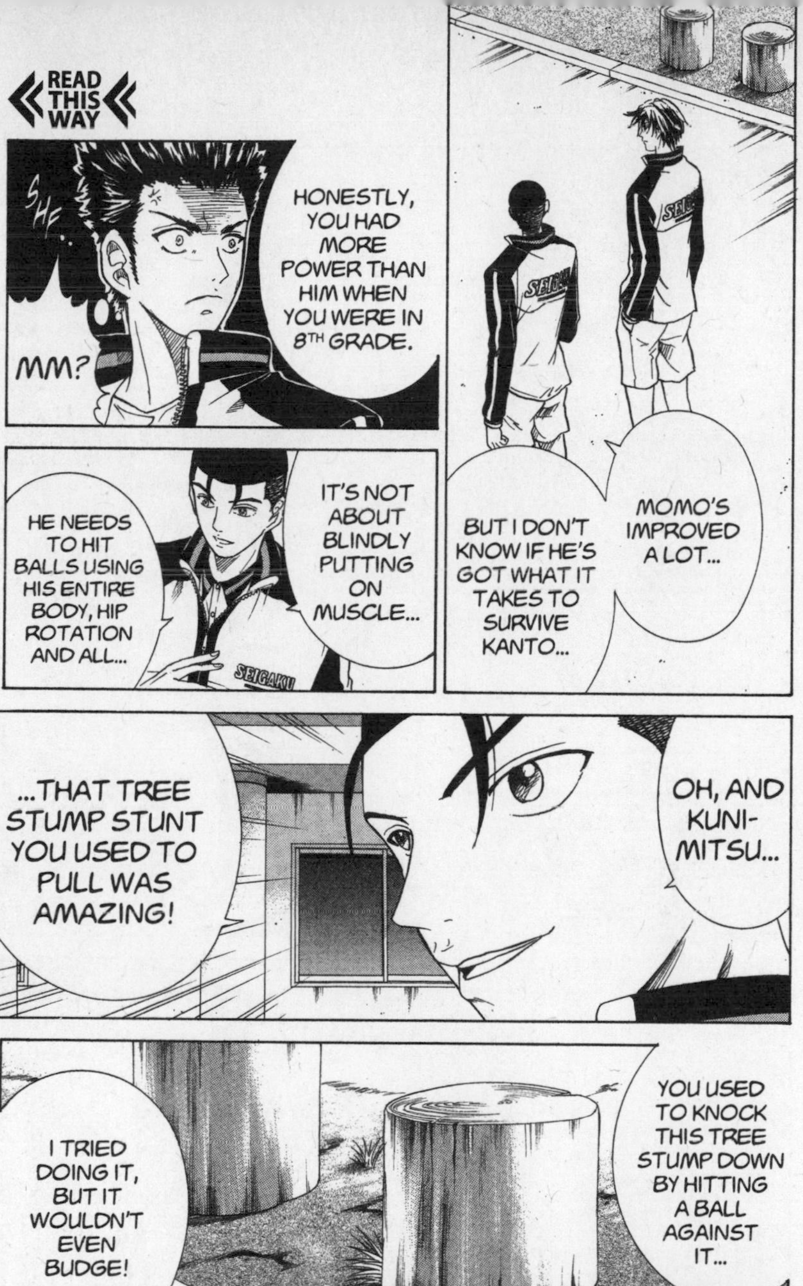
MOMO'S IMPROVED A LOT...
BUT I DON'T KNOW IF HE'S GOT WHAT IT TAKES TO SURVIVE KANTO...
SHF
HONESTLY, YOU HAD MORE POWER THAN HIM WHEN YOU WERE IN 8TH GRADE.
MM?
IT'S NOT ABOUT BLINDLY PUTTING ON MUSCLE...
HE NEEDS TO HIT BALLS USING HIS ENTIRE BODY, HIP ROTATION AND ALL...
OH, AND KUNIMITSU...
...THAT TREE STUMP STUNT YOU USED TO PULL WAS AMAZING!
YOU USED TO KNOCK THIS TREE STUMP DOWN BY HITTING A BALL AGAINST IT...
I TRIED DOING IT, BUT IT WOULDN'T EVEN BUDGE!

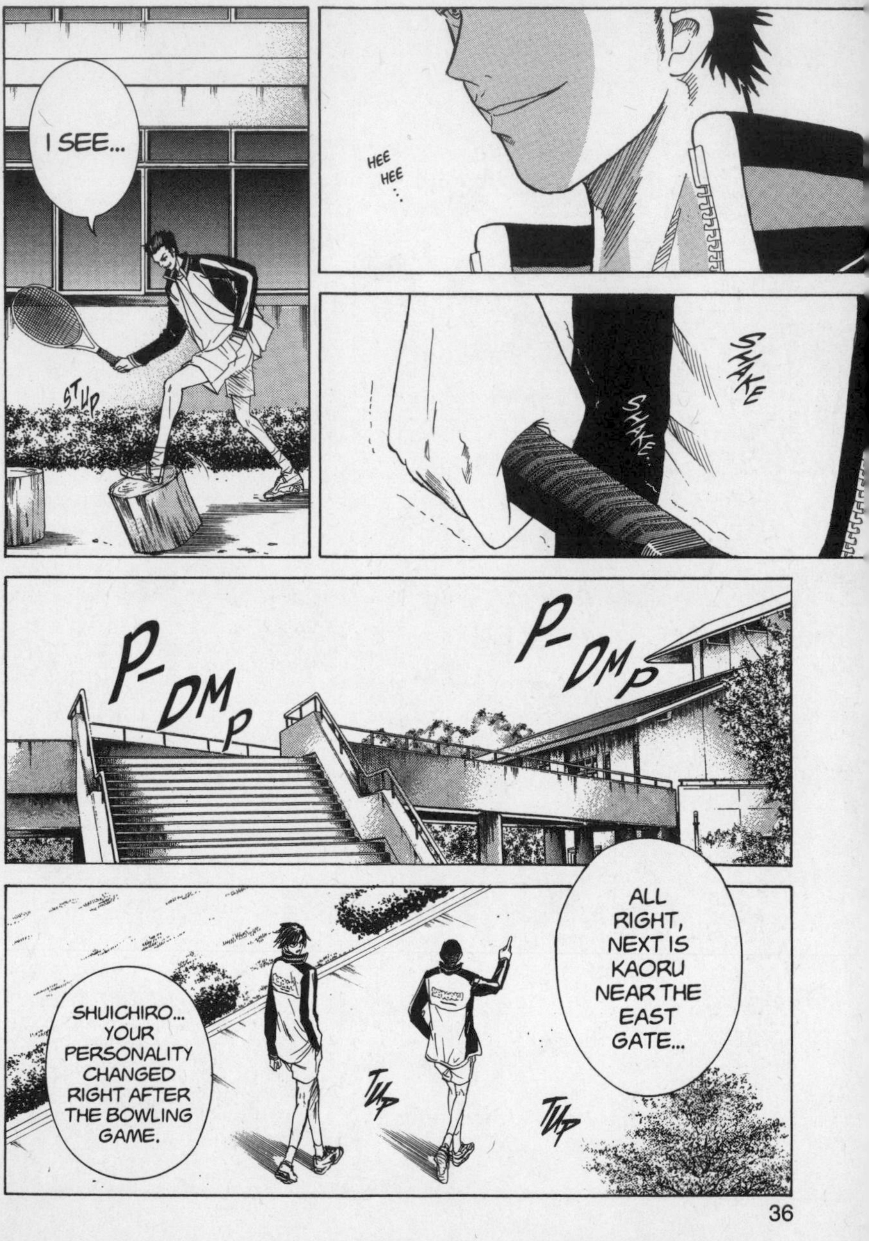
HEE HEE...
SHAKE
SHAKE
I SEE...
STUP
P-DMP
P-DMP
ALL RIGHT, NEXT IS KAORU NEAR THE EAST GATE...
SHUICHIRO... YOUR PERSONALITY CHANGED RIGHT AFTER THE BOWLING GAME.
TMP
TMP

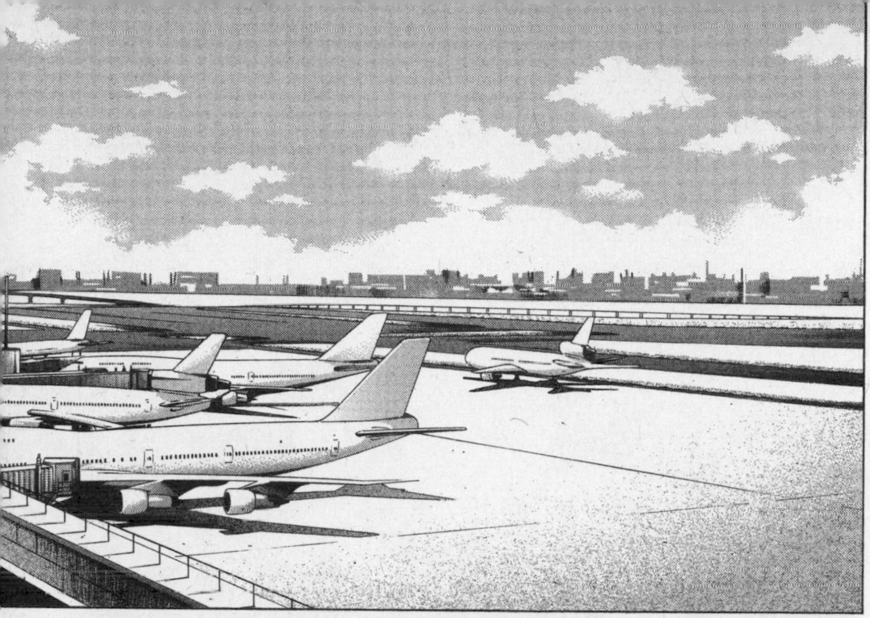
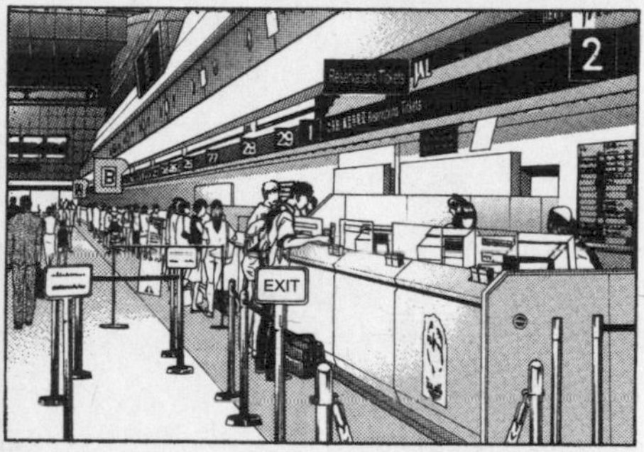
Reservations Tickets
JAL
2
B
EXIT
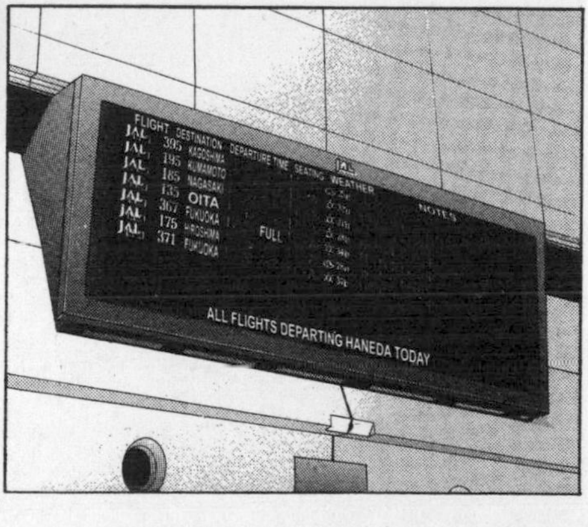
FLIGHT DESTINATION DEPARTURE TIME SEATING WEATHER NOTES
JAL
JAL 395 KAGOSHIMA
JAL 195 KUMAMOTO
JAL 185 NAGASAKI
JAL 135 OITA
JAL 367 FUKUOKA
JAL 175 HIROSHIMA
371 FUKUOKA
FULL
ALL FLIGHTS DEPARTING HANEDA TODAY
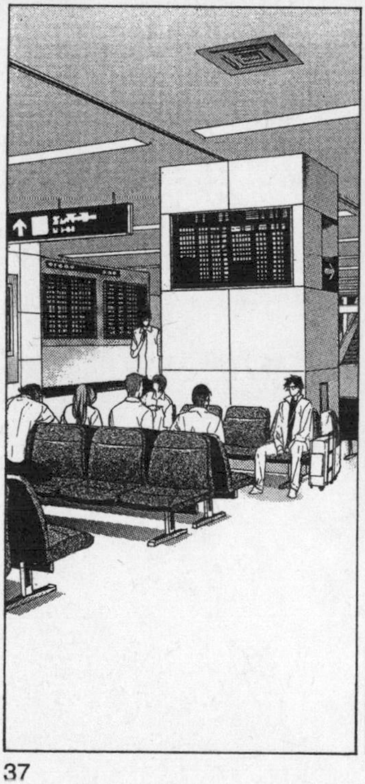

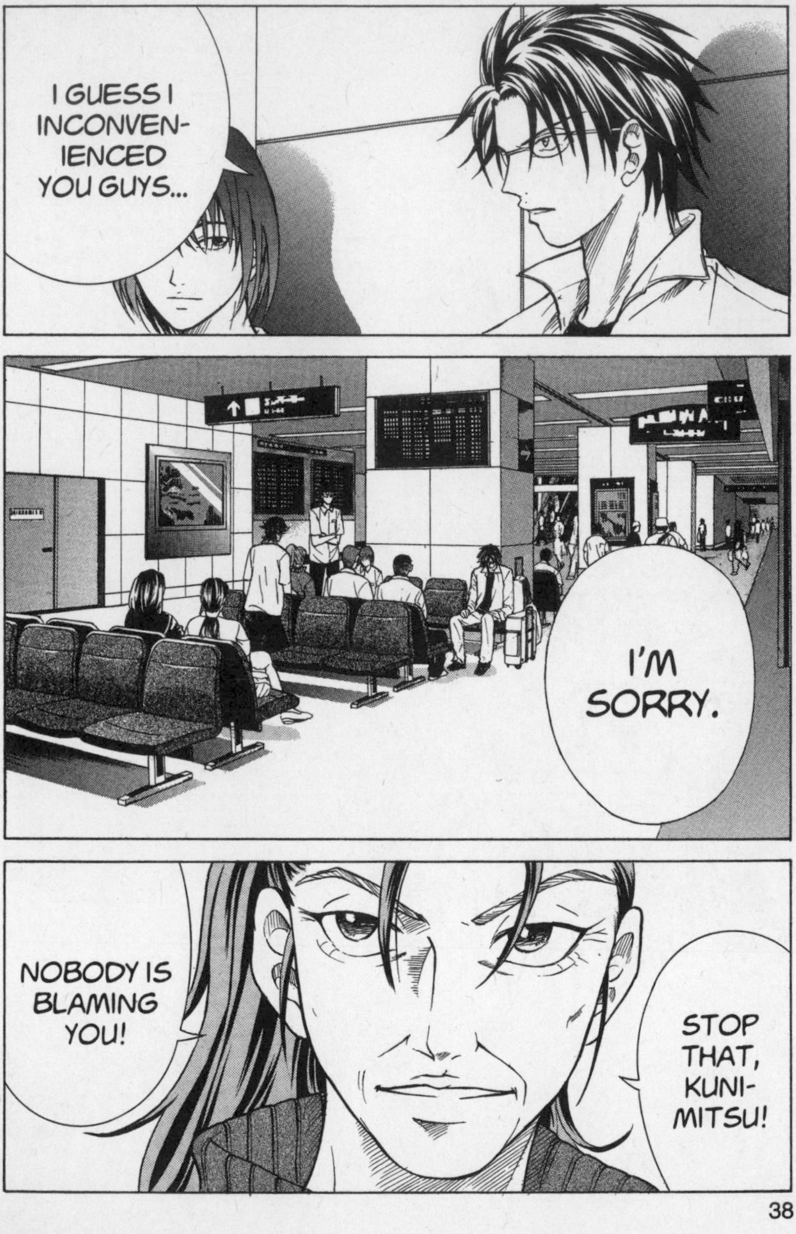
I GUESS I INCONVEN-IENCED YOU GUYS...
I'M SORRY.
STOP THAT, KUNI-MITSU!
NOBODY IS BLAMING YOU!

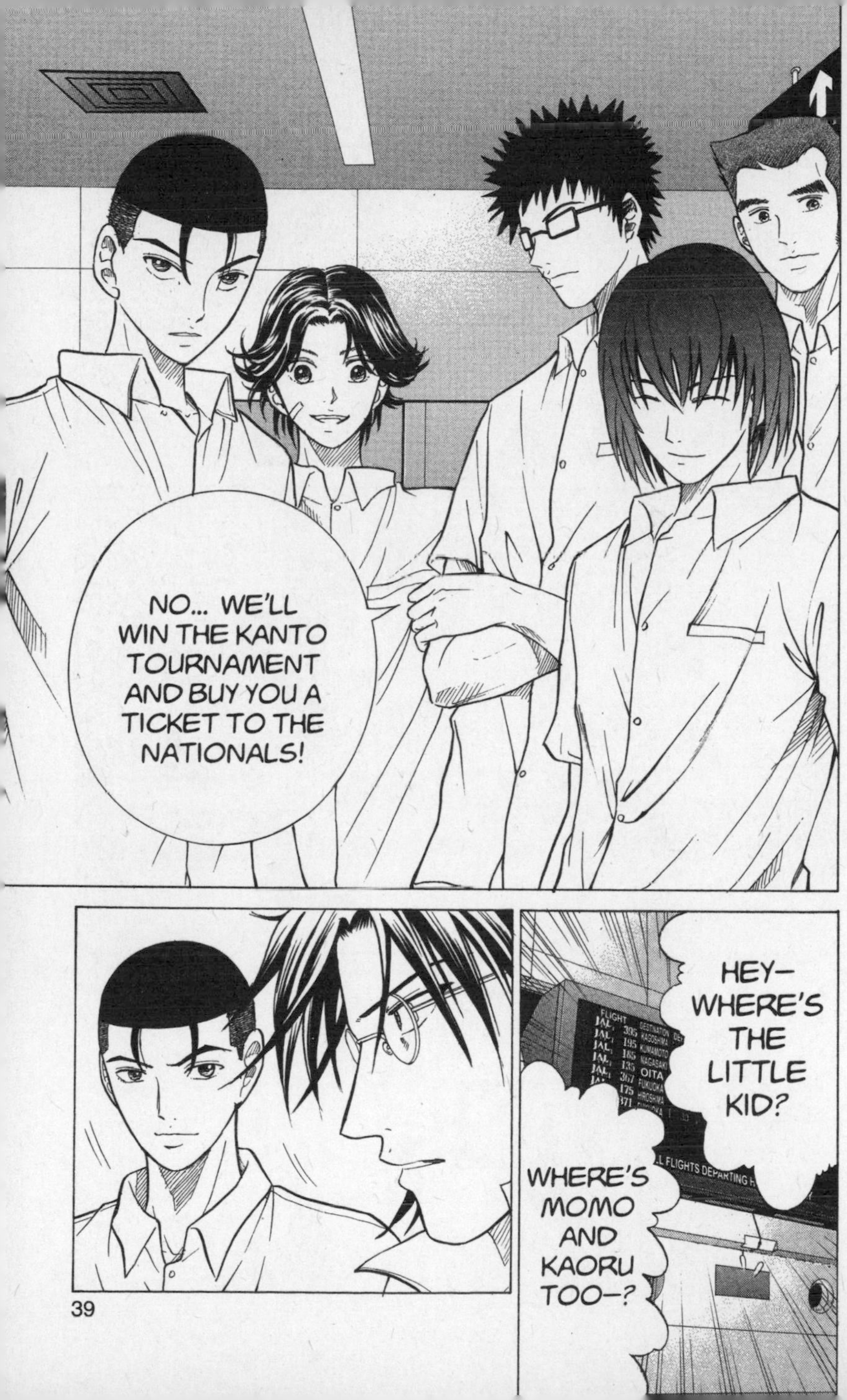
NO... WE'LL WIN THE KANTO TOURNAMENT AND BUY YOU A TICKET TO THE NATIONALS!
HEY— WHERE'S THE LITTLE KID?
WHERE'S MOMO AND KAORU TOO—?

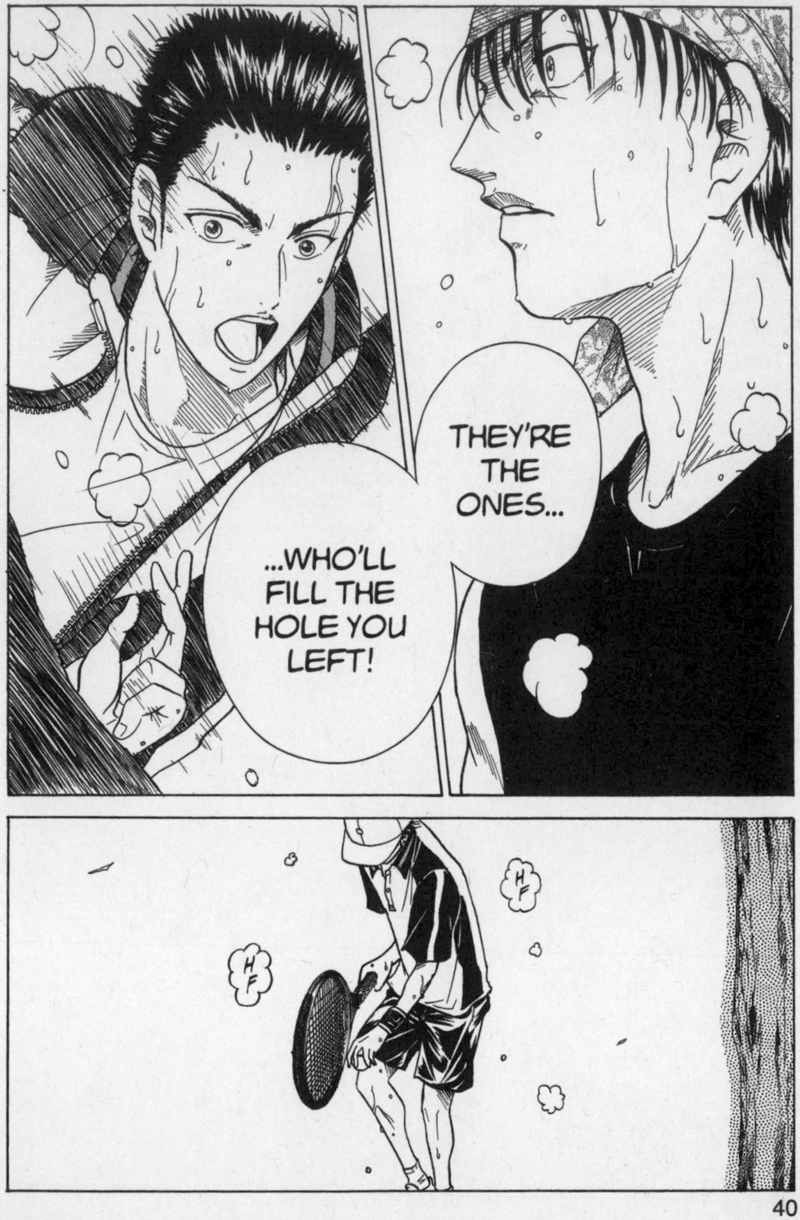
THEY'RE THE ONES...
...WHO'LL FILL THE HOLE YOU LEFT!
HF
HF

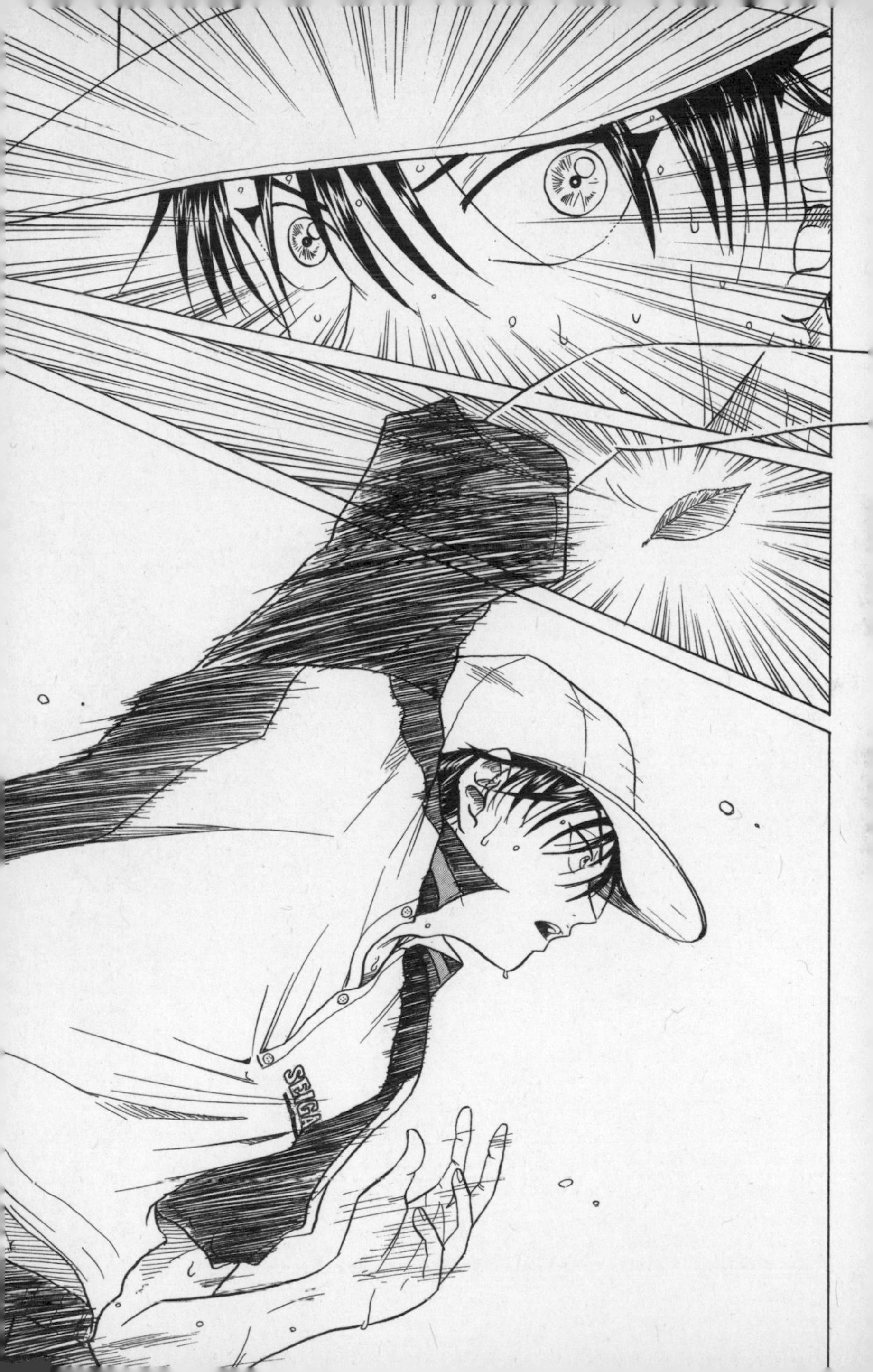
SEIGA

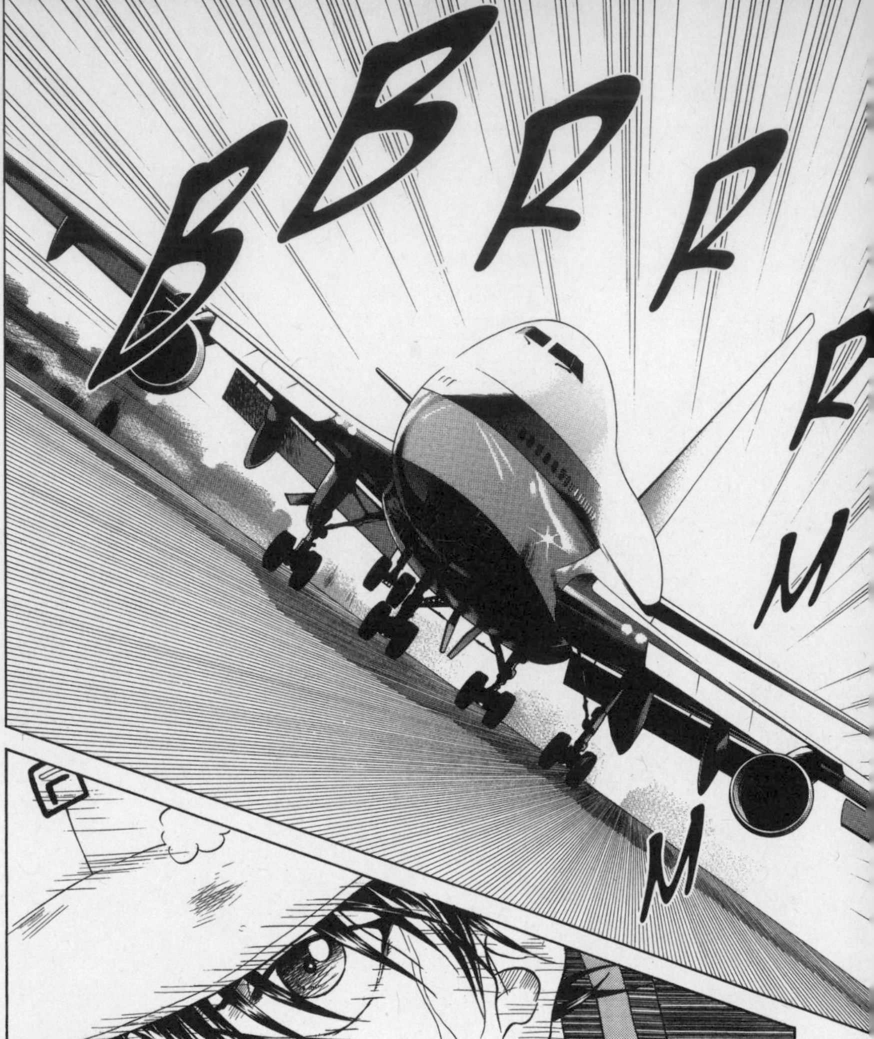
BBRRRRMM
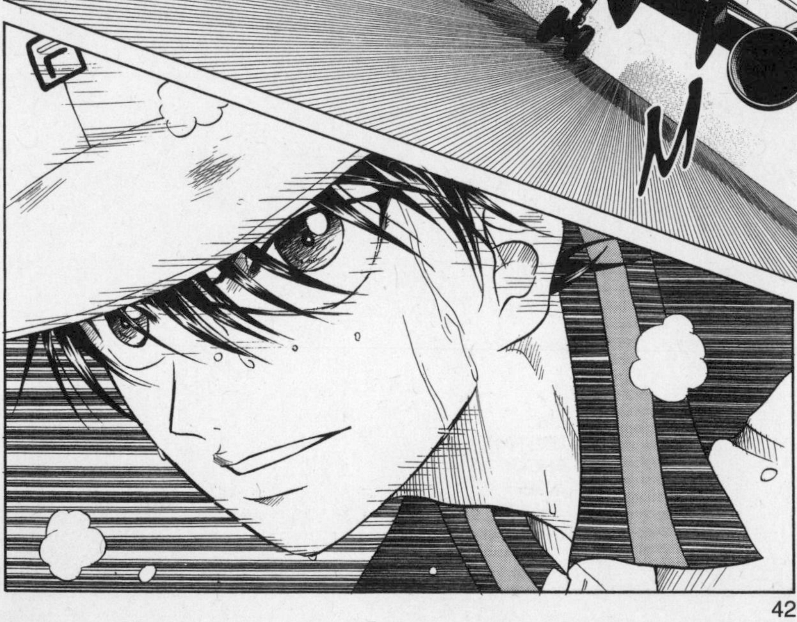

READ THIS WAY

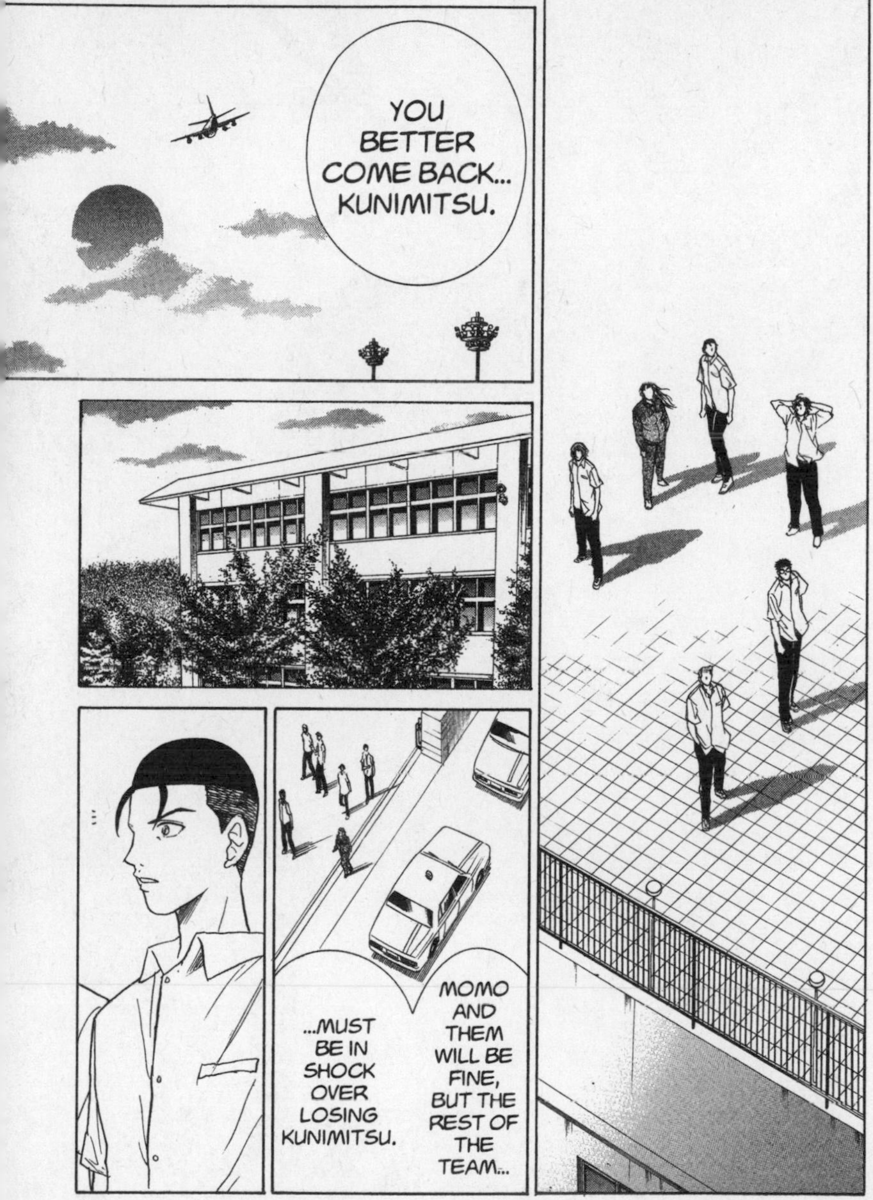
YOU BETTER COME BACK... KUNIMITSU.
MOMO AND THEM WILL BE FINE, BUT THE REST OF THE TEAM...
...MUST BE IN SHOCK OVER LOSING KUNIMITSU.

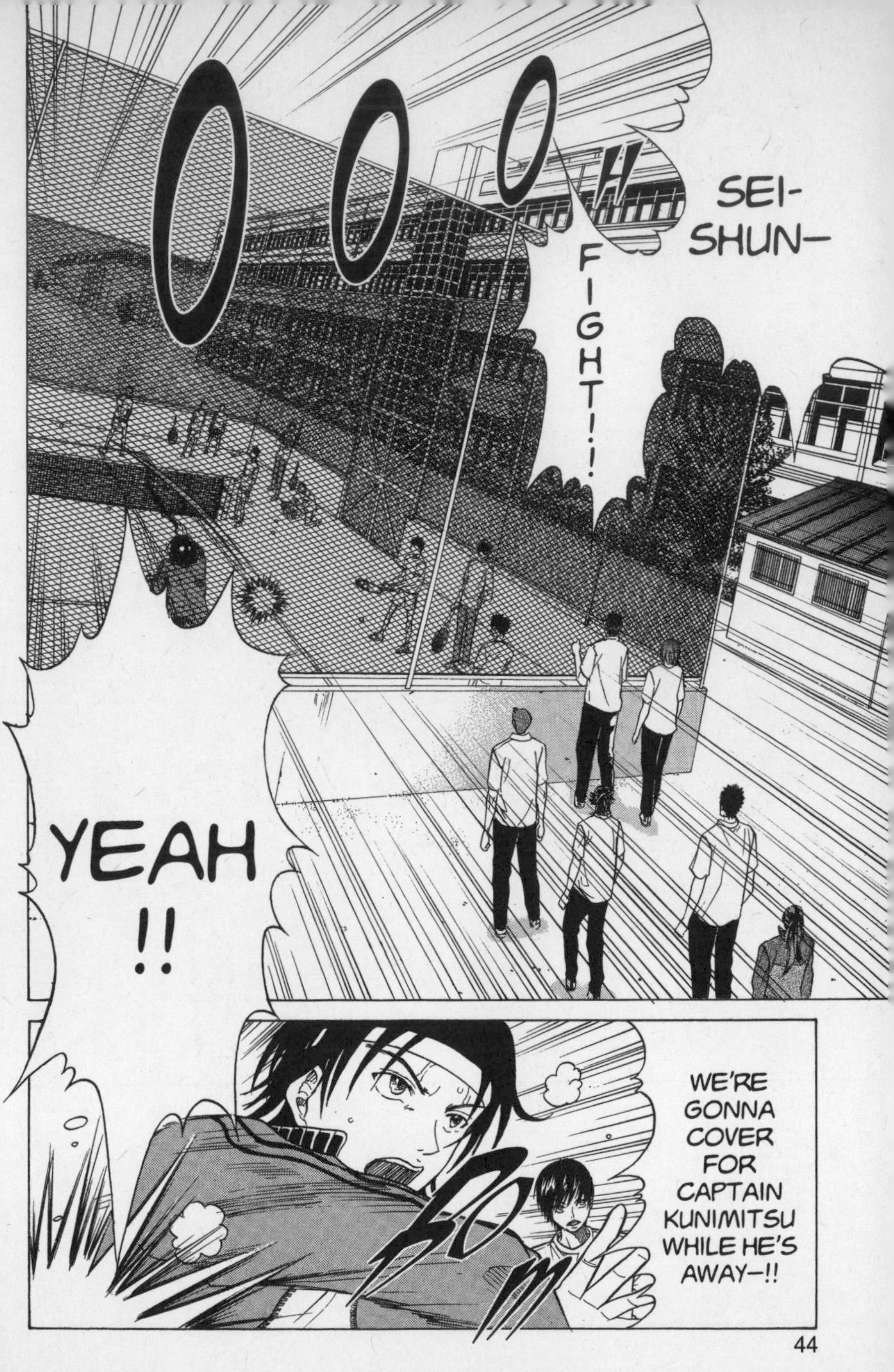
SEI-
SHUN-
FIGHT!!!
OOOH!
YEAH
!!
WE'RE GONNA COVER FOR CAPTAIN KUNIMITSU WHILE HE'S AWAY-!!

READ THIS WAY

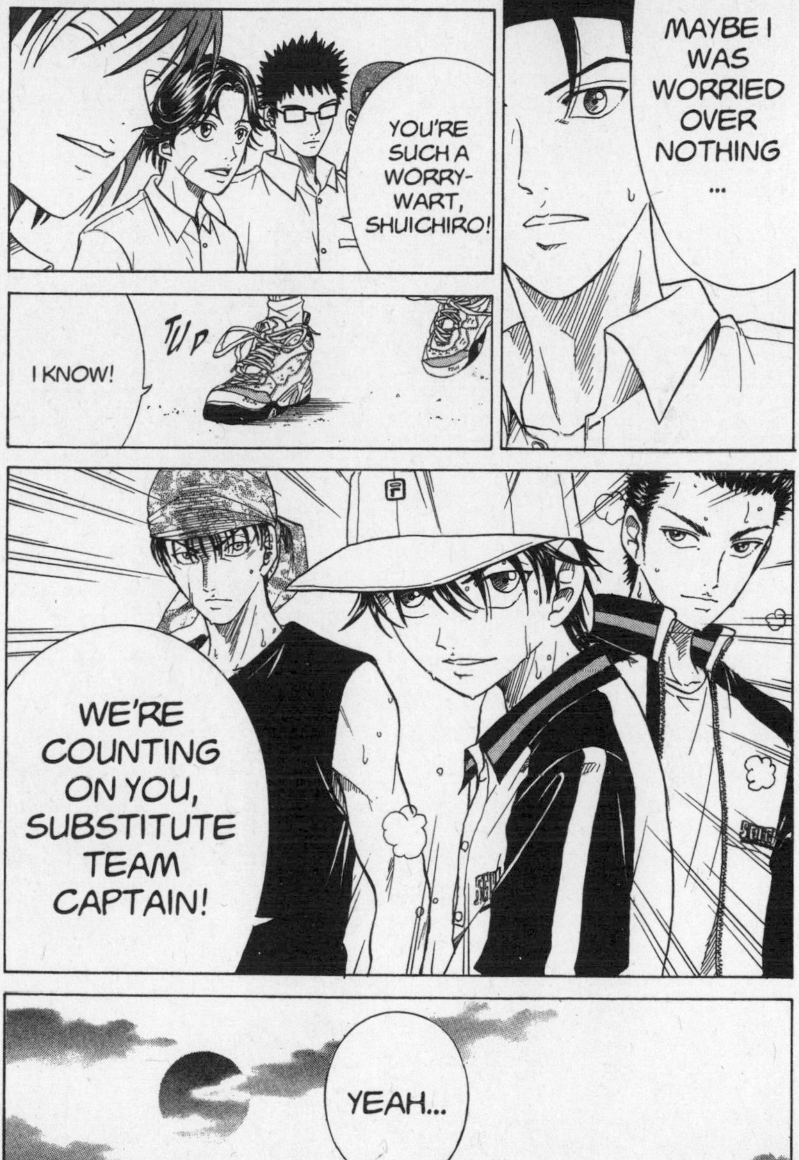
MAYBE I WAS WORRIED OVER NOTHING ...
YOU'RE SUCH A WORRY-WART, SHUICHIRO!
TUD
I KNOW!
WE'RE COUNTING ON YOU, SUBSTITUTE TEAM CAPTAIN!
YEAH...

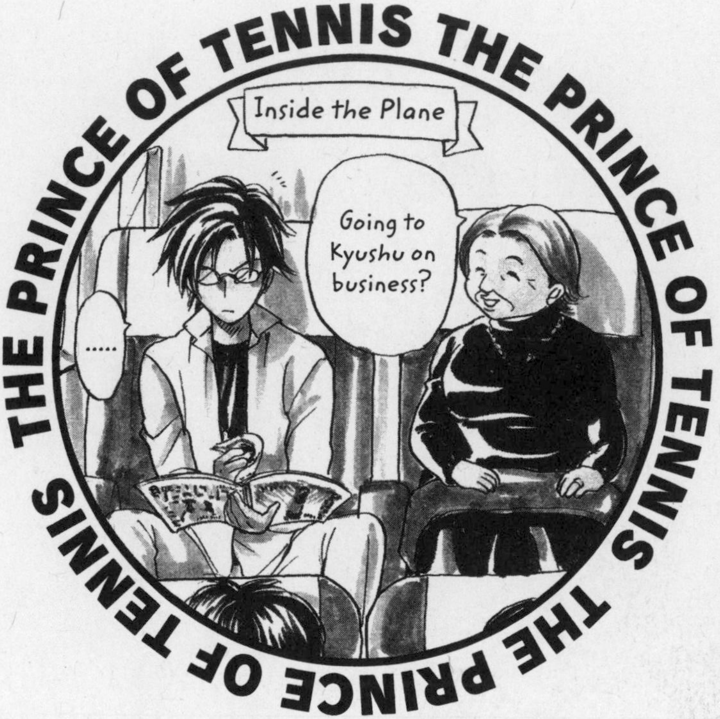
THE PRINCE OF TENNIS THE PRINCE OF TENNIS THE PRINCE OF TENNIS
Inside the Plane
Going to Kyushu on business?
......

GENIUS 161: OISHI'S NEW REGIME

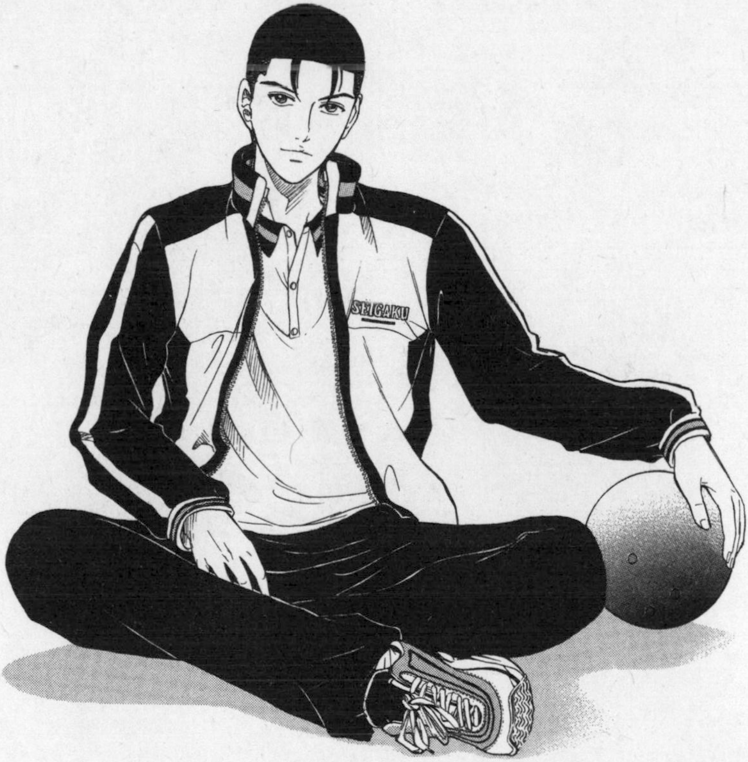
SEIGAKU

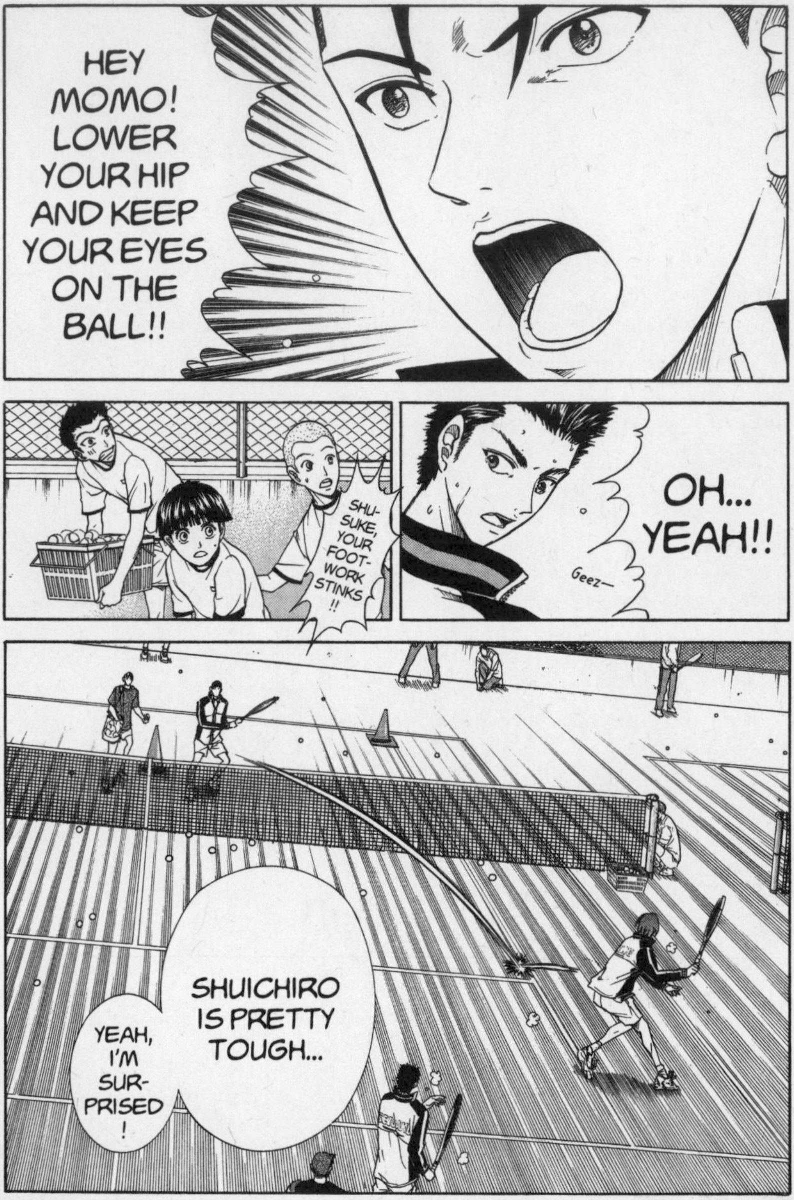
HEY MOMO! LOWER YOUR HIP AND KEEP YOUR EYES ON THE BALL!!
OH... YEAH!!
Geez~
SHU-SUKE, YOUR FOOT-WORK STINKS!!
SHUICHIRO IS PRETTY TOUGH...
YEAH, I'M SUR-PRISED!

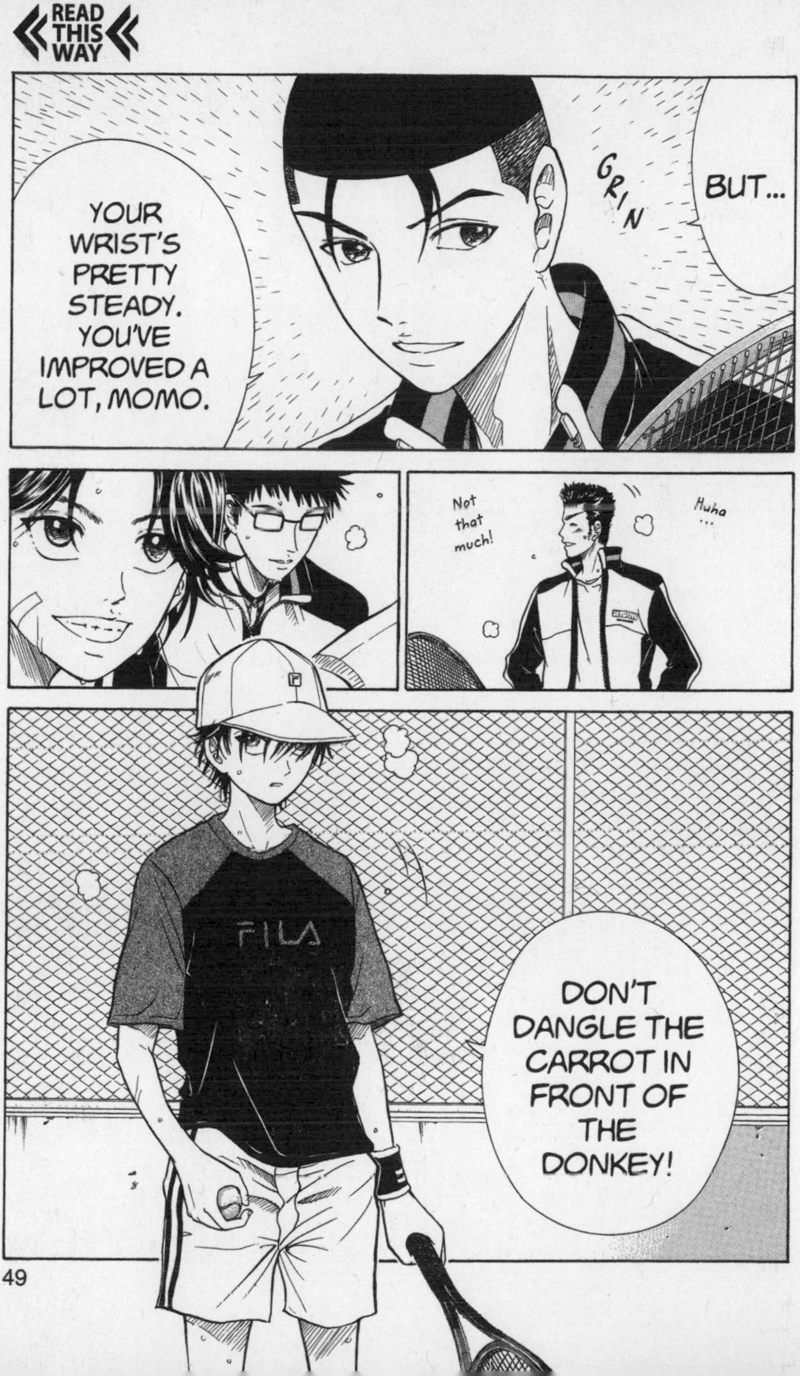
READ THIS WAY
YOUR WRIST'S PRETTY STEADY. YOU'VE IMPROVED A LOT, MOMO.
GRIN
BUT...
Not that much!
Huha ...
DON'T DANGLE THE CARROT IN FRONT OF THE DONKEY!

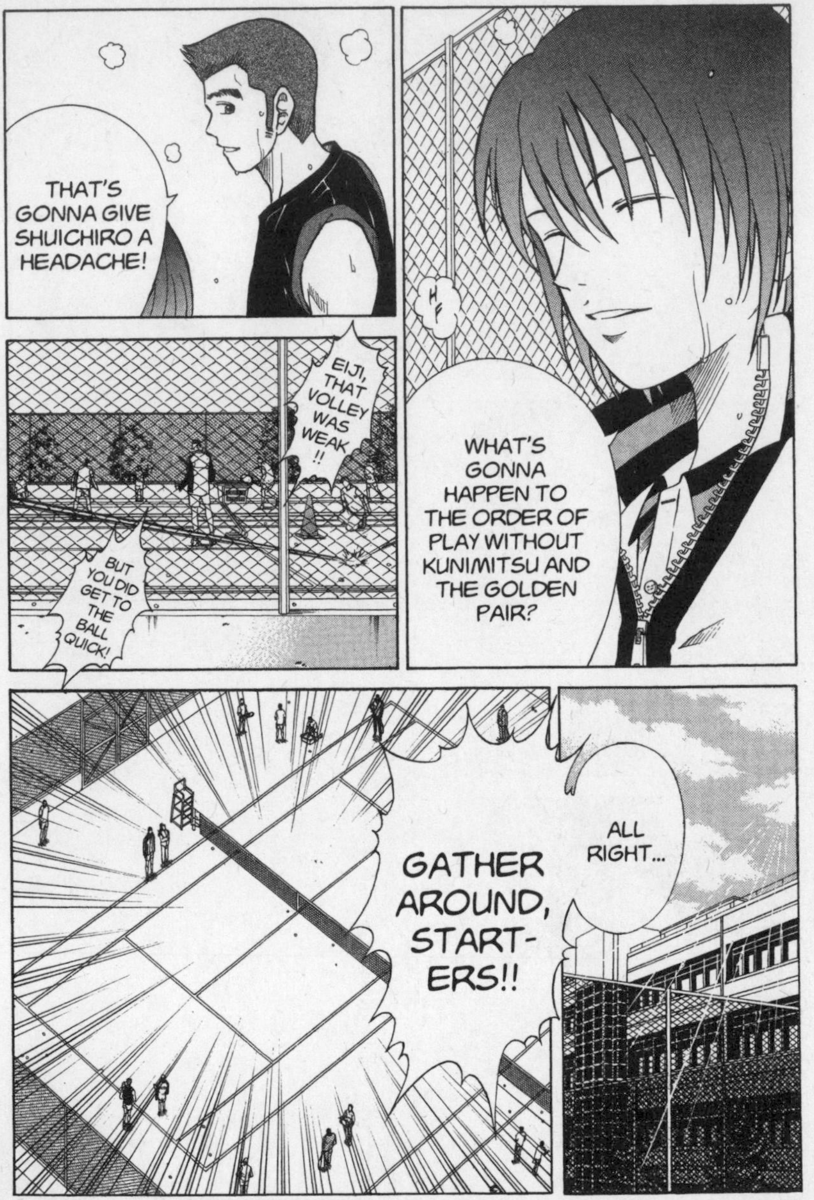
HF
WHAT'S GONNA HAPPEN TO THE ORDER OF PLAY WITHOUT KUNIMITSU AND THE GOLDEN PAIR?
THAT'S GONNA GIVE SHUICHIRO A HEADACHE!
EIJI, THAT VOLLEY WAS WEAK!!
BUT YOU DID GET TO THE BALL QUICK!
ALL RIGHT...
GATHER AROUND, STARTERS!!

READ THIS WAY

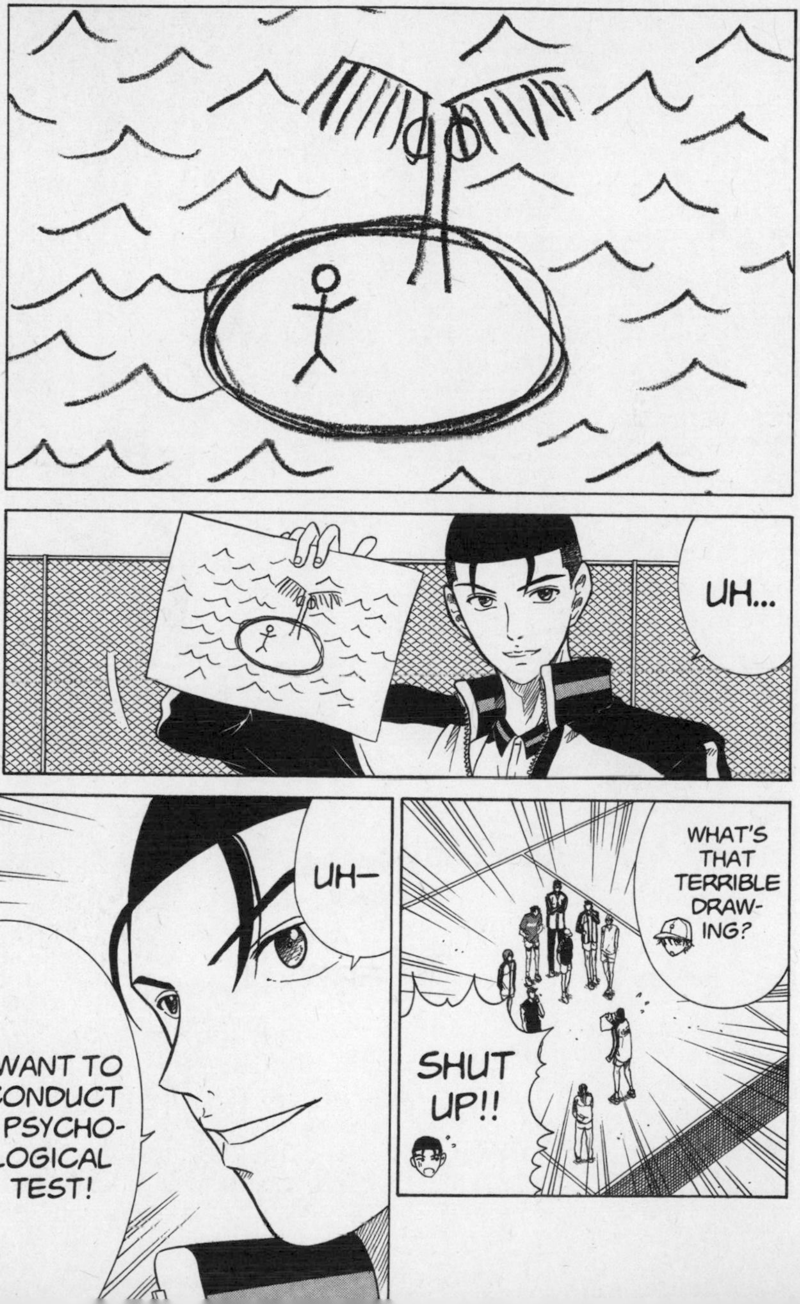
UH...
WHAT'S THAT TERRIBLE DRAWING?
SHUT UP!!
UH–
I WANT TO CONDUCT A PSYCHOLOGICAL TEST!

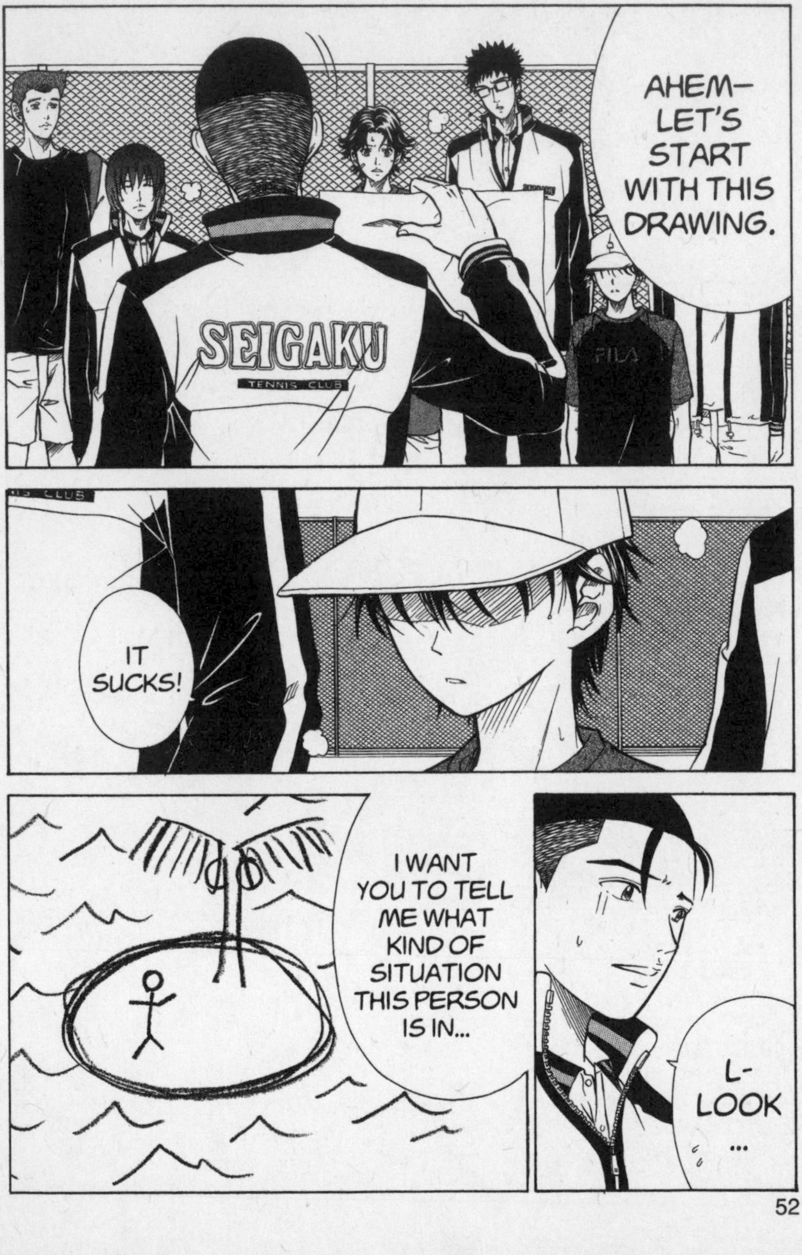
AHEM— LET'S START WITH THIS DRAWING.
SEIGAKU
TENNIS CLUB
FILA
IT SUCKS!
L- LOOK ...
I WANT YOU TO TELL ME WHAT KIND OF SITUATION THIS PERSON IS IN...

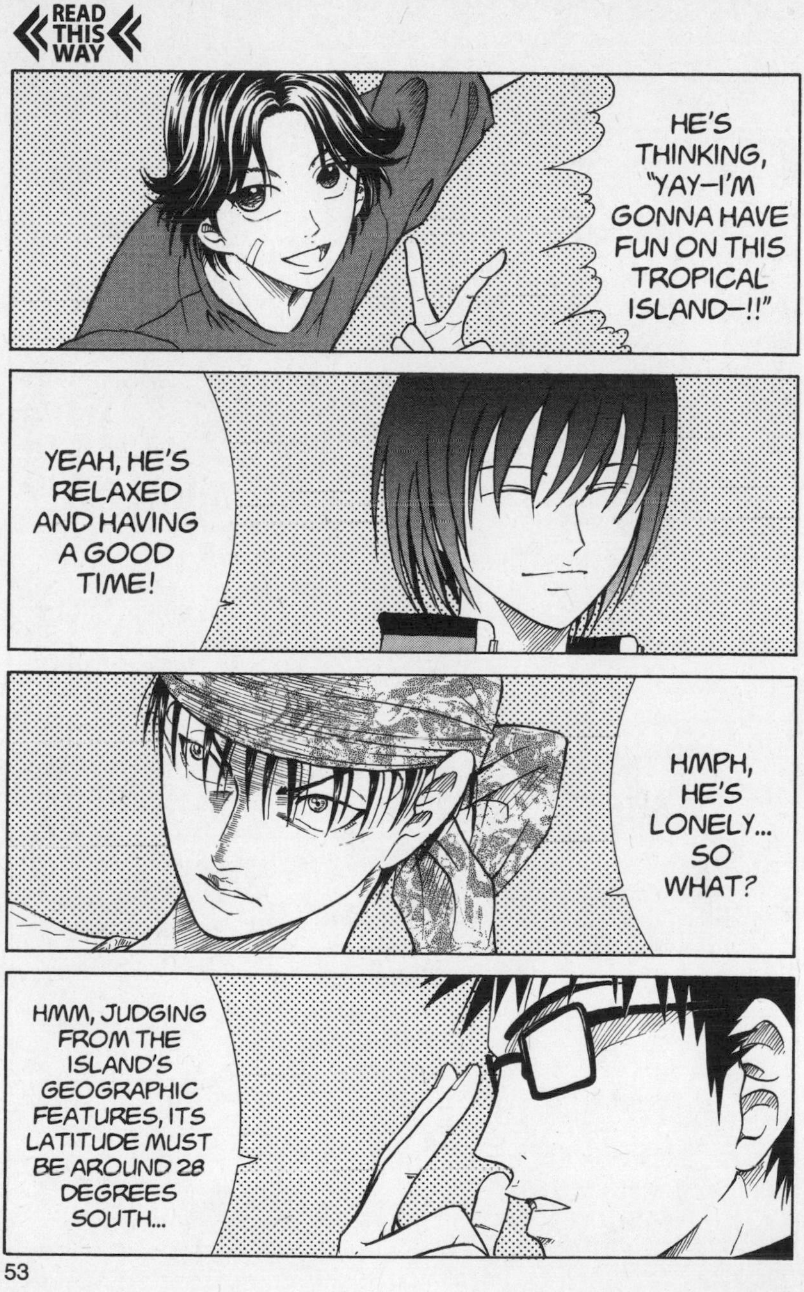
READ THIS WAY
HE'S THINKING, "YAY—I'M GONNA HAVE FUN ON THIS TROPICAL ISLAND—!!"
YEAH, HE'S RELAXED AND HAVING A GOOD TIME!
HMPH, HE'S LONELY... SO WHAT?
HMM, JUDGING FROM THE ISLAND'S GEOGRAPHIC FEATURES, ITS LATITUDE MUST BE AROUND 28 DEGREES SOUTH...

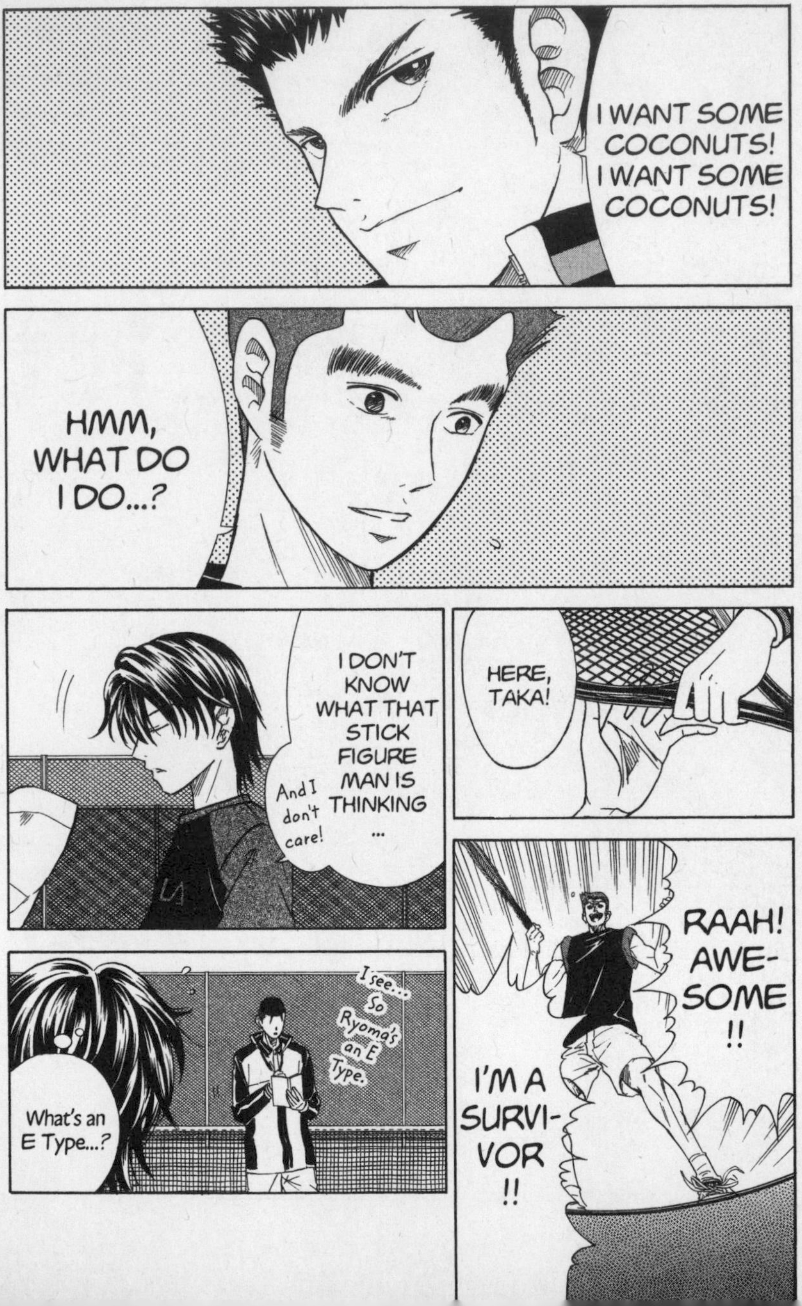
I WANT SOME COCONUTS! I WANT SOME COCONUTS!
HMM, WHAT DO I DO...?
HERE, TAKA!
I DON'T KNOW WHAT THAT STICK FIGURE MAN IS THINKING ...
And I don't care!
RAAH! AWESOME !!
I'M A SURVIVOR !!
I see... So Ryoma's an E Type.
What's an E Type...?

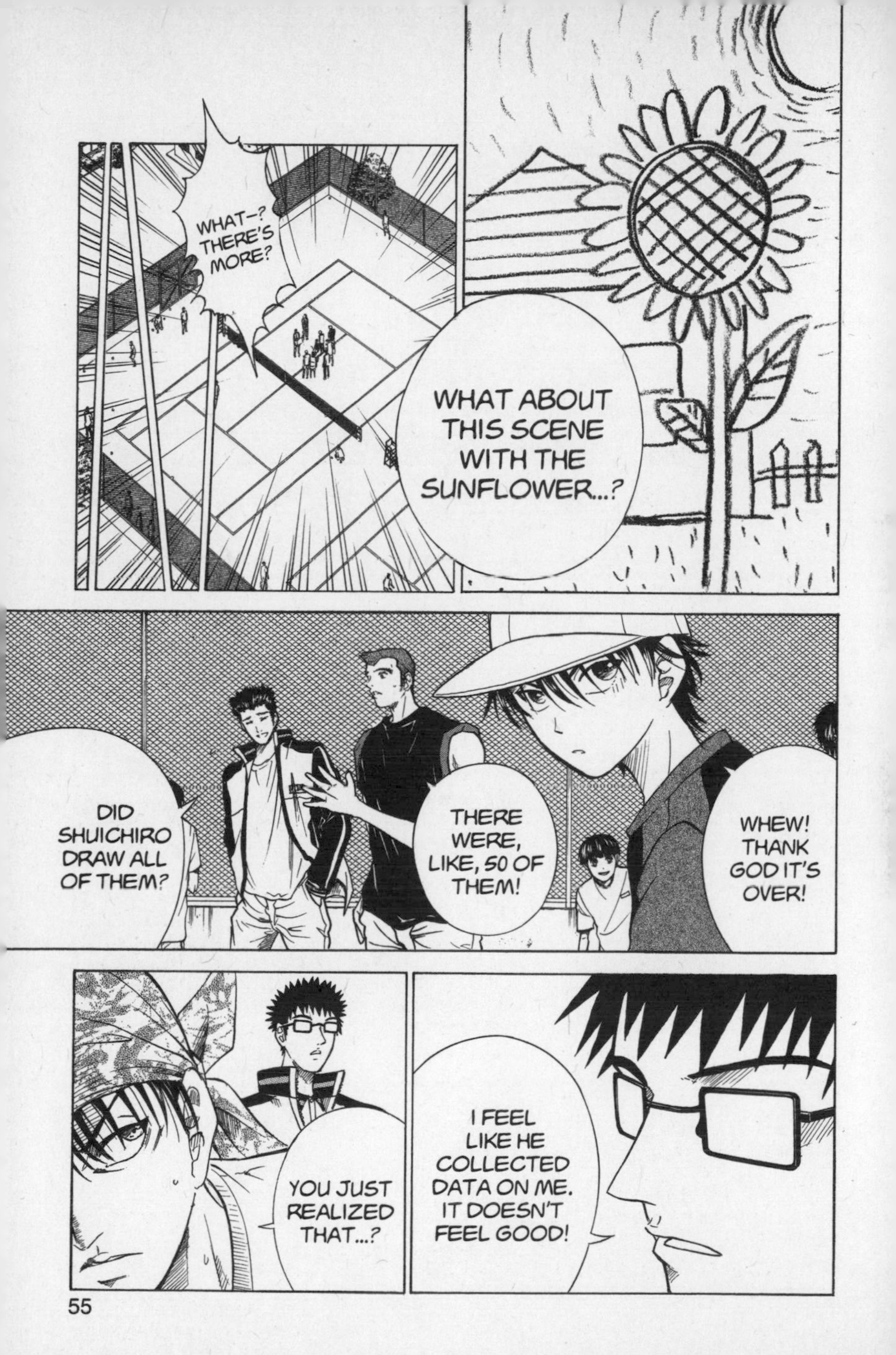
WHAT ABOUT THIS SCENE WITH THE SUNFLOWER...?
WHAT–? THERE'S MORE?
WHEW! THANK GOD IT'S OVER!
THERE WERE, LIKE, 50 OF THEM!
DID SHUICHIRO DRAW ALL OF THEM?
I FEEL LIKE HE COLLECTED DATA ON ME. IT DOESN'T FEEL GOOD!
YOU JUST REALIZED THAT...?

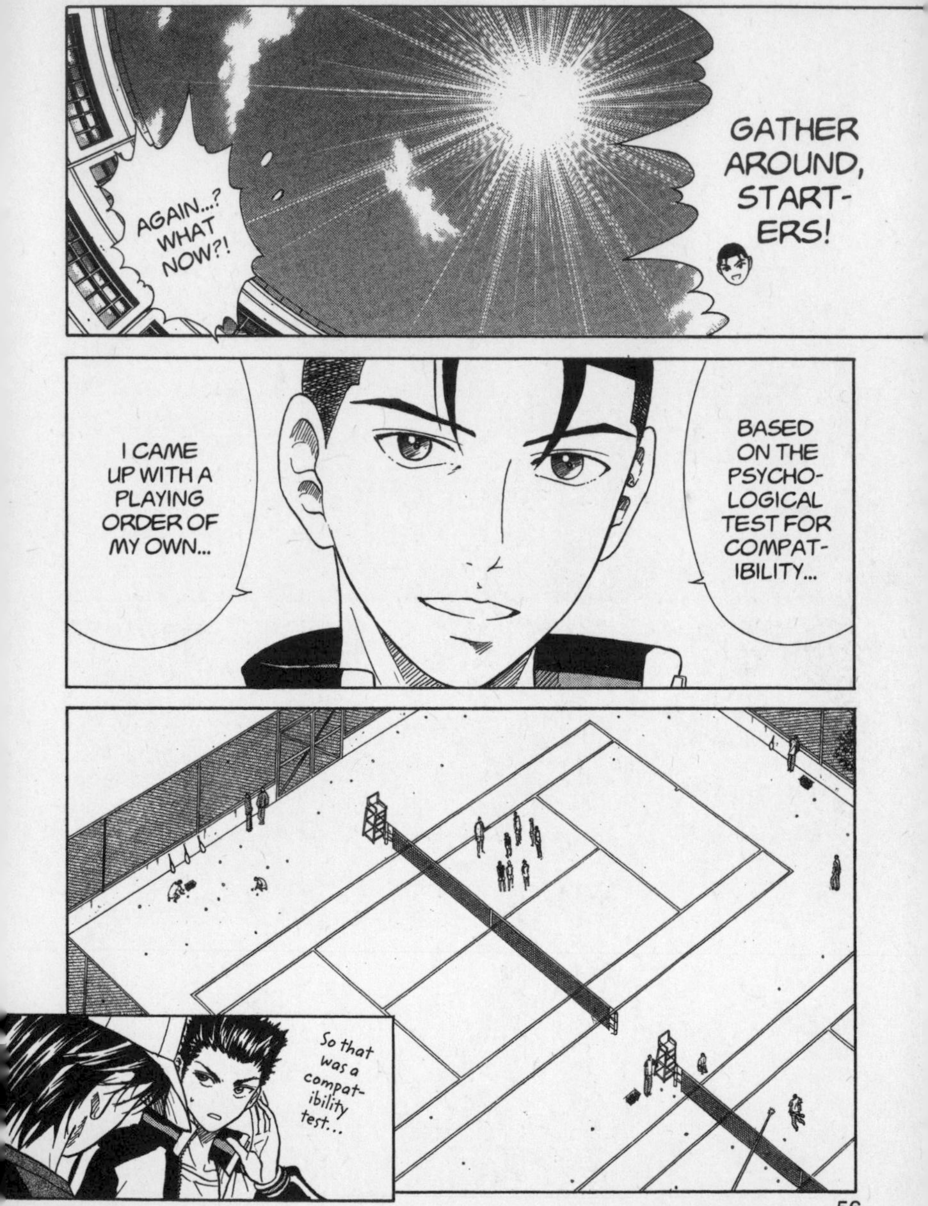
GATHER AROUND, START-ERS!
AGAIN...? WHAT NOW?!
BASED ON THE PSYCHO-LOGICAL TEST FOR COMPAT-IBILITY...
I CAME UP WITH A PLAYING ORDER OF MY OWN...
So that was a compat-ibility test...

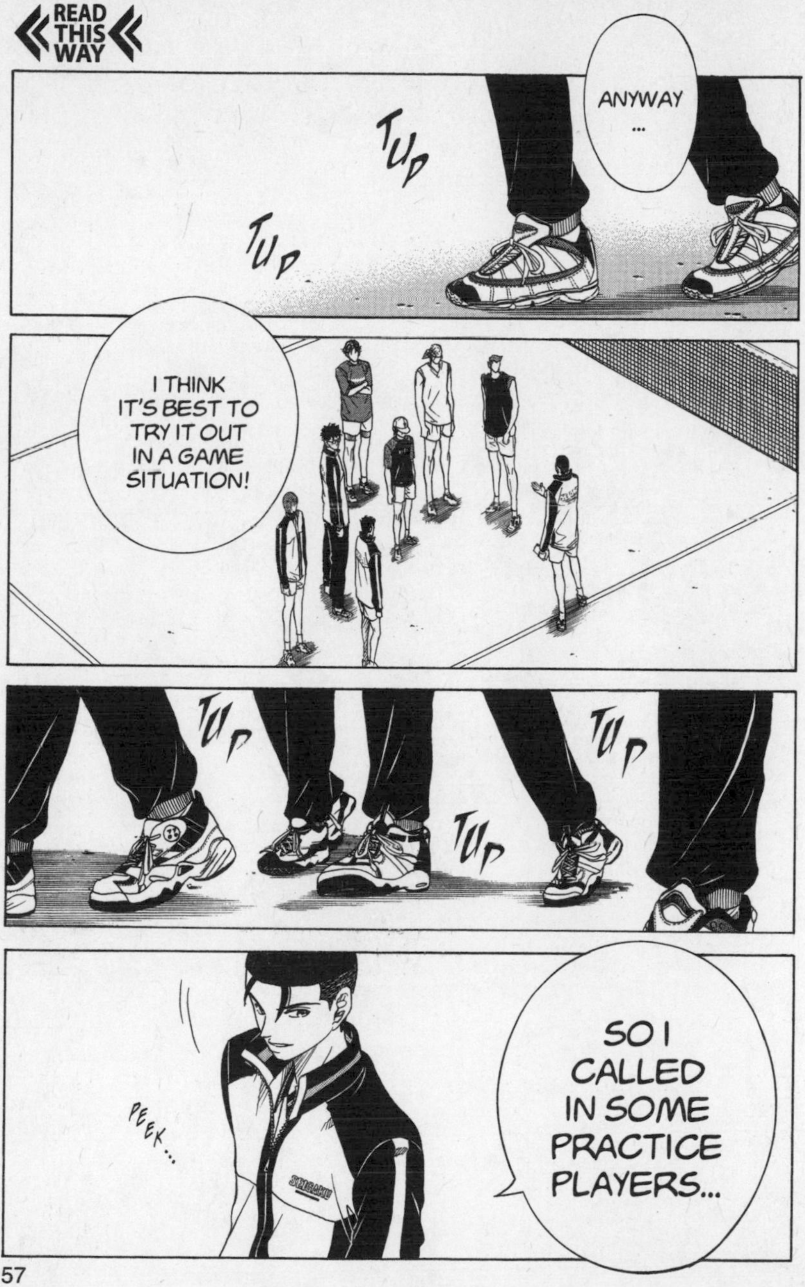
READ THIS WAY
ANYWAY ...
TUP
TUP
I THINK IT'S BEST TO TRY IT OUT IN A GAME SITUATION!
TUP
TUP
TUP
SO I CALLED IN SOME PRACTICE PLAYERS...
PEEK...

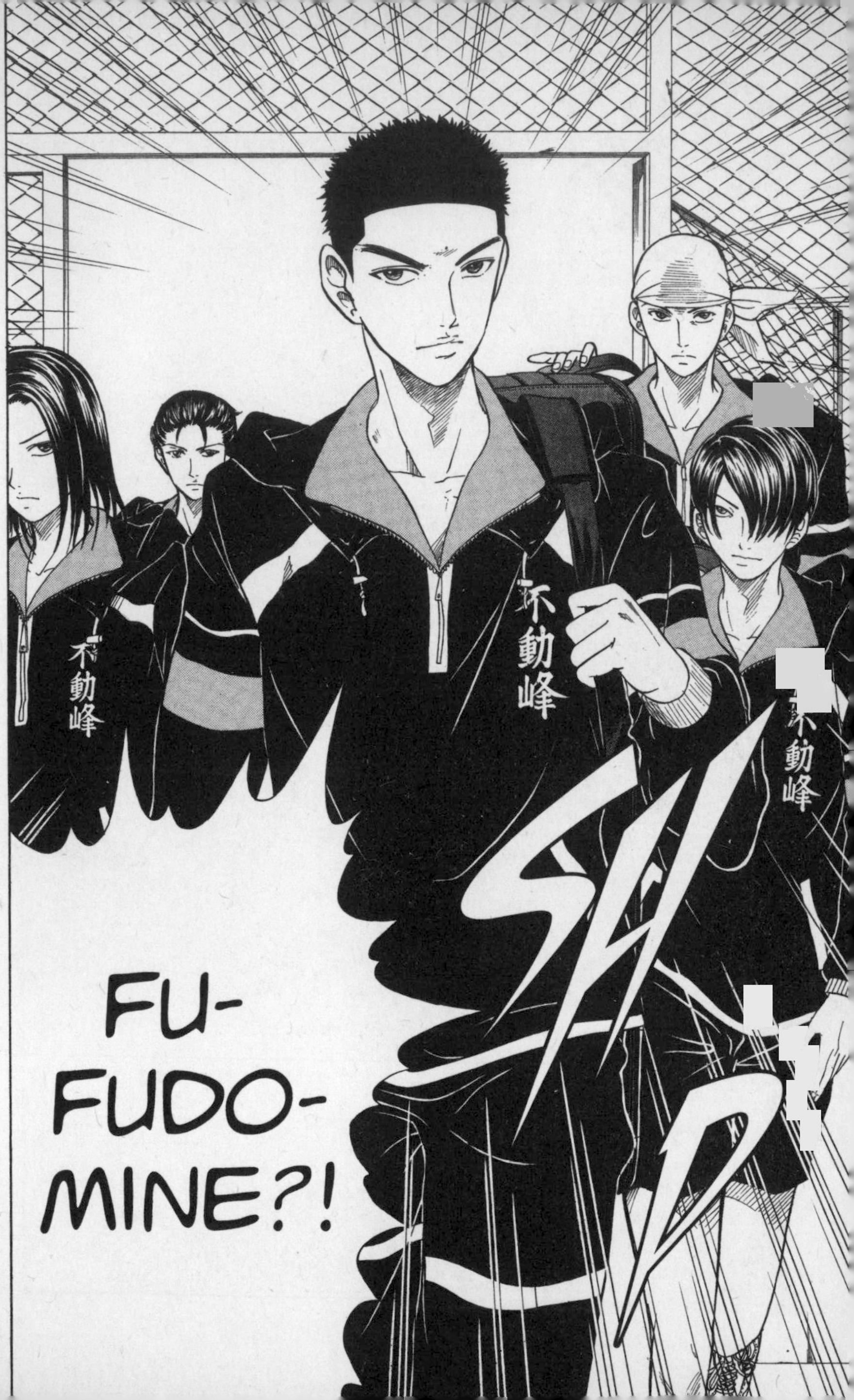
FU-
FUDO-
MINE?!
不動峰

READ THIS WAY

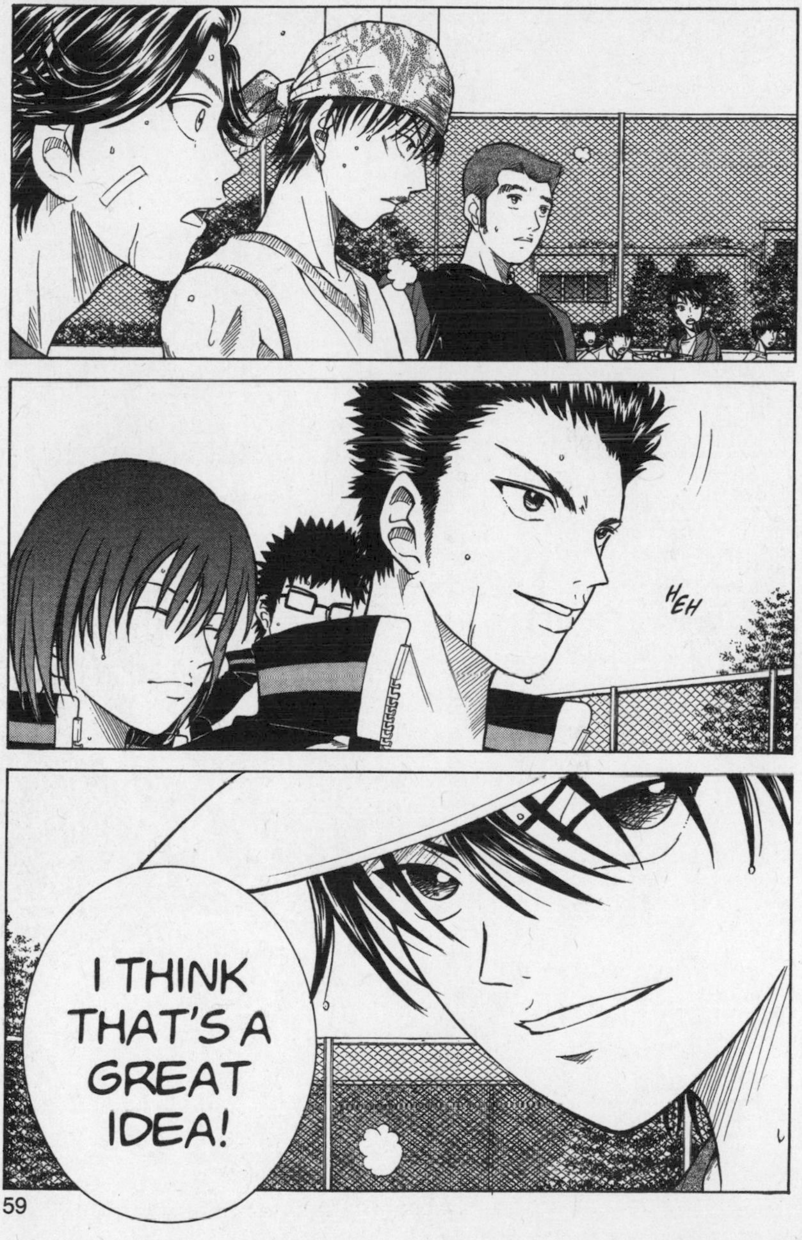
HEH
I THINK THAT'S A GREAT IDEA!

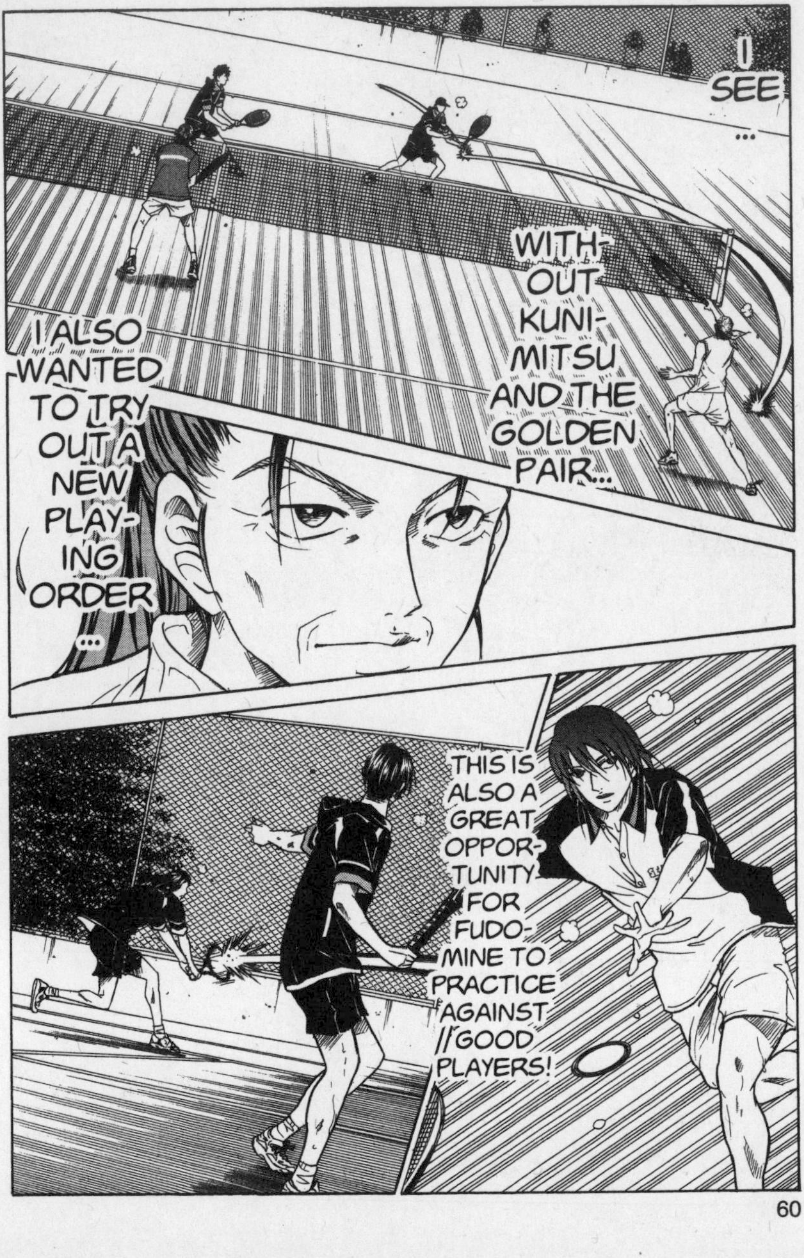
I SEE ...
WITHOUT KUNIMITSU AND THE GOLDEN PAIR...
I ALSO WANTED TO TRY OUT A NEW PLAYING ORDER ...
THIS IS ALSO A GREAT OPPORTUNITY FOR FUDOMINE TO PRACTICE AGAINST GOOD PLAYERS!

READ THIS WAY

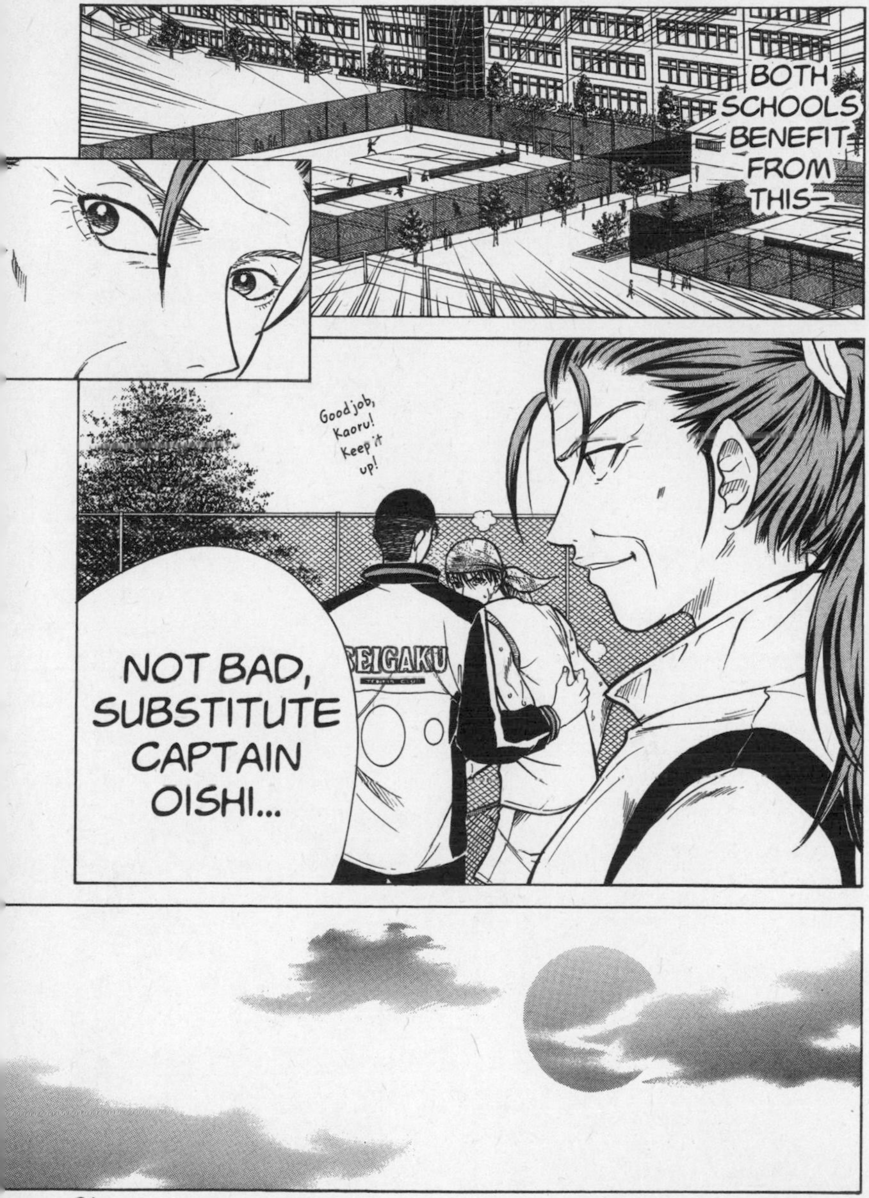
BOTH SCHOOLS BENEFIT FROM THIS—
Good job, Kaoru! Keep it up!
SEIGAKU
NOT BAD, SUBSTITUTE CAPTAIN OISHI...

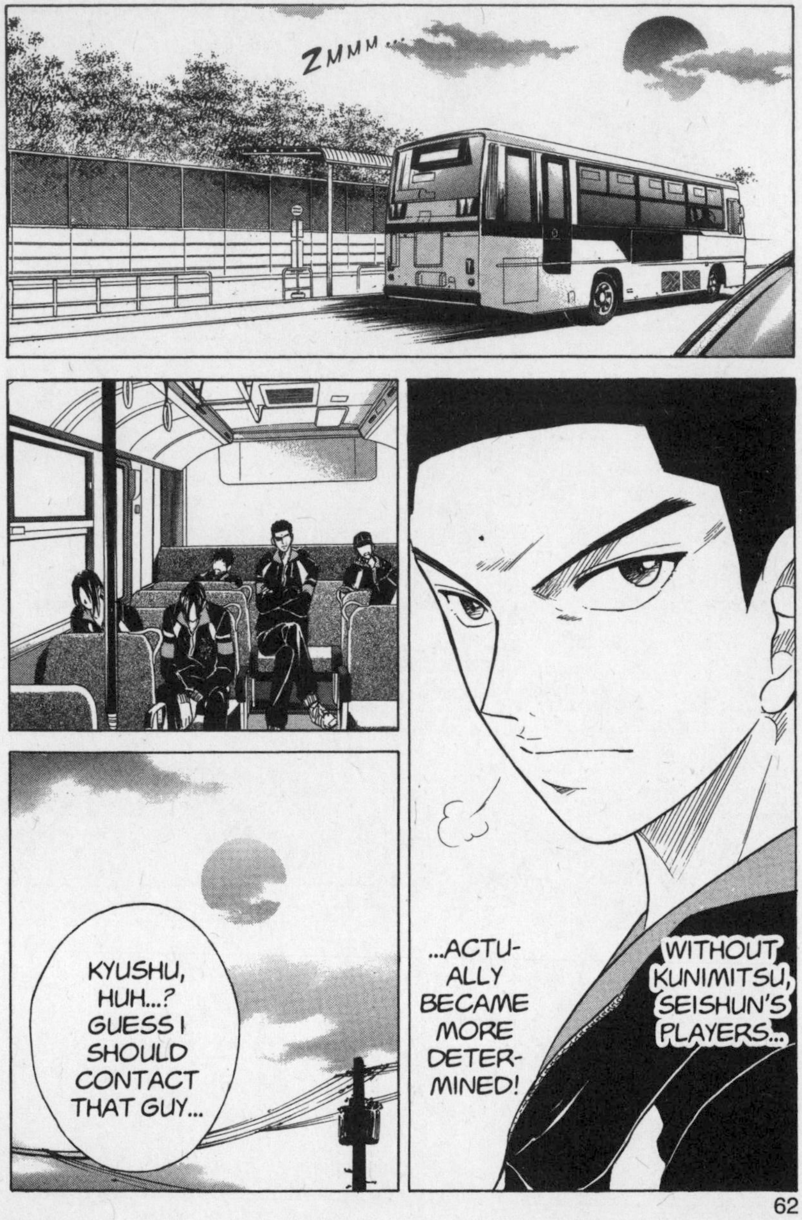
ZMMM...
WITHOUT KUNIMITSU, SEISHUN'S PLAYERS...
...ACTU-ALLY BECAME MORE DETER-MINED!
KYUSHU, HUH...? GUESS I SHOULD CONTACT THAT GUY...

READ THIS WAY

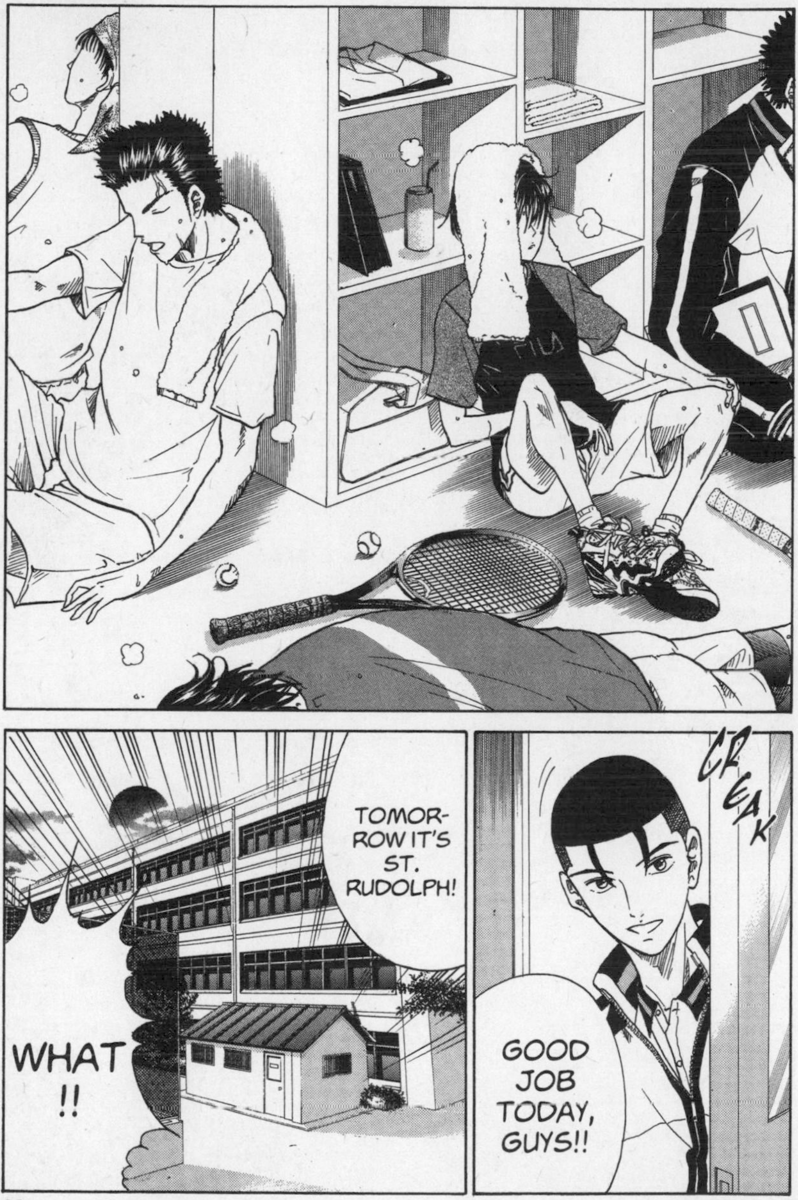
CREAK
GOOD JOB TODAY, GUYS!!
TOMOR-ROW IT'S ST. RUDOLPH!
WHAT !!

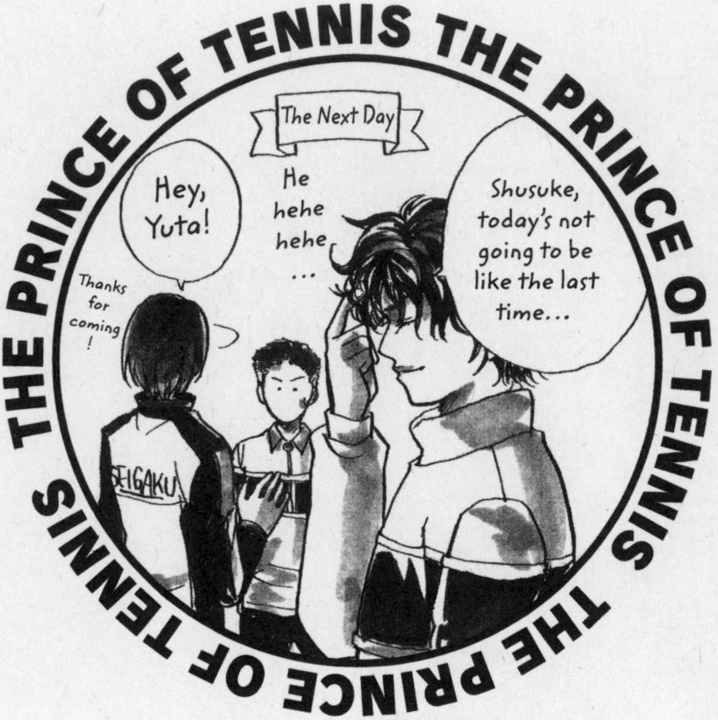
THE PRINCE OF TENNIS THE PRINCE OF TENNIS THE PRINCE OF TENNIS
The Next Day
Shusuke, today's not going to be like the last time...
He hehe hehe...
Hey, Yuta!
Thanks for coming!
SEIGAKU

Genius 162: Saitama Midoriyama's Ability

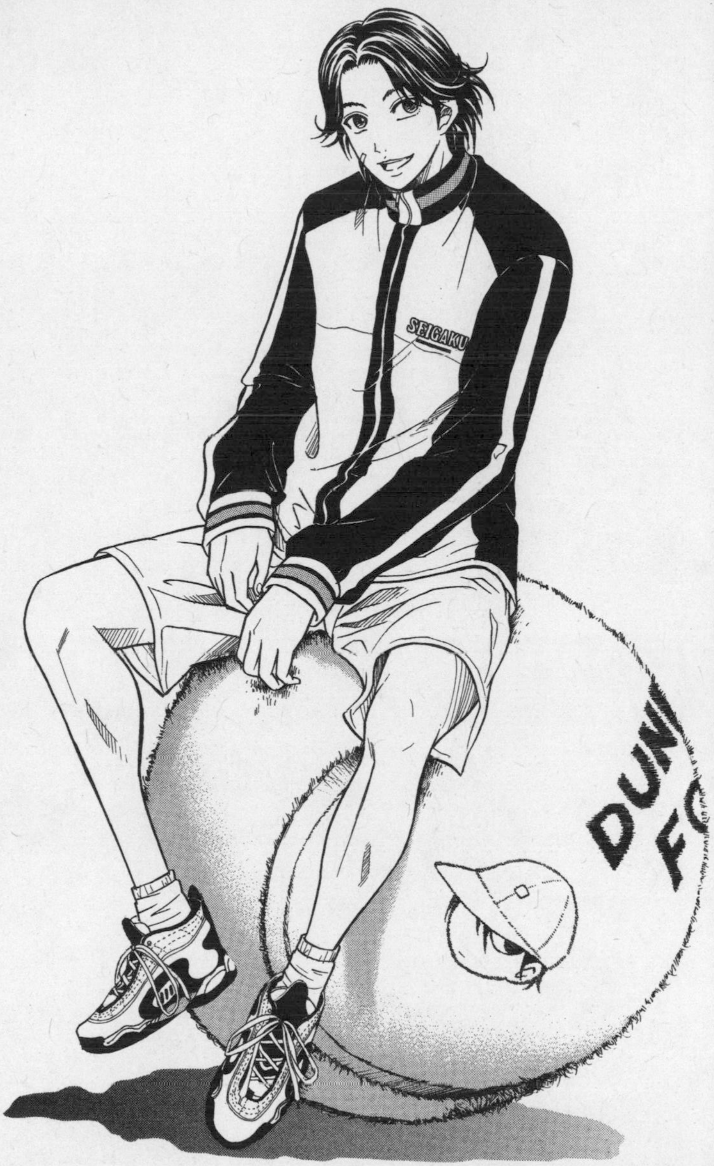
SEIGAKU

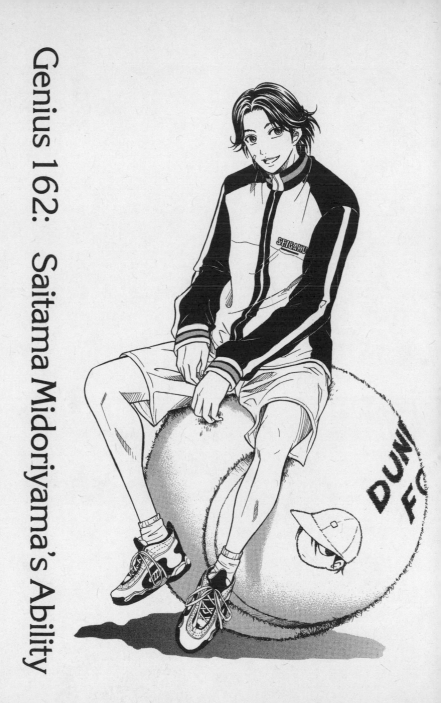

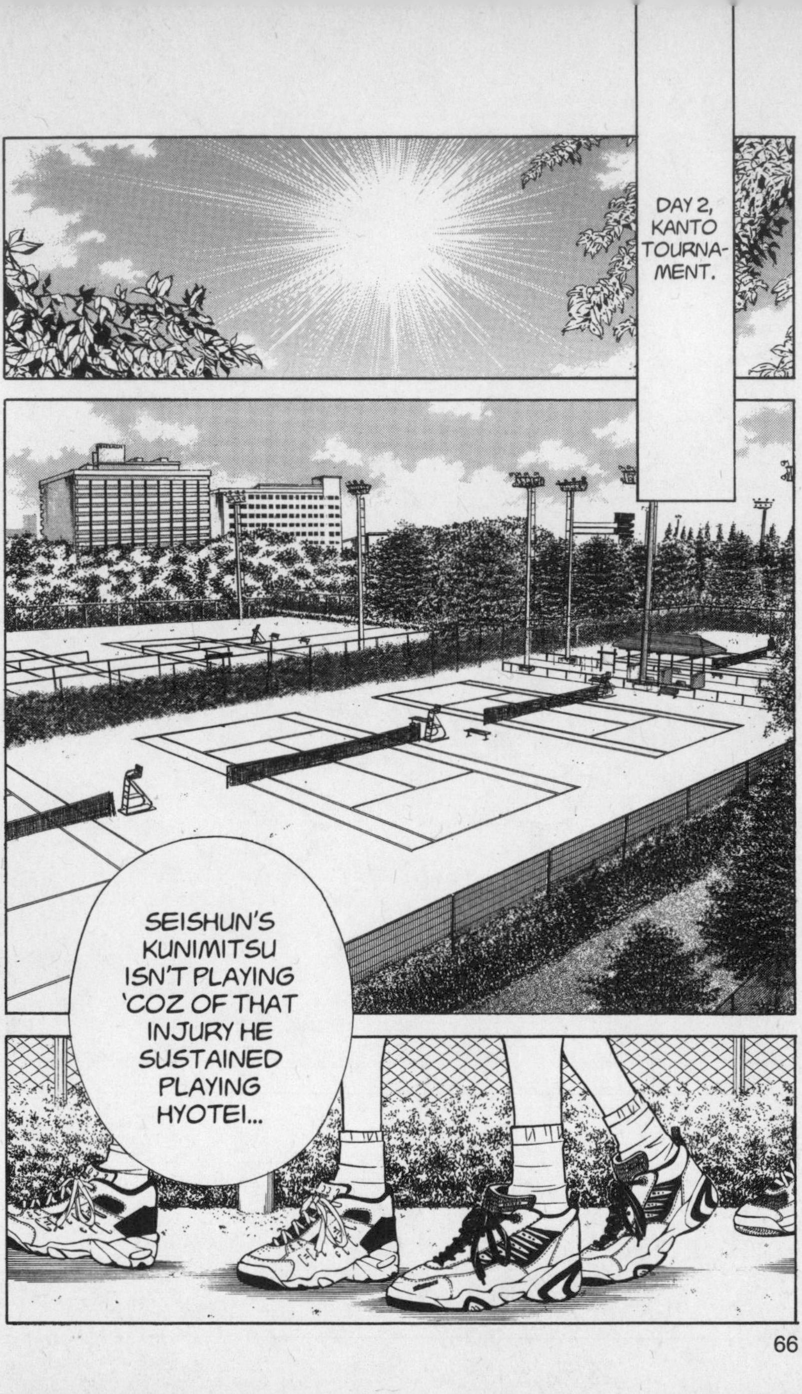
DAY 2, KANTO TOURNAMENT.
SEISHUN'S KUNIMITSU ISN'T PLAYING 'COZ OF THAT INJURY HE SUSTAINED PLAYING HYOTEI...

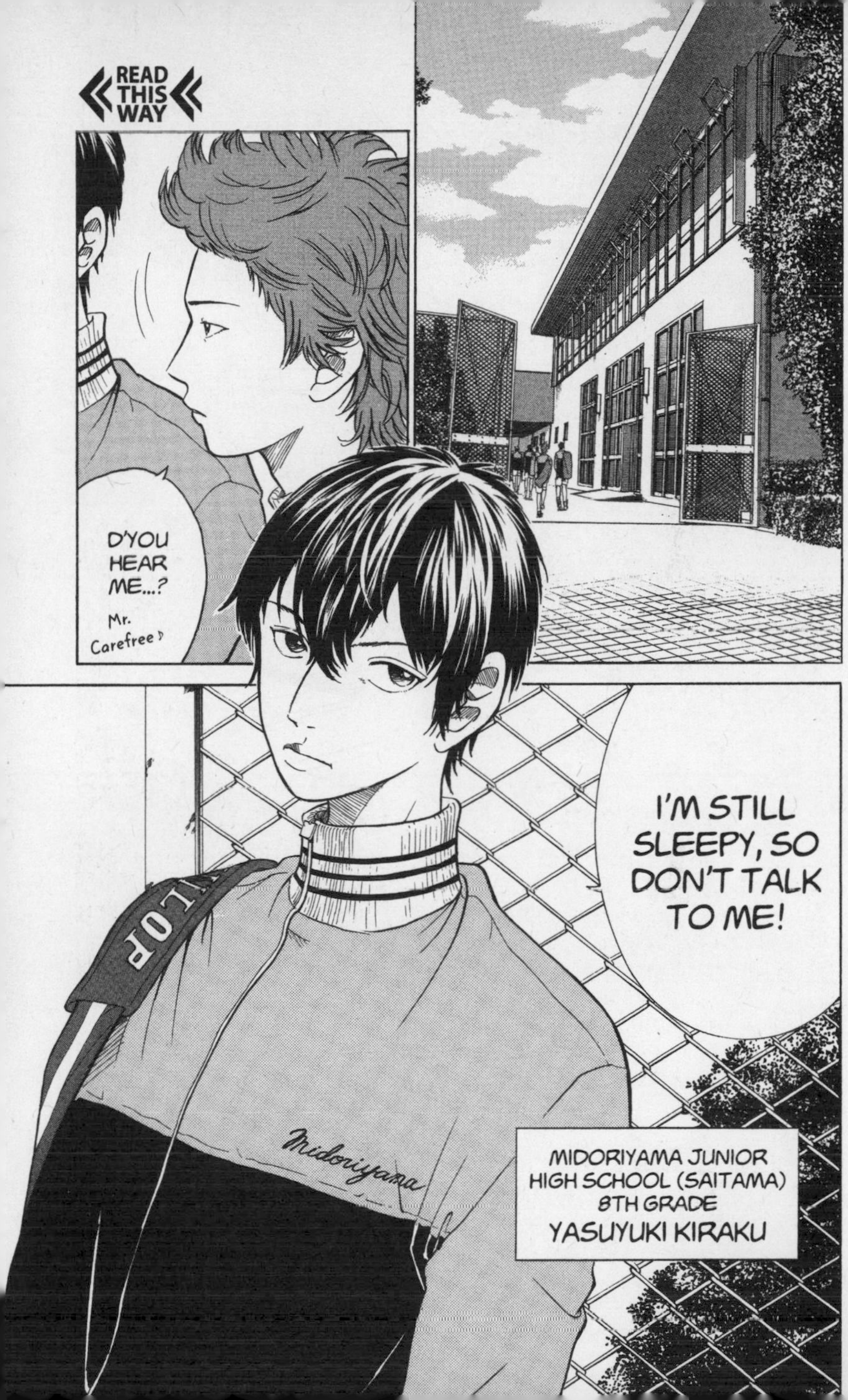
READ THIS WAY
D'YOU HEAR ME...?
Mr. Carefree
I'M STILL SLEEPY, SO DON'T TALK TO ME!
Midoriyama
MIDORIYAMA JUNIOR HIGH SCHOOL (SAITAMA) 8TH GRADE YASUYUKI KIRAKU

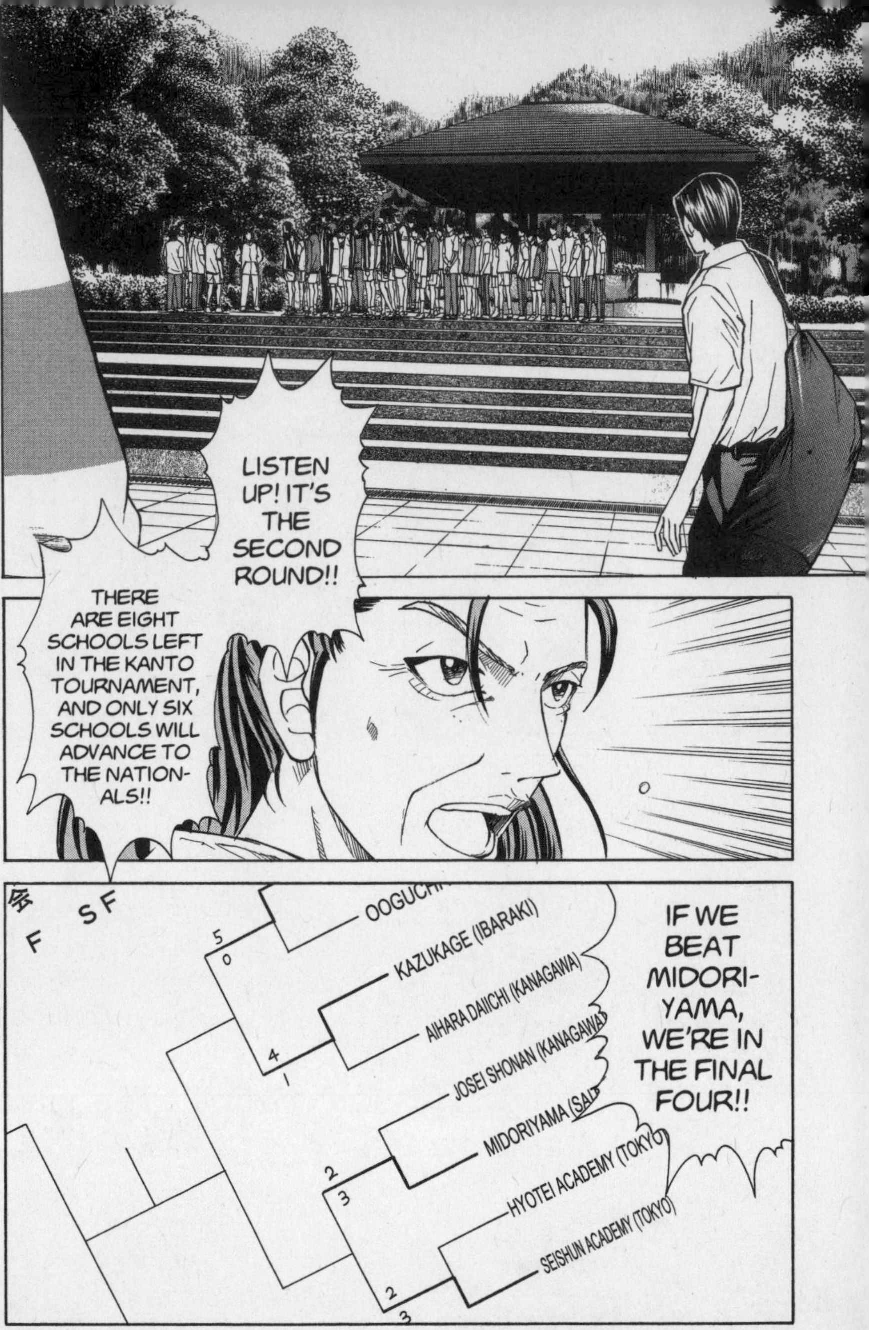
LISTEN UP! IT'S THE SECOND ROUND!!
THERE ARE EIGHT SCHOOLS LEFT IN THE KANTO TOURNAMENT, AND ONLY SIX SCHOOLS WILL ADVANCE TO THE NATION-ALS!!
IF WE BEAT MIDORI-YAMA, WE'RE IN THE FINAL FOUR!!
OOGUCHI
KAZUKAGE (IBARAKI)
AIHARA DAIICHI (KANAGAWA)
JOSEI SHONAN (KANAGAWA
MIDORIYAMA (SAI
HYOTEI ACADEMY (TOKYO
SEISHUN ACADEMY (TOKYO)

READ THIS WAY

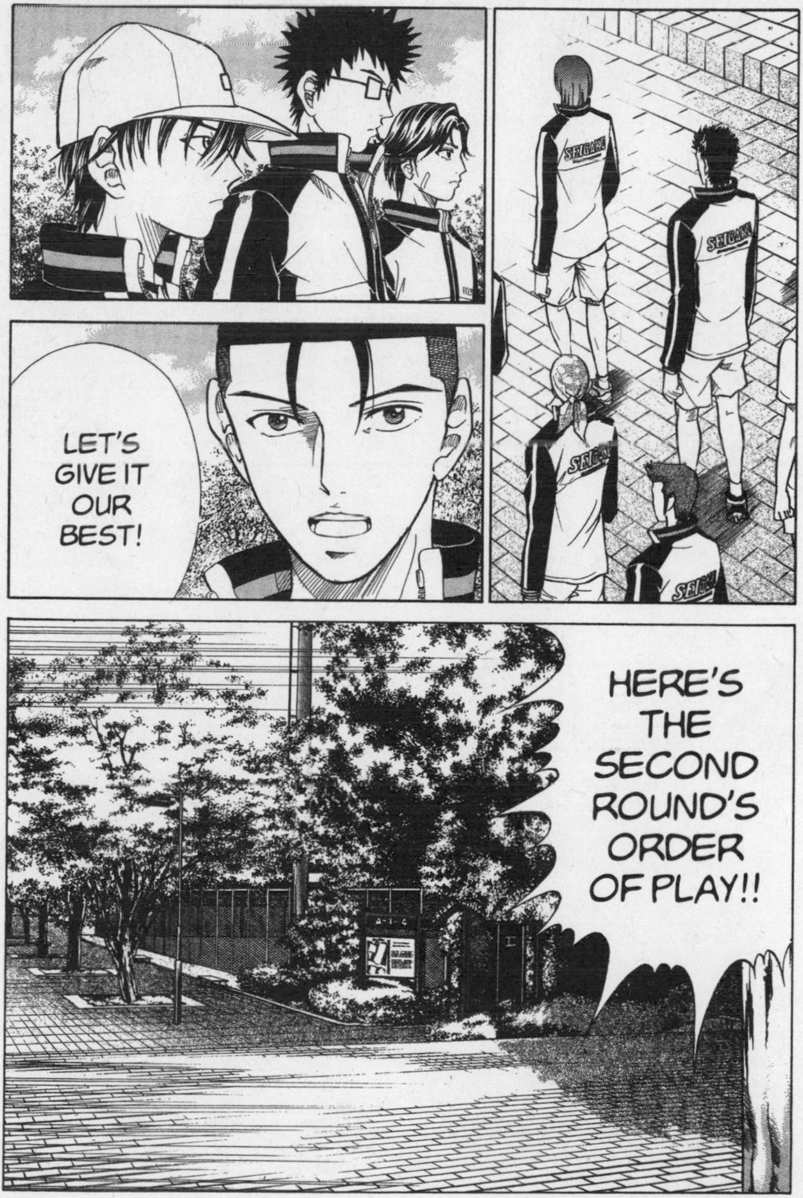
LET'S GIVE IT OUR BEST!
HERE'S THE SECOND ROUND'S ORDER OF PLAY!!

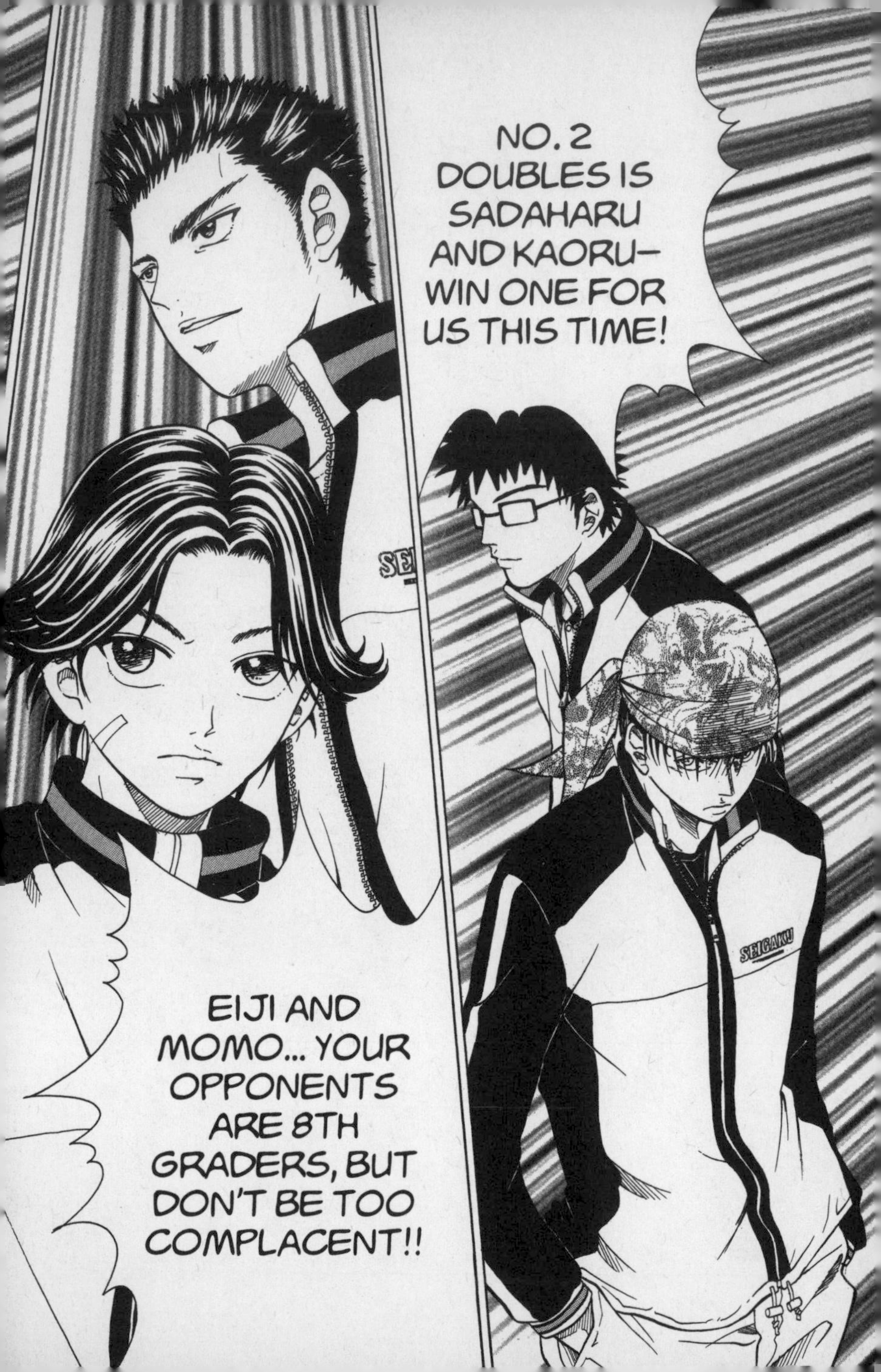
NO. 2 DOUBLES IS SADAHARU AND KAORU– WIN ONE FOR US THIS TIME!
SEIGAKU
EIJI AND MOMO... YOUR OPPONENTS ARE 8TH GRADERS, BUT DON'T BE TOO COMPLACENT!!

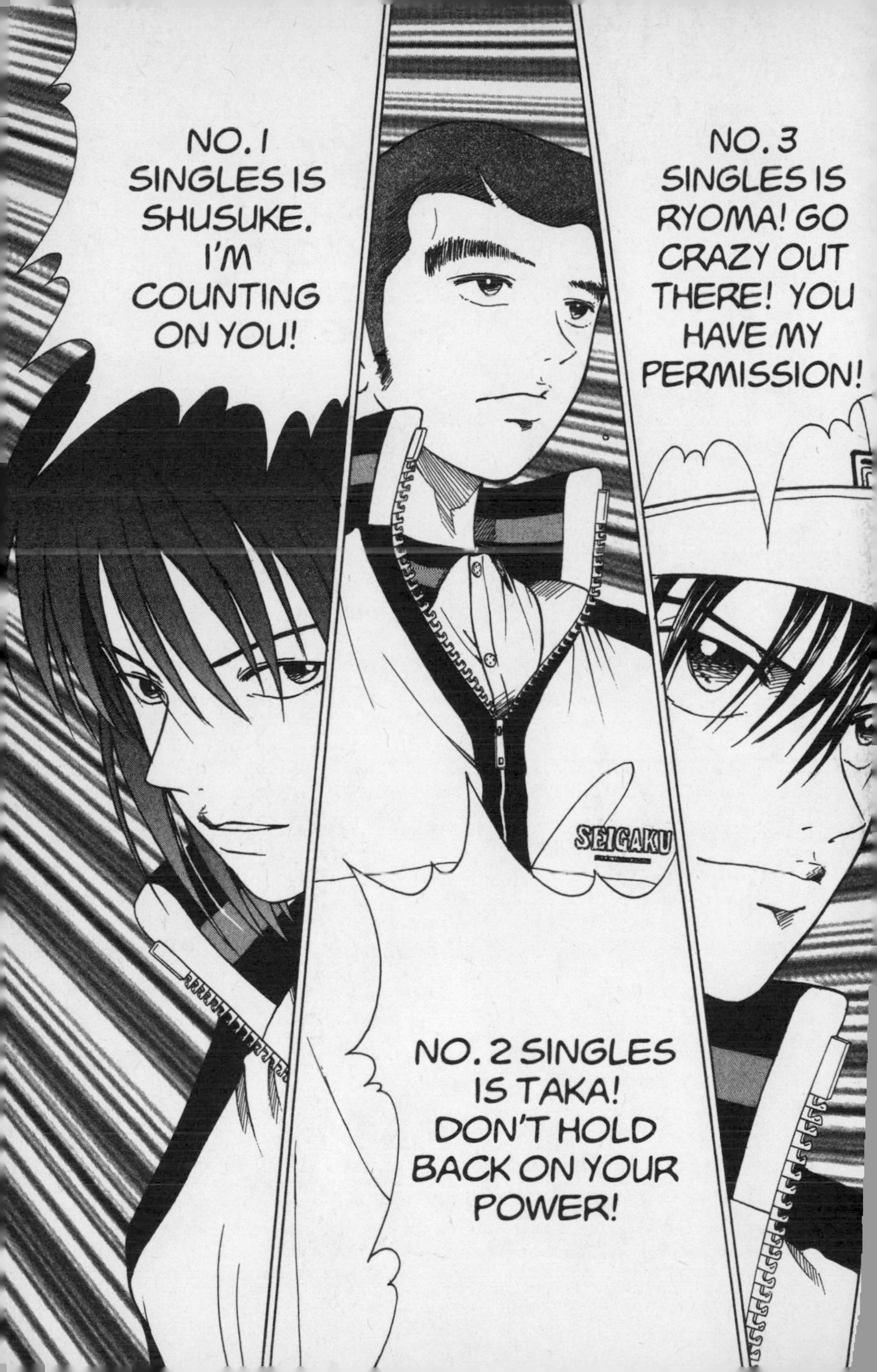
NO. 3 SINGLES IS RYOMA! GO CRAZY OUT THERE! YOU HAVE MY PERMISSION!
SEIGAKU
NO. 2 SINGLES IS TAKA! DON'T HOLD BACK ON YOUR POWER!
NO. 1 SINGLES IS SHUSUKE. I'M COUNTING ON YOU!

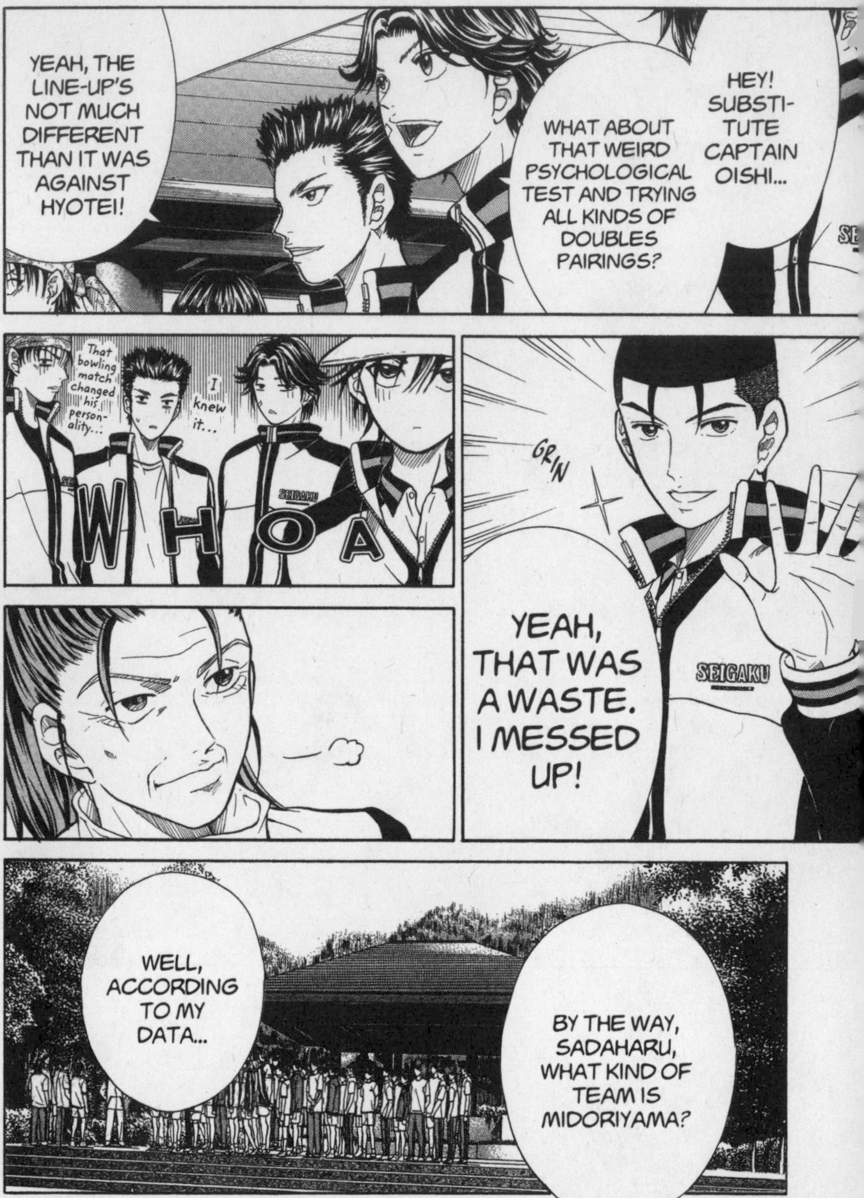
HEY! SUBSTI-TUTE CAPTAIN OISHI...
WHAT ABOUT THAT WEIRD PSYCHOLOGICAL TEST AND TRYING ALL KINDS OF DOUBLES PAIRINGS?
YEAH, THE LINE-UP'S NOT MUCH DIFFERENT THAN IT WAS AGAINST HYOTEI!
GRIN
YEAH, THAT WAS A WASTE. I MESSED UP!
I knew it...
That bowling match changed his personality...
WHOA
BY THE WAY, SADAHARU, WHAT KIND OF TEAM IS MIDORIYAMA?
WELL, ACCORDING TO MY DATA...

READ THIS WAY

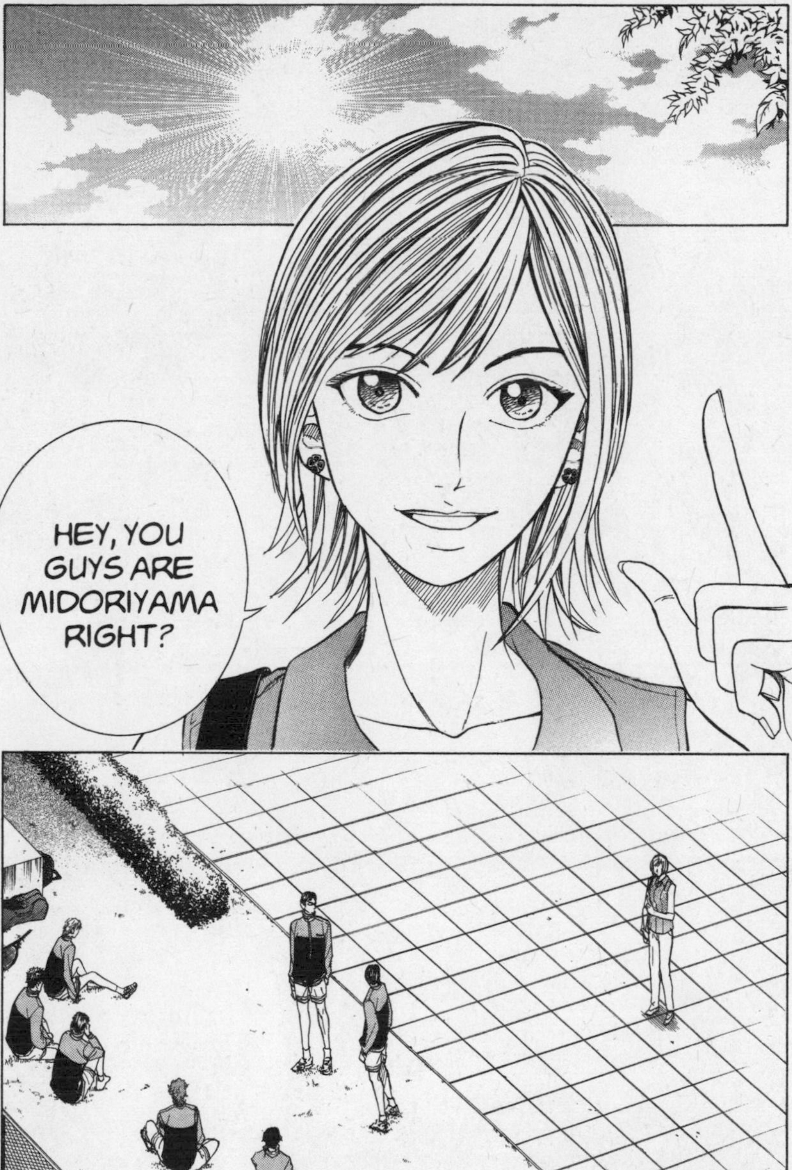
HEY, YOU GUYS ARE MIDORIYAMA RIGHT?

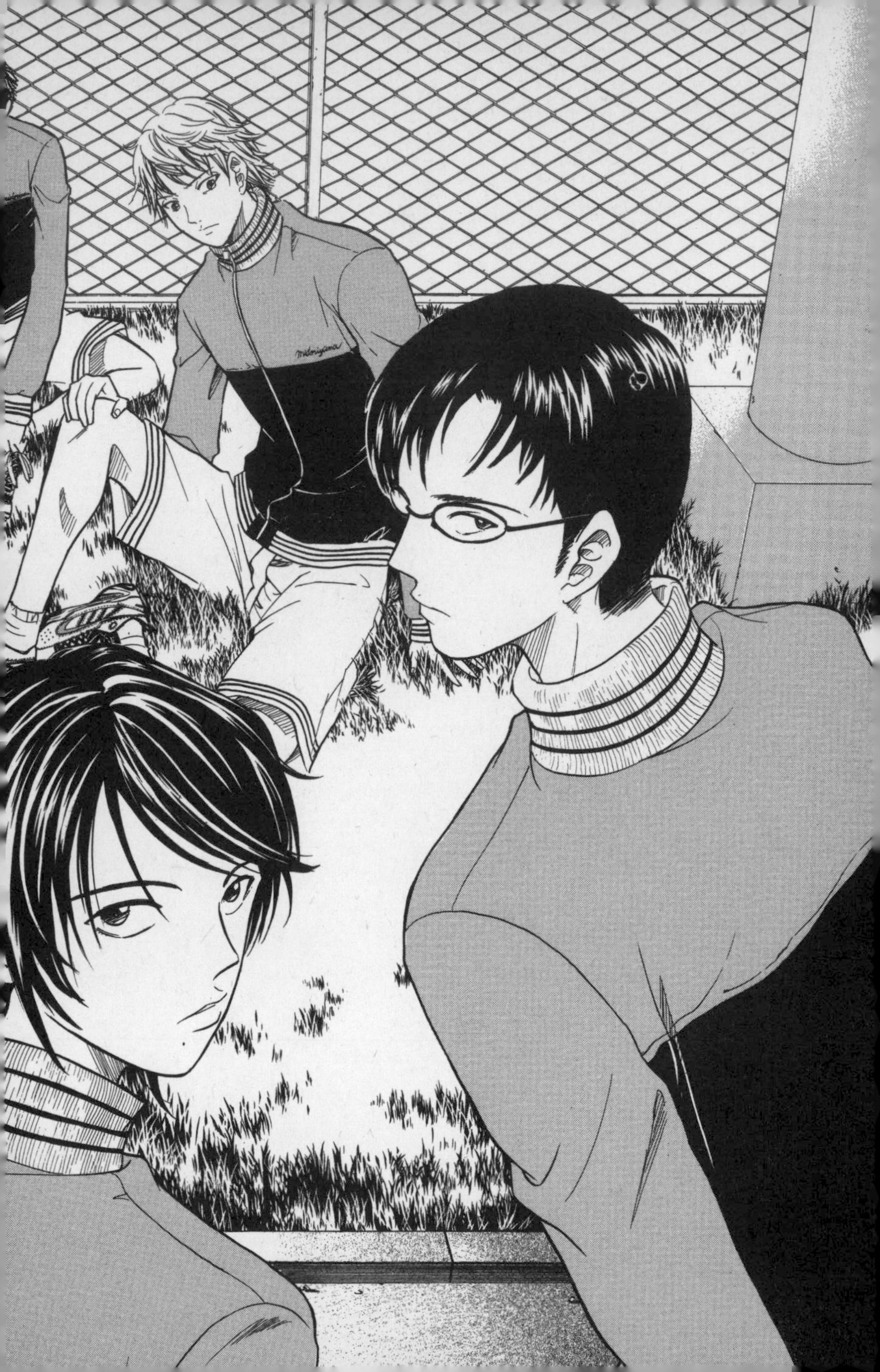
Midoriyama

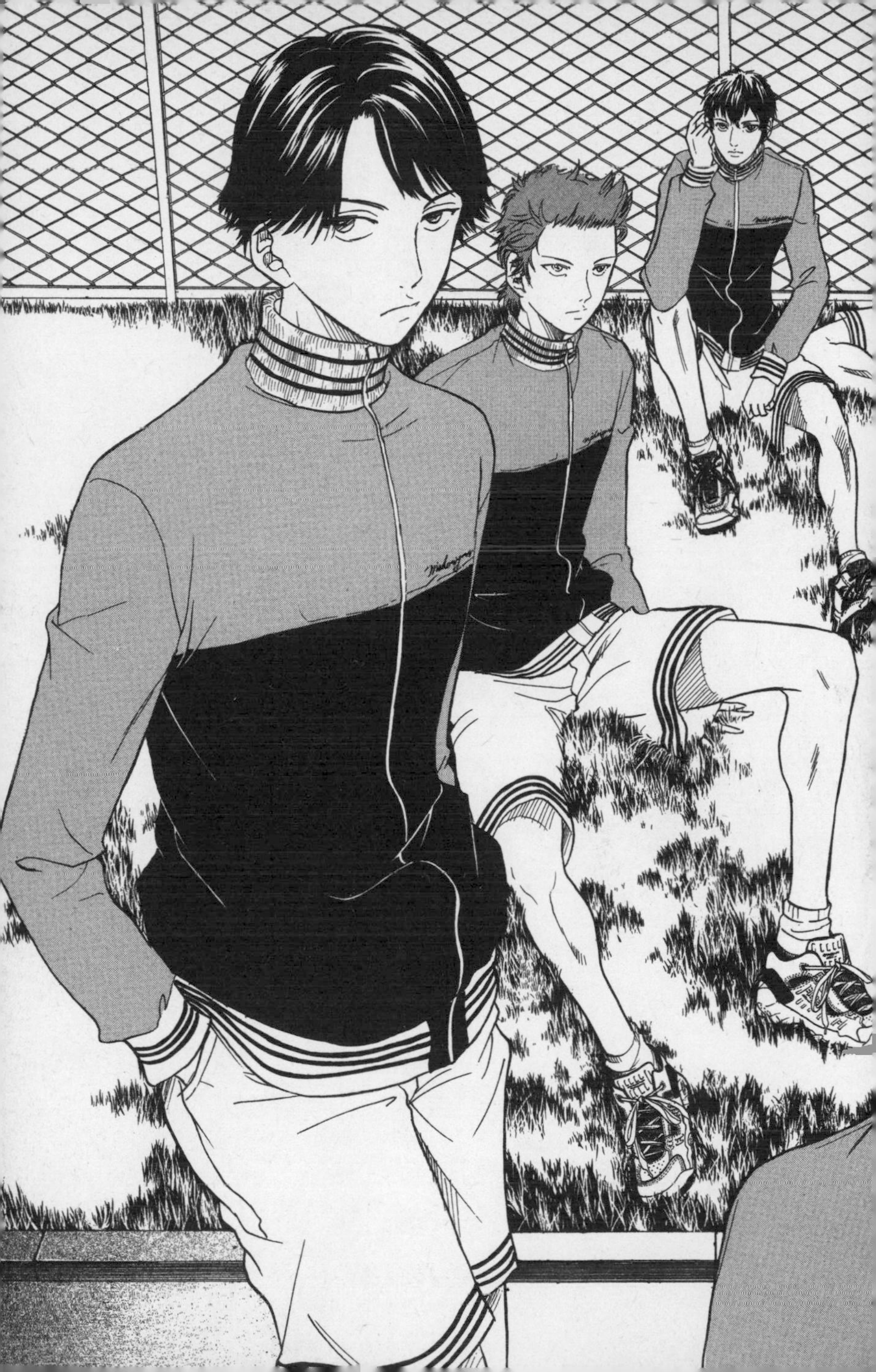

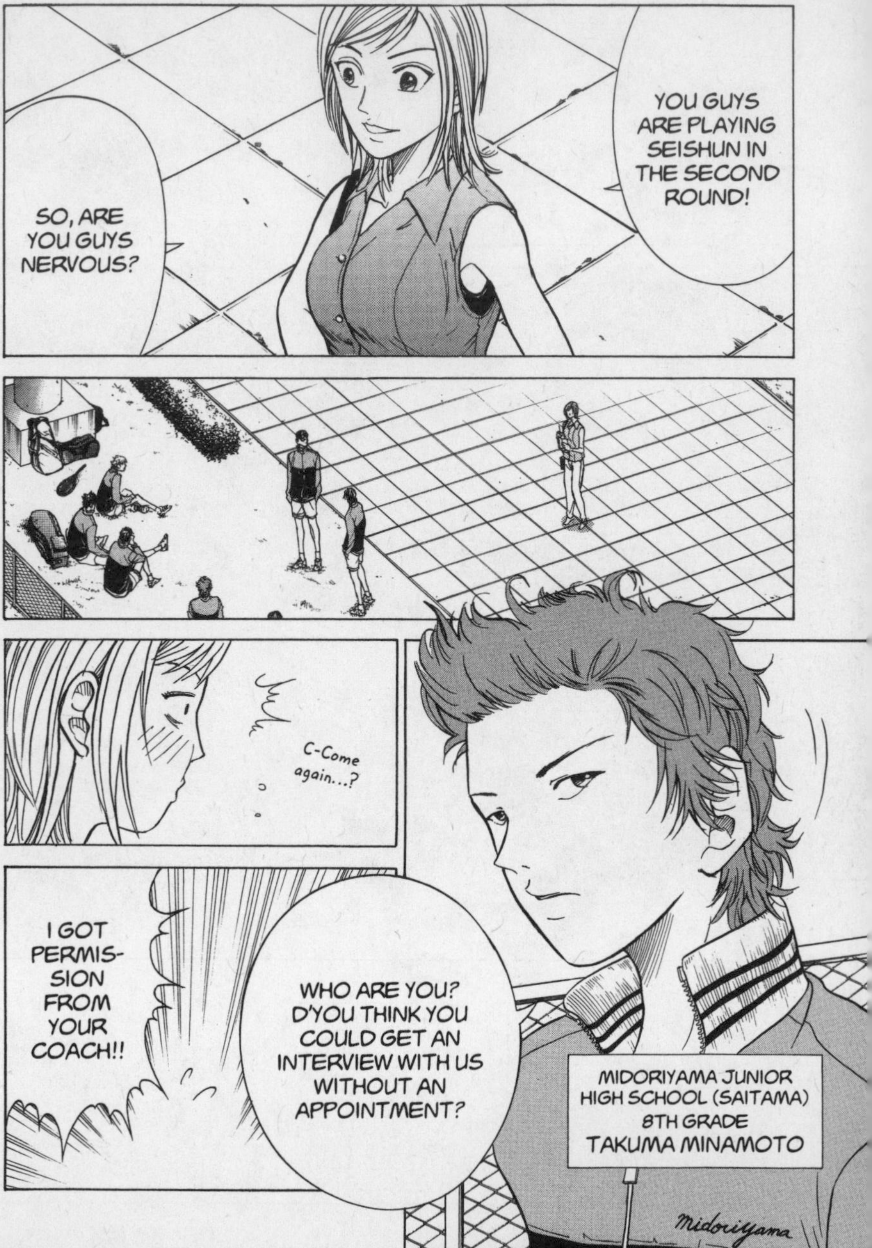
YOU GUYS ARE PLAYING SEISHUN IN THE SECOND ROUND!
SO, ARE YOU GUYS NERVOUS?
MIDORIYAMA JUNIOR HIGH SCHOOL (SAITAMA) 8TH GRADE TAKUMA MINAMOTO
Midoriyama
WHO ARE YOU? D'YOU THINK YOU COULD GET AN INTERVIEW WITH US WITHOUT AN APPOINTMENT?
C-Come again...?
I GOT PERMIS-SION FROM YOUR COACH!!

READ THIS WAY

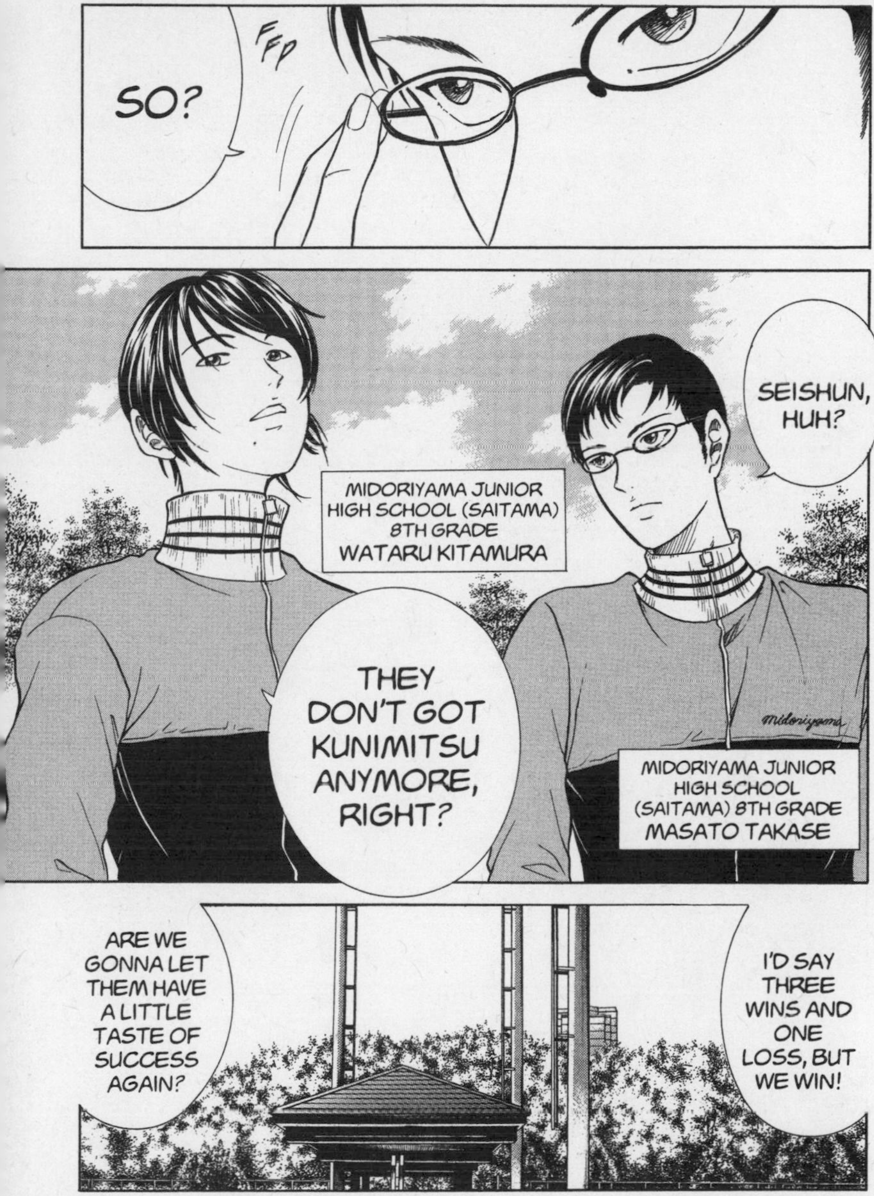
FFP
SO?
SEISHUN, HUH?
MIDORIYAMA JUNIOR HIGH SCHOOL (SAITAMA) 8TH GRADE MASATO TAKASE
MIDORIYAMA JUNIOR HIGH SCHOOL (SAITAMA) 8TH GRADE WATARU KITAMURA
THEY DON'T GOT KUNIMITSU ANYMORE, RIGHT?
midoriyama
I'D SAY THREE WINS AND ONE LOSS, BUT WE WIN!
ARE WE GONNA LET THEM HAVE A LITTLE TASTE OF SUCCESS AGAIN?

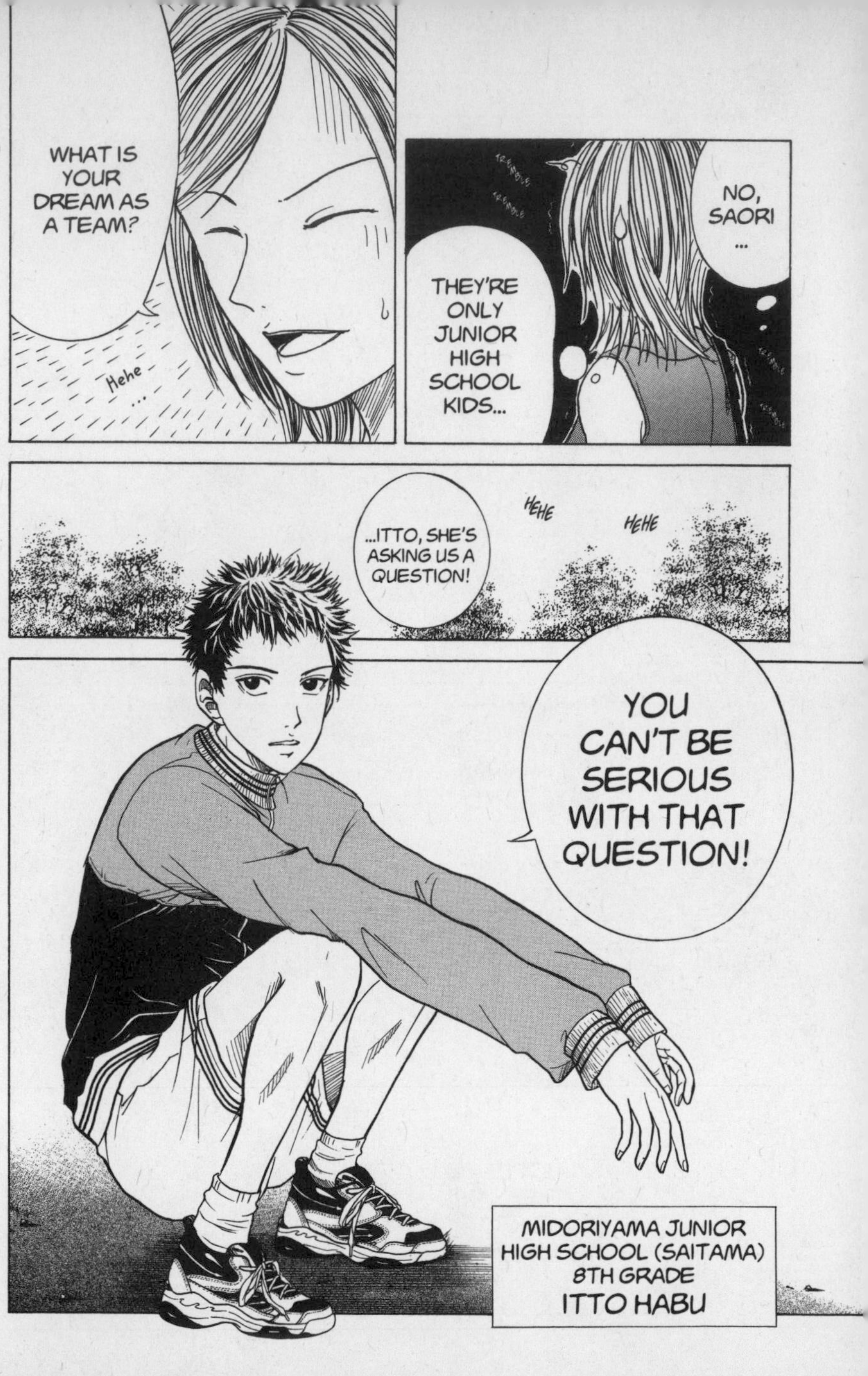
WHAT IS YOUR DREAM AS A TEAM?
Hehe ...
THEY'RE ONLY JUNIOR HIGH SCHOOL KIDS...
NO, SAORI ...
HEHE
HEHE
...ITTO, SHE'S ASKING US A QUESTION!
YOU CAN'T BE SERIOUS WITH THAT QUESTION!
MIDORIYAMA JUNIOR HIGH SCHOOL (SAITAMA) 8TH GRADE ITTO HABU

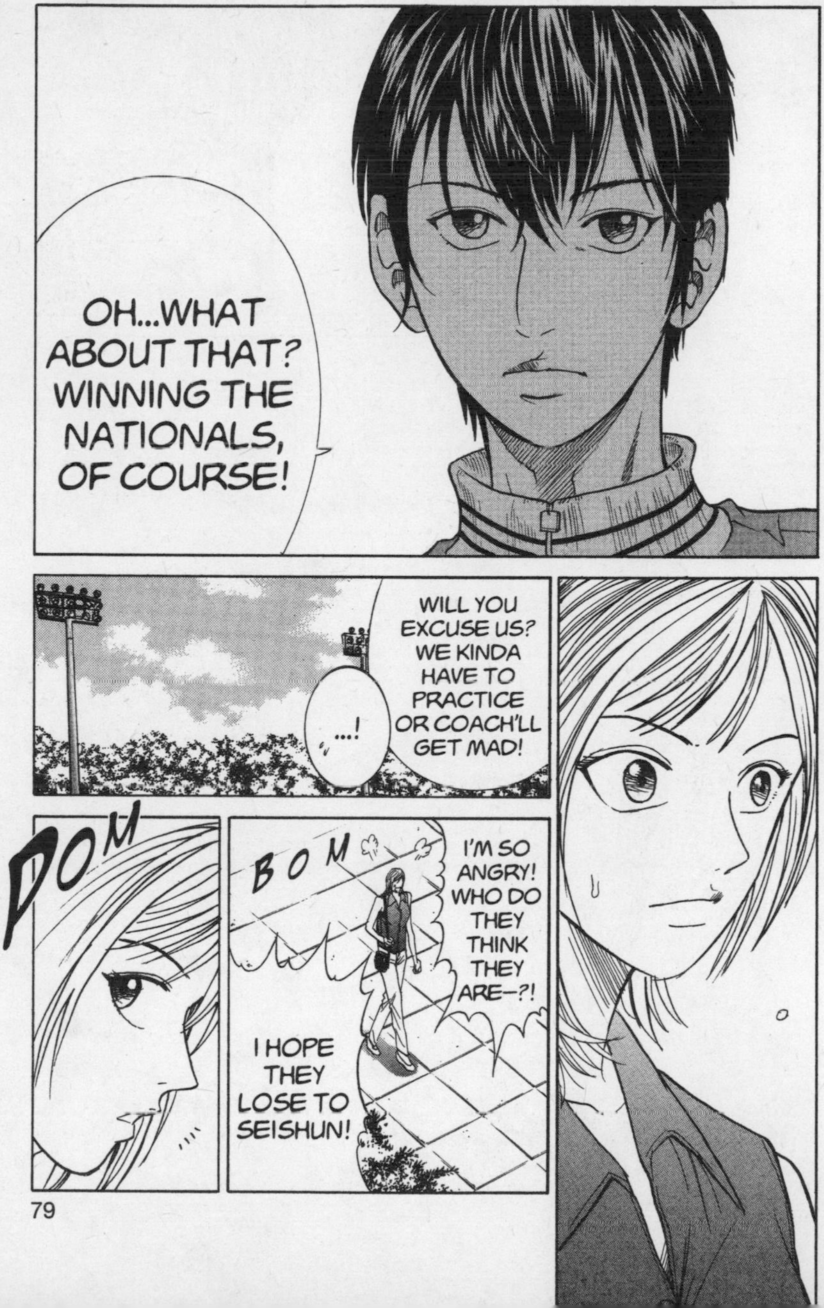
OH...WHAT ABOUT THAT? WINNING THE NATIONALS, OF COURSE!
WILL YOU EXCUSE US? WE KINDA HAVE TO PRACTICE OR COACH'LL GET MAD!
...!
BOM
I'M SO ANGRY! WHO DO THEY THINK THEY ARE--?!
I HOPE THEY LOSE TO SEISHUN!
DOM

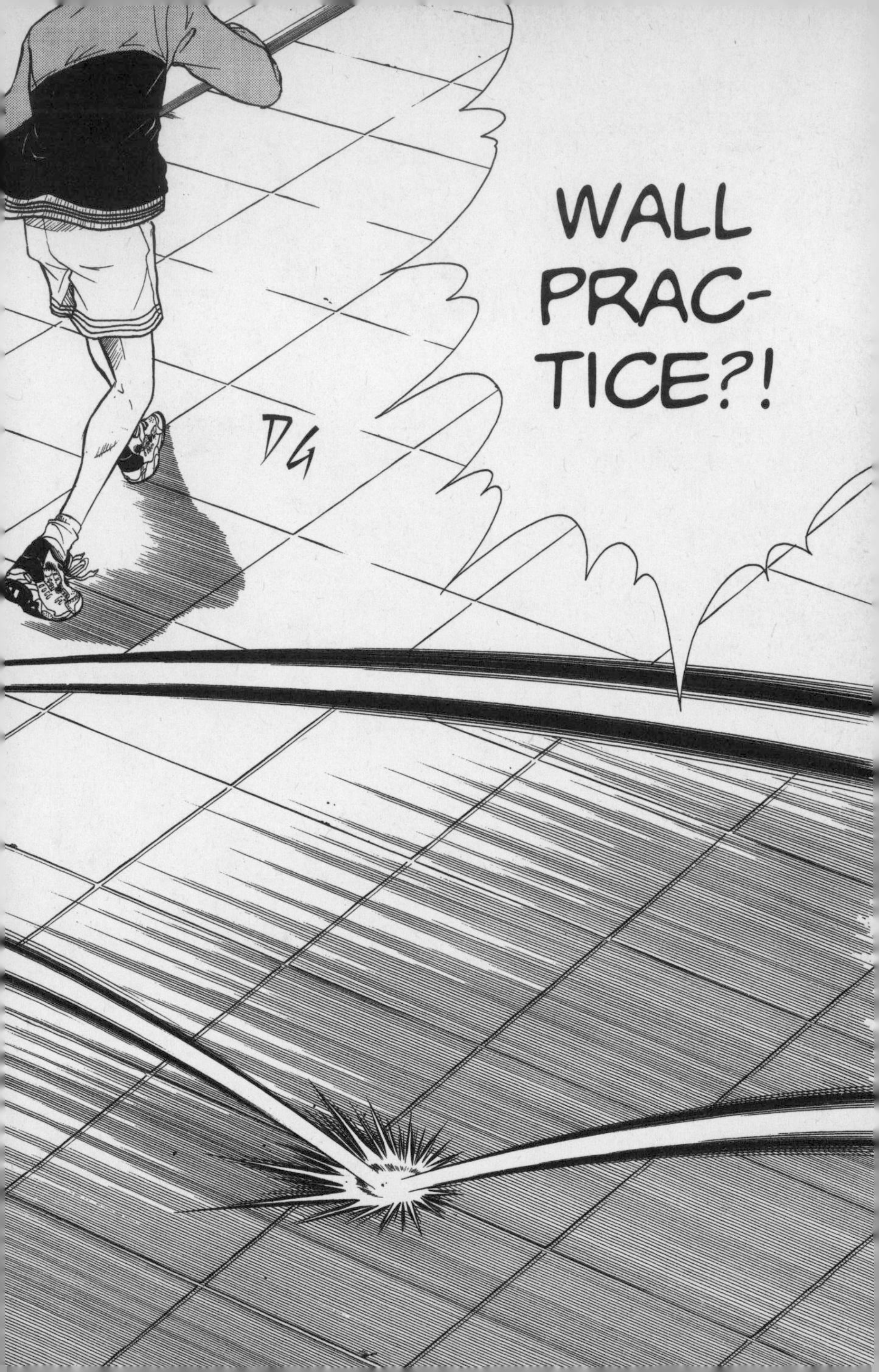
WALL PRAC-TICE?!
DG

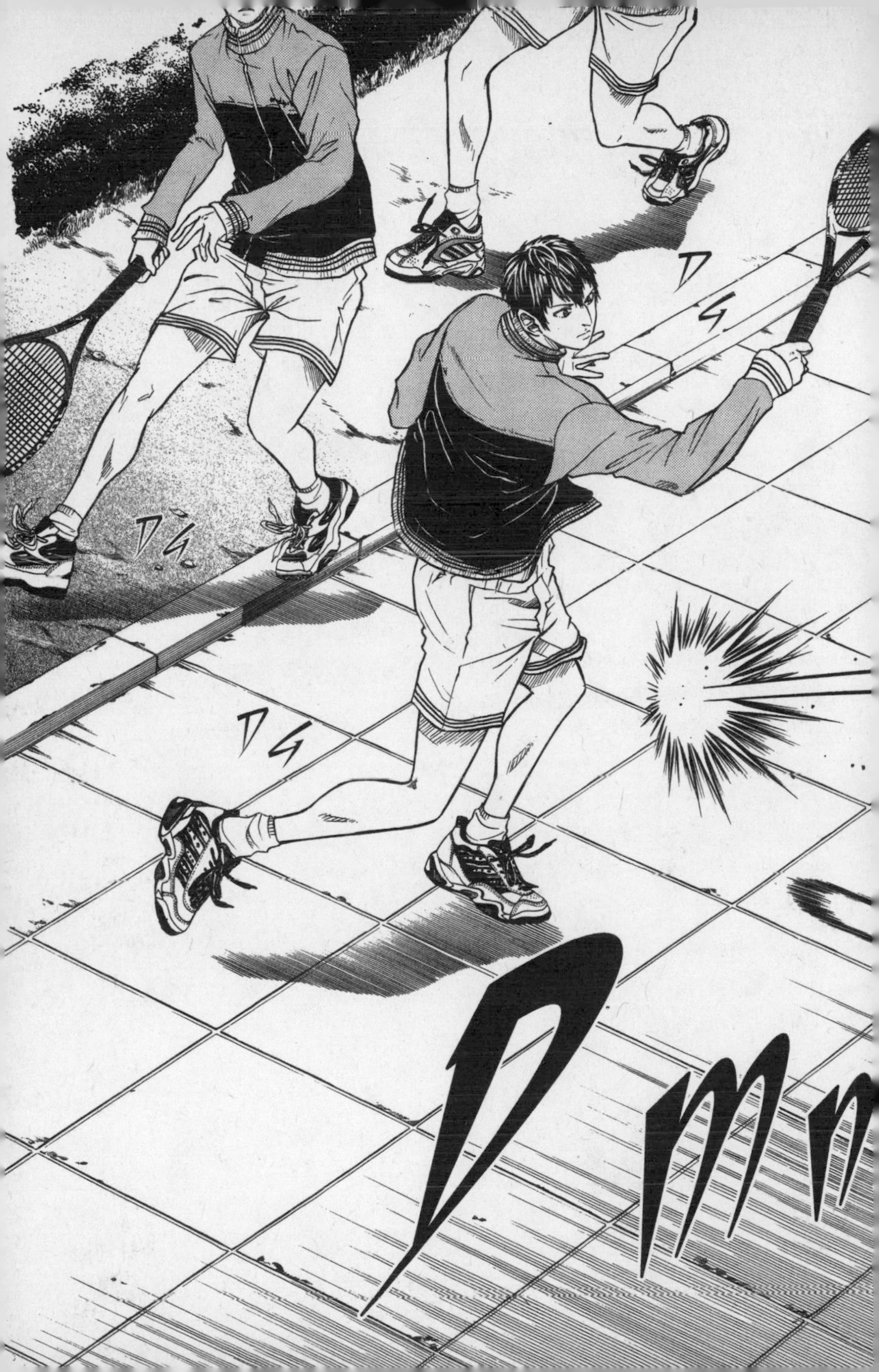

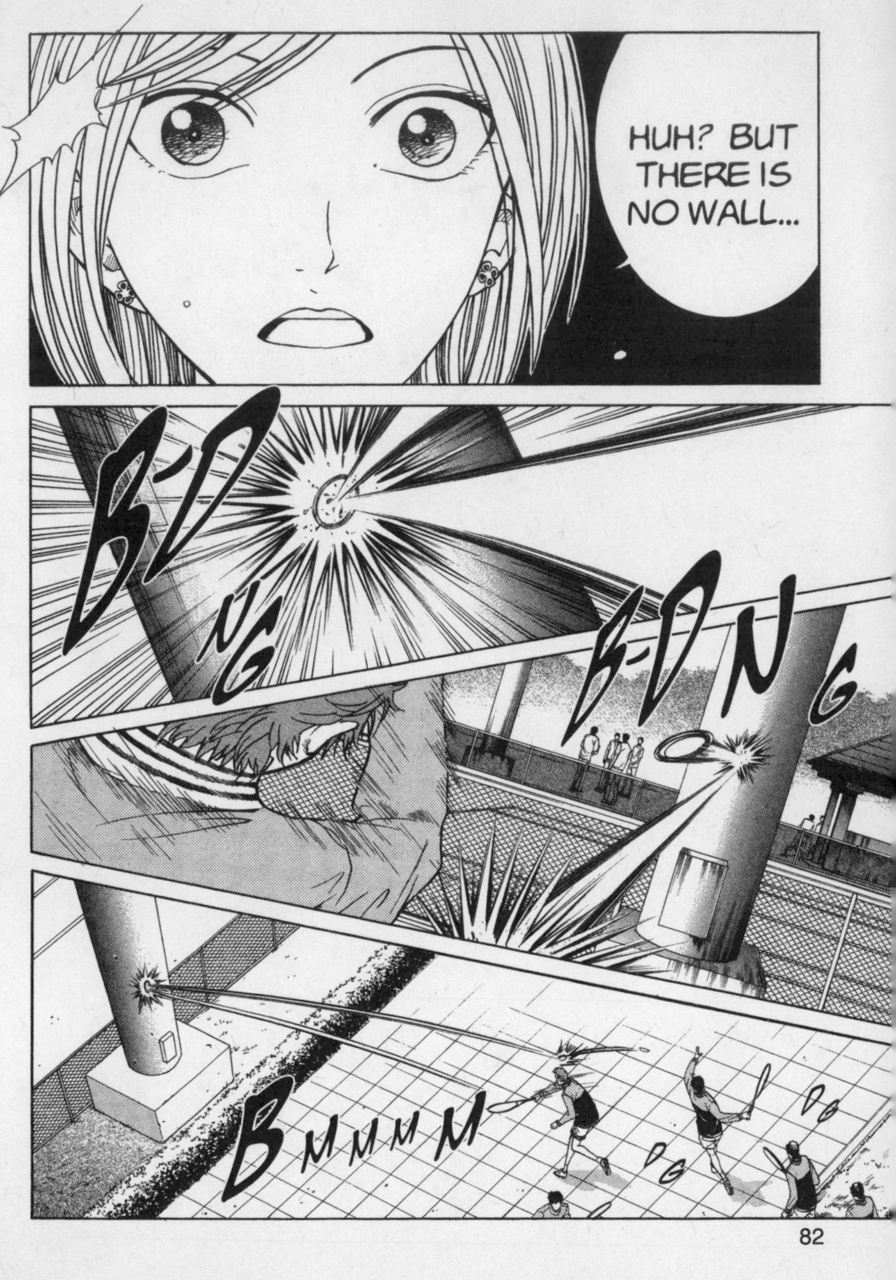
HUH? BUT THERE IS NO WALL...
B-DNG
B-DNG
BMMMM
DG
DG

READ THIS WAY

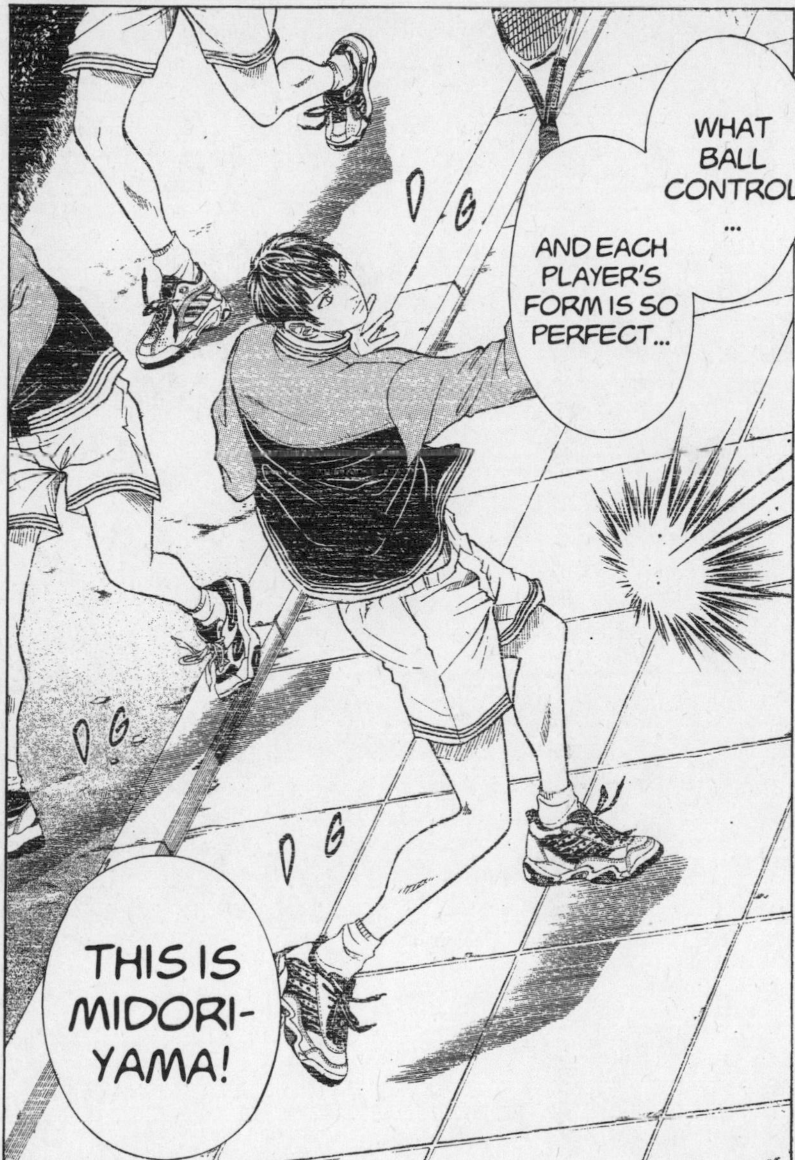
WHAT BALL CONTROL ...
AND EACH PLAYER'S FORM IS SO PERFECT...
THIS IS MIDORI-YAMA!

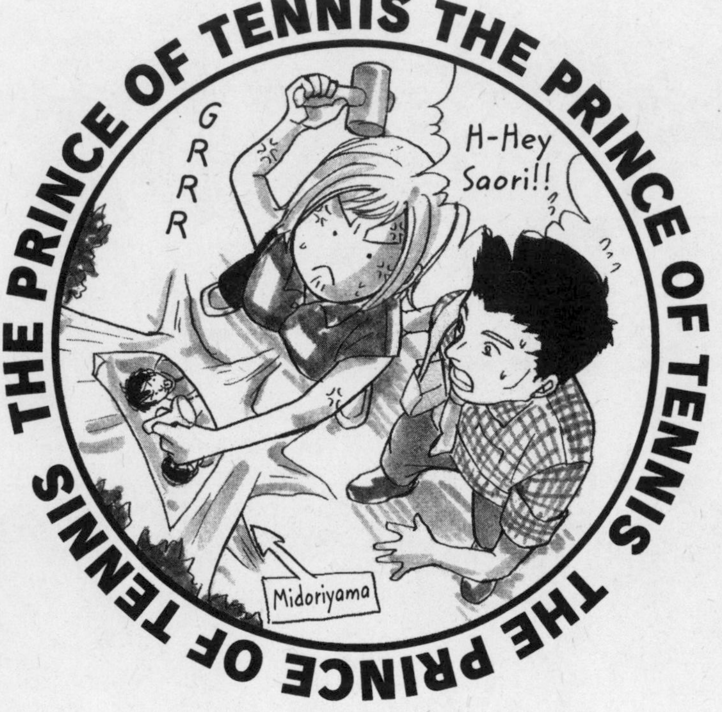
THE PRINCE OF TENNIS THE PRINCE OF TENNIS THE PRINCE OF TENNIS
H-Hey Saori!!
GRRR
Midoriyama

5th Match — No. 1 Singles	4th Match — No. 2 Singles	3rd Match — No. 3 Singles	2nd Match — No. 1 Doubles		1st Match — No. 2 Doubles	
SHUSUKE FUJI (9th Grade) Blood Type: B	TAKASHI KAWAMURA (9th Grade) Blood Type: A	RYOMA ECHIZEN (7th Grade) Blood Type: O	TAKESHI MOMOSHIRO (8th Grade) Blood Type: O	EIJI KIKUMARU (9th Grade) Blood Type: A	KAORU KAIDO (8th Grade) Blood Type: B	SADAHARU INUI (9th Grade) Blood Type: AB

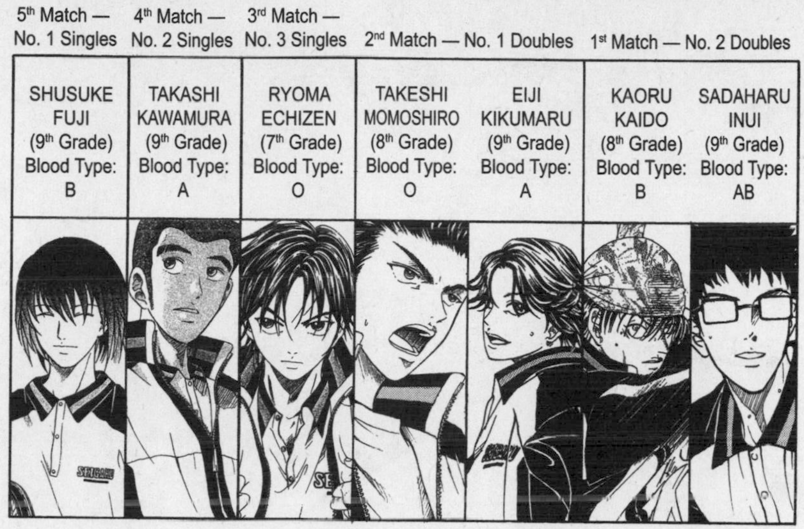

GENIUS 163: TENACITY

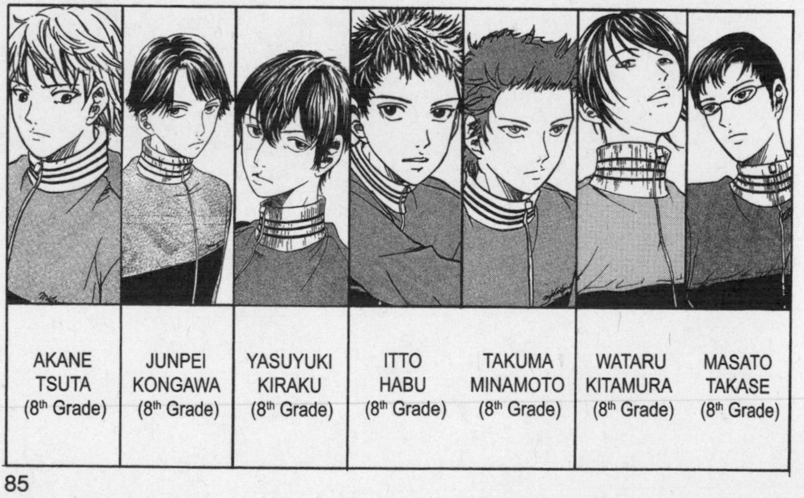

AKANE TSUTA (8th Grade)	JUNPEI KONGAWA (8th Grade)	YASUYUKI KIRAKU (8th Grade)	ITTO HABU (8th Grade)	TAKUMA MINAMOTO (8th Grade)	WATARU KITAMURA (8th Grade)	MASATO TAKASE (8th Grade)

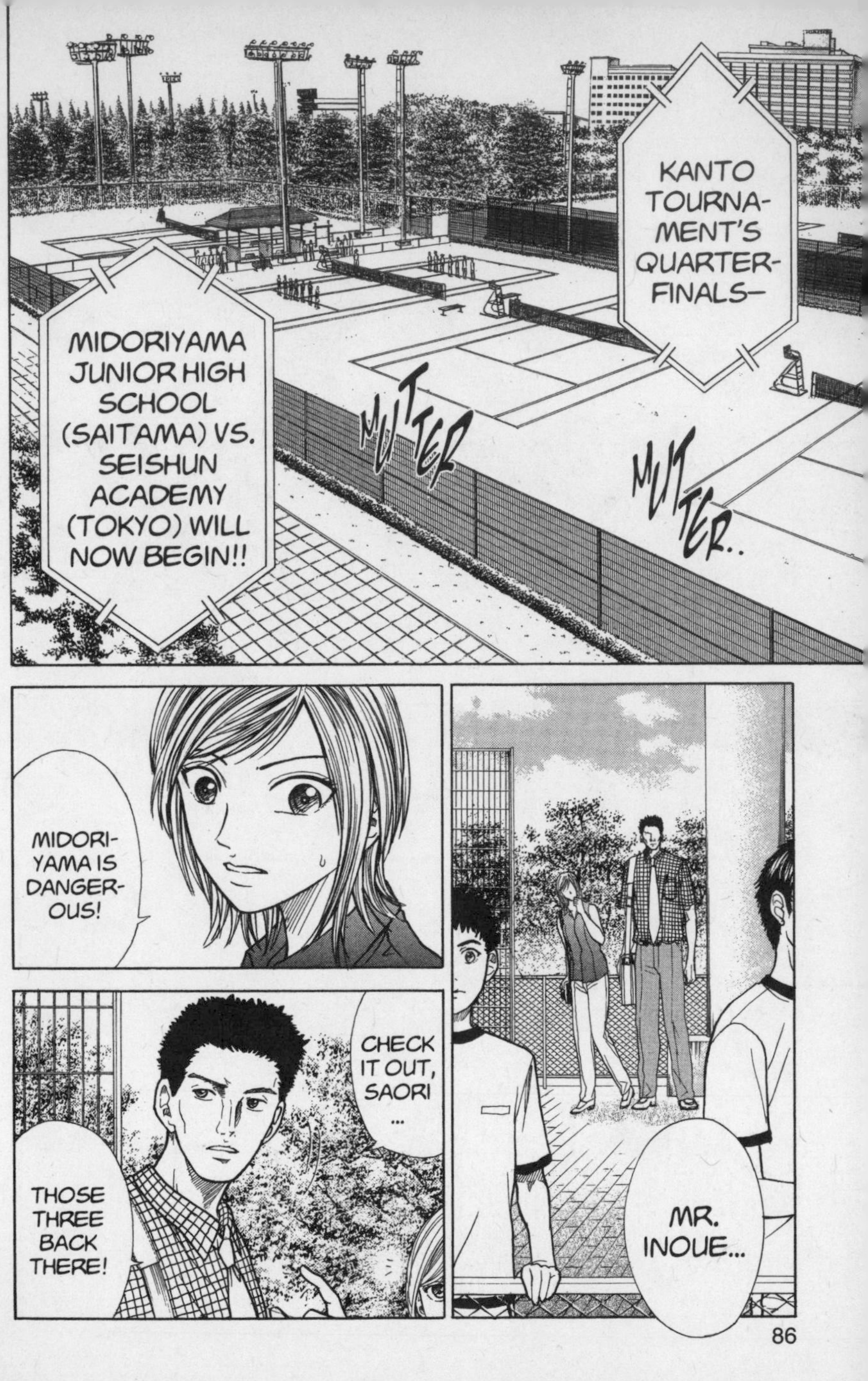
KANTO TOURNAMENT'S QUARTER-FINALS—
MIDORIYAMA JUNIOR HIGH SCHOOL (SAITAMA) VS. SEISHUN ACADEMY (TOKYO) WILL NOW BEGIN!!
MUTTER
MUTTER...
MR. INOUE...
MIDORIYAMA IS DANGEROUS!
CHECK IT OUT, SAORI...
THOSE THREE BACK THERE!

READ THIS WAY

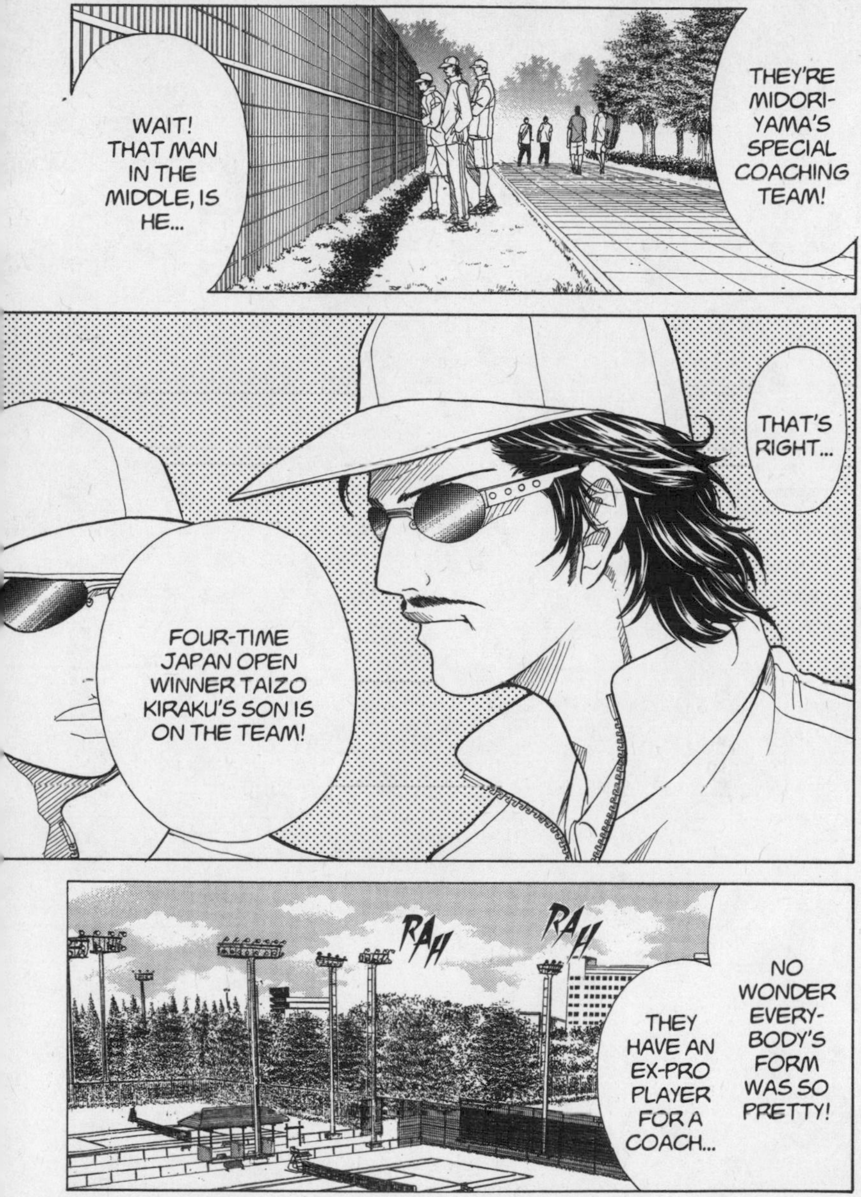
THEY'RE MIDORI-YAMA'S SPECIAL COACHING TEAM!
WAIT! THAT MAN IN THE MIDDLE, IS HE...
THAT'S RIGHT...
FOUR-TIME JAPAN OPEN WINNER TAIZO KIRAKU'S SON IS ON THE TEAM!
RAH
RAH
NO WONDER EVERY-BODY'S FORM WAS SO PRETTY!
THEY HAVE AN EX-PRO PLAYER FOR A COACH...

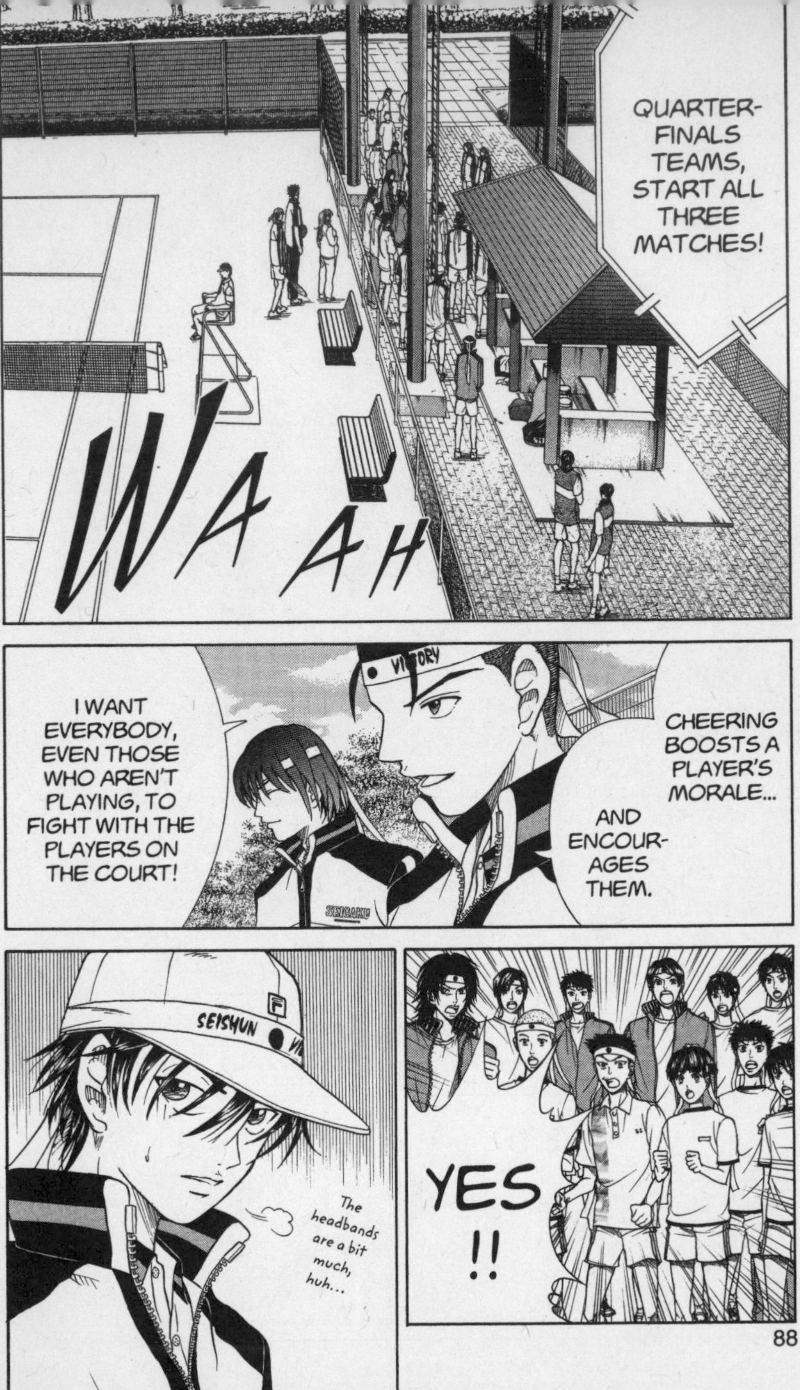
QUARTER-FINALS TEAMS, START ALL THREE MATCHES!
WAAH
CHEERING BOOSTS A PLAYER'S MORALE...
AND ENCOURAGES THEM.
I WANT EVERYBODY, EVEN THOSE WHO AREN'T PLAYING, TO FIGHT WITH THE PLAYERS ON THE COURT!
YES!!
SEISHUN
The headbands are a bit much, huh...

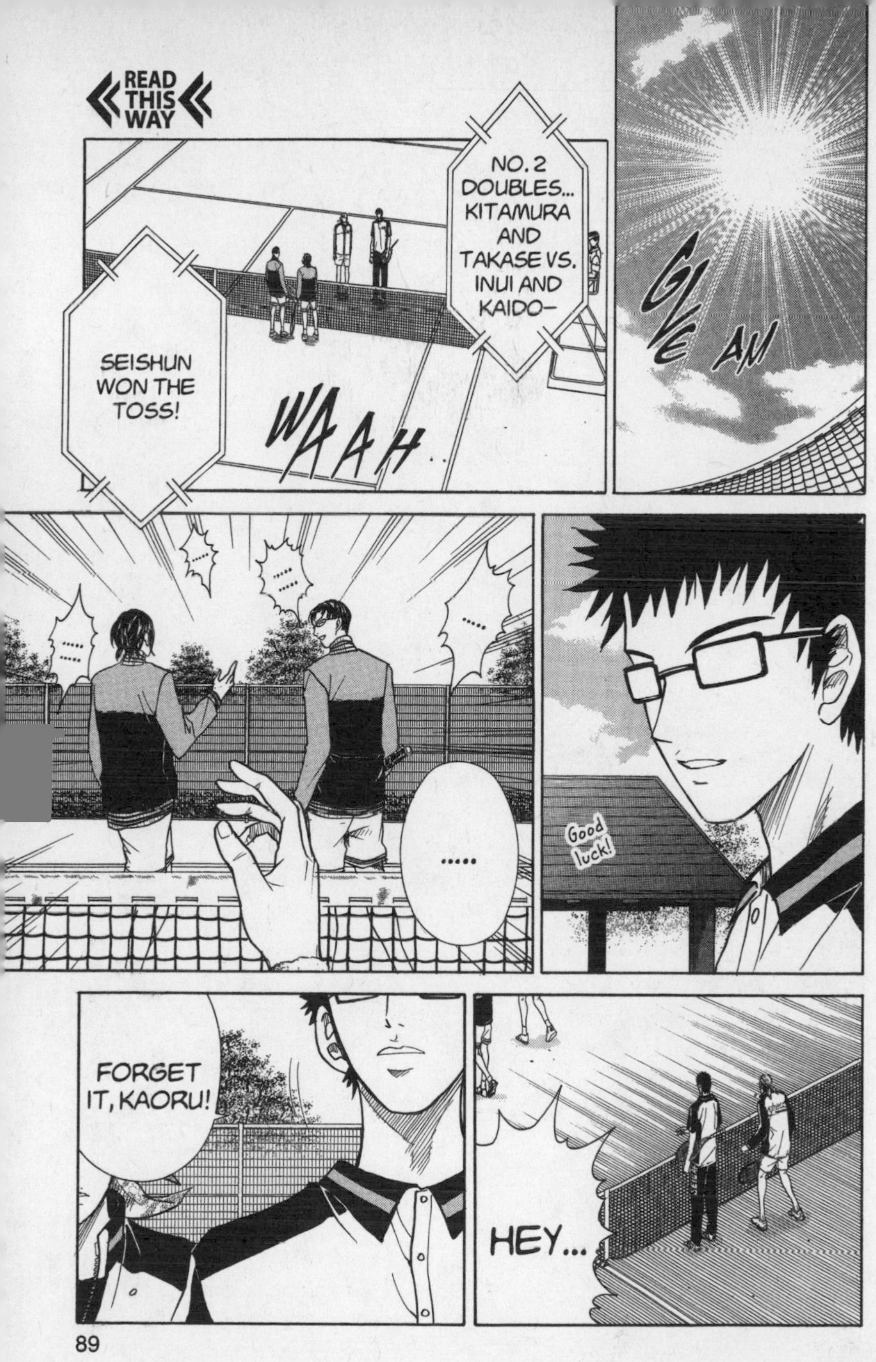
READ THIS WAY
NO. 2 DOUBLES... KITAMURA AND TAKASE VS. INUI AND KAIDO–
SEISHUN WON THE TOSS!
WAAAH
Good luck!
.....
HEY...
FORGET IT, KAORU!

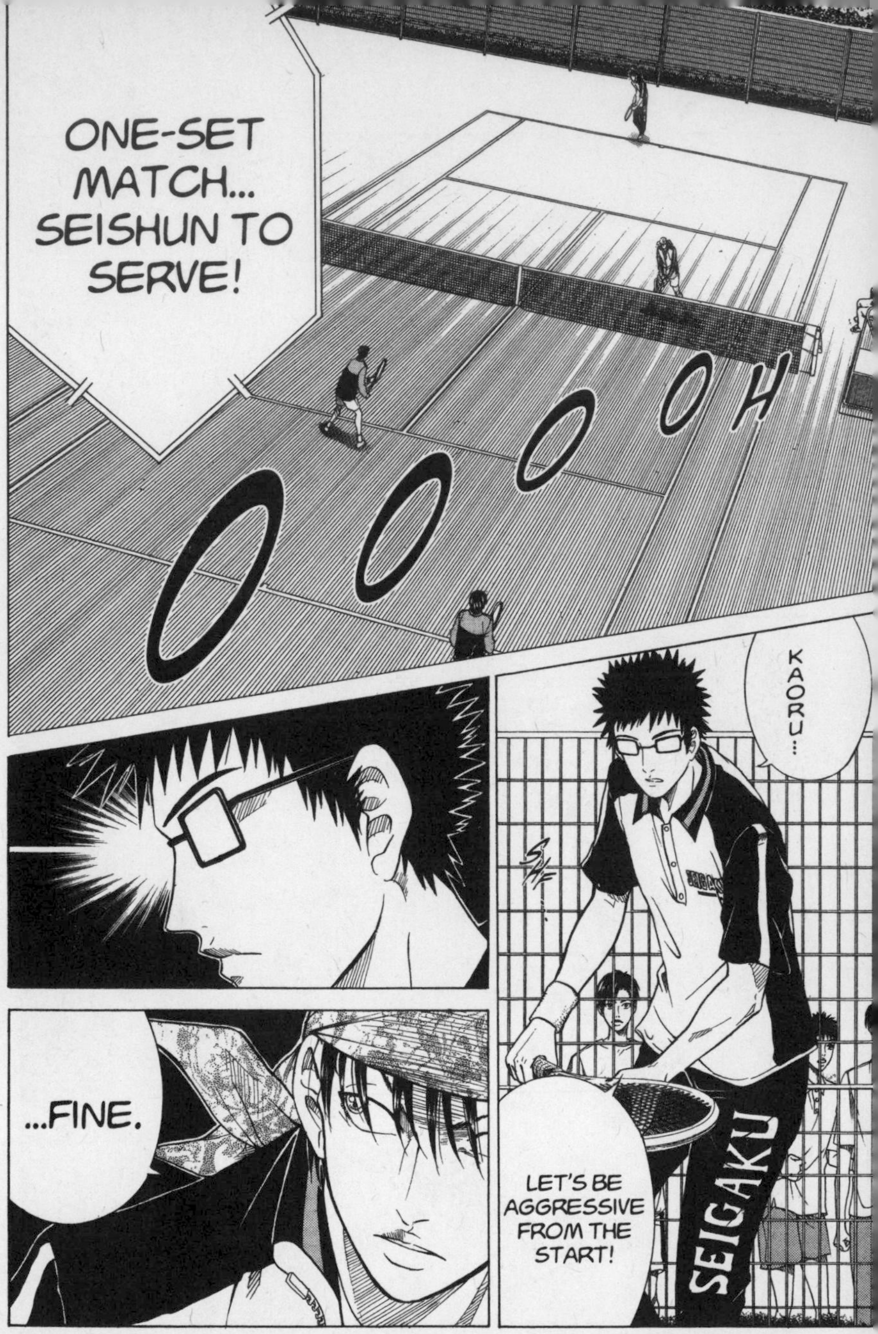
ONE-SET MATCH... SEISHUN TO SERVE!
OOOOH
KAORU...
LET'S BE AGGRESSIVE FROM THE START!
...FINE.

READ THIS WAY

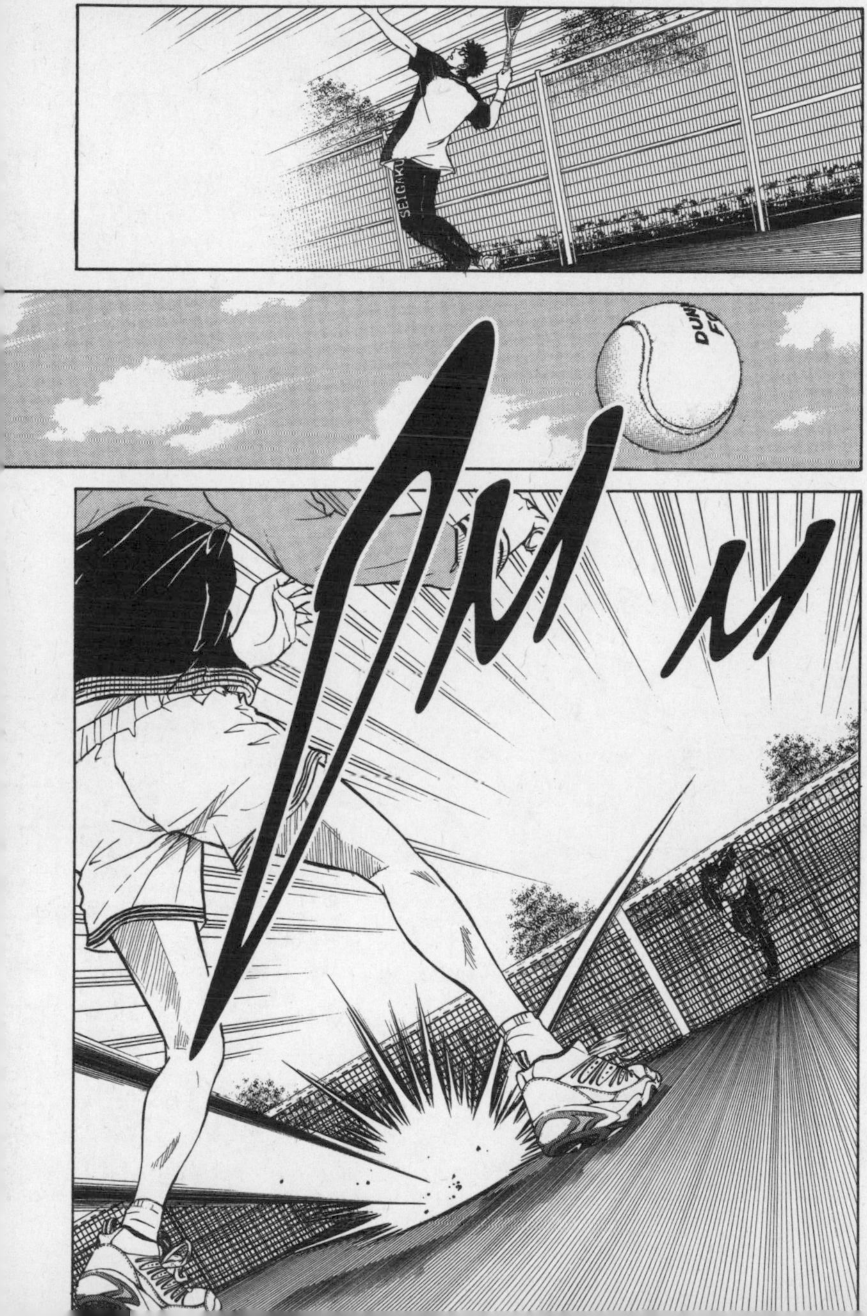
SEIGAKU

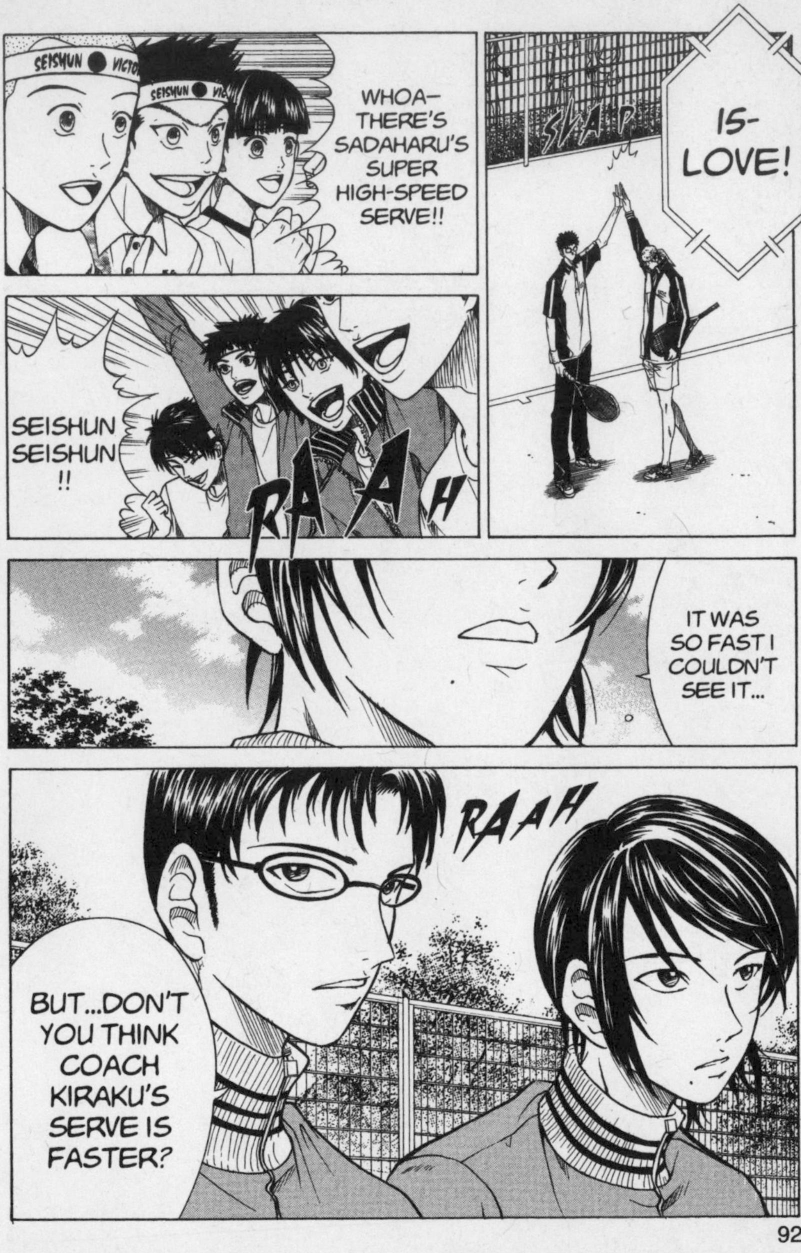
SLAP
15-
LOVE!
WHOA-
THERE'S
SADAHARU'S
SUPER
HIGH-SPEED
SERVE!!
SEISHUN
SEISHUN
SEISHUN
SEISHUN
!!
RAAH
IT WAS
SO FAST I
COULDN'T
SEE IT...
RAAH
BUT...DON'T
YOU THINK
COACH
KIRAKU'S
SERVE IS
FASTER?

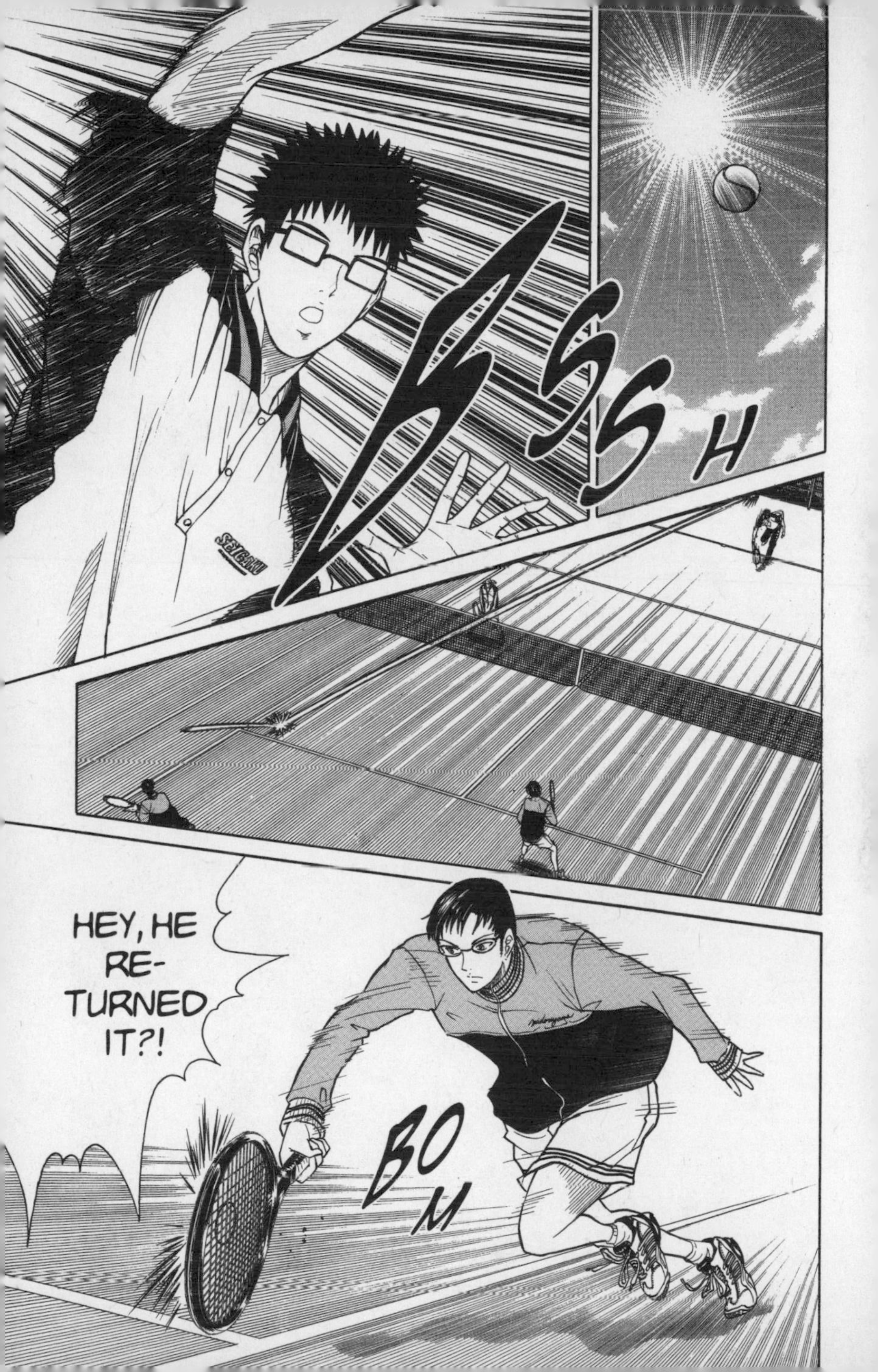
VSSSH
HEY, HE RE-TURNED IT?!
BOOM

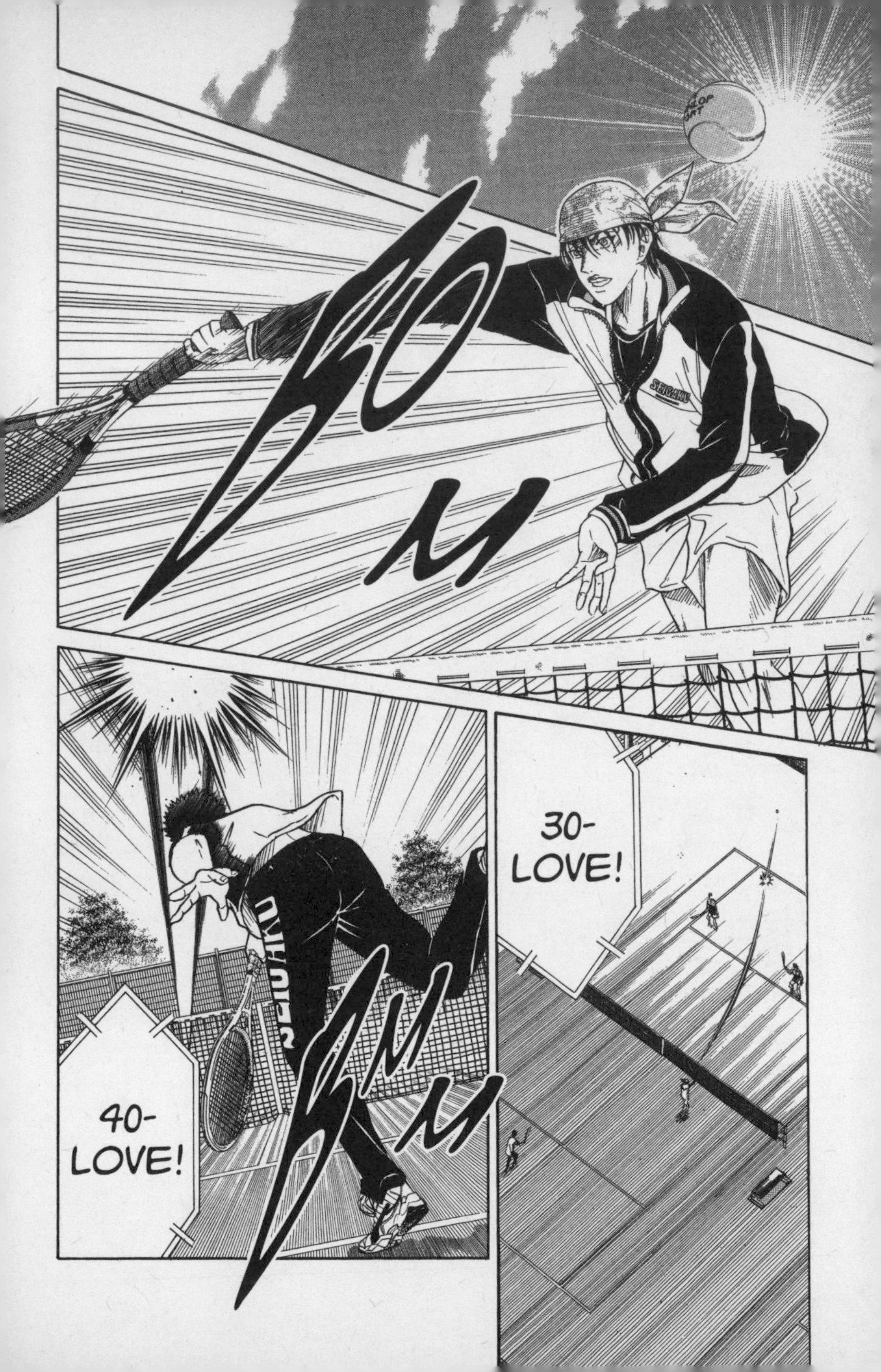
SEIGAKU
30-
LOVE!
40-
LOVE!

READ THIS WAY

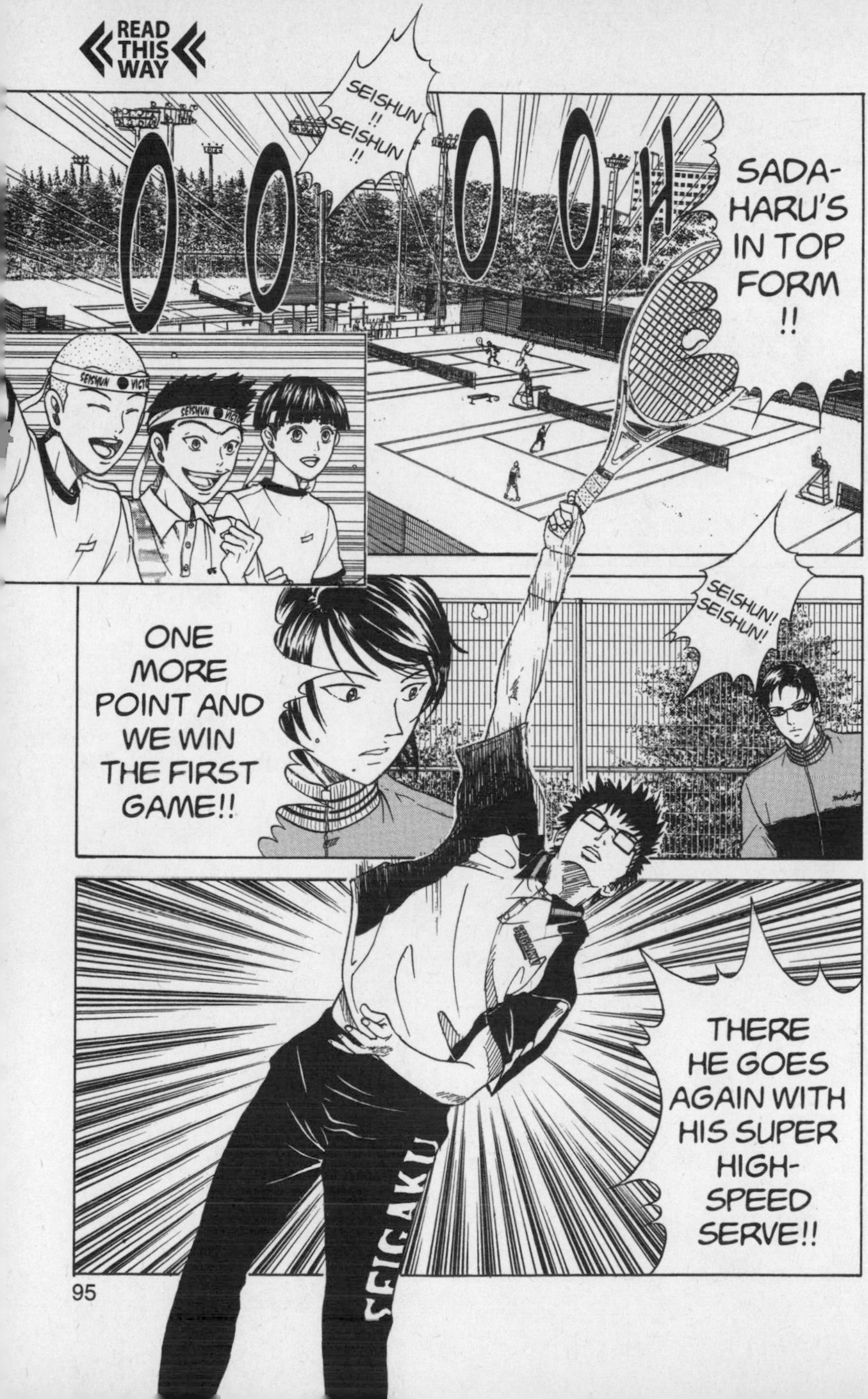
SADAHARU'S IN TOP FORM!!
OOOOH
SEISHUN!! SEISHUN!!
SEISHUN! SEISHUN!
ONE MORE POINT AND WE WIN THE FIRST GAME!!
THERE HE GOES AGAIN WITH HIS SUPER HIGH-SPEED SERVE!!

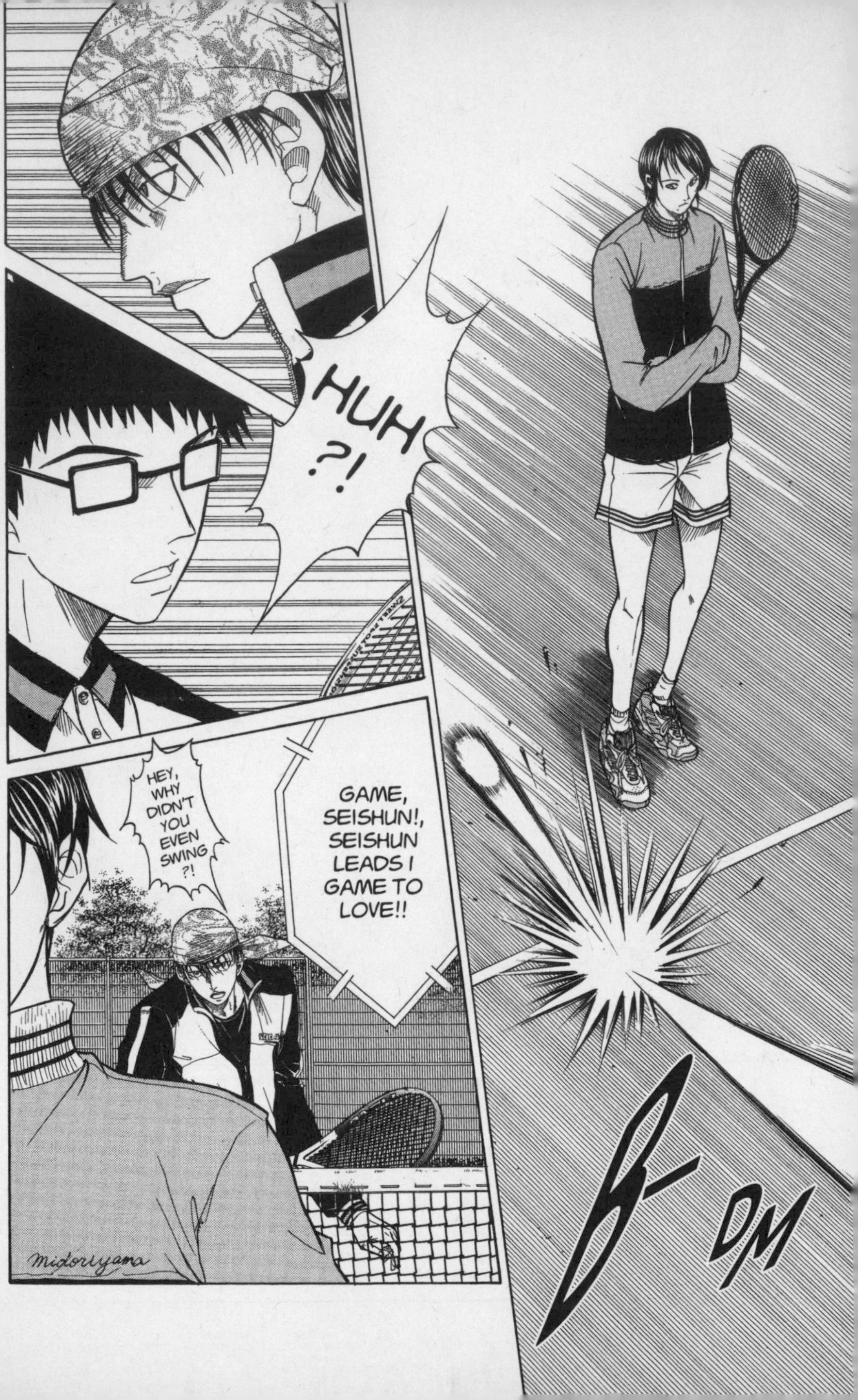
B-DM
HUH?!
GAME, SEISHUN!, SEISHUN LEADS 1 GAME TO LOVE!!
HEY, WHY DIDN'T YOU EVEN SWING?!
midoriyama

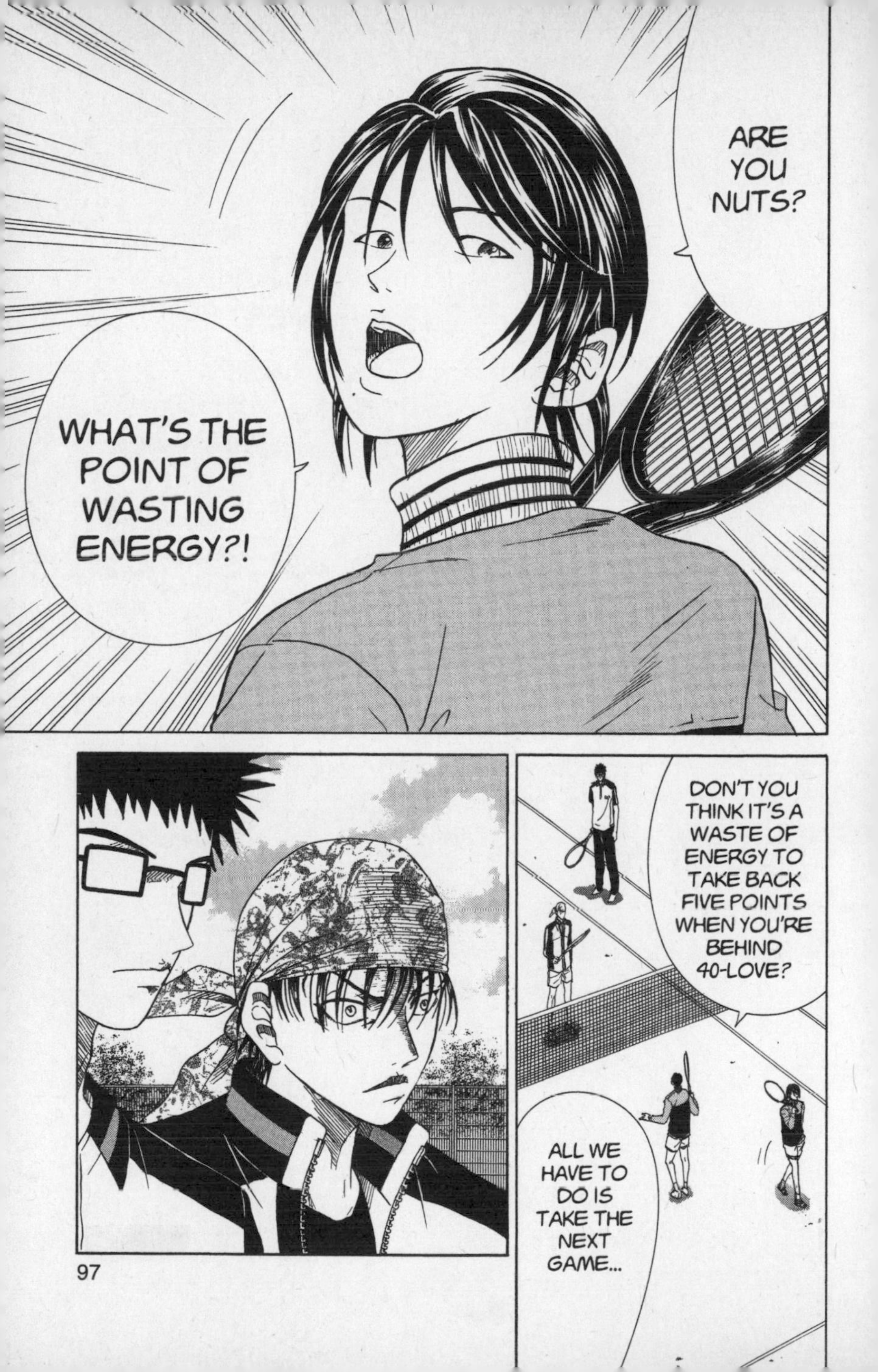
ARE YOU NUTS?
WHAT'S THE POINT OF WASTING ENERGY?!
DON'T YOU THINK IT'S A WASTE OF ENERGY TO TAKE BACK FIVE POINTS WHEN YOU'RE BEHIND 40-LOVE?
ALL WE HAVE TO DO IS TAKE THE NEXT GAME...

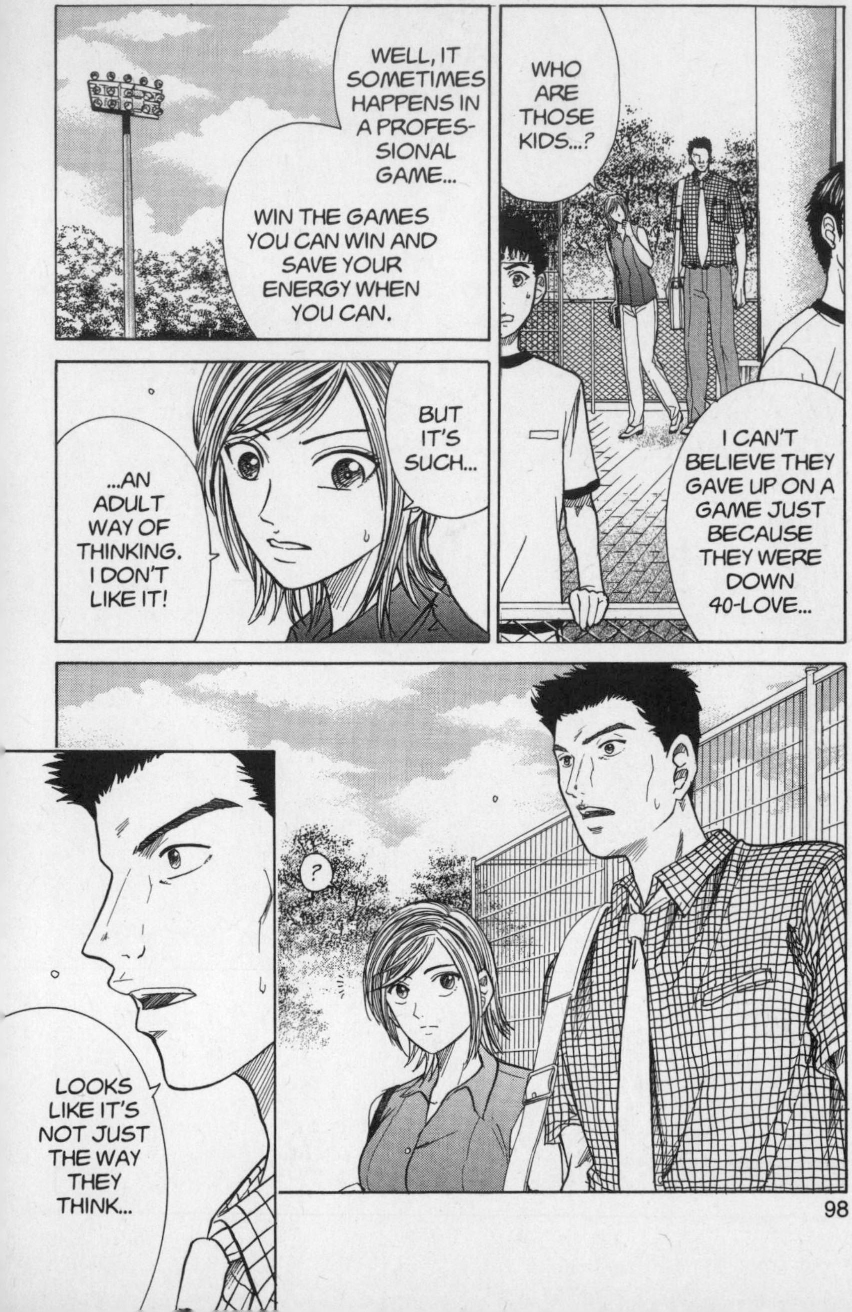
WHO ARE THOSE KIDS...?
I CAN'T BELIEVE THEY GAVE UP ON A GAME JUST BECAUSE THEY WERE DOWN 40-LOVE...
WELL, IT SOMETIMES HAPPENS IN A PROFES-SIONAL GAME...
WIN THE GAMES YOU CAN WIN AND SAVE YOUR ENERGY WHEN YOU CAN.
BUT IT'S SUCH...
...AN ADULT WAY OF THINKING. I DON'T LIKE IT!
?
LOOKS LIKE IT'S NOT JUST THE WAY THEY THINK...

READ THIS WAY

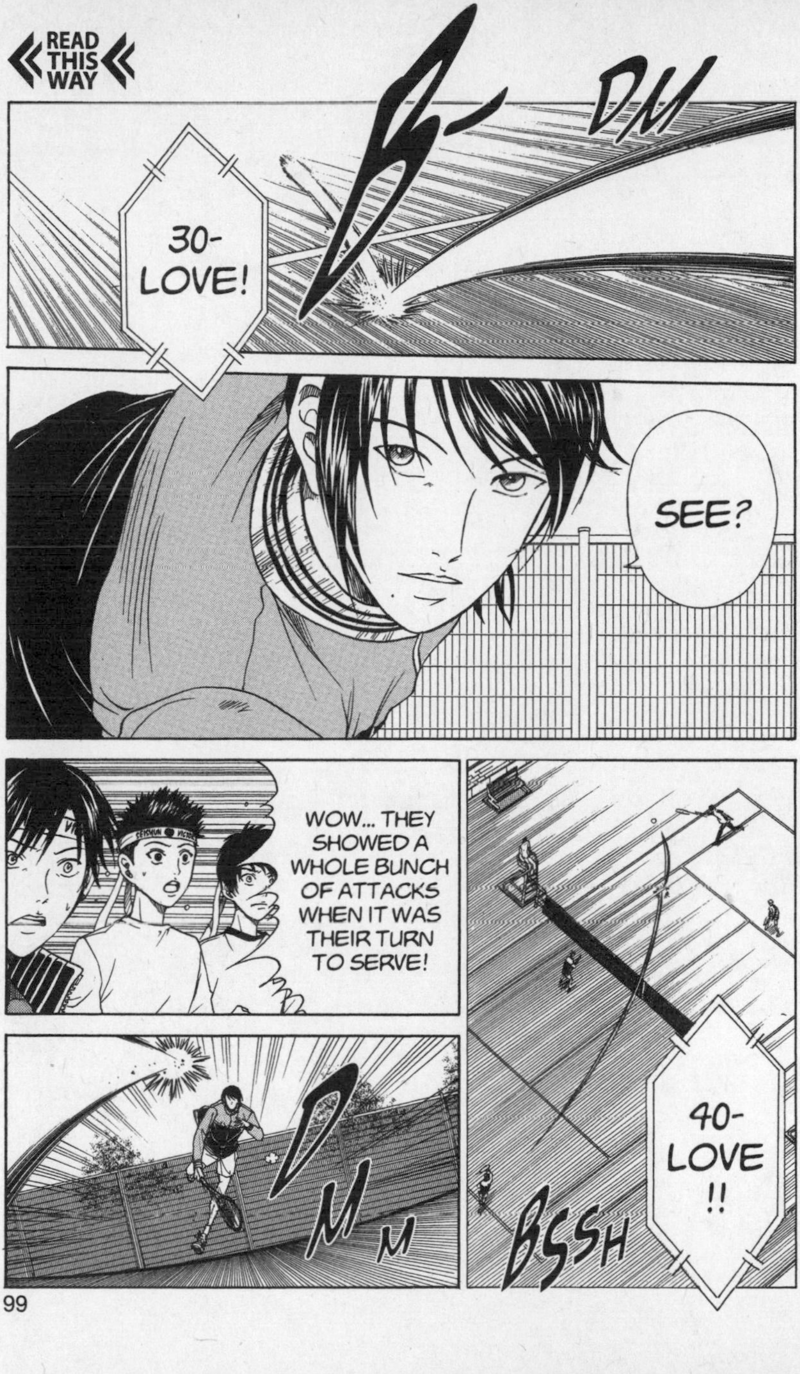

B- DM
30-LOVE!
SEE?
40-LOVE!!
BSSH
WOW... THEY SHOWED A WHOLE BUNCH OF ATTACKS WHEN IT WAS THEIR TURN TO SERVE!
DMM

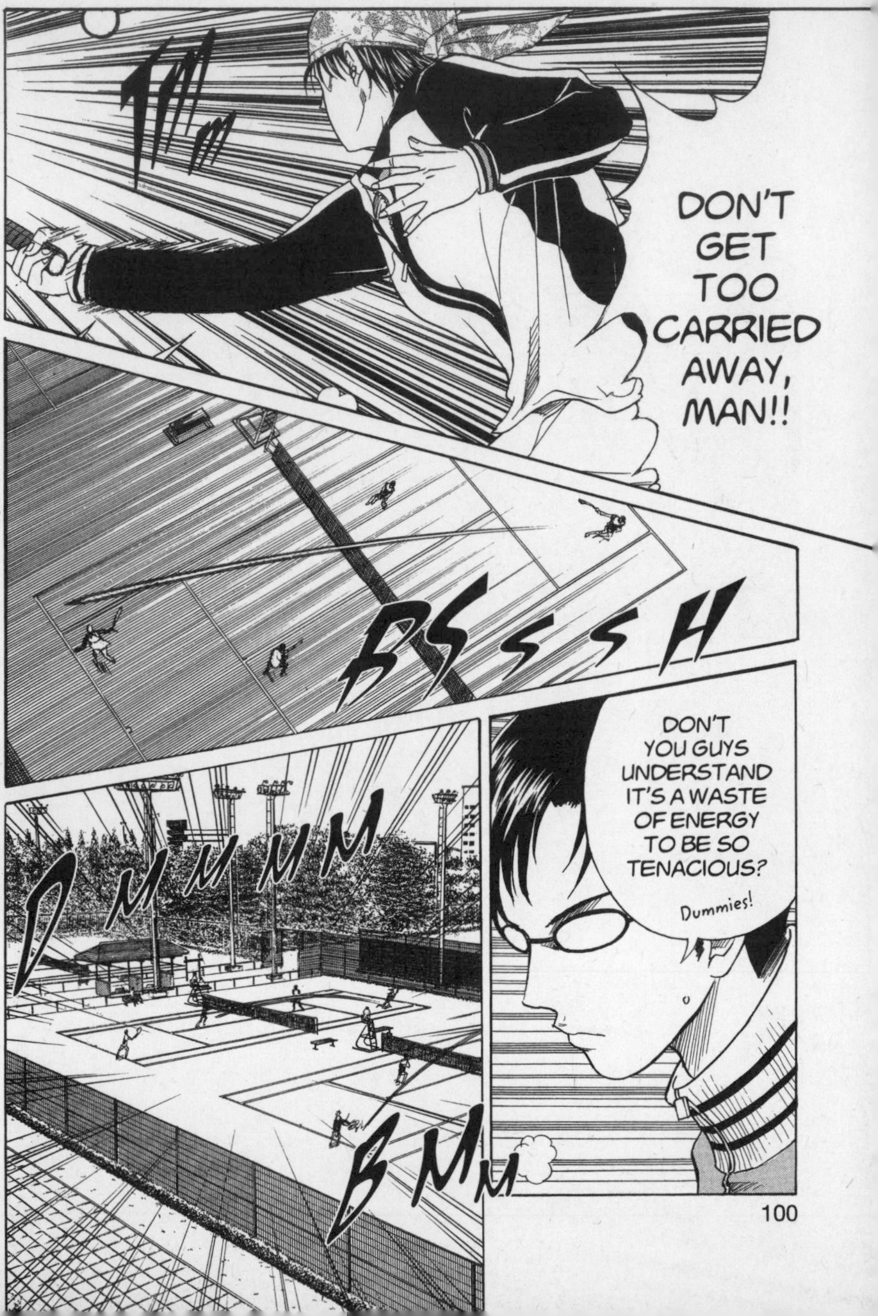
DON'T GET TOO CARRIED AWAY, MAN!!
BSSSH
DON'T YOU GUYS UNDERSTAND IT'S A WASTE OF ENERGY TO BE SO TENACIOUS?
Dummies!
DMMMMM
BMM

READ THIS WAY

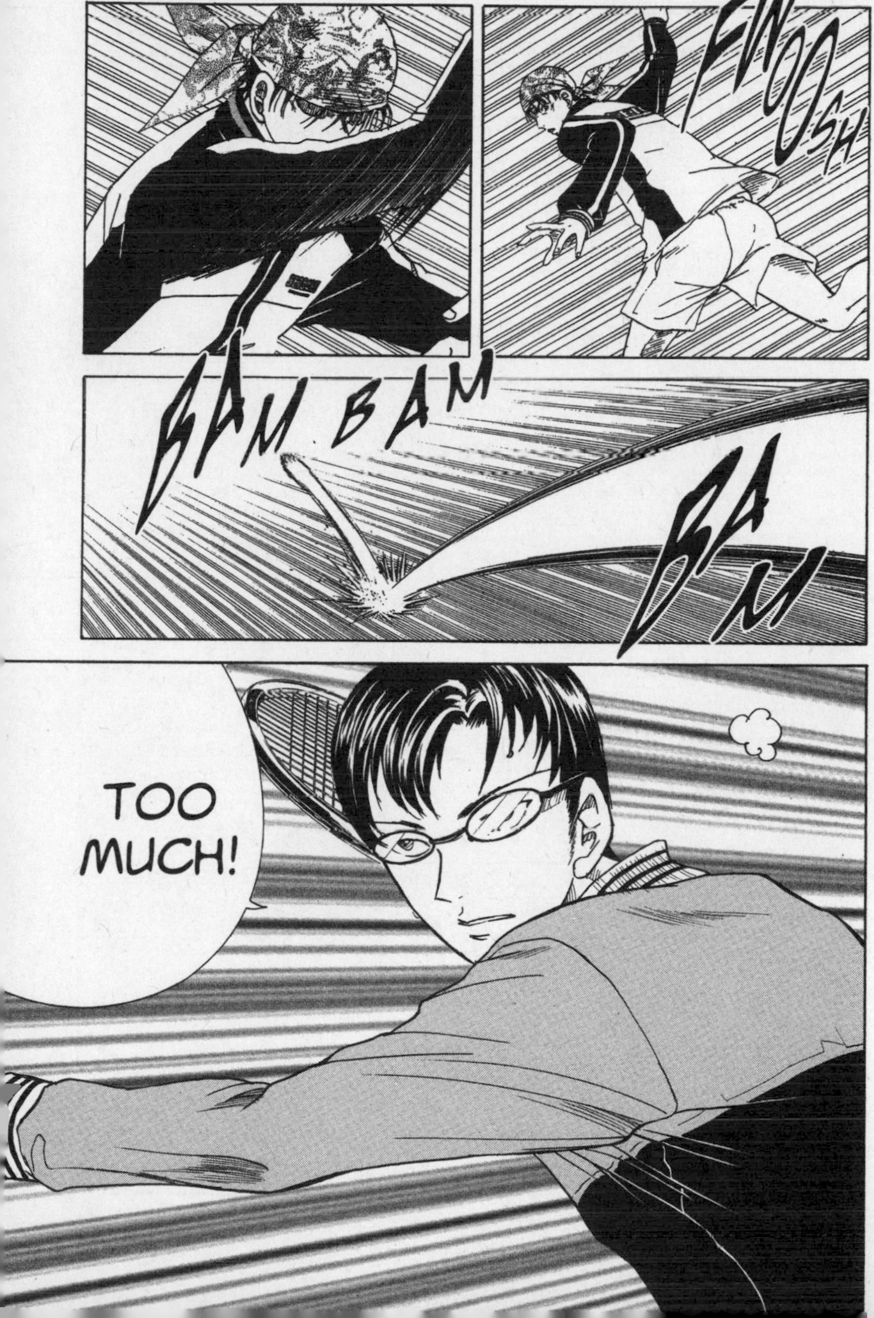
FWOOSH
BAM BAM
BAM
TOO MUCH!

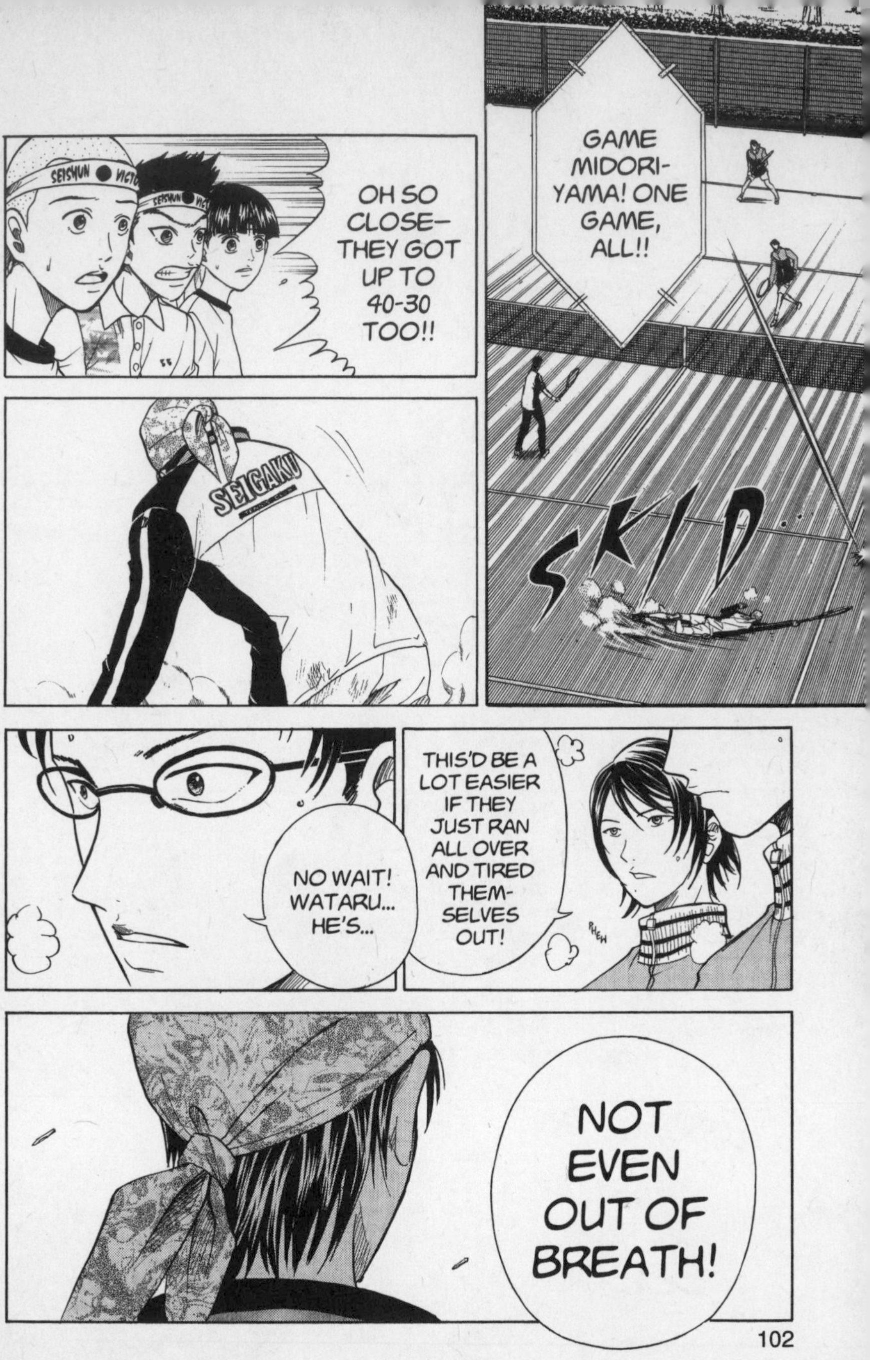
GAME MIDORI-YAMA! ONE GAME, ALL!!
SKID
OH SO CLOSE—THEY GOT UP TO 40-30 TOO!!
SEIGAKU
THIS'D BE A LOT EASIER IF THEY JUST RAN ALL OVER AND TIRED THEM-SELVES OUT!
NO WAIT! WATARU... HE'S...
NOT EVEN OUT OF BREATH!

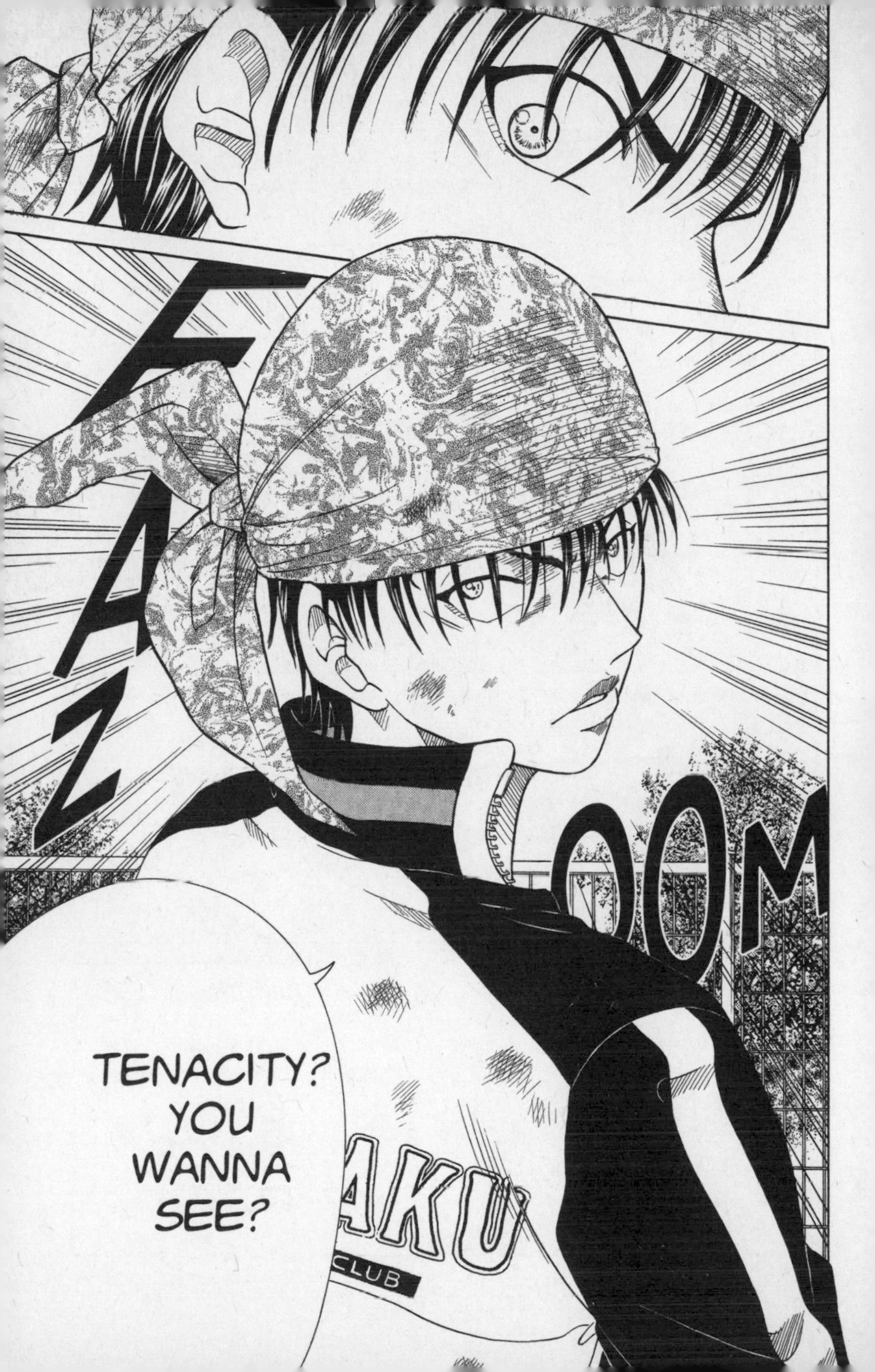
FAZOOM
TENACITY? YOU WANNA SEE?
AKU
CLUB

テニスの王子様

THE PRINCE OF TENNIS™

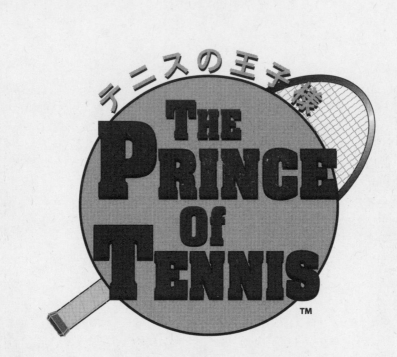

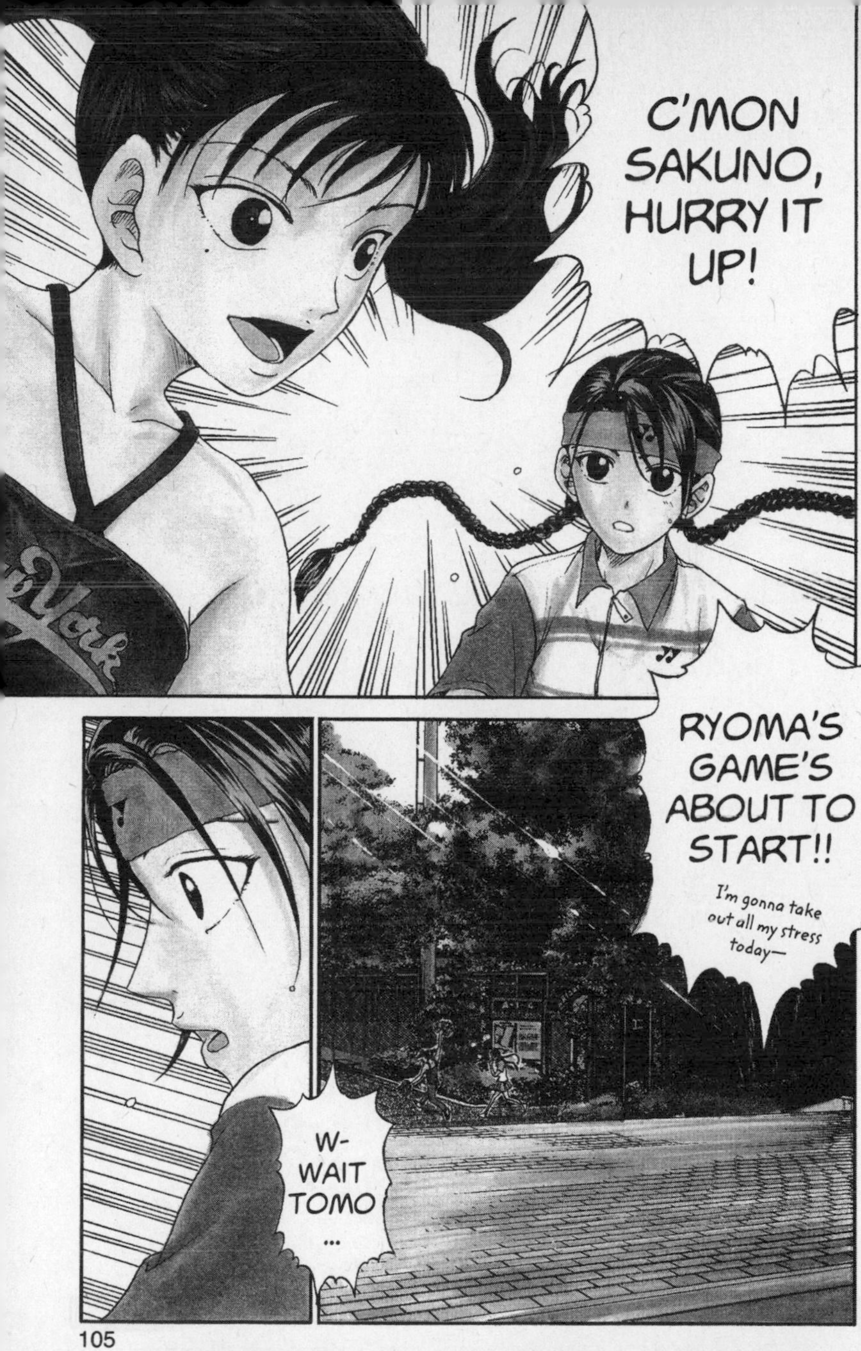
C'MON SAKUNO, HURRY IT UP!
RYOMA'S GAME'S ABOUT TO START!!
I'm gonna take out all my stress today—
W-WAIT TOMO ...

GENIUS 164: EVERYBODY'S BATTLES

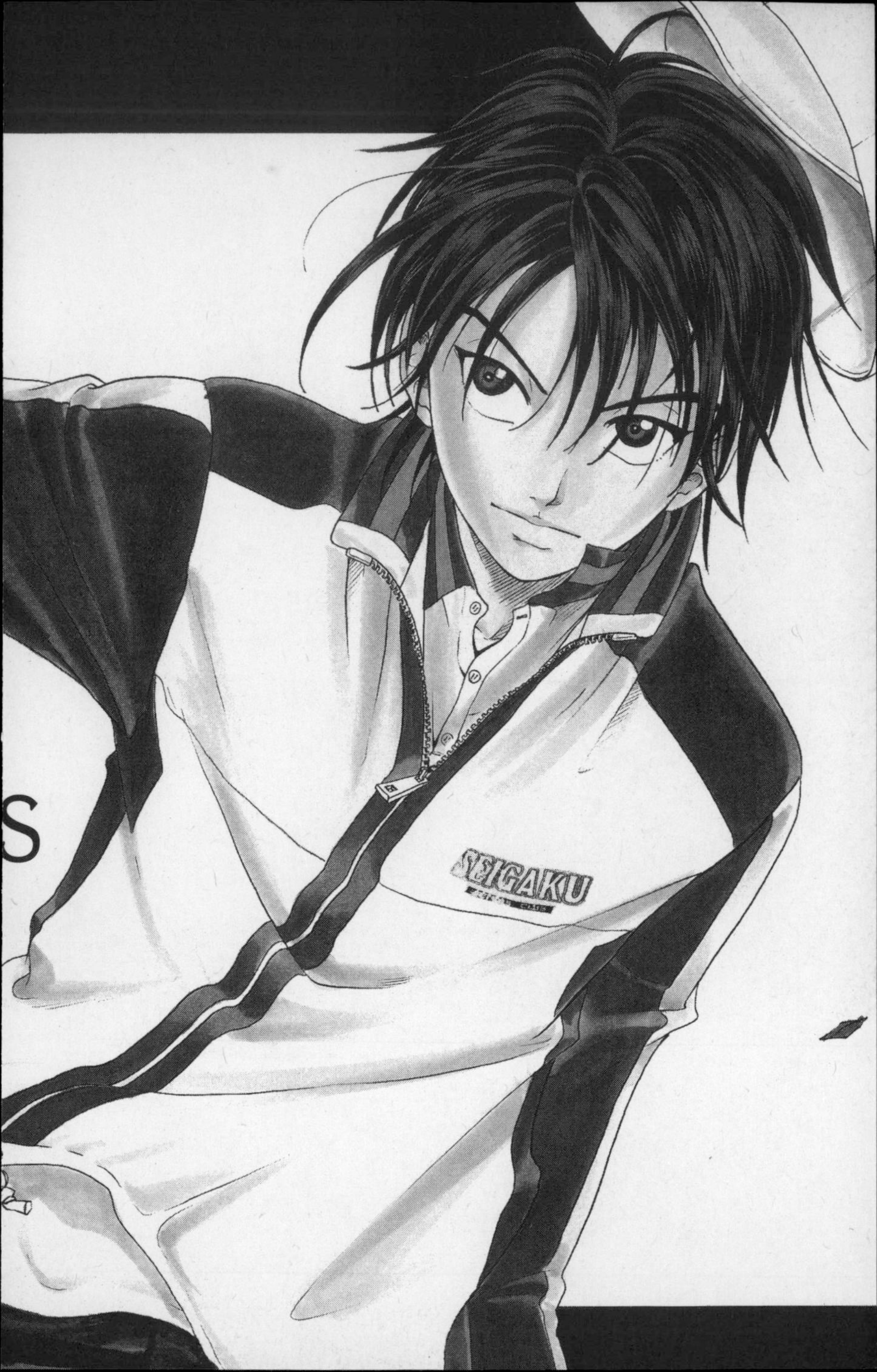
S
SEIGAKU

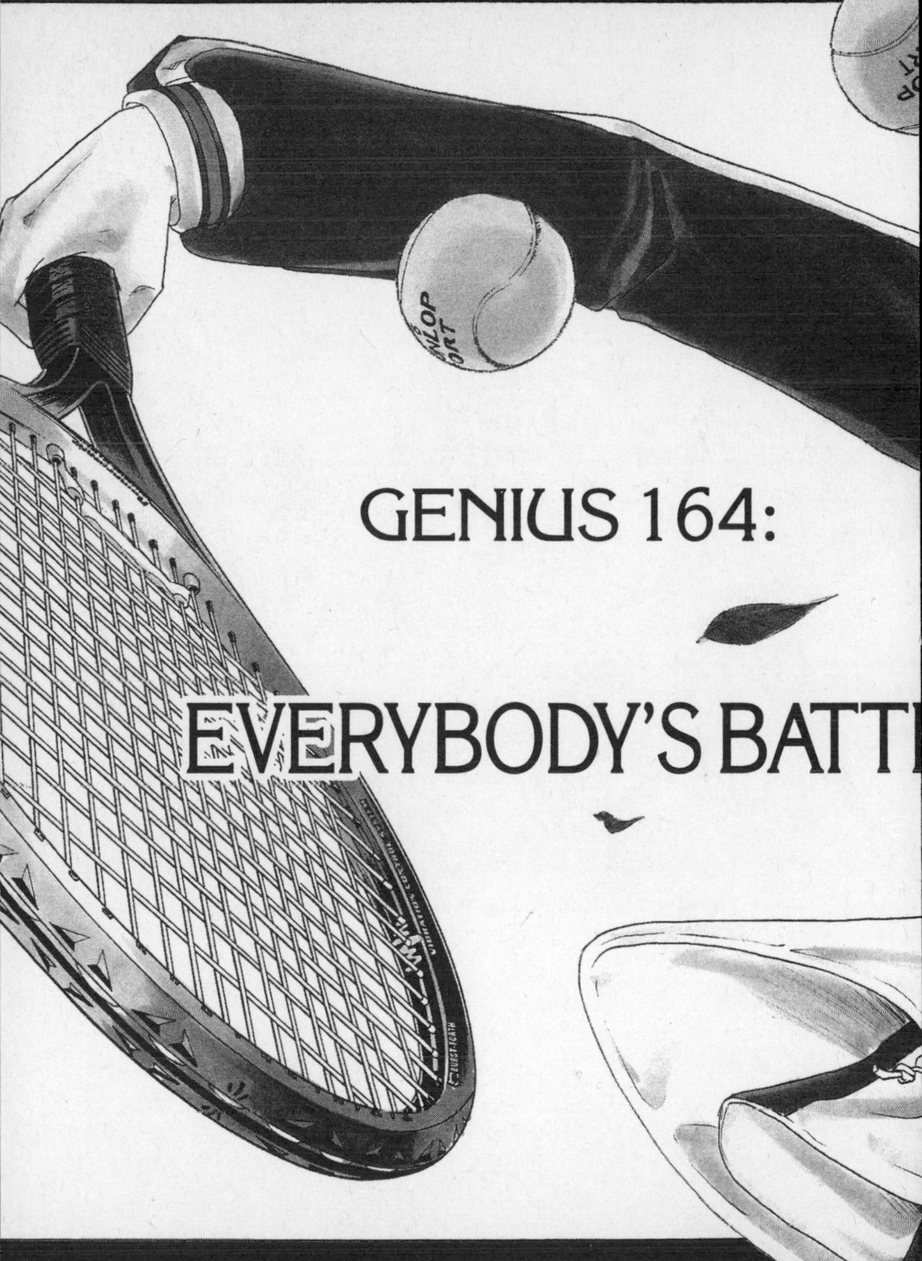
GENIUS 164:
EVERYBODY'S BATT

テニスの王子様

THE PRINCE OF TENNIS™

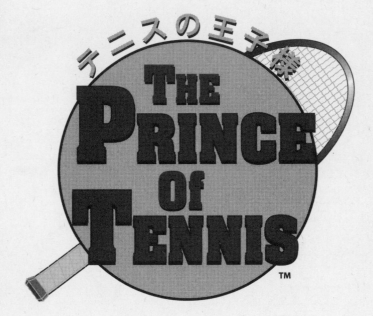

READ THIS WAY

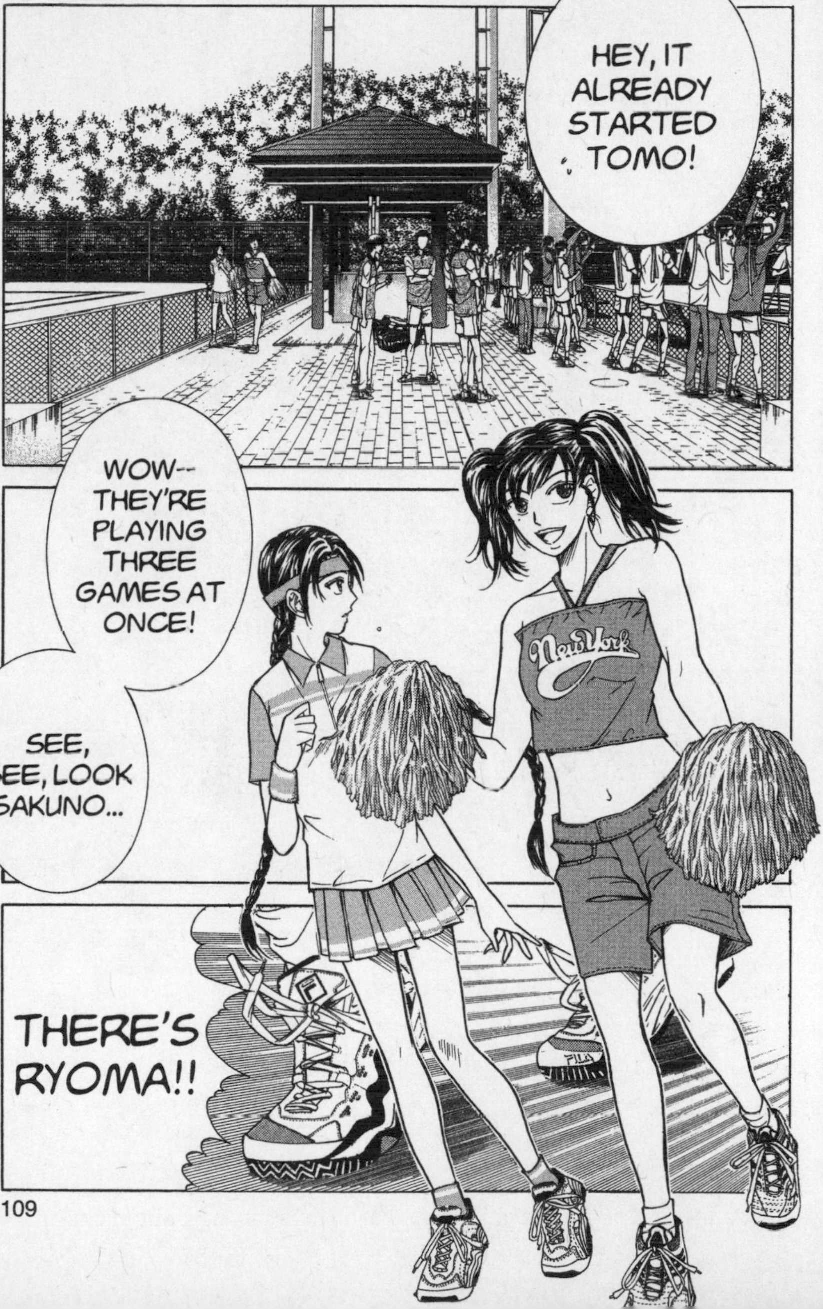
HEY, IT ALREADY STARTED TOMO!
WOW-- THEY'RE PLAYING THREE GAMES AT ONCE!
SEE, SEE, LOOK SAKUNO...
THERE'S RYOMA!!

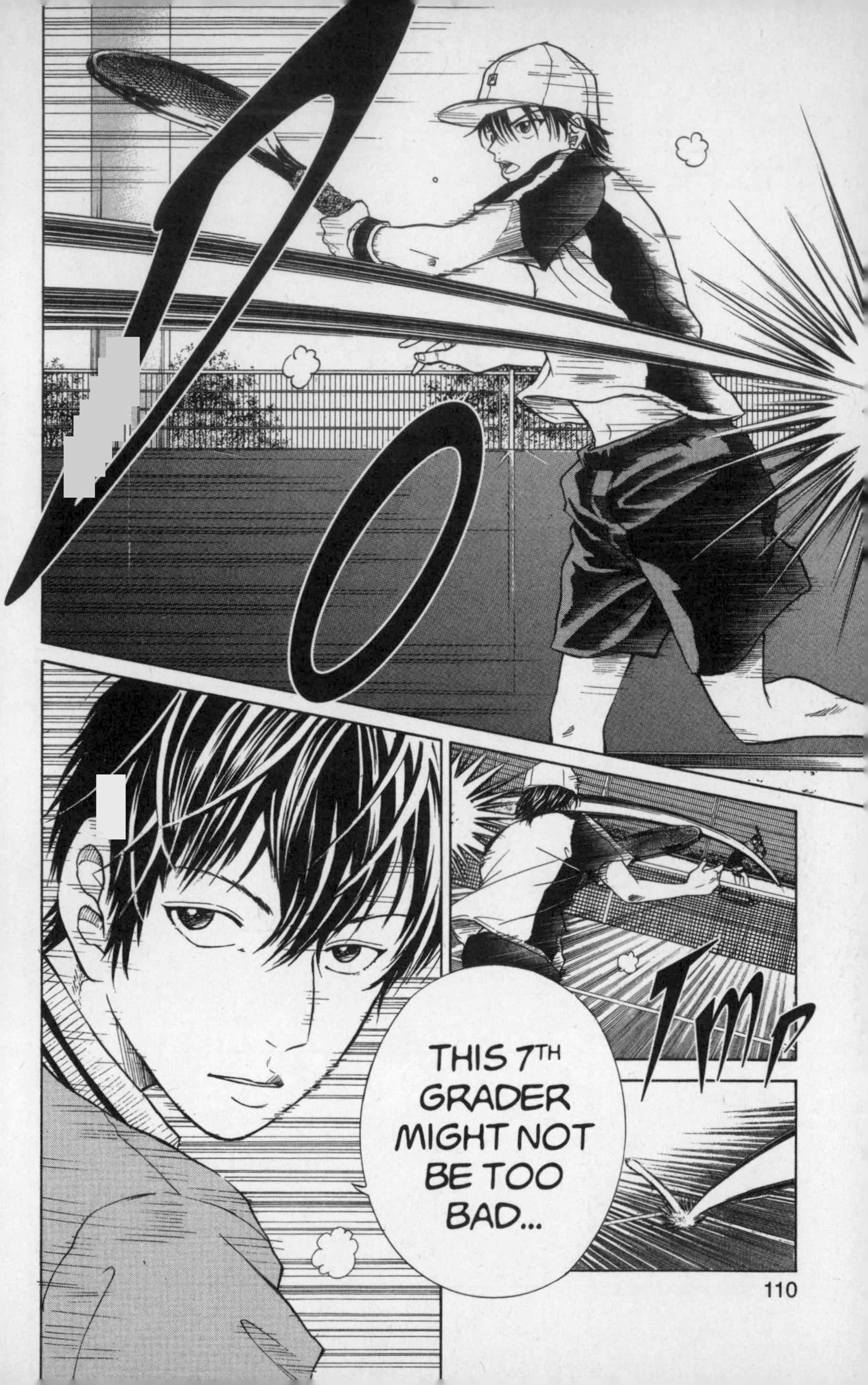
Tmp
THIS 7TH GRADER MIGHT NOT BE TOO BAD...

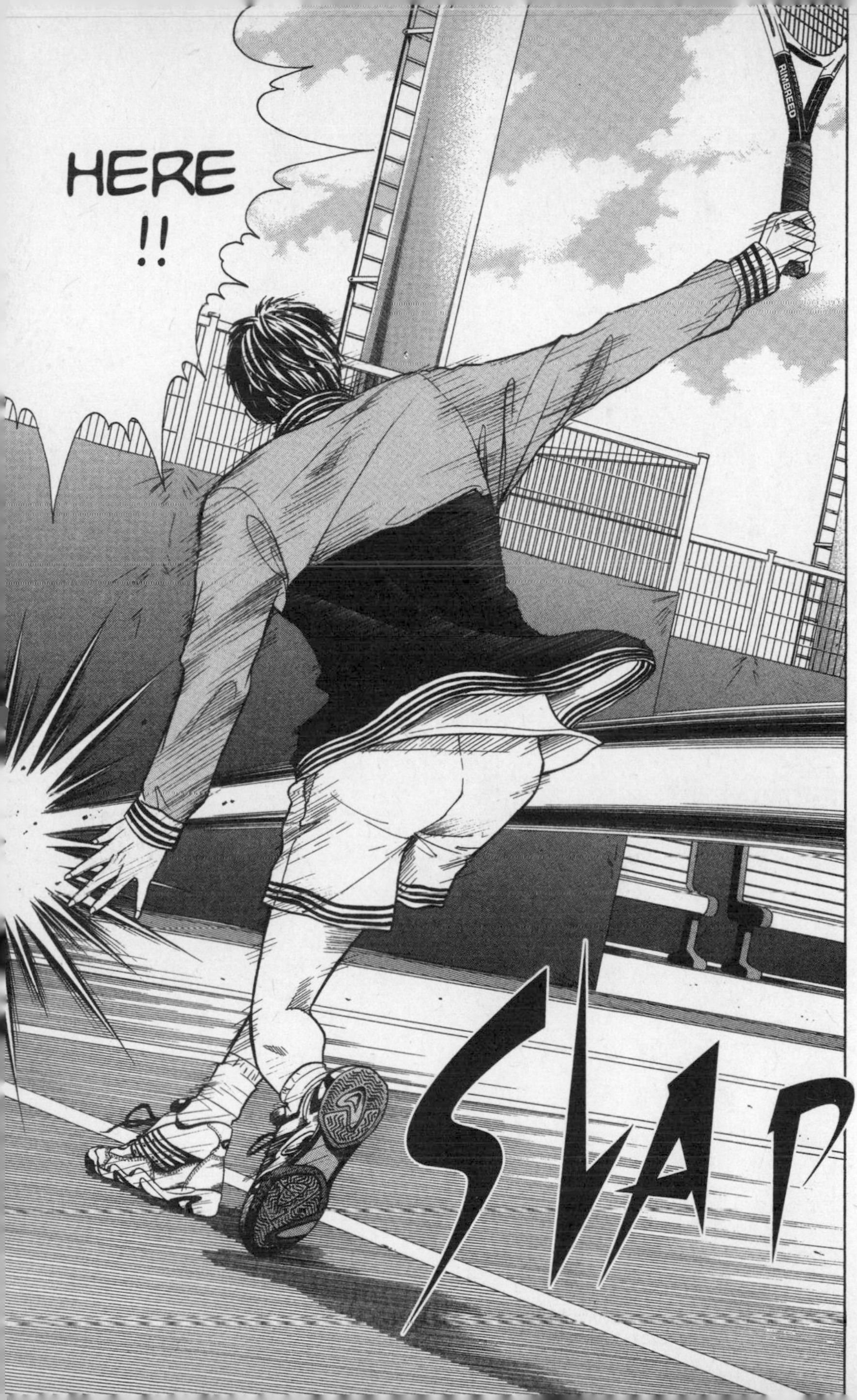
RIMBREED
HERE !!
SLAP

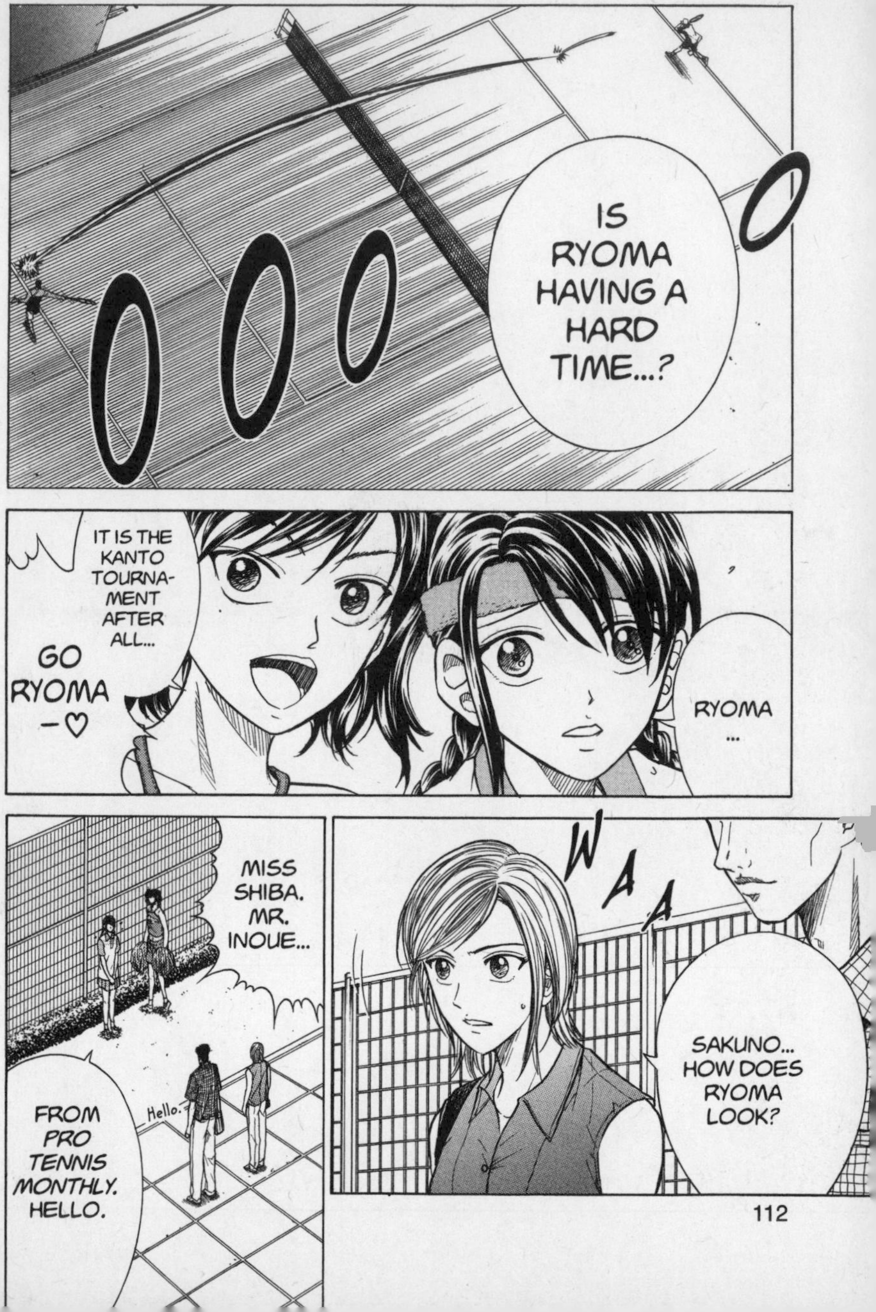
IS RYOMA HAVING A HARD TIME...?
RYOMA ...
IT IS THE KANTO TOURNAMENT AFTER ALL...
GO RYOMA —♡
WAA
SAKUNO... HOW DOES RYOMA LOOK?
MISS SHIBA. MR. INOUE...
Hello.
FROM PRO TENNIS MONTHLY. HELLO.

READ THIS WAY

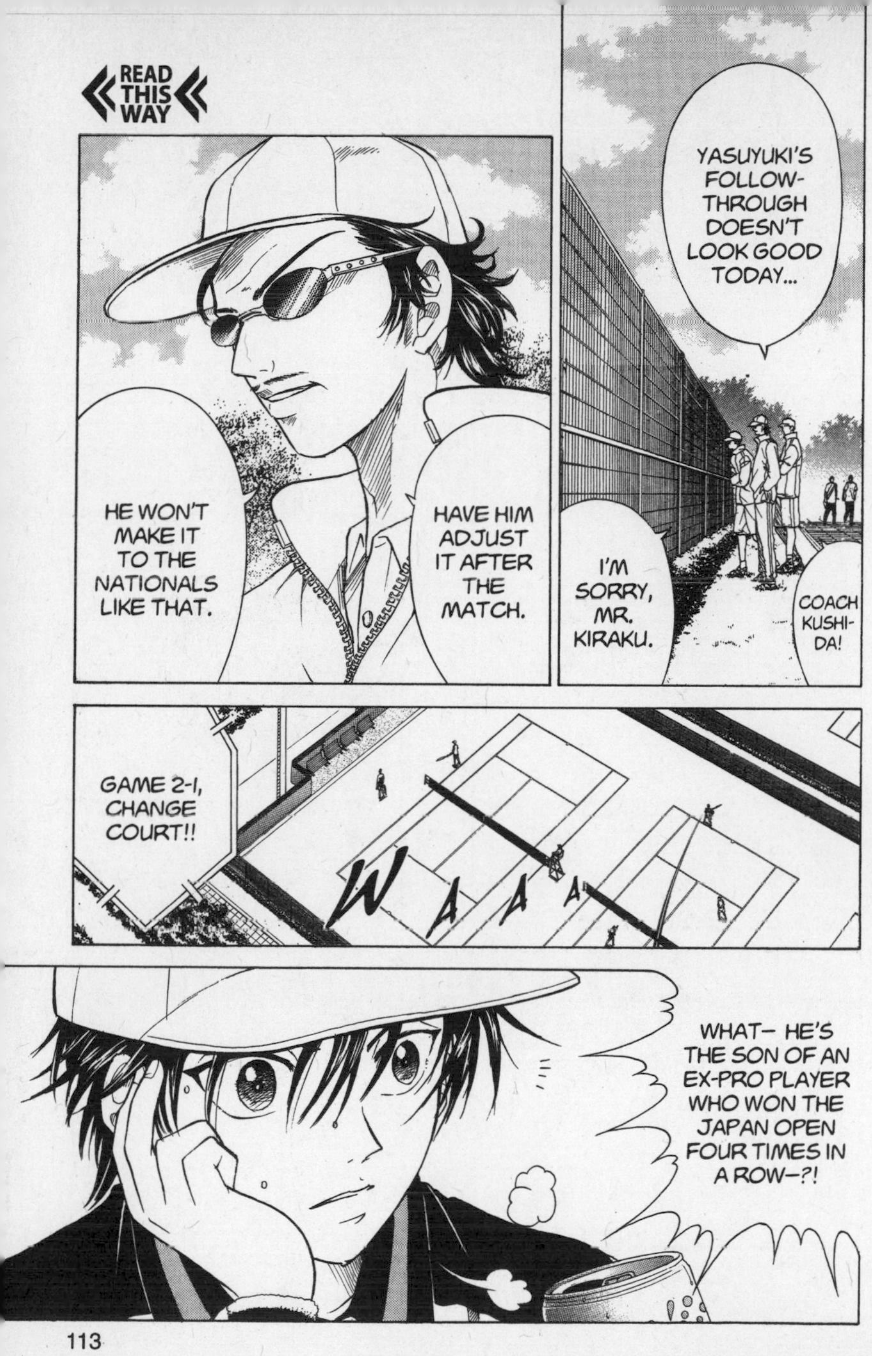
YASUYUKI'S FOLLOW-THROUGH DOESN'T LOOK GOOD TODAY...
COACH KUSHIDA!
I'M SORRY, MR. KIRAKU.
HAVE HIM ADJUST IT AFTER THE MATCH.
HE WON'T MAKE IT TO THE NATIONALS LIKE THAT.
GAME 2-1, CHANGE COURT!!
WAAAA
WHAT– HE'S THE SON OF AN EX-PRO PLAYER WHO WON THE JAPAN OPEN FOUR TIMES IN A ROW–?!

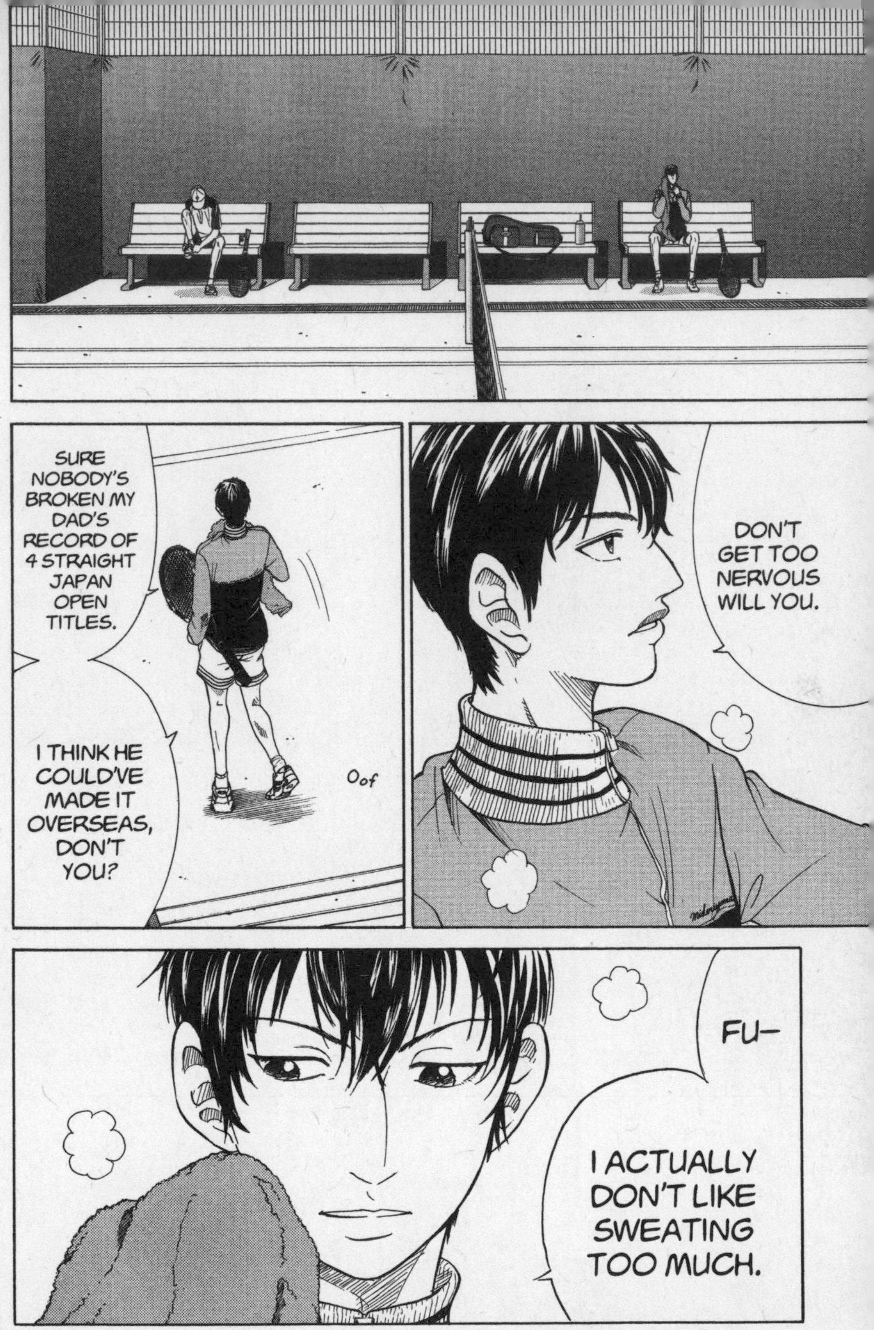
DON'T GET TOO NERVOUS WILL YOU.
SURE NOBODY'S BROKEN MY DAD'S RECORD OF 4 STRAIGHT JAPAN OPEN TITLES.
I THINK HE COULD'VE MADE IT OVERSEAS, DON'T YOU?
Oof
FU-
I ACTUALLY DON'T LIKE SWEATING TOO MUCH.

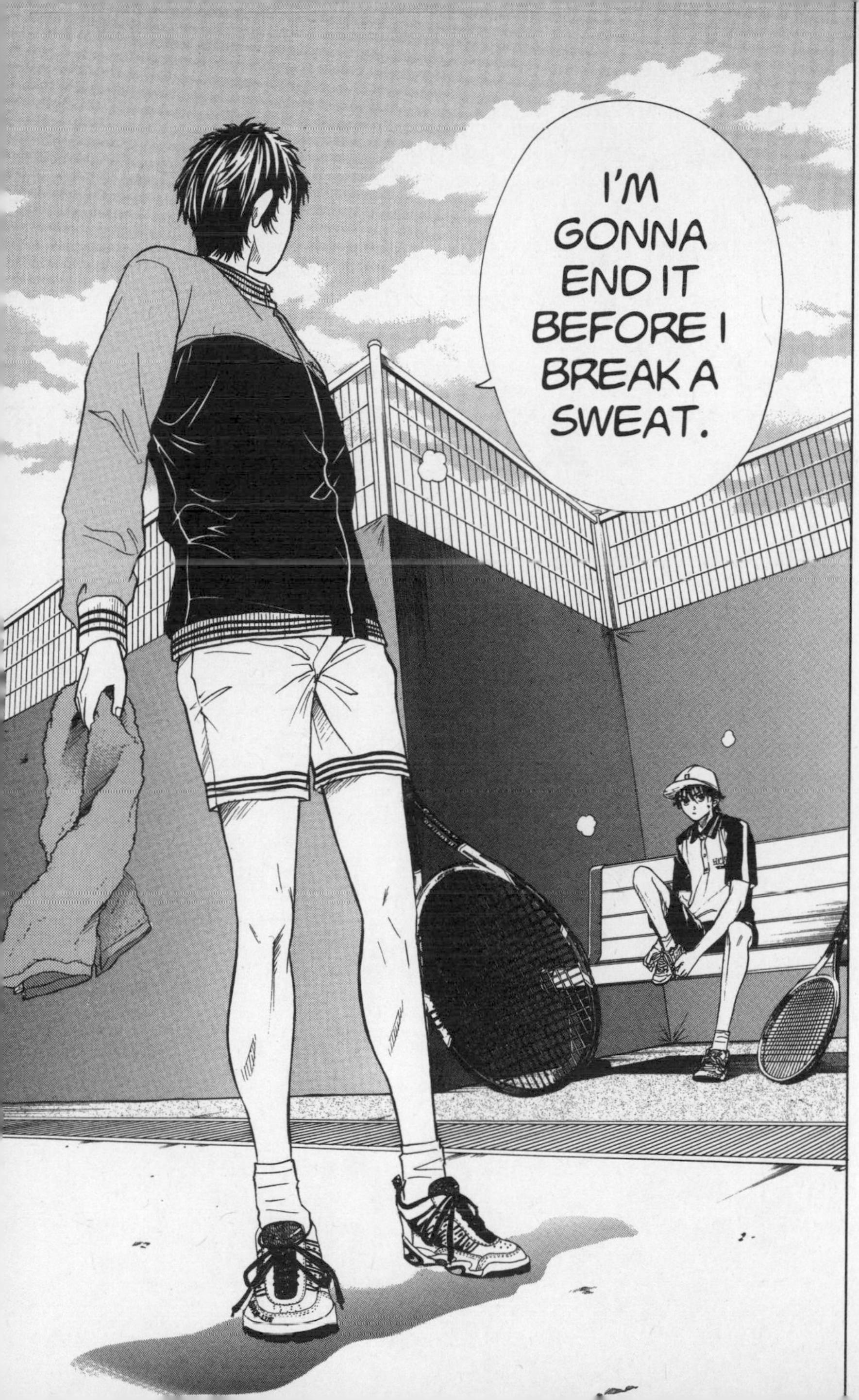
I'M GONNA END IT BEFORE I BREAK A SWEAT.

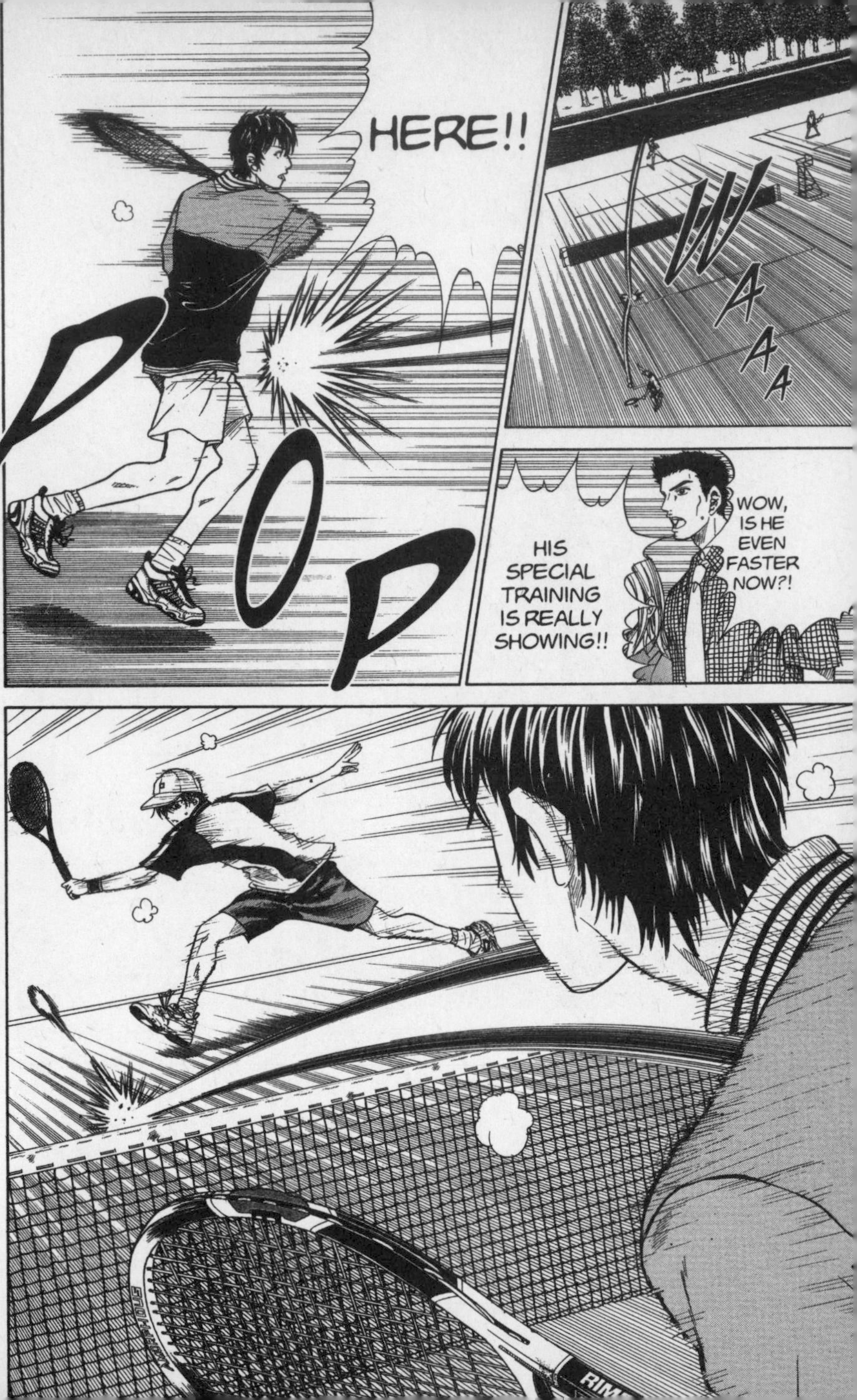
WAAAA
WOW, IS HE EVEN FASTER NOW?!
HIS SPECIAL TRAINING IS REALLY SHOWING!!
HERE!!
POP

READ THIS WAY

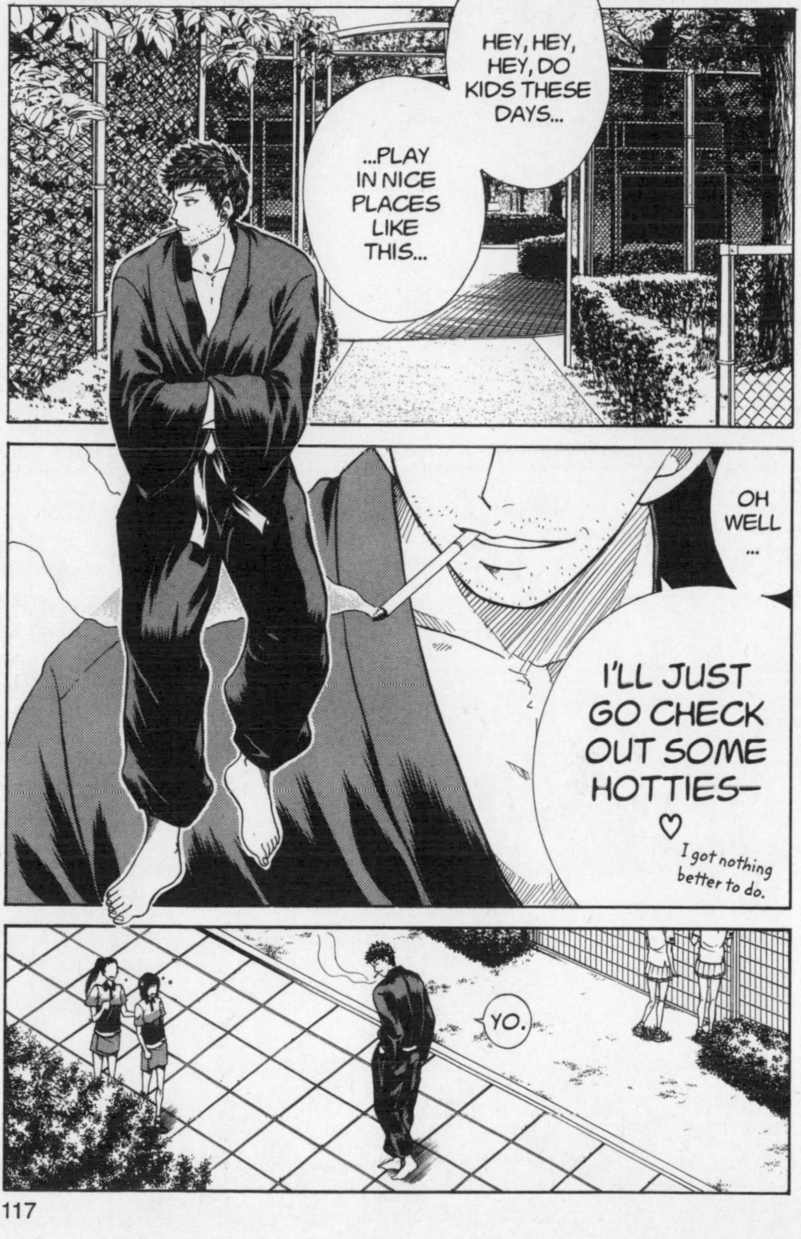
HEY, HEY, HEY, DO KIDS THESE DAYS...
...PLAY IN NICE PLACES LIKE THIS...
OH WELL ...
I'LL JUST GO CHECK OUT SOME HOTTIES— ♡
I got nothing better to do.
YO.

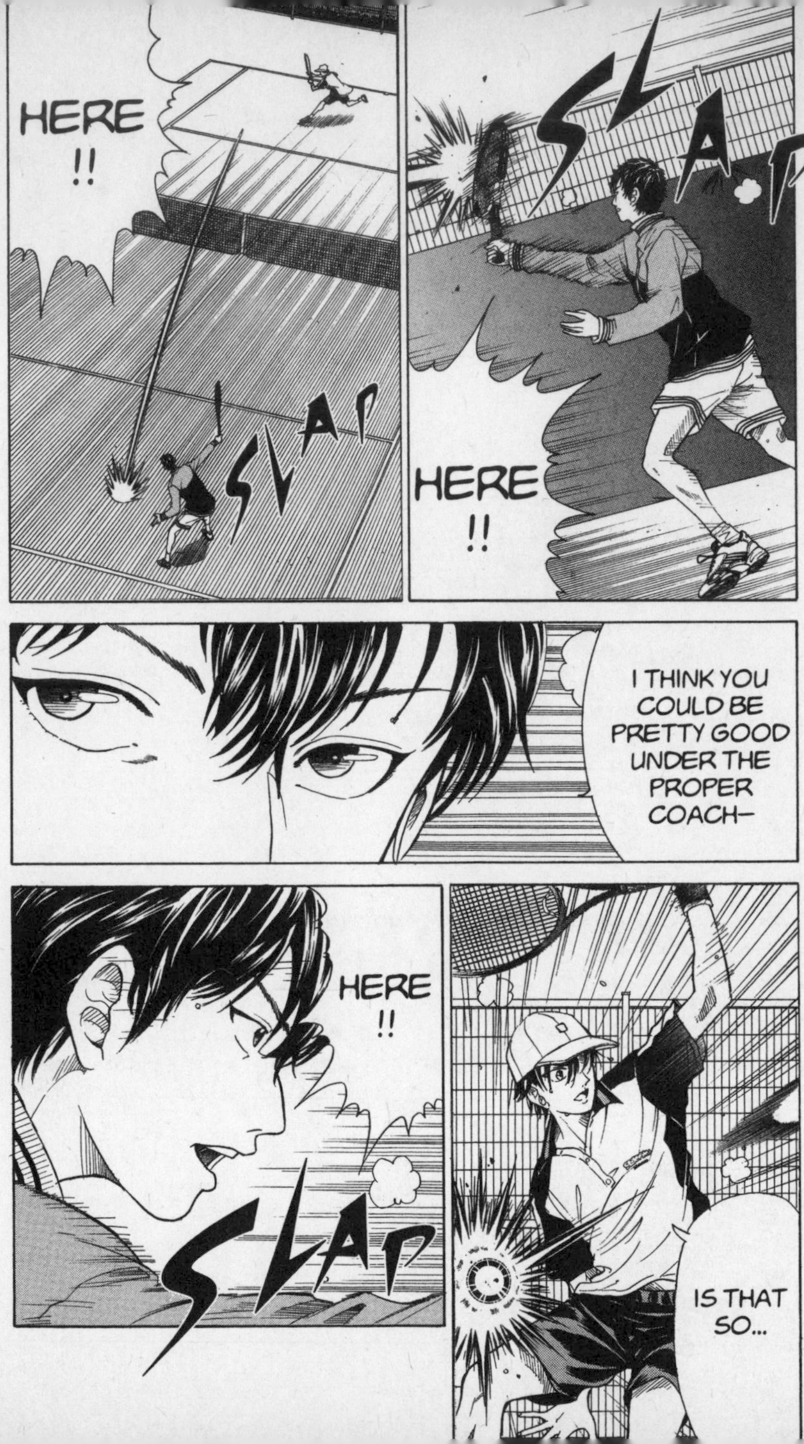
SLAP
HERE !!
HERE !!
SLAP
I THINK YOU COULD BE PRETTY GOOD UNDER THE PROPER COACH–
IS THAT SO...
HERE !!
SLAP

READ THIS WAY

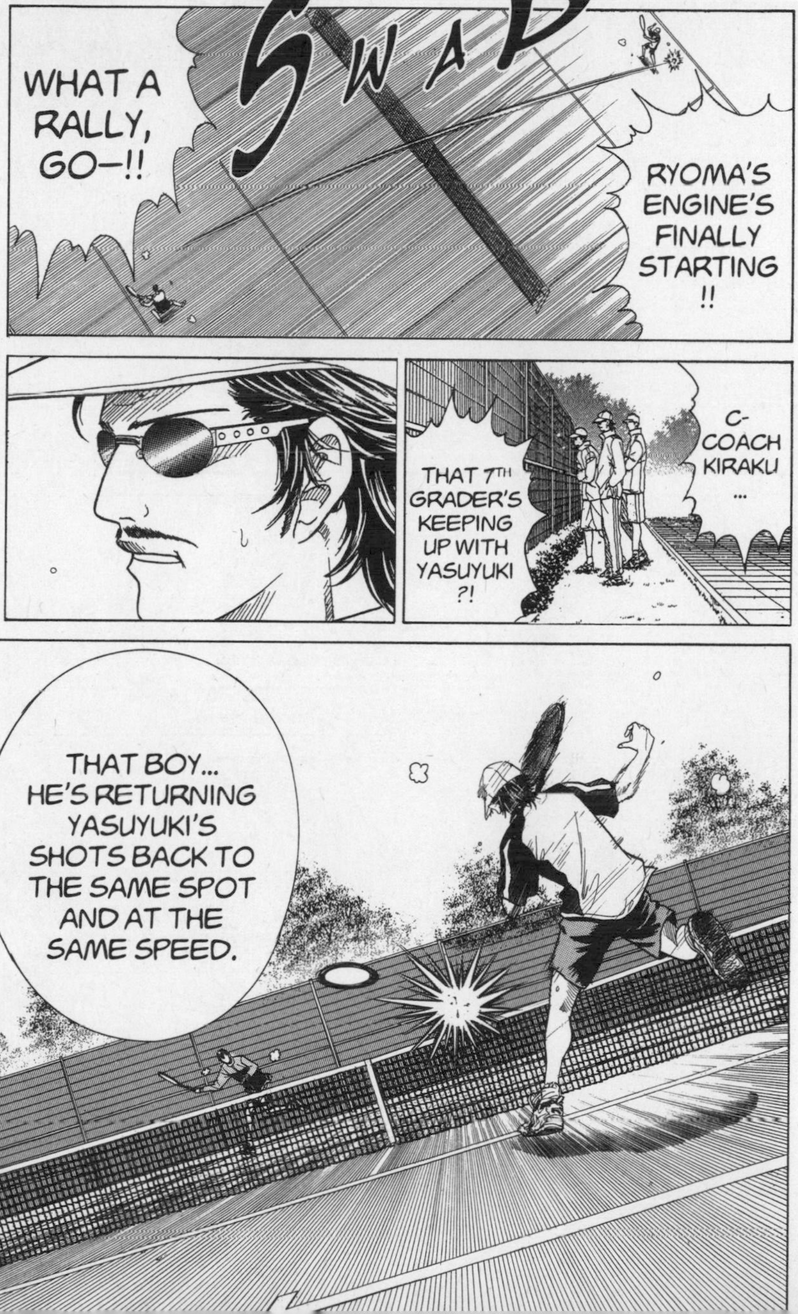
RYOMA'S ENGINE'S FINALLY STARTING !!
SWAP
WHAT A RALLY, GO-!!
C-COACH KIRAKU ...
THAT 7TH GRADER'S KEEPING UP WITH YASUYUKI ?!
THAT BOY... HE'S RETURNING YASUYUKI'S SHOTS BACK TO THE SAME SPOT AND AT THE SAME SPEED.

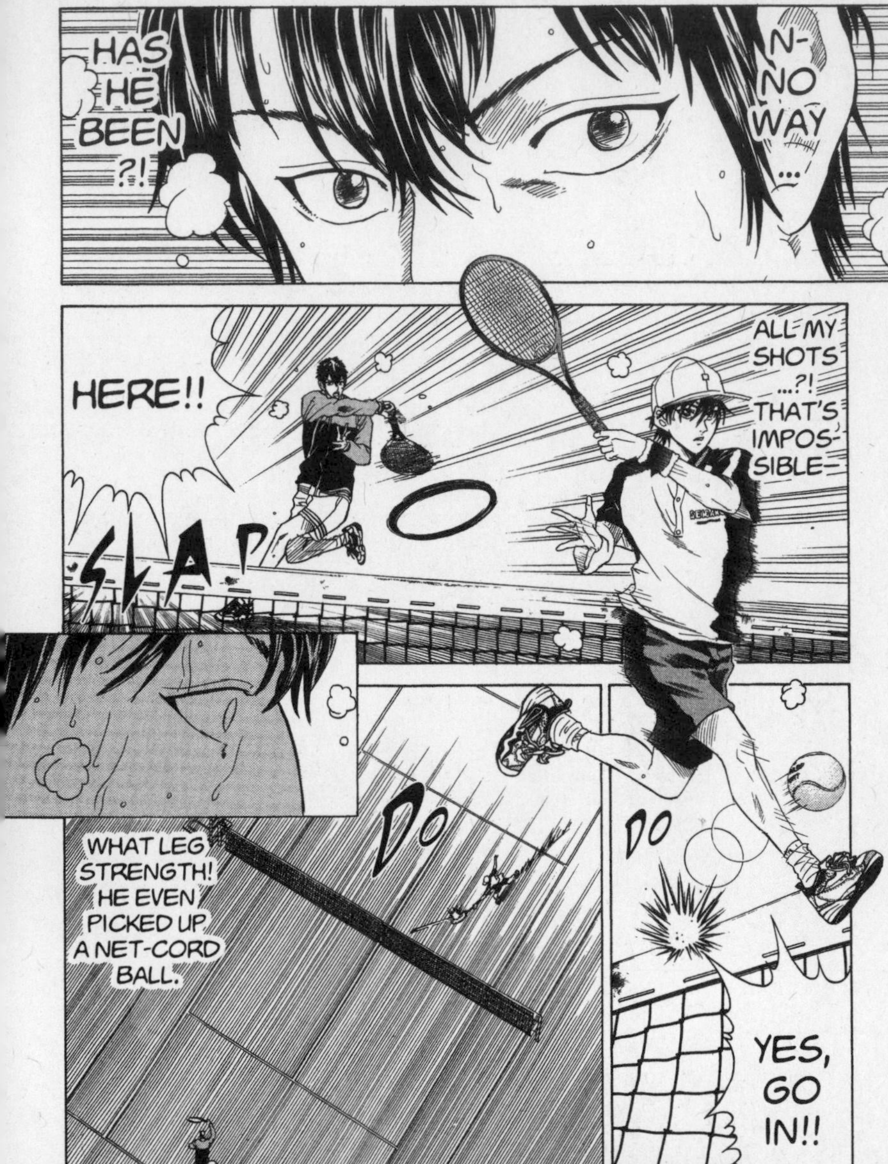
N-NO WAY...
HAS HE BEEN ?!
ALL MY SHOTS ...?! THAT'S IMPOSSIBLE
HERE!!
SLAP
DO
YES, GO IN!!
DO
WHAT LEG STRENGTH! HE EVEN PICKED UP A NET-CORD BALL.

READ THIS WAY

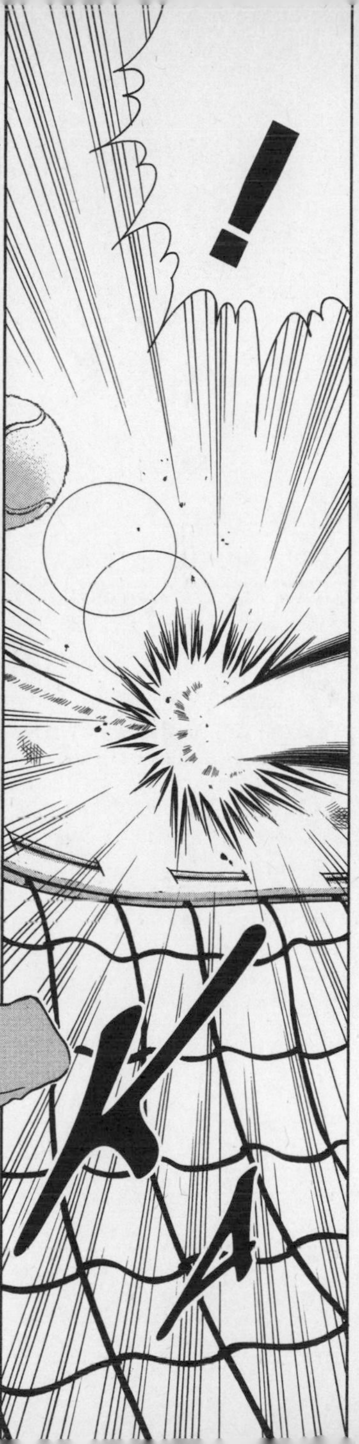
!

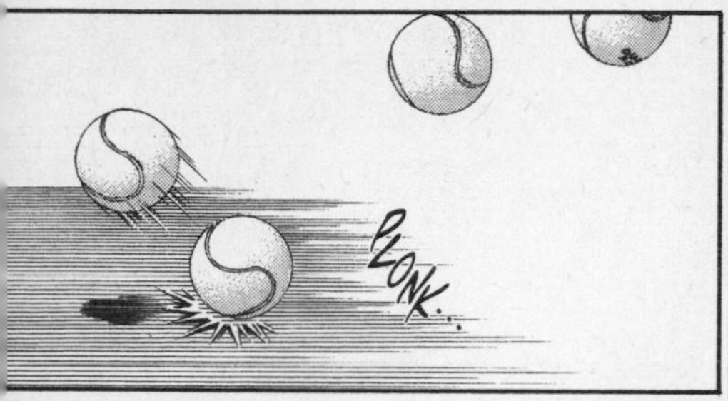
PLONK...

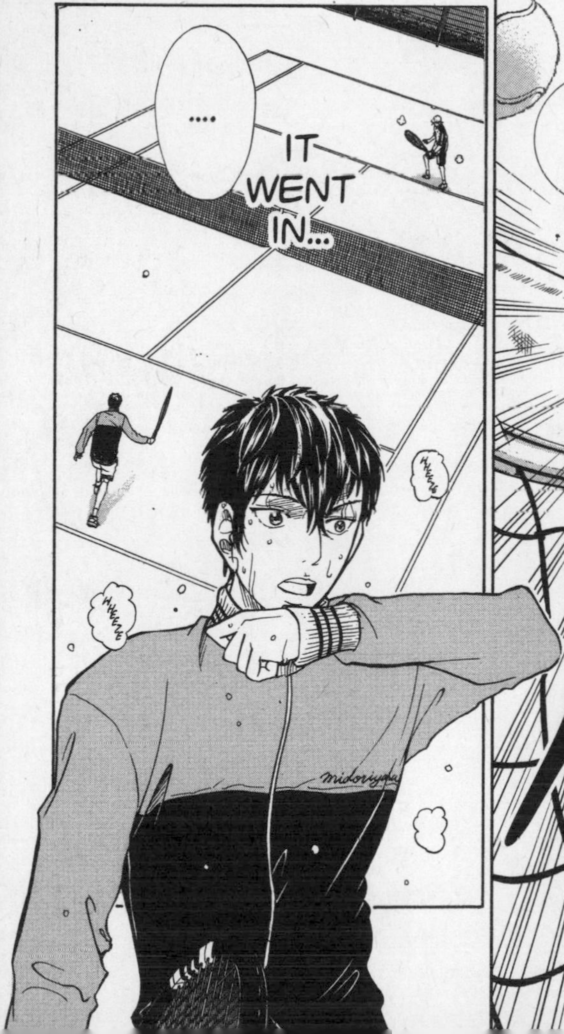
....
IT WENT IN...
WHEEZE

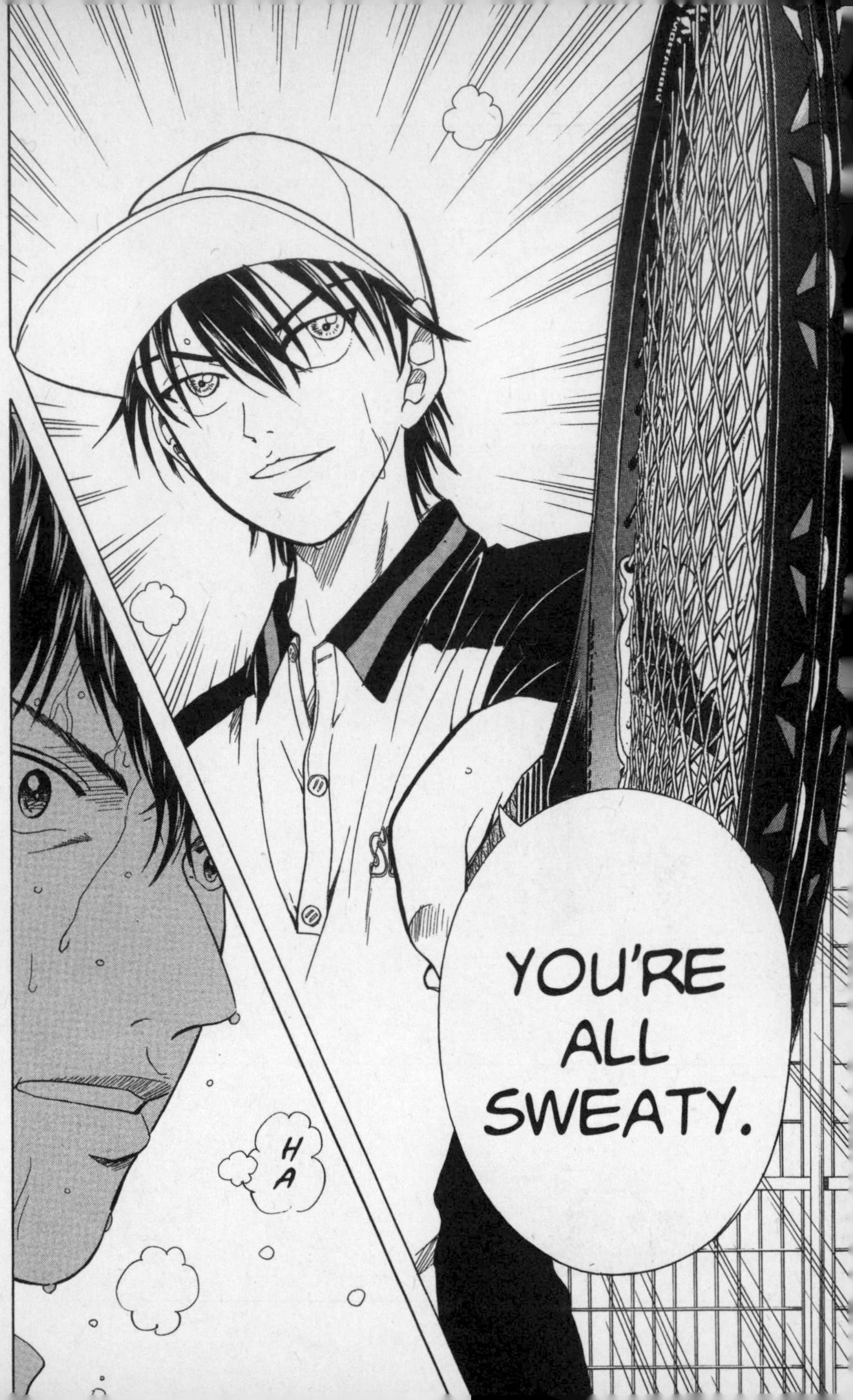
YOU'RE ALL SWEATY.
HA

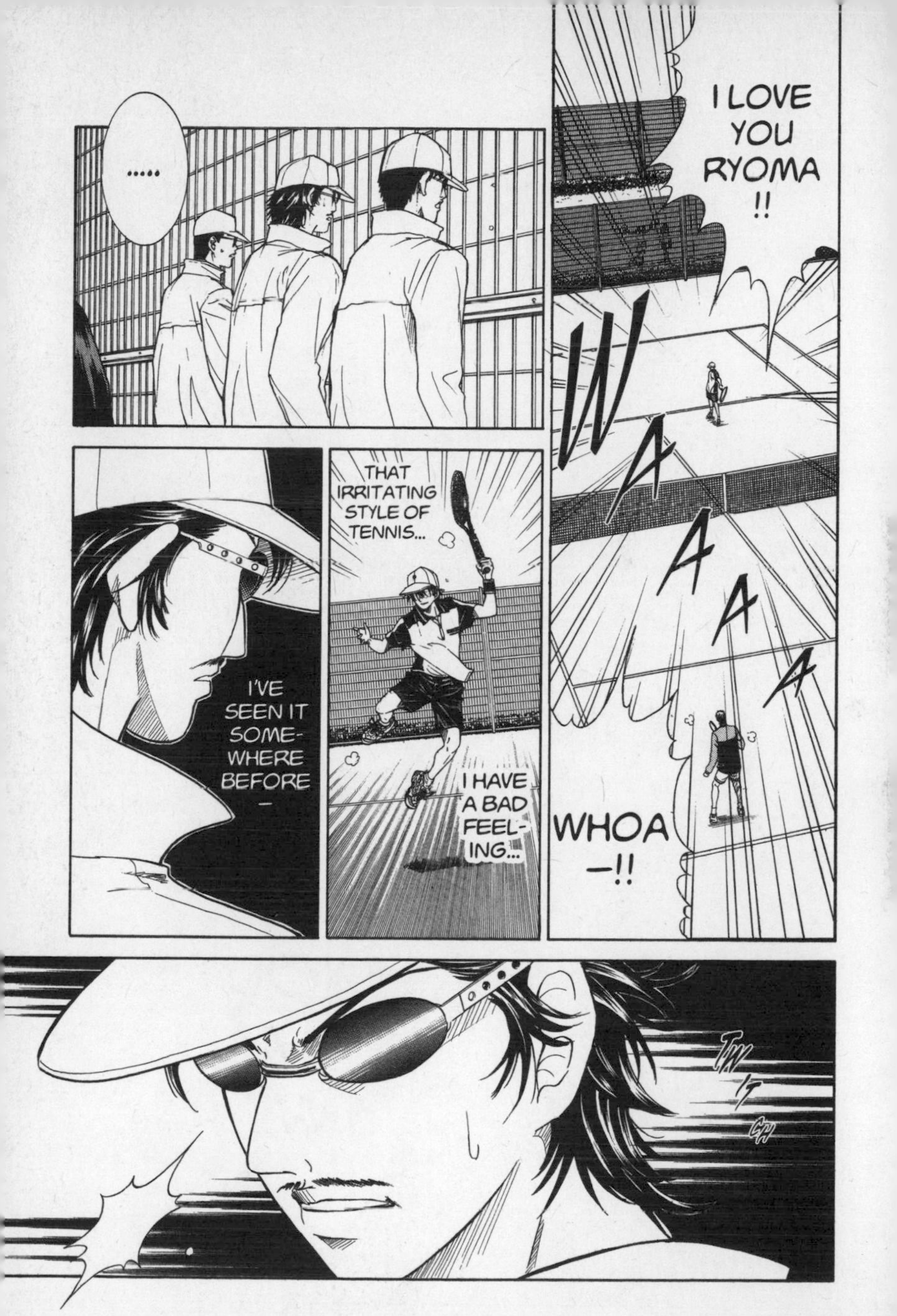
I LOVE YOU RYOMA !!
WAAAAA
WHOA-!!
......
THAT IRRITATING STYLE OF TENNIS...
I HAVE A BAD FEELING...
I'VE SEEN IT SOMEWHERE BEFORE -
TWITCH

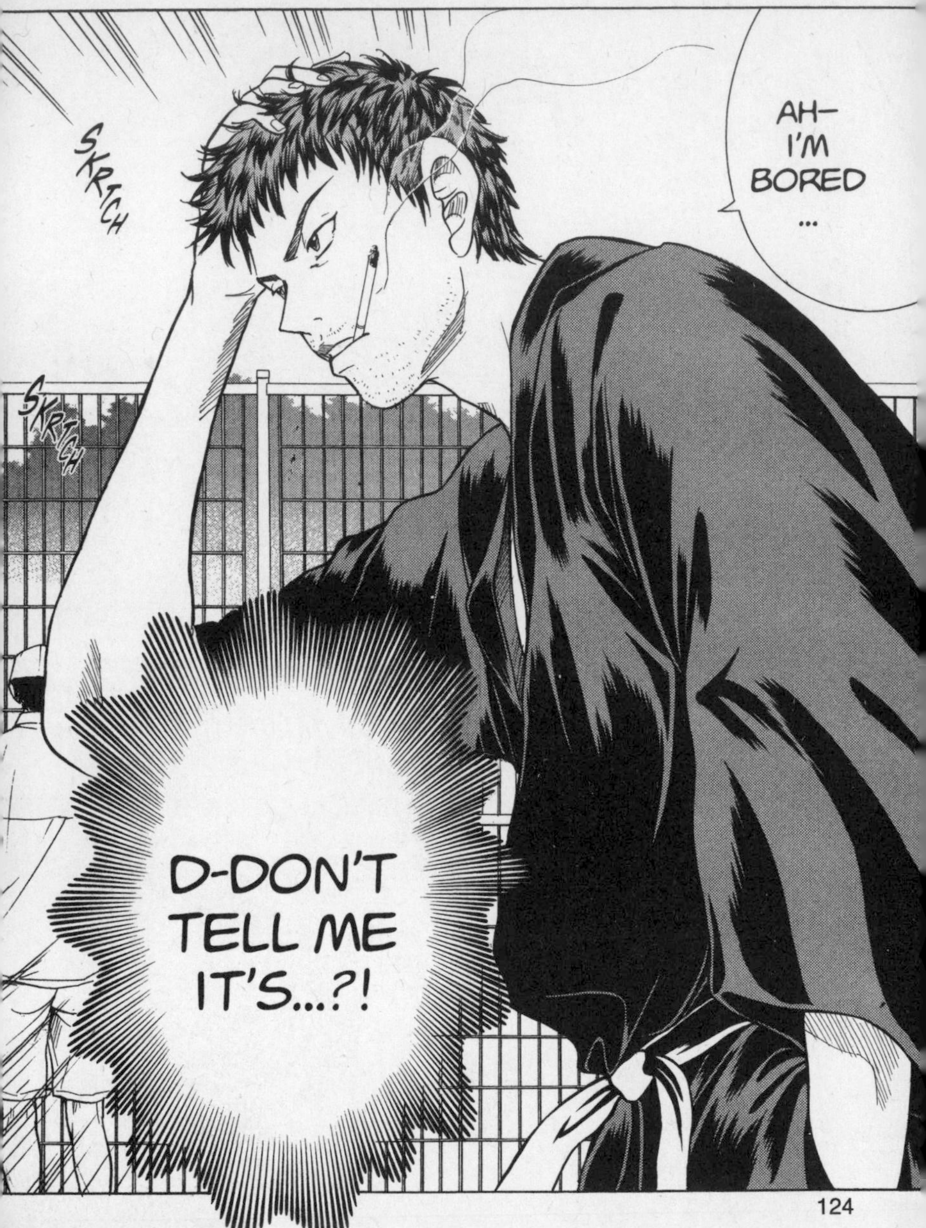
AH— I'M BORED ...
SKRITCH
SKRITCH
D-DON'T TELL ME IT'S...?!

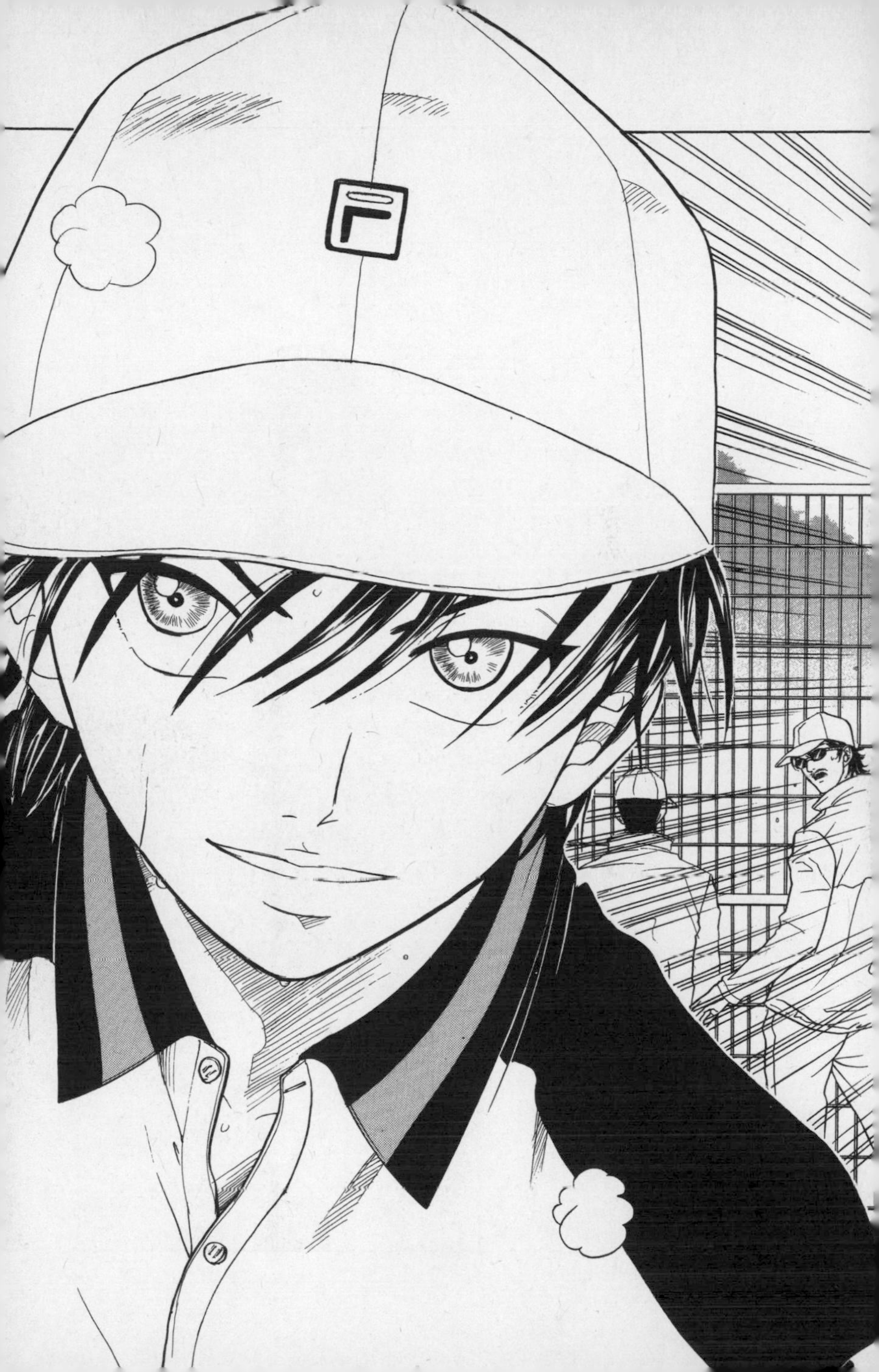

Thank you for reading *The Prince of Tennis*, volume 19.

Hello, everybody. I already announced this at the "Prince of Tennis Tennis Festival" held in late March, but here it is again. In *Shonen Jump*, issue 32, on sale July 8th, 2003, the four-year anniversary issue, I will write a "Prince of Tennis Special Edition Episode". I cannot be more pleased. It is all due to the fans. I really thank all of you!! After June, when I'm finished writing it, I'm sure I'll be hit by a dreadful schedule, but I'll use your fan letters as energy!! I hope all of you pick up a copy of issue 32!!

Last year, faced with a new medium called "anime," I tried to experience it as much as I could while maintaining the manga. This year, as a sign of appreciation, I will focus my efforts on the manga. But I recently felt a decline in my health. I get tired easily and it takes me longer to recuperate. So I've taken up jogging, though I'm lucky if I can run once a week. Exercising makes my body feel more refreshed than any massage! I hope to have more time to exercise.

Well then, I'll see you in the next volume...volume 20 (I'm so happy—!!)!! Keep supporting *The Prince of Tennis* and Ryoma!!

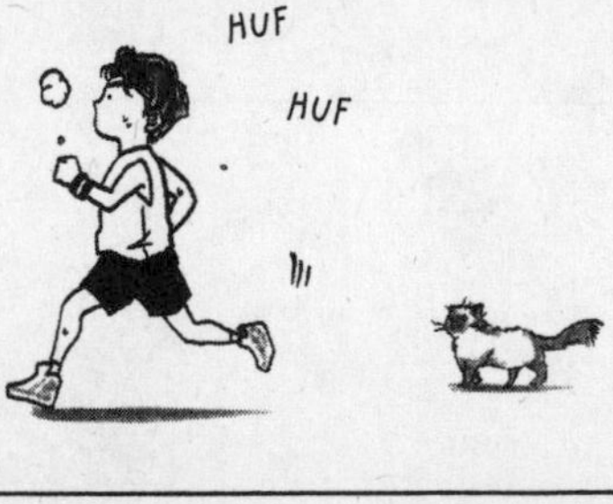
HUF
HUF

テニスの王子様
T.Konomi
2003.6.6

Send fan letters to: Takeshi Konomi c/o VIZ Media, LLC P.O. Box 77010 San Francisco, CA 94107

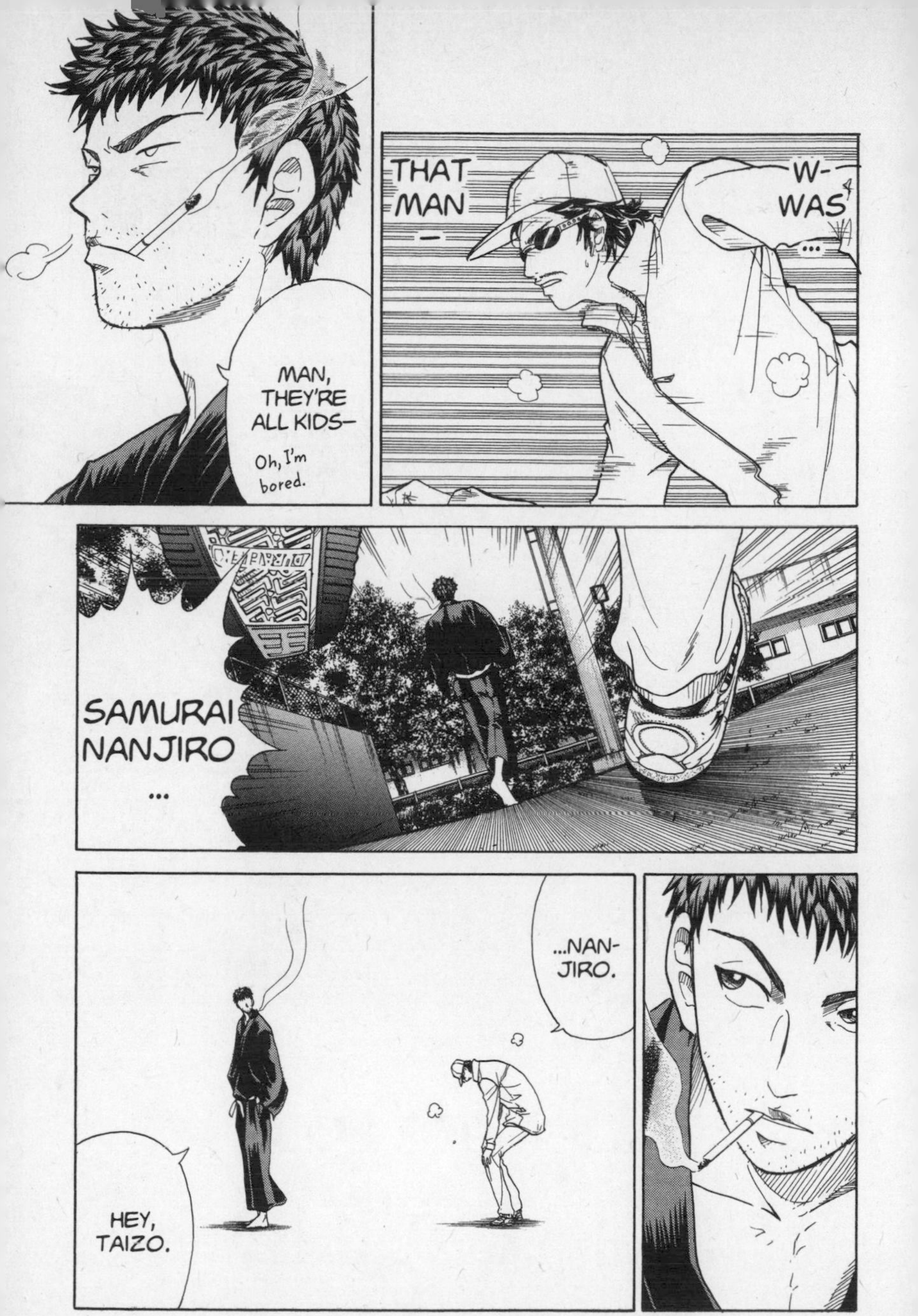
THAT MAN —
W-WAS ...
MAN, THEY'RE ALL KIDS—
Oh, I'm bored.
SAMURAI NANJIRO ...
...NAN-JIRO.
HEY, TAIZO.

GENIUS 165: JUST A KID

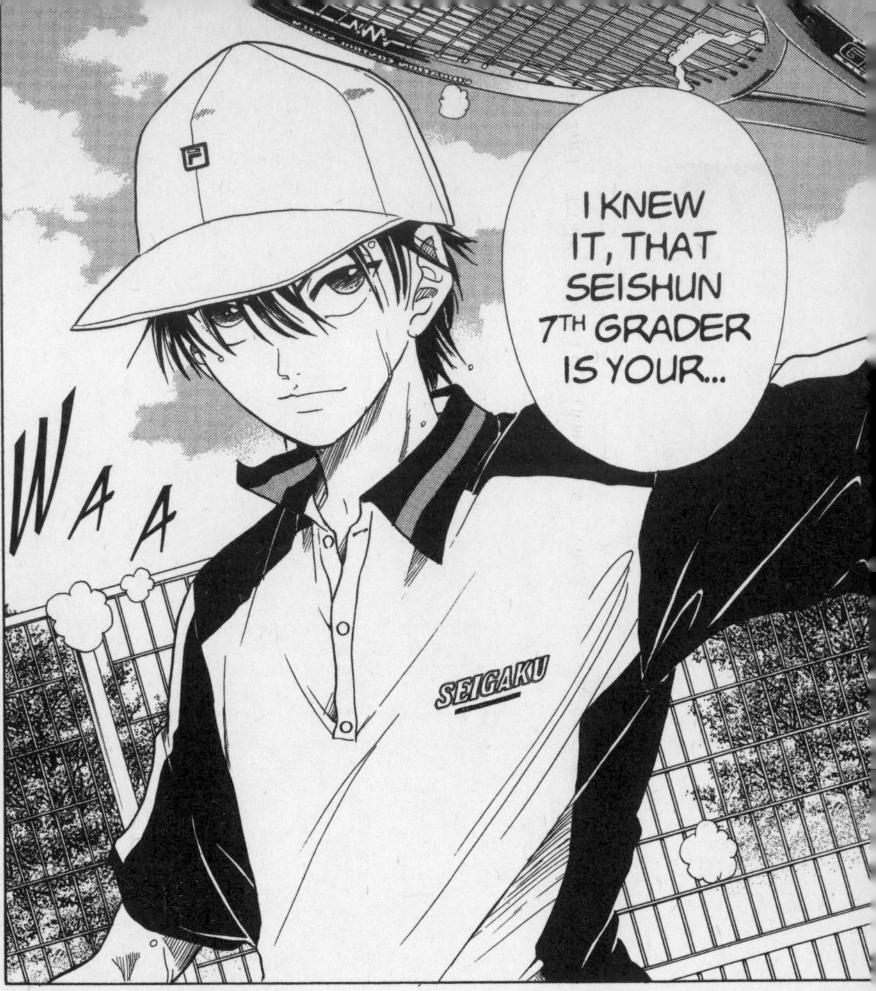
I KNEW IT, THAT SEISHUN 7TH GRADER IS YOUR...
WAA
SEIGAKU

GENIUS 165: JUST A KID

READ THIS WAY

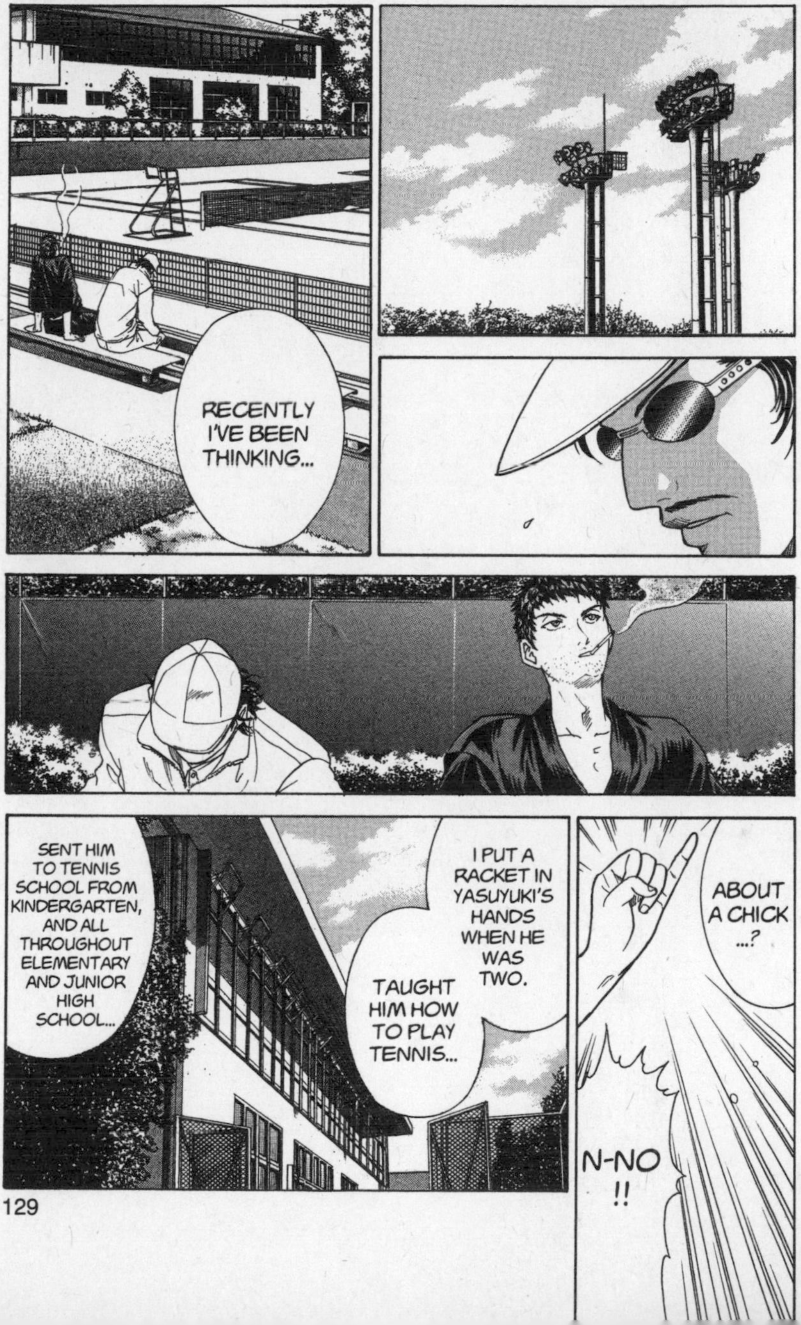

RECENTLY I'VE BEEN THINKING...
ABOUT A CHICK ...?
N-NO !!
I PUT A RACKET IN YASUYUKI'S HANDS WHEN HE WAS TWO.
TAUGHT HIM HOW TO PLAY TENNIS...
SENT HIM TO TENNIS SCHOOL FROM KINDERGARTEN, AND ALL THROUGHOUT ELEMENTARY AND JUNIOR HIGH SCHOOL...

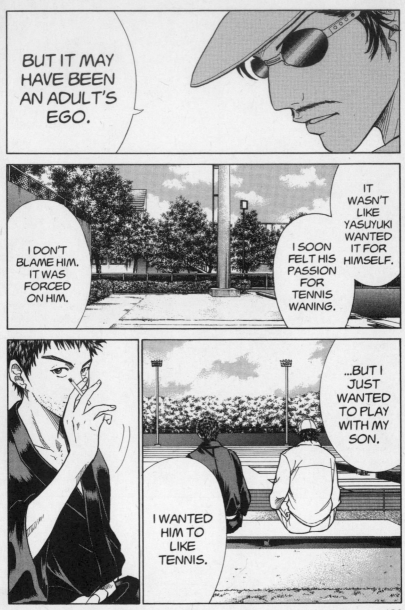

BUT IT MAY HAVE BEEN AN ADULT'S EGO.
IT WASN'T LIKE YASUYUKI WANTED IT FOR HIMSELF.
I SOON FELT HIS PASSION FOR TENNIS WANING.
I DON'T BLAME HIM. IT WAS FORCED ON HIM.
...BUT I JUST WANTED TO PLAY WITH MY SON.
I WANTED HIM TO LIKE TENNIS.

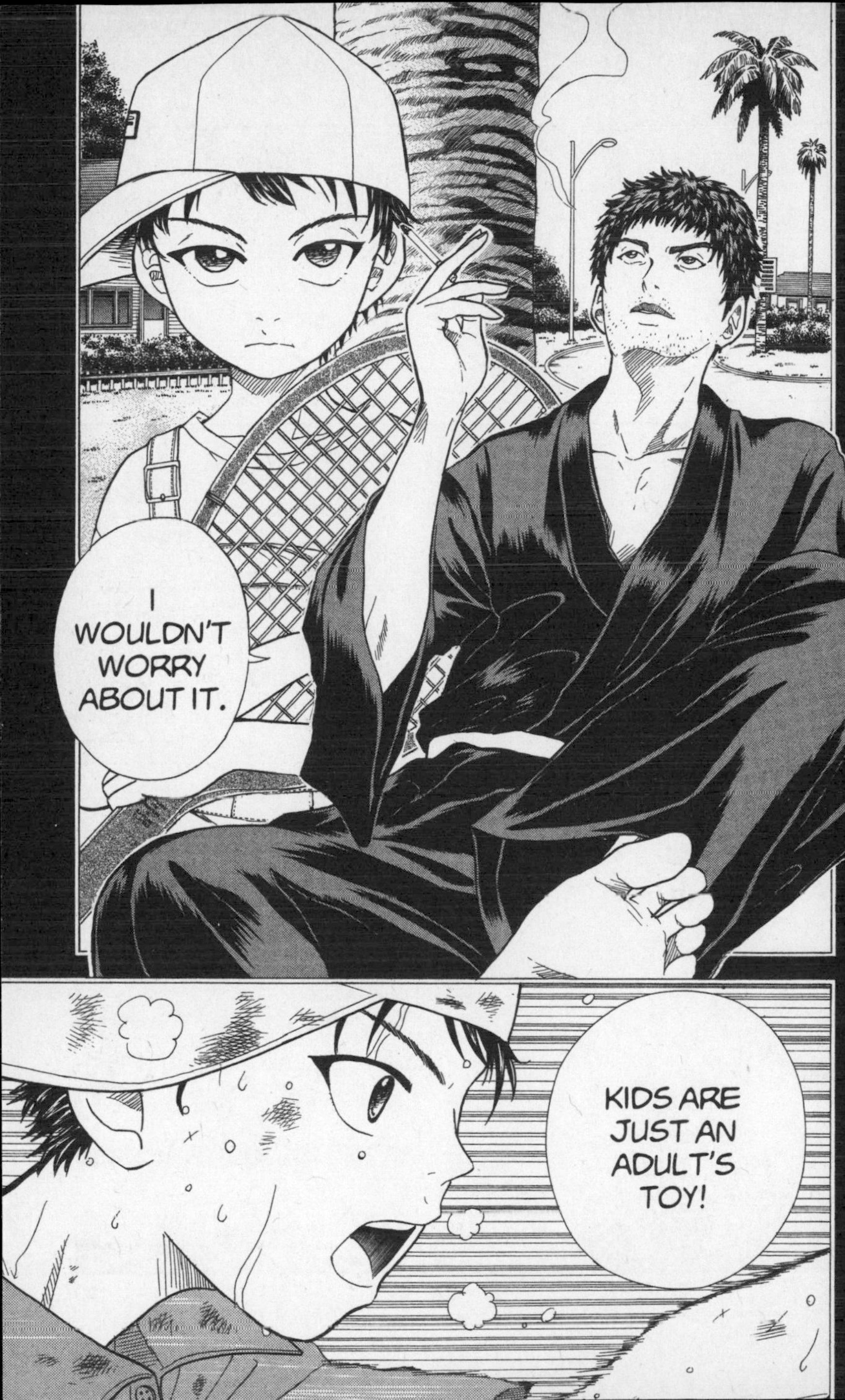
I WOULDN'T WORRY ABOUT IT.
KIDS ARE JUST AN ADULT'S TOY!

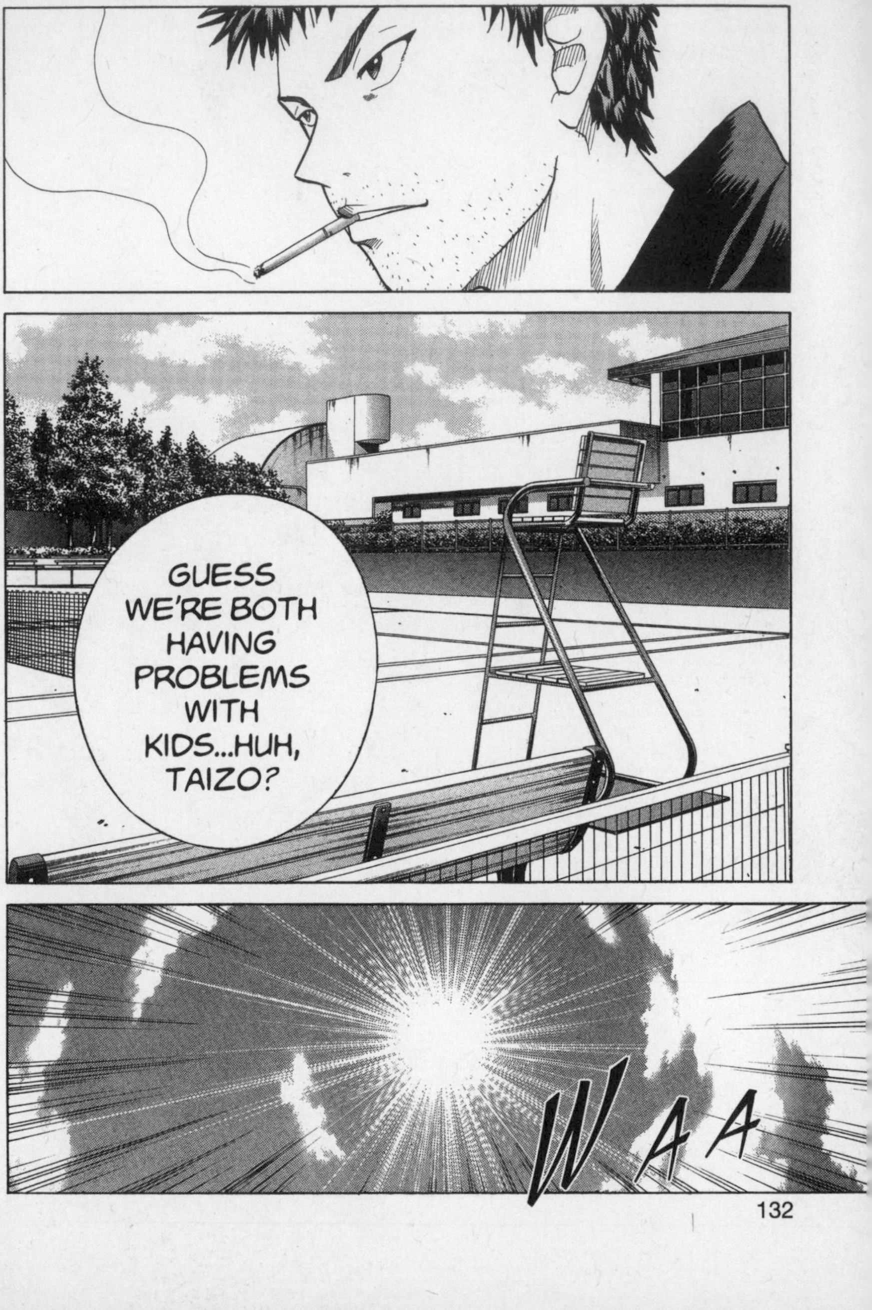
GUESS WE'RE BOTH HAVING PROBLEMS WITH KIDS...HUH, TAIZO?
WAA

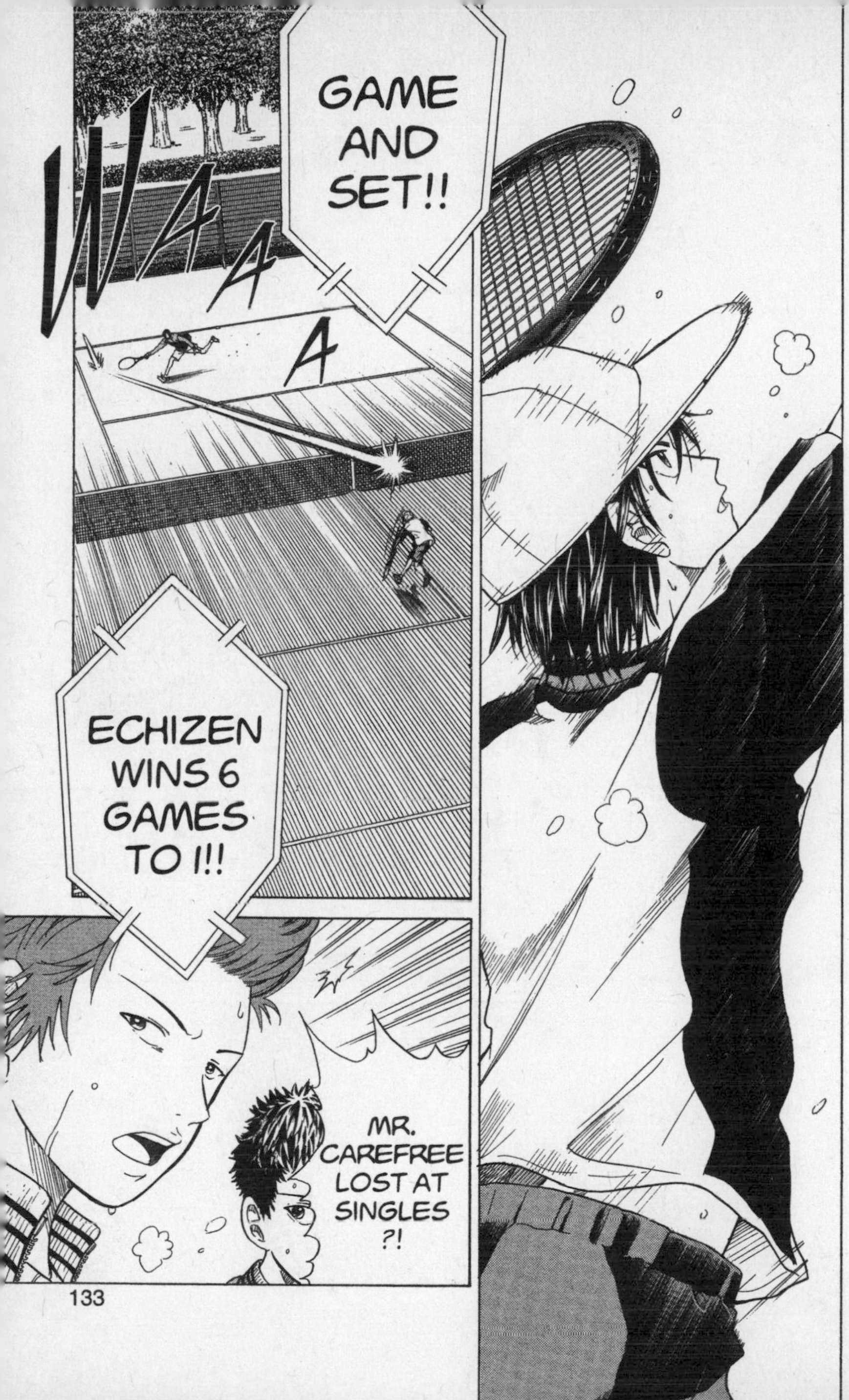
GAME AND SET!!
WAAA
ECHIZEN WINS 6 GAMES TO 1!!
MR. CAREFREE LOST AT SINGLES ?!

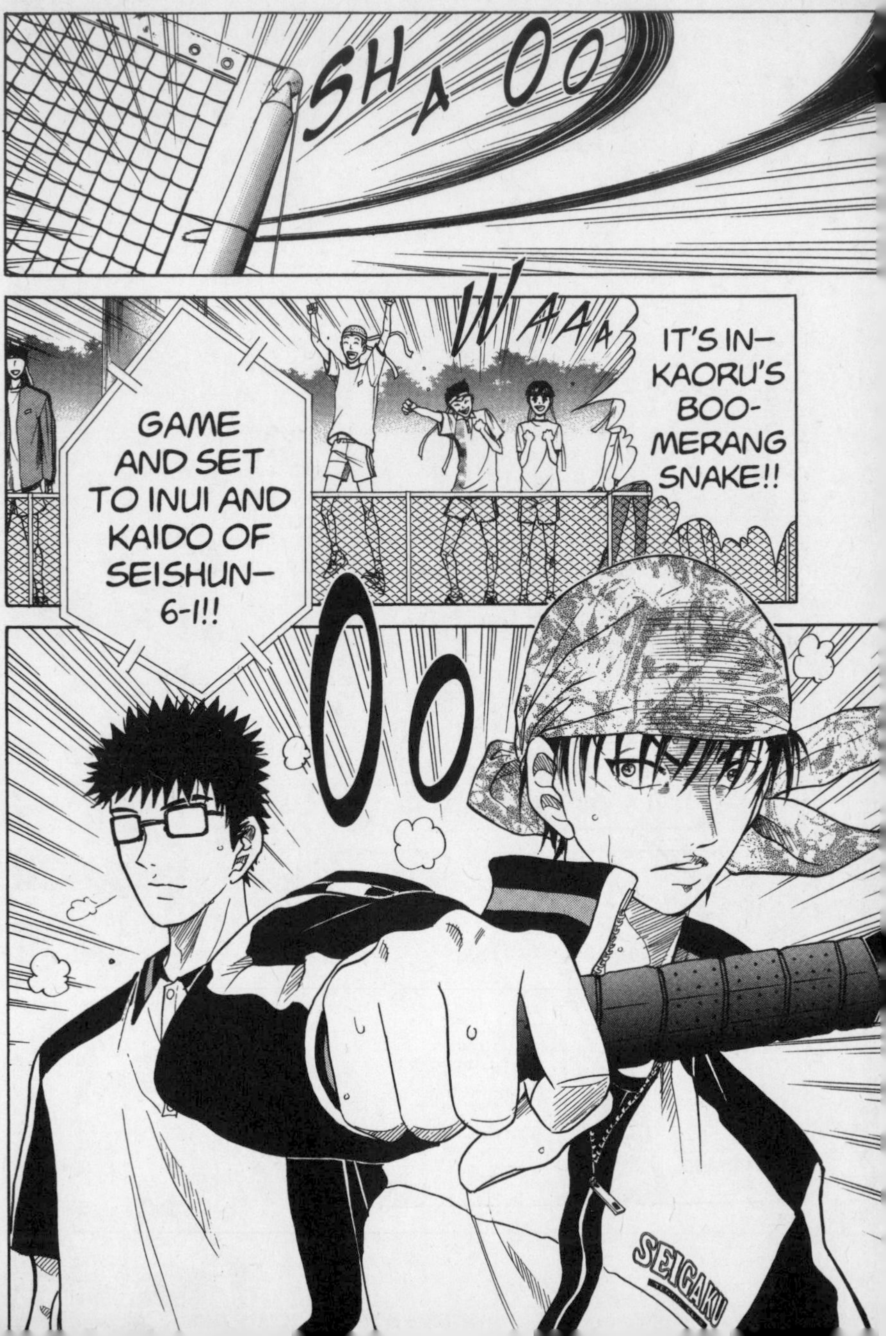
SHAOO
WAAA
IT'S IN-KAORU'S BOO-MERANG SNAKE!!
GAME AND SET TO INUI AND KAIDO OF SEISHUN- 6-1!!
OO
SEIGAKU

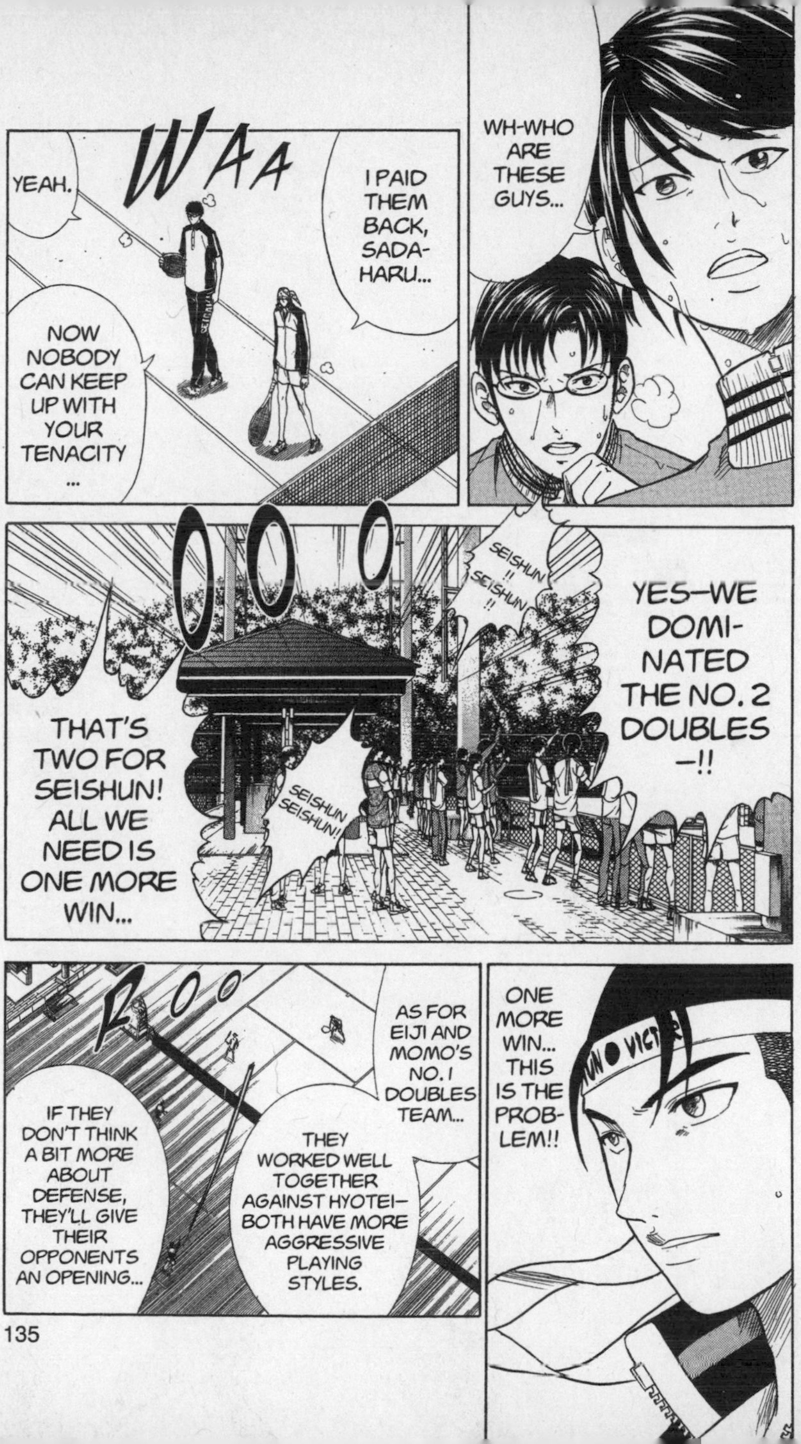
WH-WHO ARE THESE GUYS...
I PAID THEM BACK, SADAHARU...
WAA
YEAH.
NOW NOBODY CAN KEEP UP WITH YOUR TENACITY ...
OOO
SEISHUN!! SEISHUN!!
YES—WE DOMINATED THE NO. 2 DOUBLES—!!
SEISHUN SEISHUN!
THAT'S TWO FOR SEISHUN! ALL WE NEED IS ONE MORE WIN...
ONE MORE WIN... THIS IS THE PROBLEM!!
AS FOR EIJI AND MOMO'S NO. 1 DOUBLES TEAM...
THEY WORKED WELL TOGETHER AGAINST HYOTEI—BOTH HAVE MORE AGGRESSIVE PLAYING STYLES.
ROO
IF THEY DON'T THINK A BIT MORE ABOUT DEFENSE, THEY'LL GIVE THEIR OPPONENTS AN OPENING...

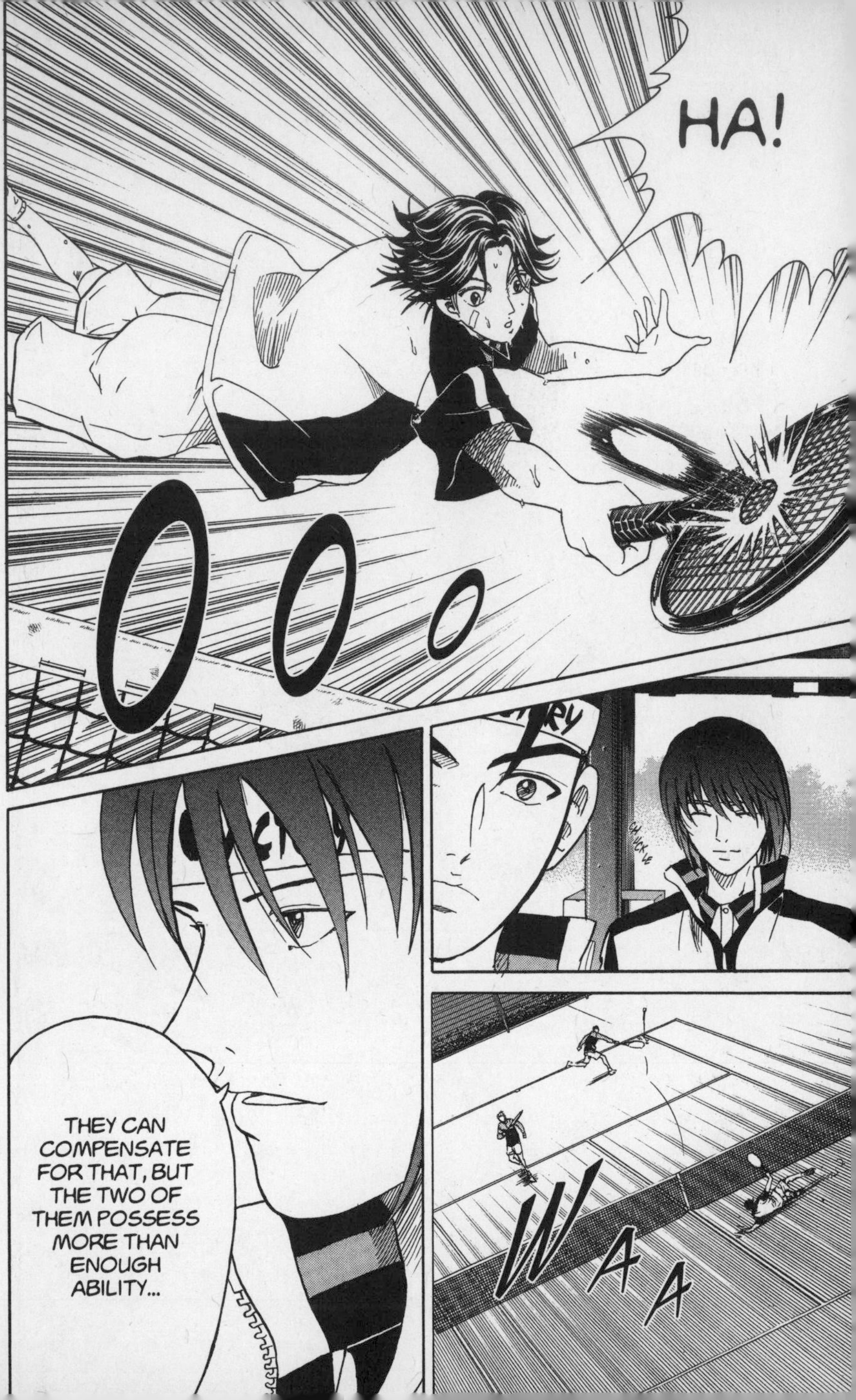
HA!
CHUCKLE
WAA
THEY CAN COMPENSATE FOR THAT, BUT THE TWO OF THEM POSSESS MORE THAN ENOUGH ABILITY...

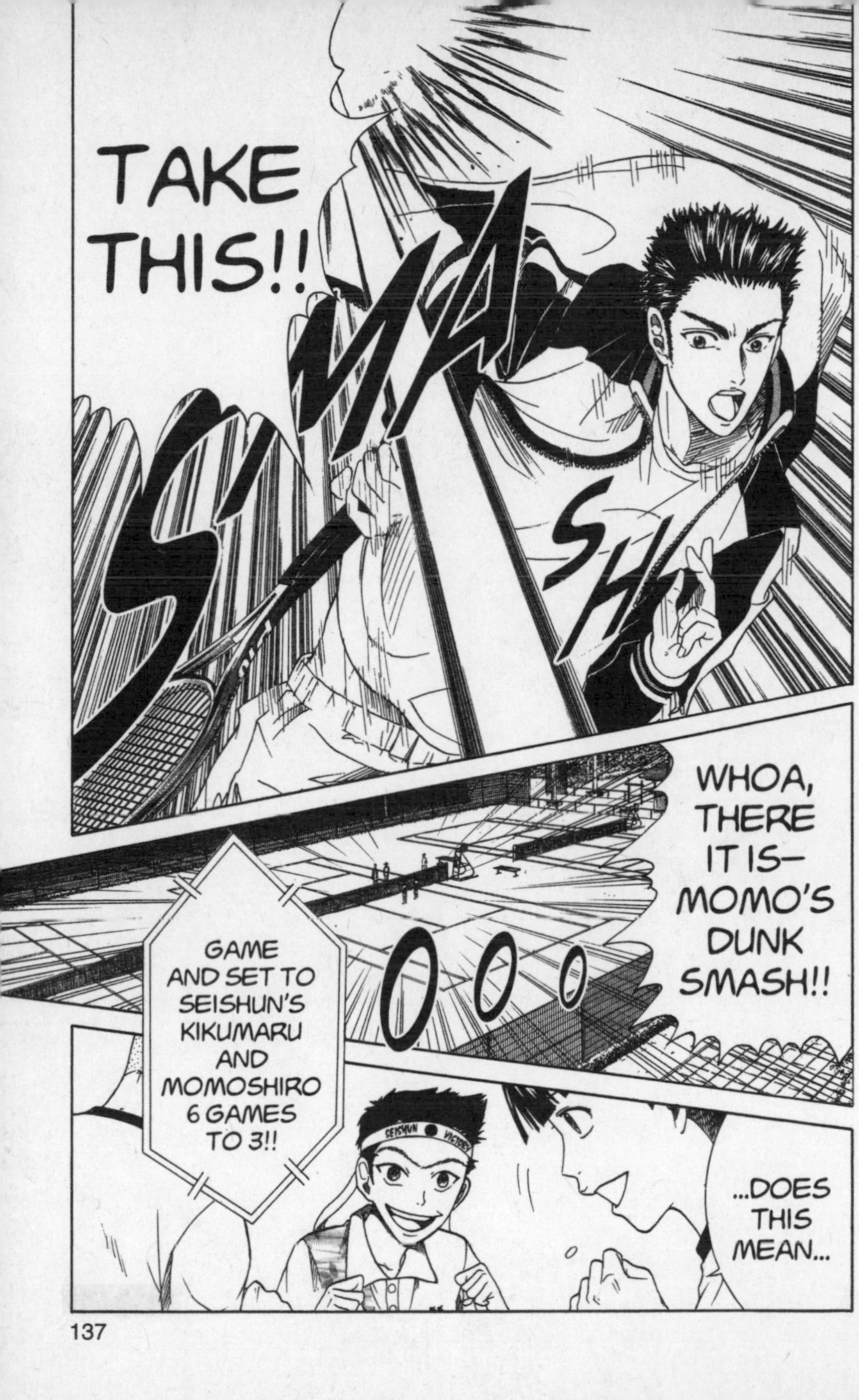
TAKE THIS!!
WHOA, THERE IT IS— MOMO'S DUNK SMASH!!
GAME AND SET TO SEISHUN'S KIKUMARU AND MOMOSHIRO 6 GAMES TO 3!!
...DOES THIS MEAN...

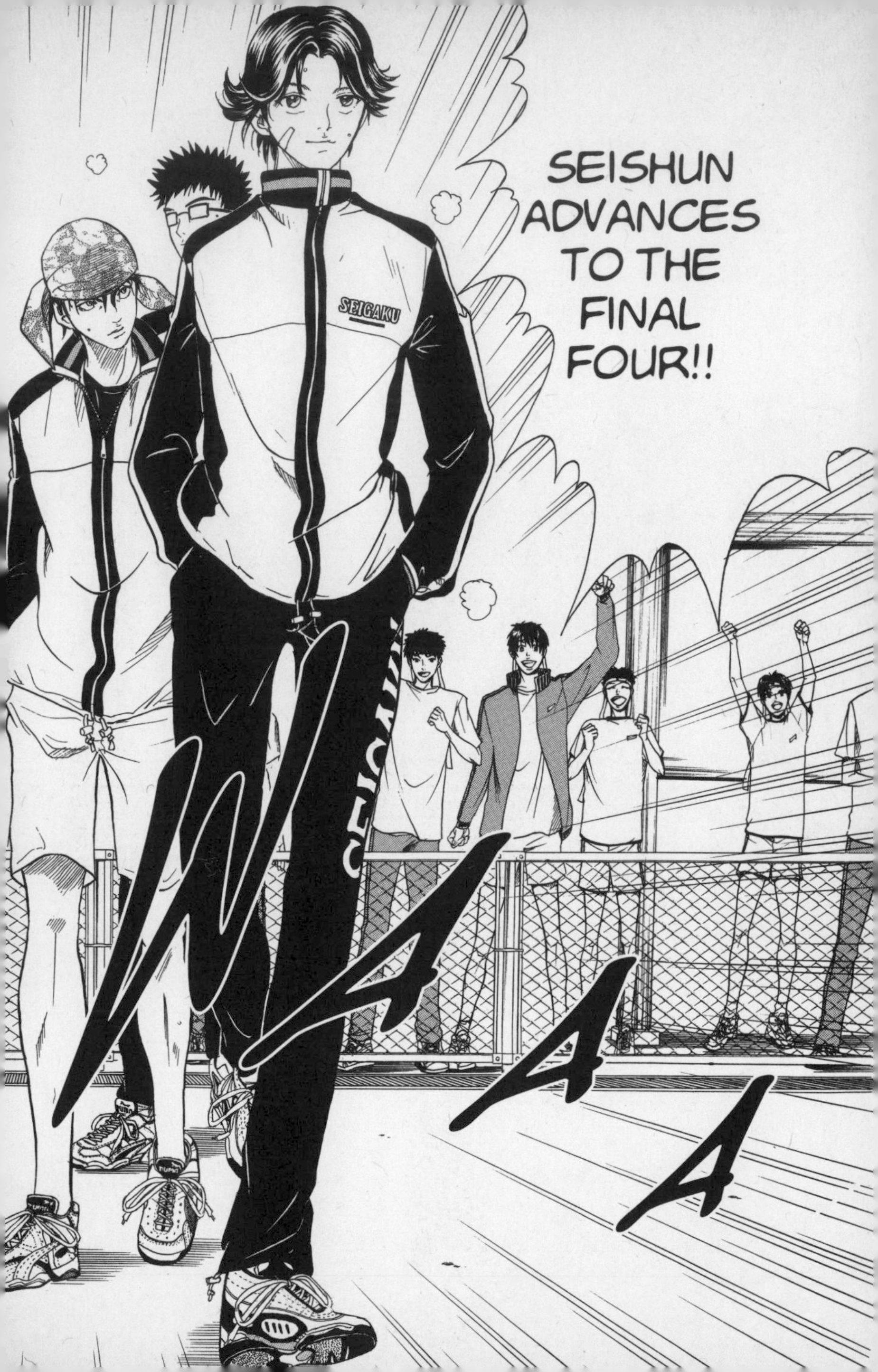
SEISHUN ADVANCES TO THE FINAL FOUR!!
WAAA

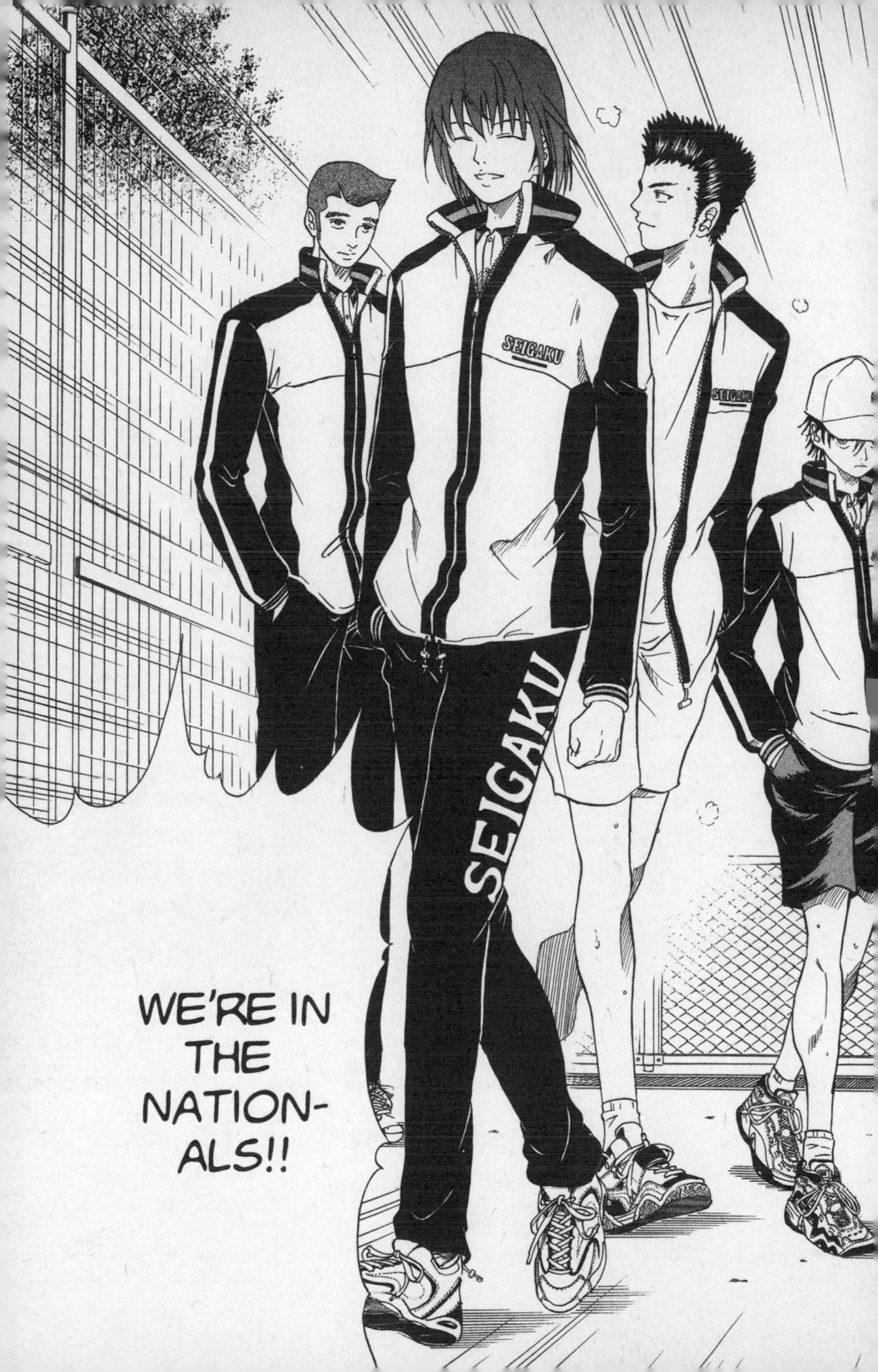
WE'RE IN THE NATION-ALS!!
SEIGAKU
SEIGAKU
SEIGAKU

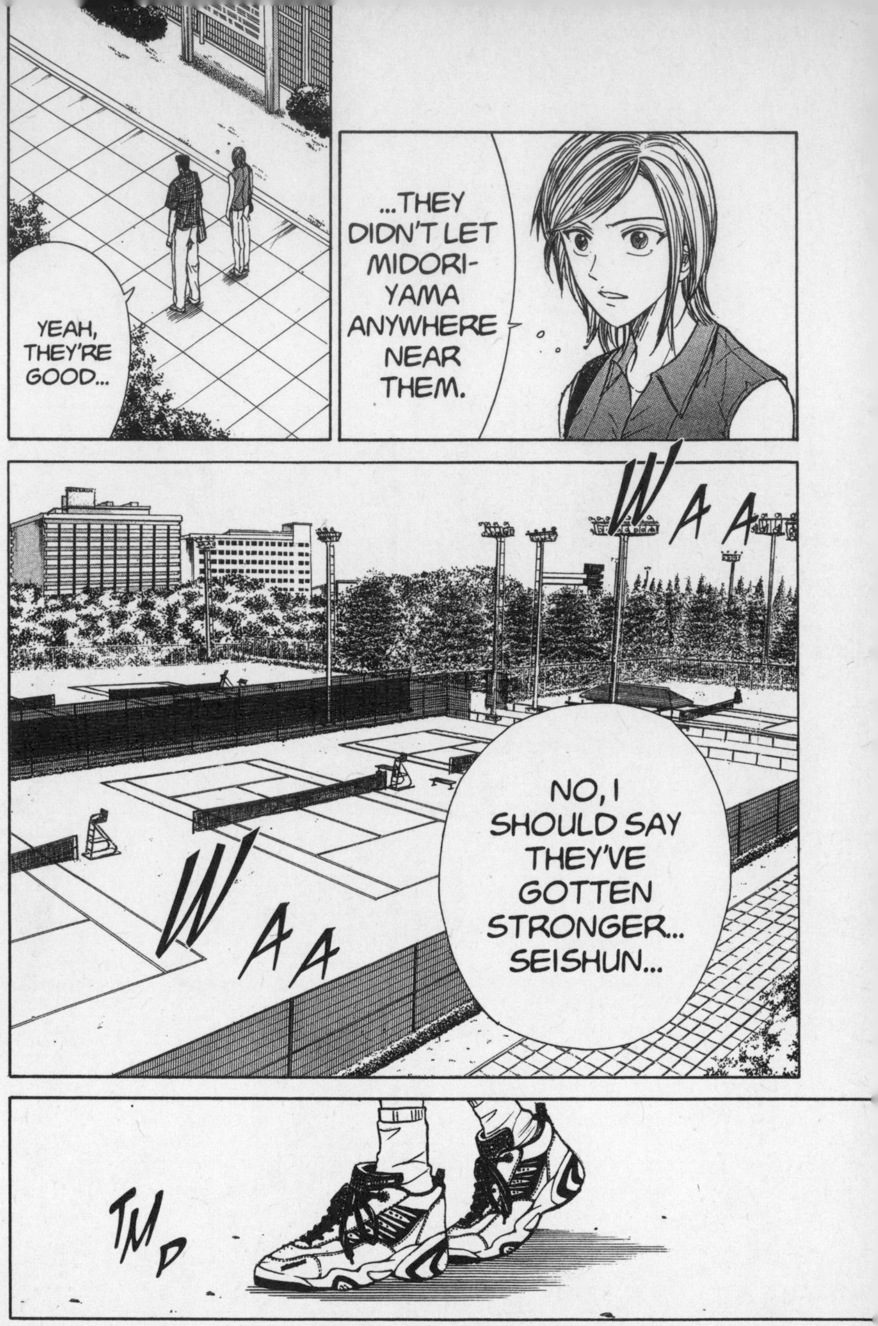
...THEY DIDN'T LET MIDORI-YAMA ANYWHERE NEAR THEM.
YEAH, THEY'RE GOOD...
WAA
NO, I SHOULD SAY THEY'VE GOTTEN STRONGER... SEISHUN...
WAA
TMP

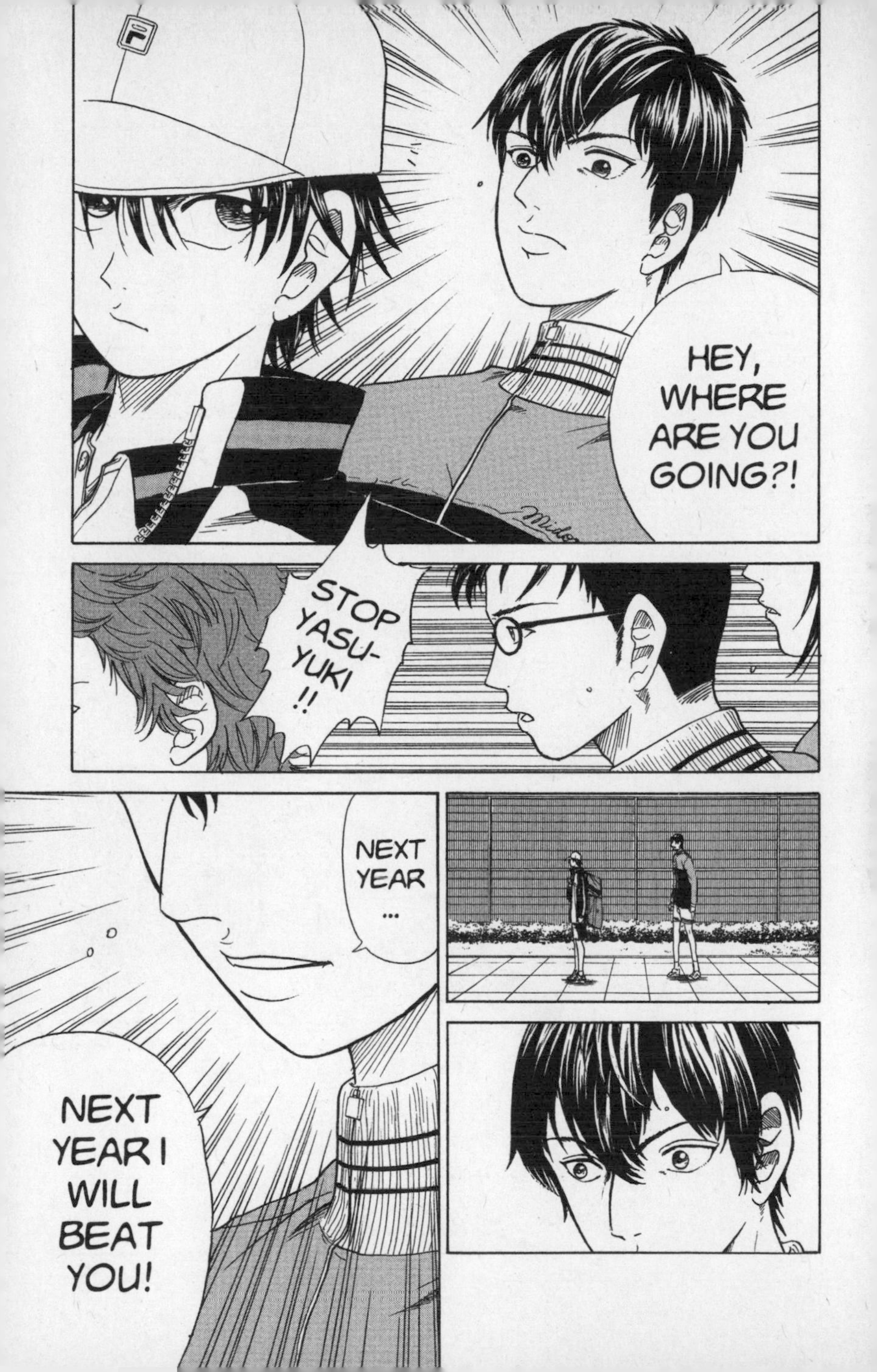
HEY, WHERE ARE YOU GOING?!
STOP YASU-YUKI !!
NEXT YEAR ...
NEXT YEAR I WILL BEAT YOU!

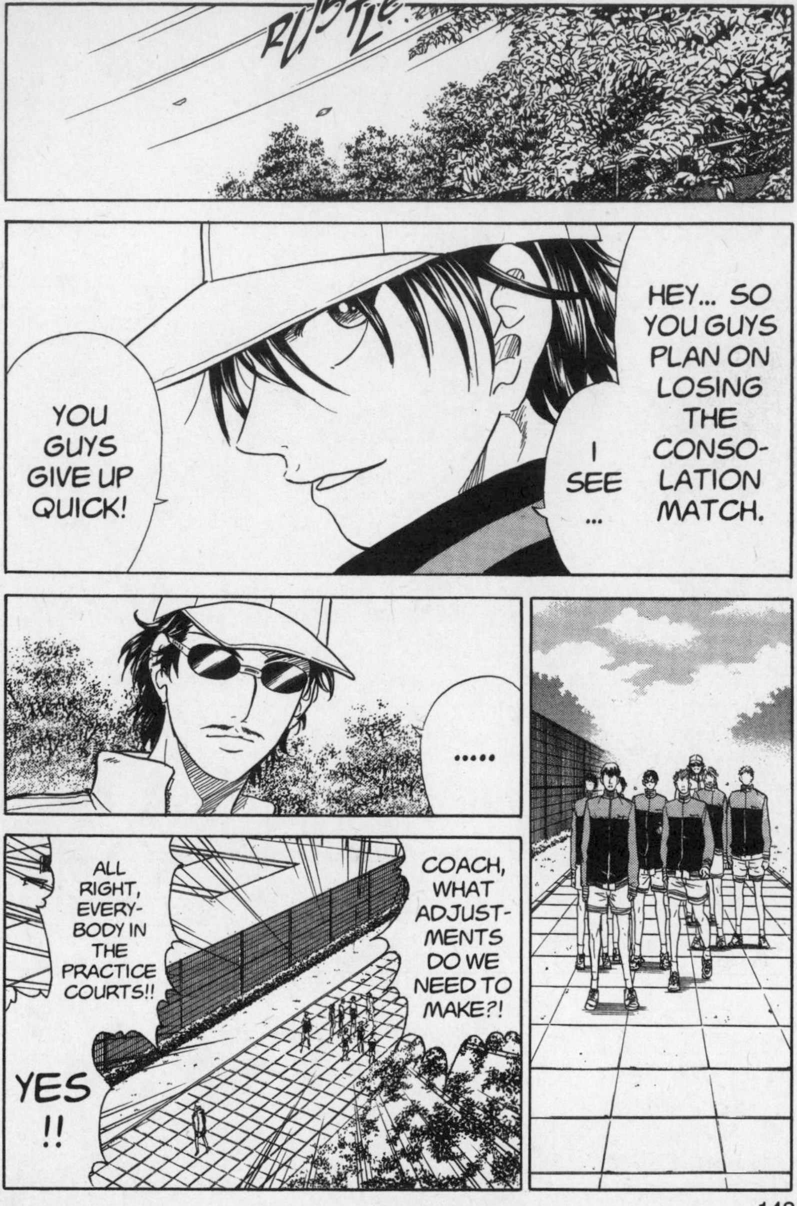
RUSTLE...
HEY... SO YOU GUYS PLAN ON LOSING THE CONSOLATION MATCH.
I SEE...
YOU GUYS GIVE UP QUICK!
.....
COACH, WHAT ADJUSTMENTS DO WE NEED TO MAKE?!
ALL RIGHT, EVERYBODY IN THE PRACTICE COURTS!!
YES!!

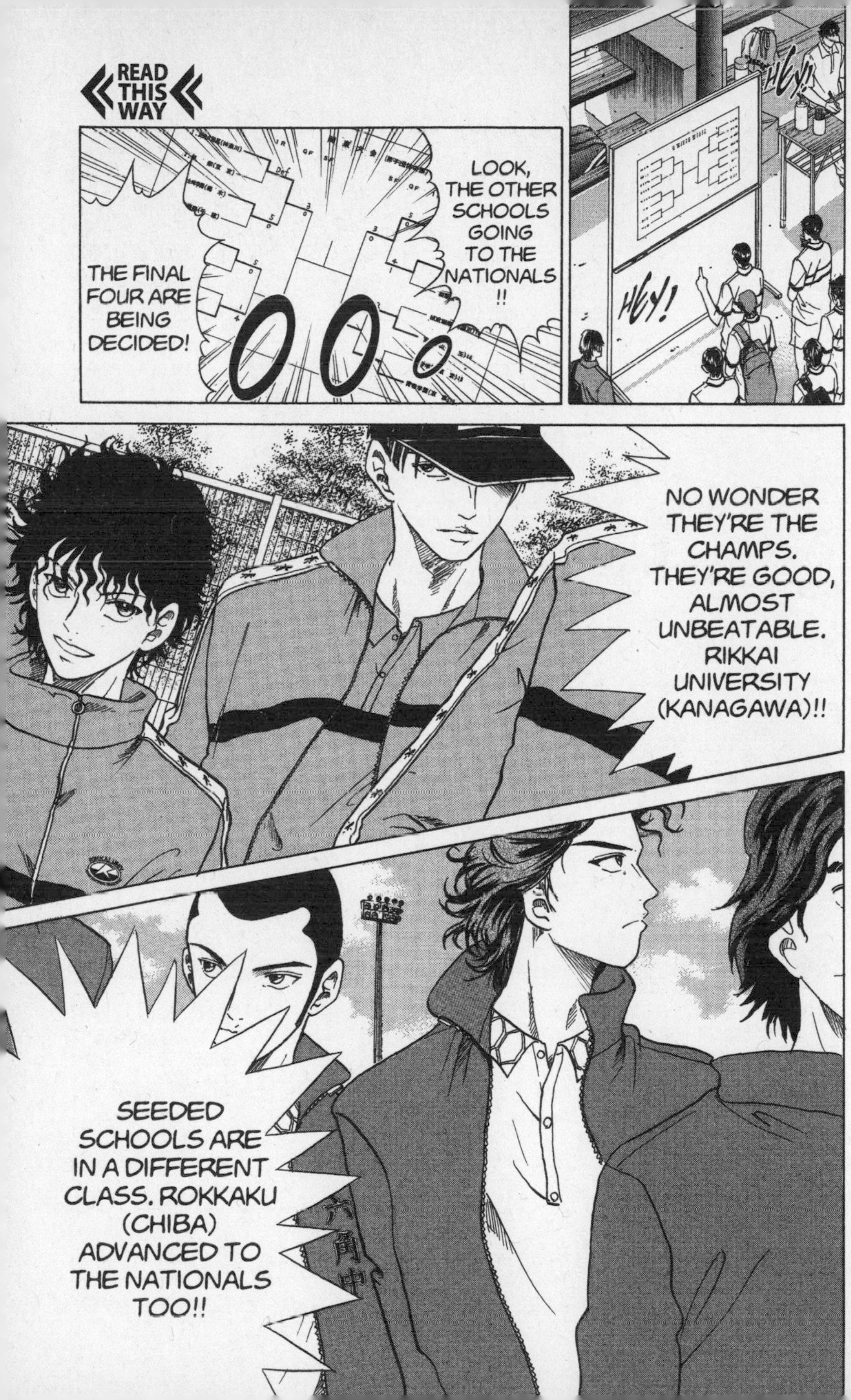
READ THIS WAY
HEY!
HEY!
LOOK, THE OTHER SCHOOLS GOING TO THE NATIONALS !!
THE FINAL FOUR ARE BEING DECIDED!
NO WONDER THEY'RE THE CHAMPS. THEY'RE GOOD, ALMOST UNBEATABLE. RIKKAI UNIVERSITY (KANAGAWA)!!
SEEDED SCHOOLS ARE IN A DIFFERENT CLASS. ROKKAKU (CHIBA) ADVANCED TO THE NATIONALS TOO!!

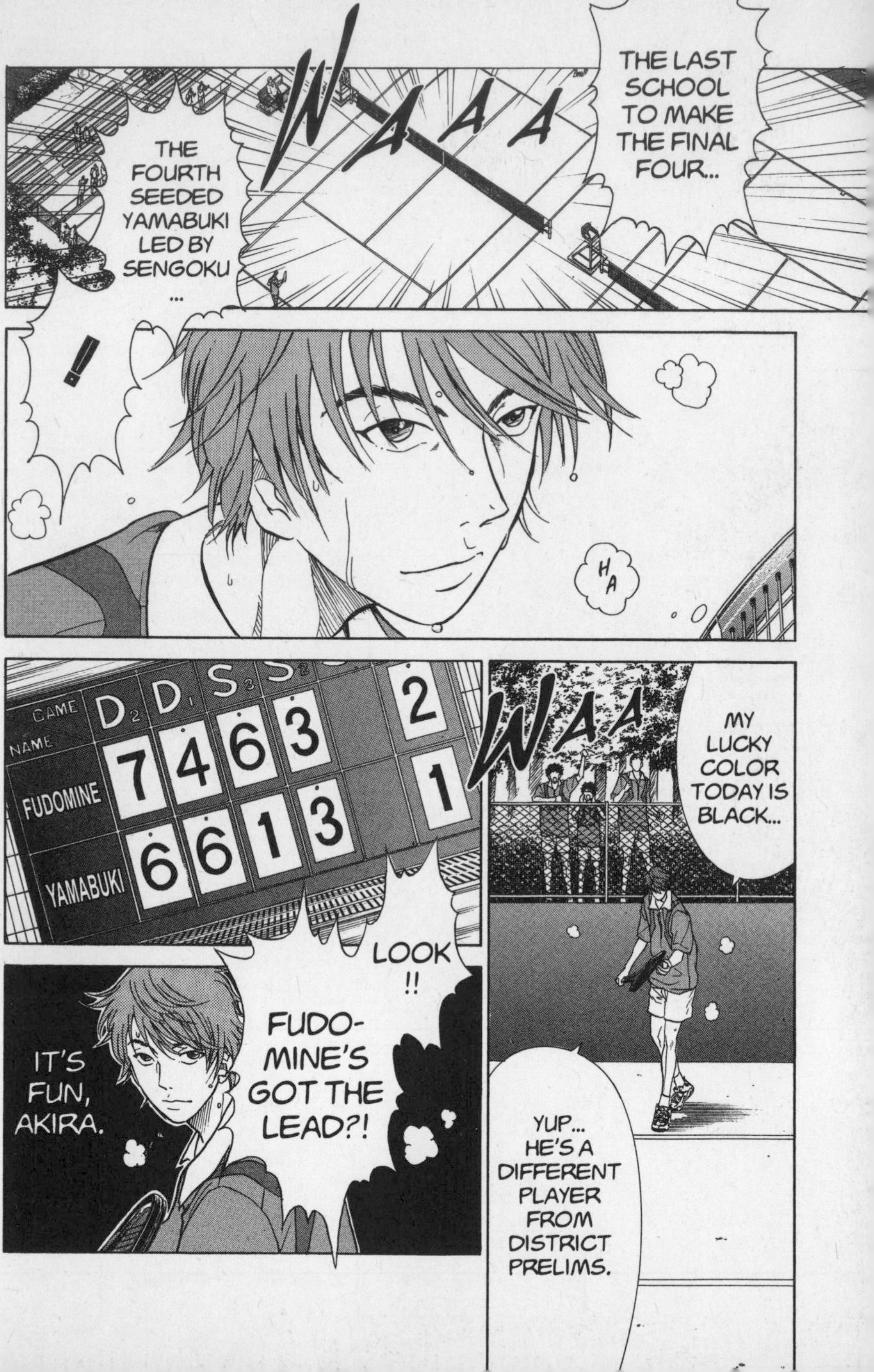
THE LAST SCHOOL TO MAKE THE FINAL FOUR...
WAAA
THE FOURTH SEEDED YAMABUKI LED BY SENGOKU ...
!
HA
MY LUCKY COLOR TODAY IS BLACK...
WAA
YUP... HE'S A DIFFERENT PLAYER FROM DISTRICT PRELIMS.
GAME D2 D1 S3 S2
NAME
FUDOMINE 7 4 6 3 2
YAMABUKI 6 6 1 3 1
LOOK!!
FUDO-MINE'S GOT THE LEAD?!
IT'S FUN, AKIRA.

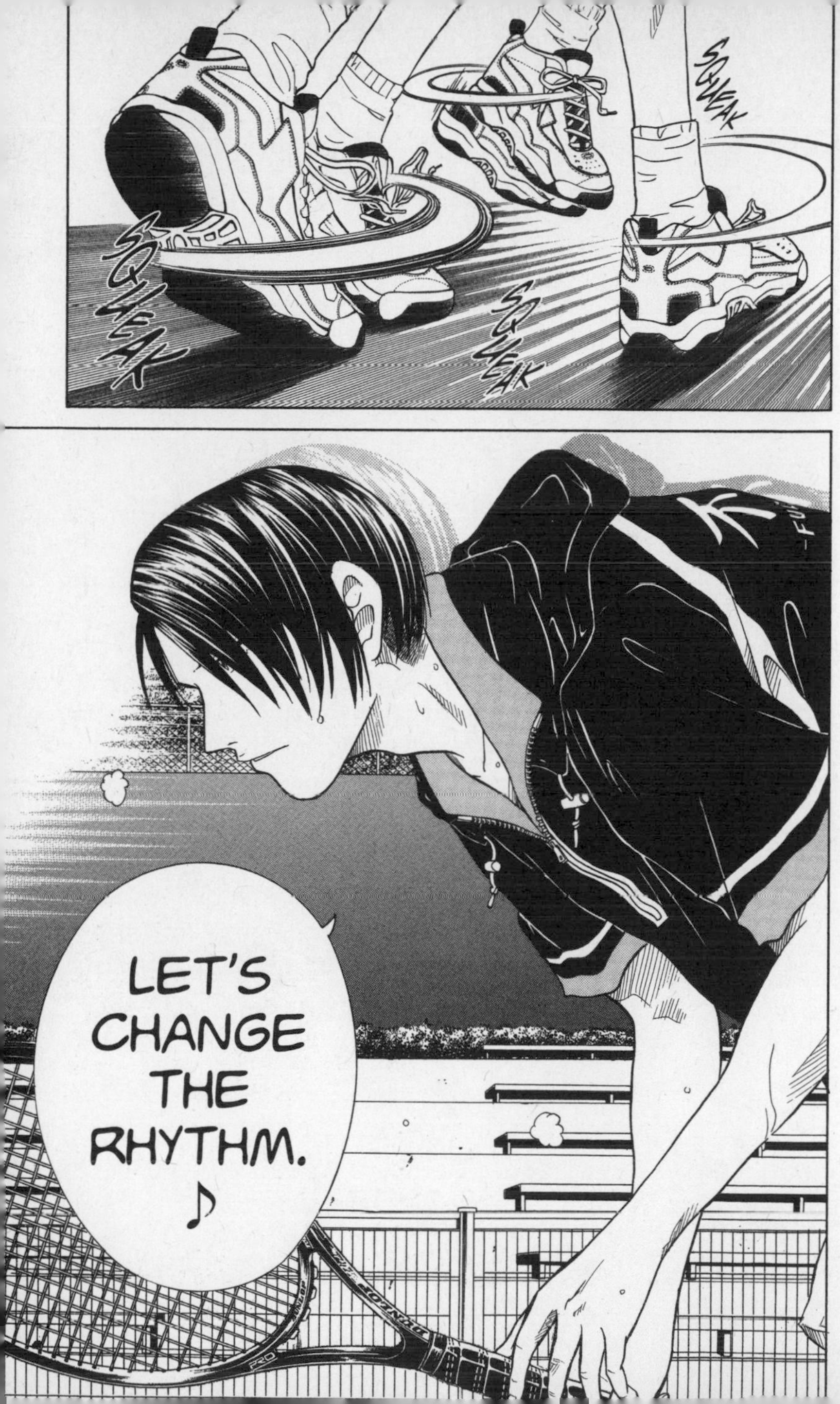
SQUEAK
SQUEAK
SQUEAK
LET'S CHANGE THE RHYTHM. ♪

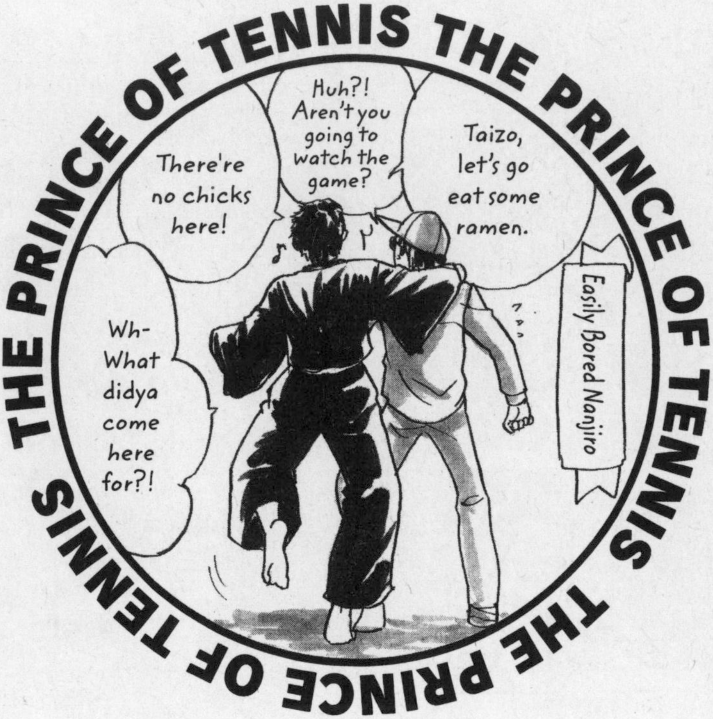
THE PRINCE OF TENNIS THE PRINCE OF TENNIS THE PRINCE OF TENNIS THE PRINCE OF TENNIS
Easily Bored Nanjiro
Taizo, let's go eat some ramen.
Huh?! Aren't you going to watch the game?
There're no chicks here!
Wh- What didya come here for?!

GENIUS 166: FEEL THE RHYTHM♪

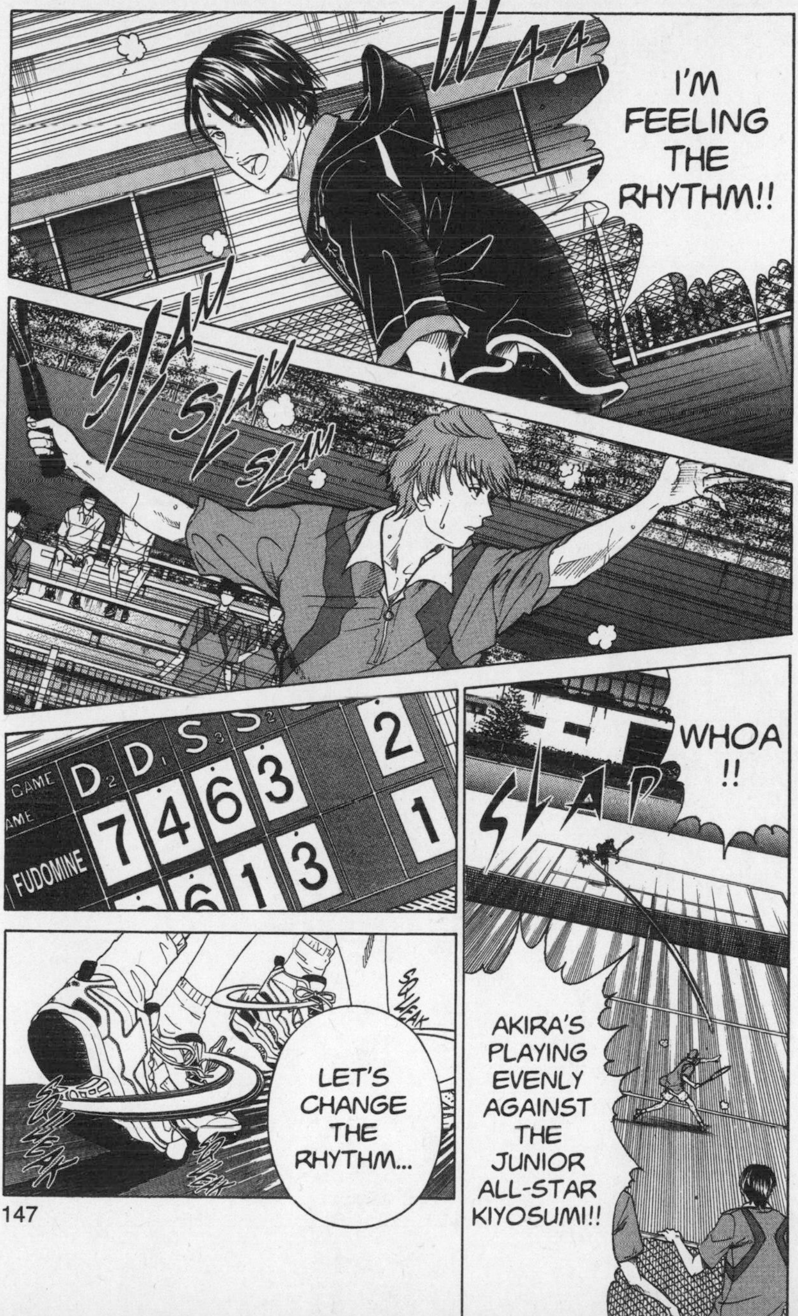
WAA
I'M FEELING THE RHYTHM!!
SLAM
SLAM
SLAM
SLAP
WHOA !!
AKIRA'S PLAYING EVENLY AGAINST THE JUNIOR ALL-STAR KIYOSUMI!!
GAME
FUDOMINE
SQUEAK
LET'S CHANGE THE RHYTHM...
SQUEAK
SQUEAK

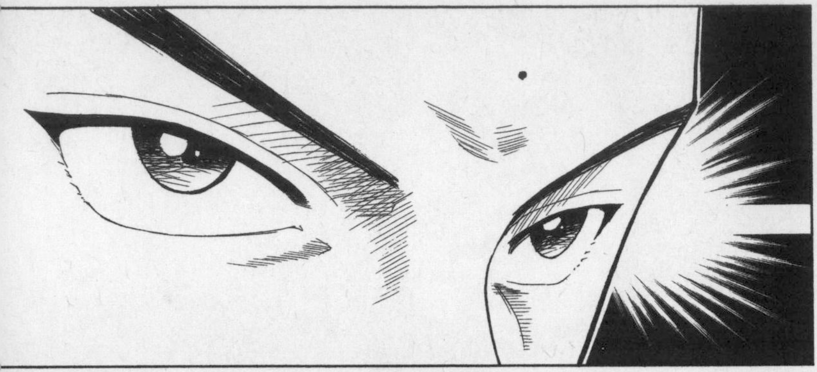

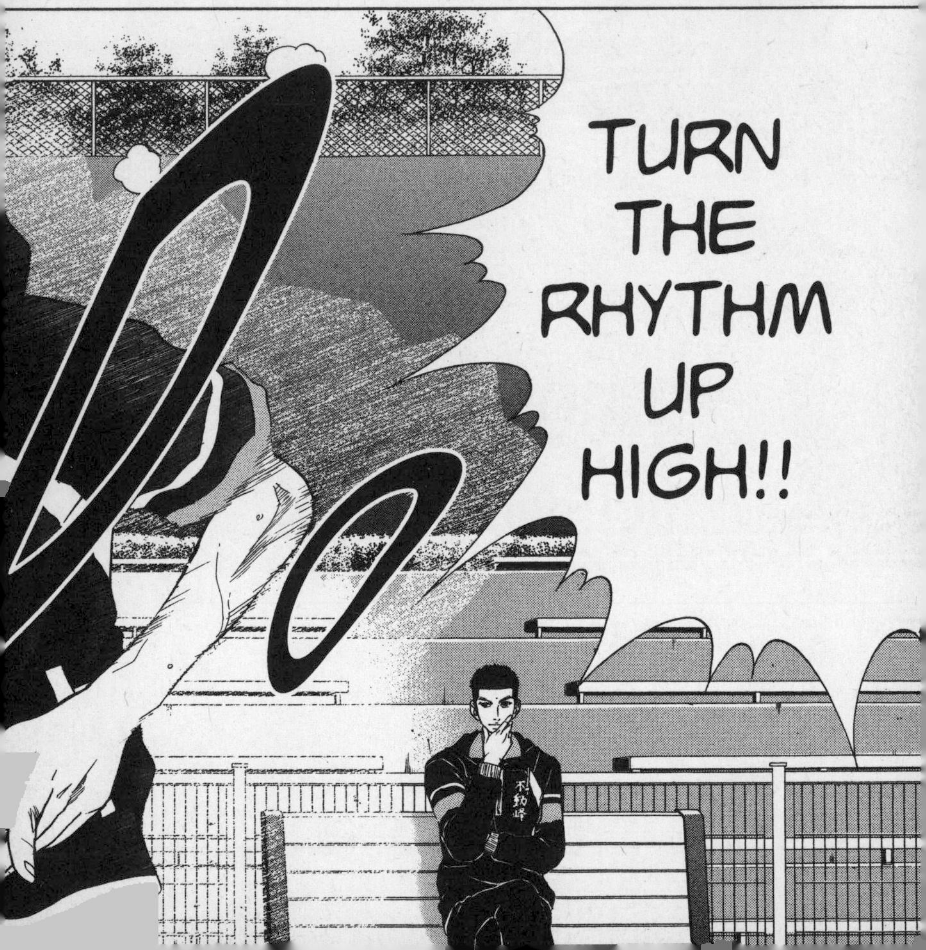
TURN THE RHYTHM UP HIGH!!

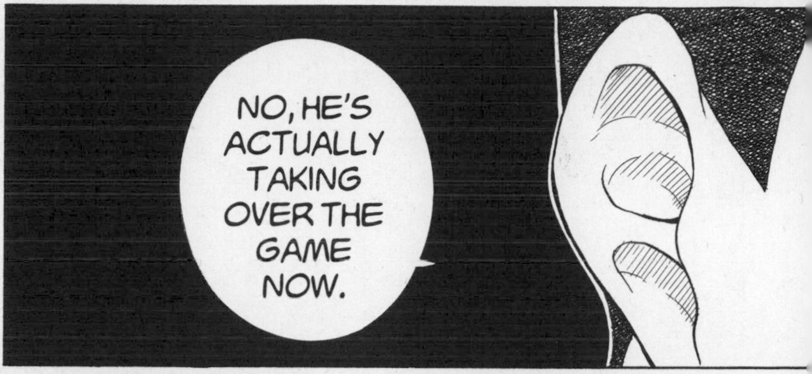
NO, HE'S ACTUALLY TAKING OVER THE GAME NOW.

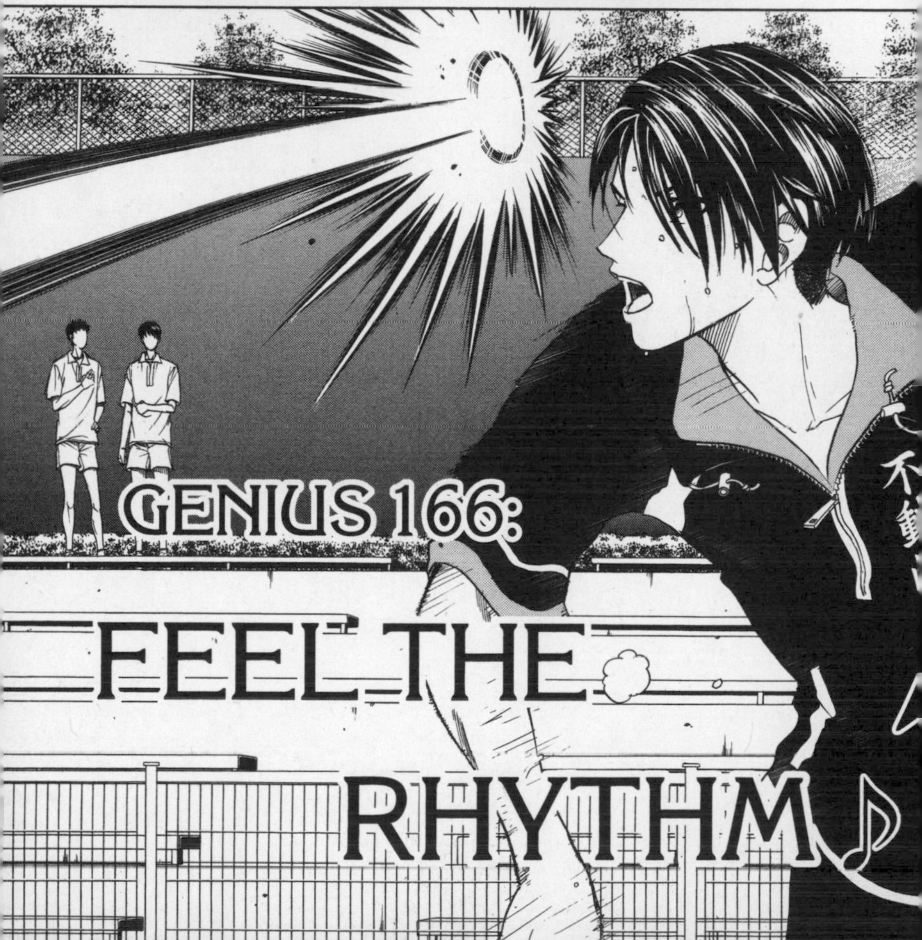
GENIUS 166:
FEEL THE RHYTHM♪

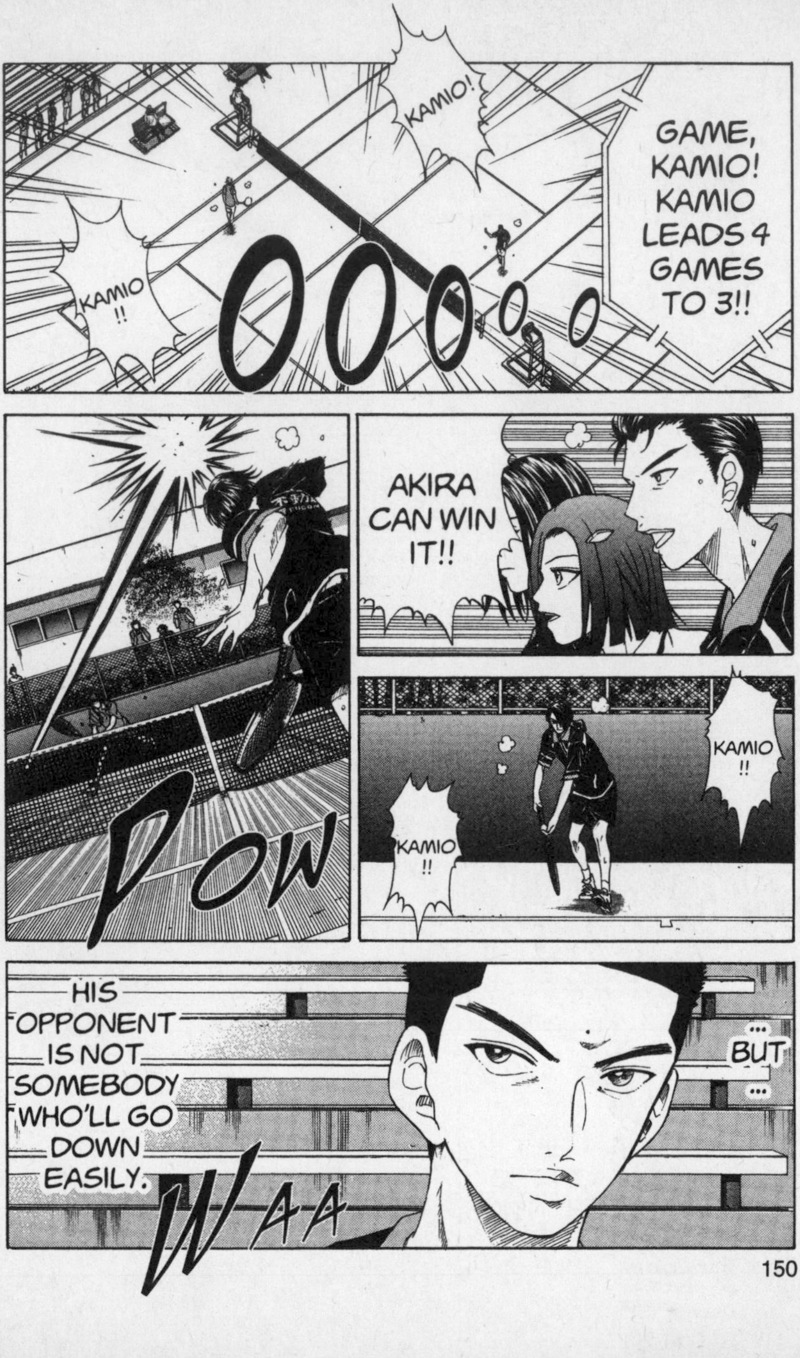
GAME, KAMIO! KAMIO LEADS 4 GAMES TO 3!!
KAMIO!
OOOOO
KAMIO !!
AKIRA CAN WIN IT!!
KAMIO !!
KAMIO !!
POW
...BUT...
HIS OPPONENT IS NOT SOMEBODY WHO'LL GO DOWN EASILY.
WAA

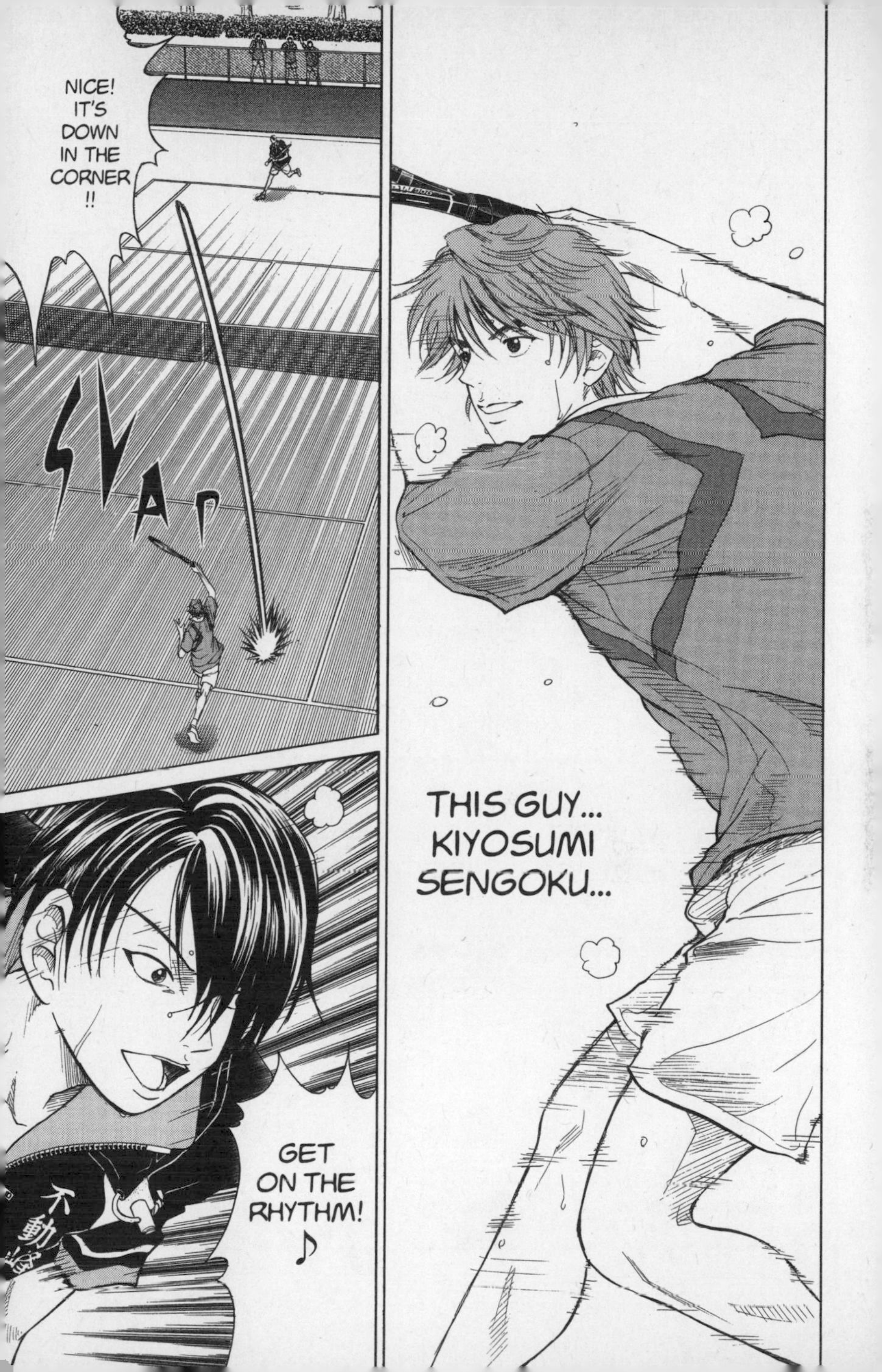
THIS GUY... KIYOSUMI SENGOKU...
NICE! IT'S DOWN IN THE CORNER !!
SNAP
GET ON THE RHYTHM! ♪

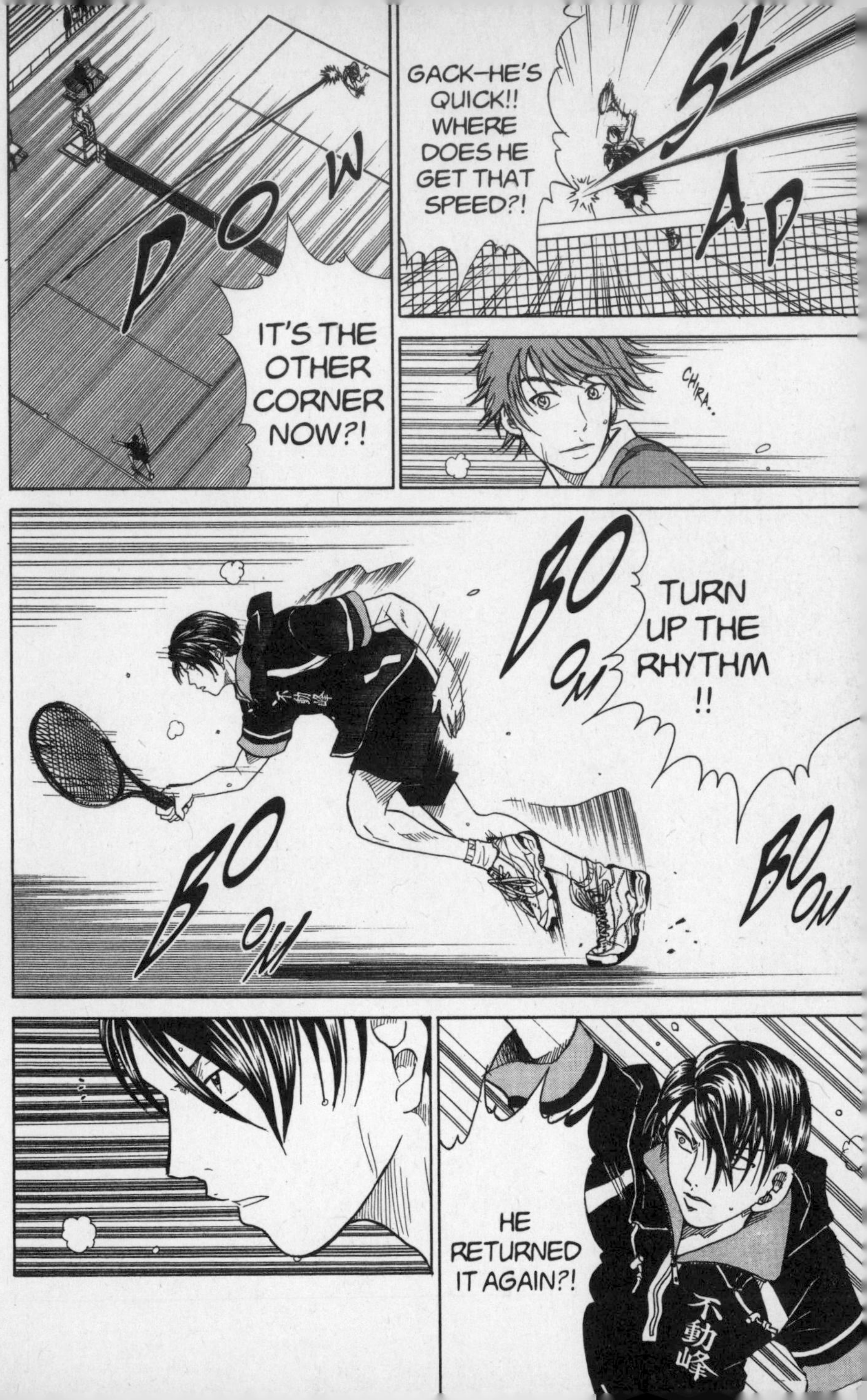
SLAP
GACK—HE'S QUICK!! WHERE DOES HE GET THAT SPEED?!
CHIRA..
DOW
IT'S THE OTHER CORNER NOW?!
BOOM
TURN UP THE RHYTHM !!
BOOM
BOOM
HE RETURNED IT AGAIN?!
不動峰

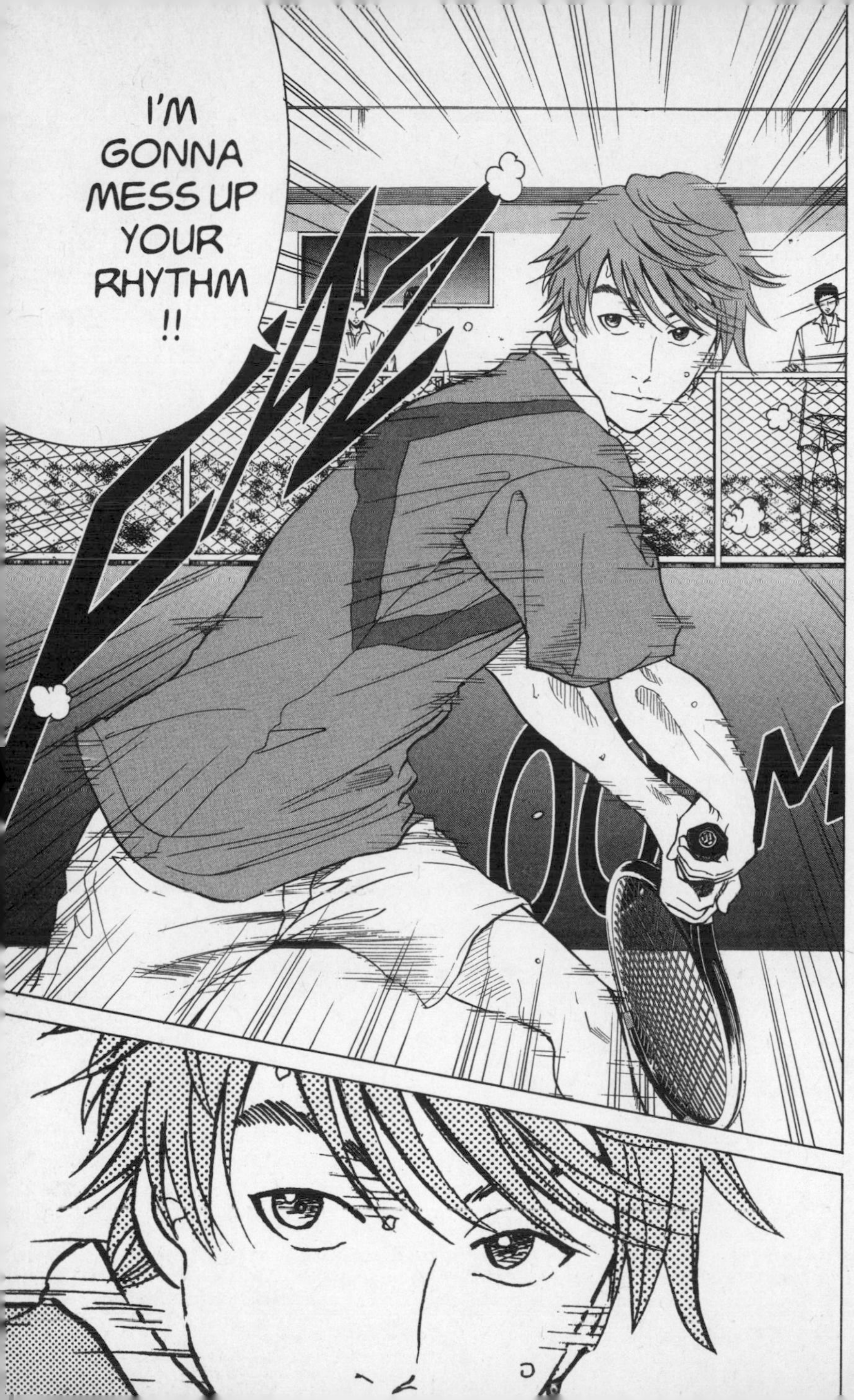
I'M GONNA MESS UP YOUR RHYTHM !!

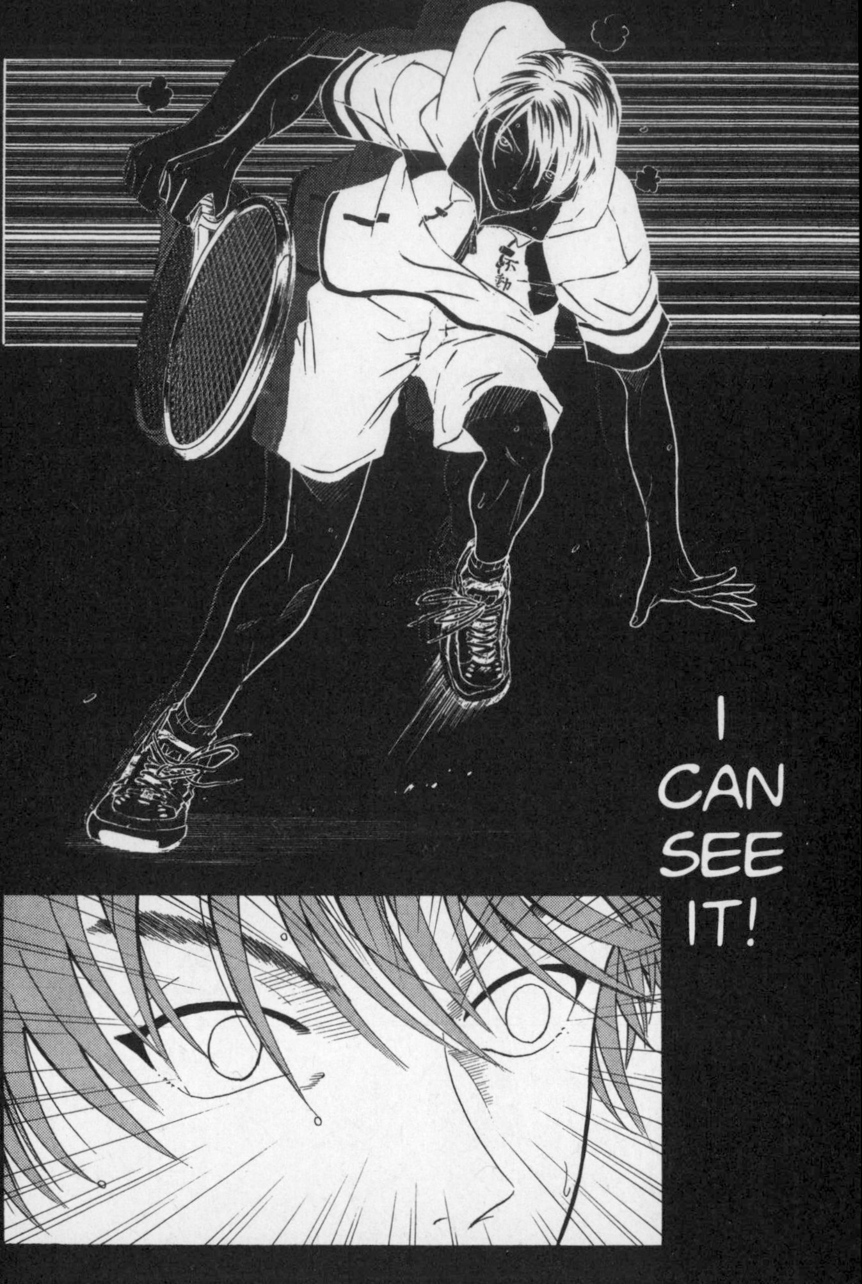
I CAN SEE IT!

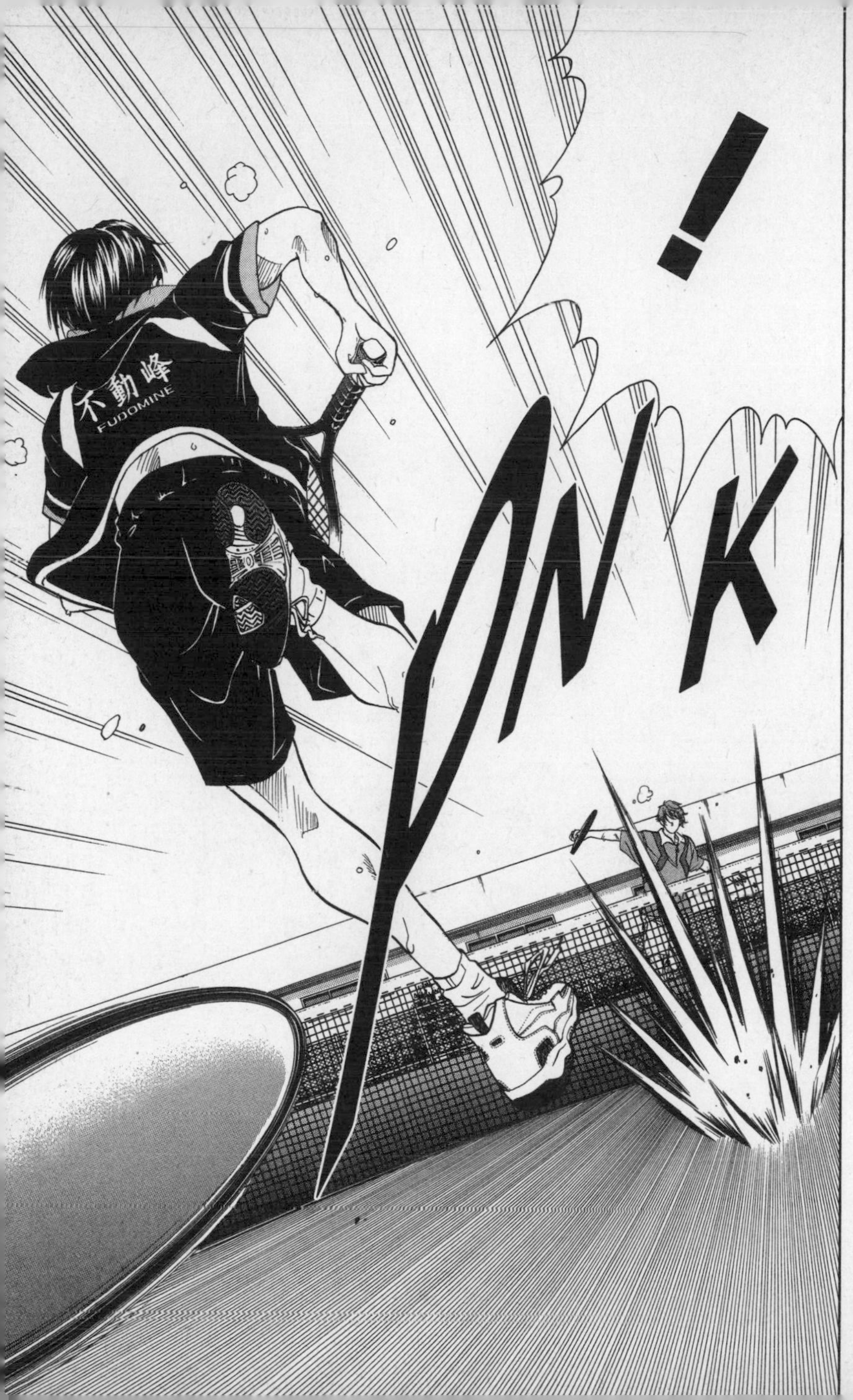
!
不動峰
FUDOMINE

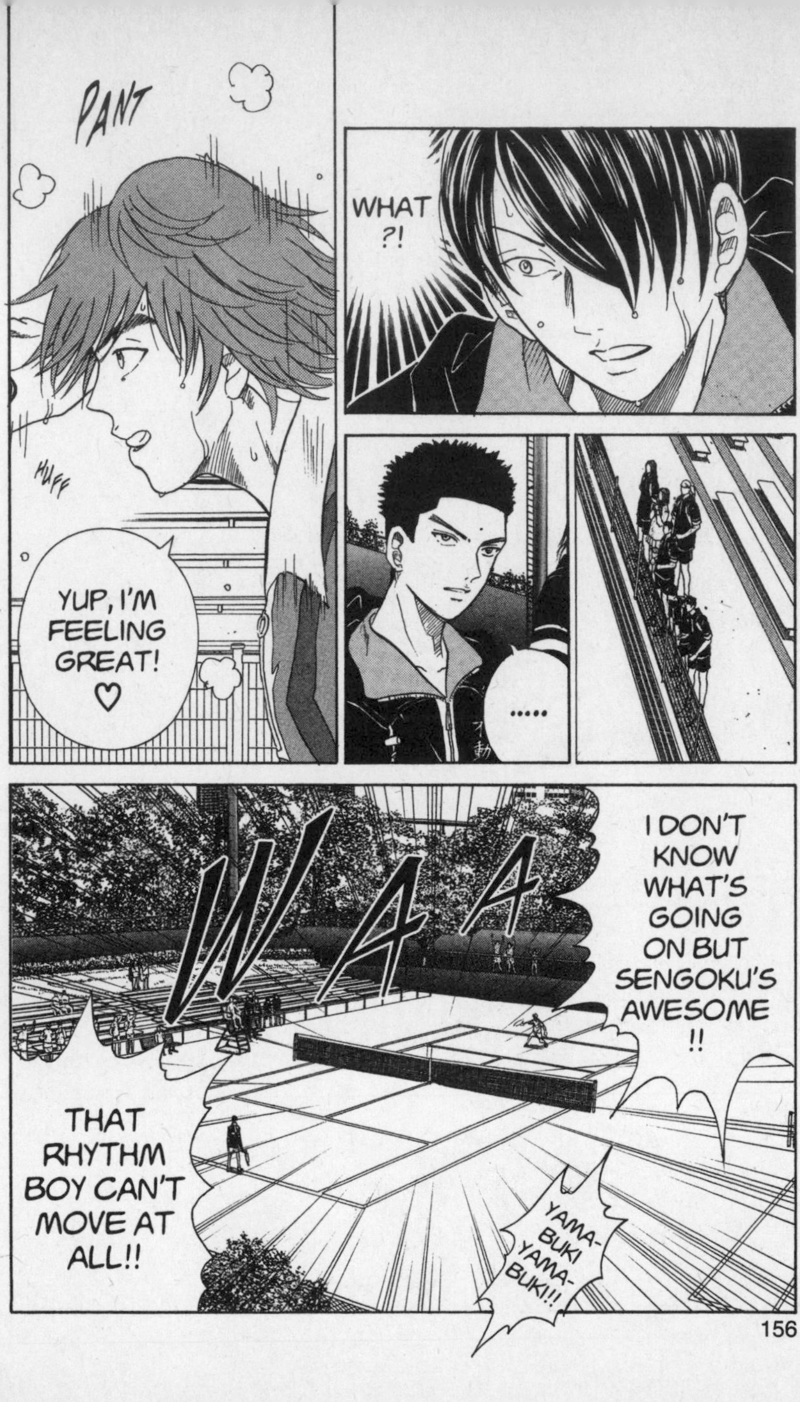
WHAT ?!
.....
PANT
HUFF
YUP, I'M FEELING GREAT! ♡
I DON'T KNOW WHAT'S GOING ON BUT SENGOKU'S AWESOME !!
WAA
YAMA-BUKI YAMA-BUKI!!!
THAT RHYTHM BOY CAN'T MOVE AT ALL!!

READ THIS WAY

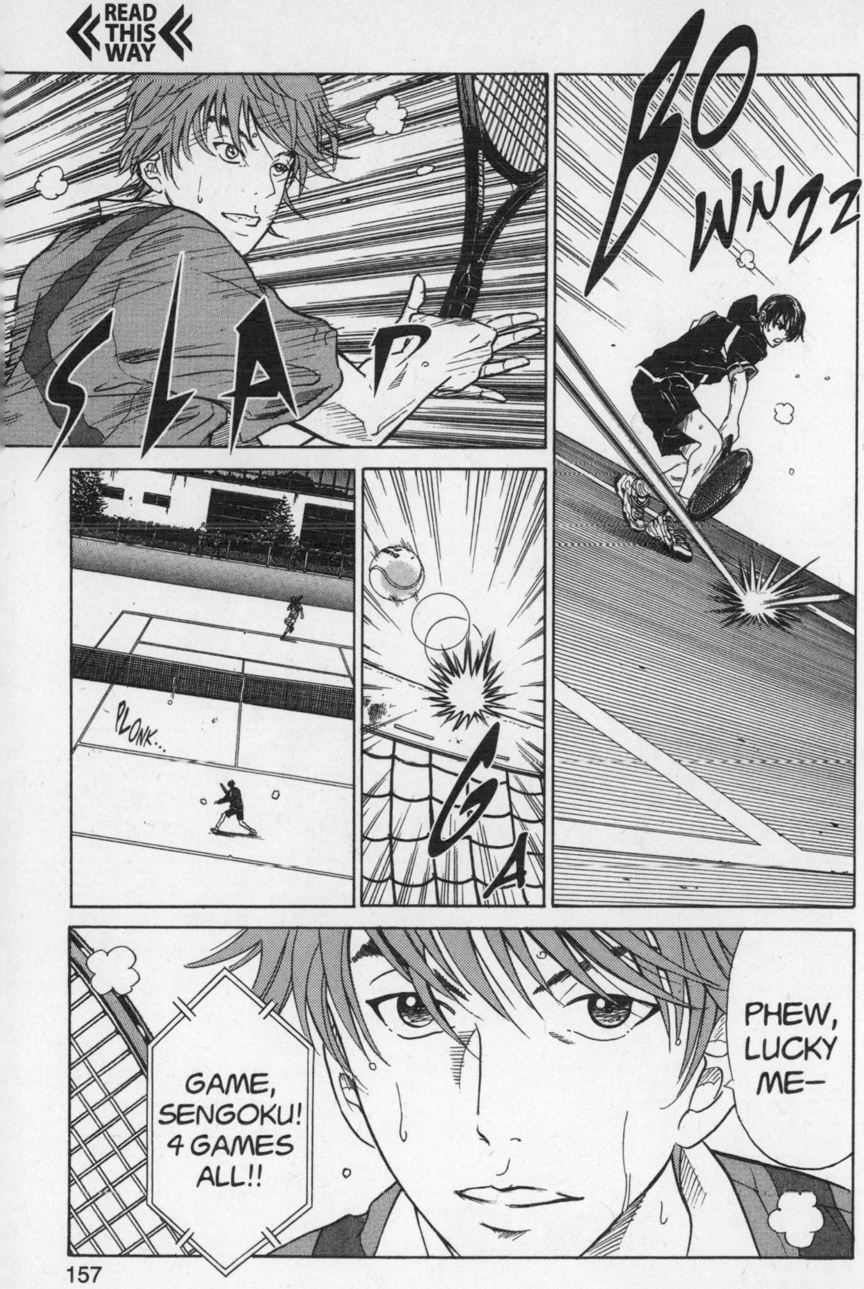
BOWNZZ
SLAP
GA
PLONK...
PHEW, LUCKY ME—
GAME, SENGOKU! 4 GAMES ALL!!

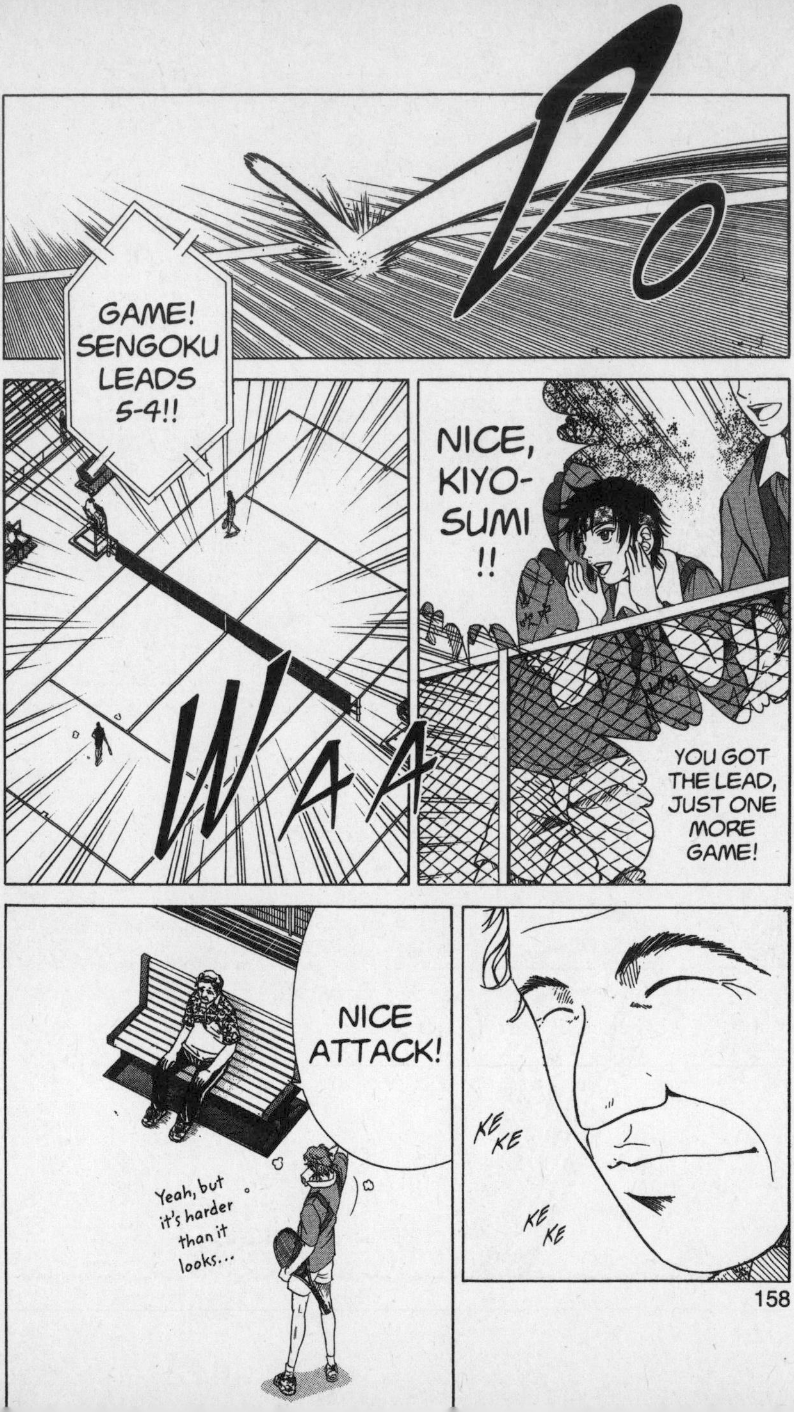
DO
GAME! SENGOKU LEADS 5-4!!
NICE, KIYO-SUMI!!
YOU GOT THE LEAD, JUST ONE MORE GAME!
WAA
KE KE
KE KE
NICE ATTACK!
Yeah, but it's harder than it looks...

READ THIS WAY

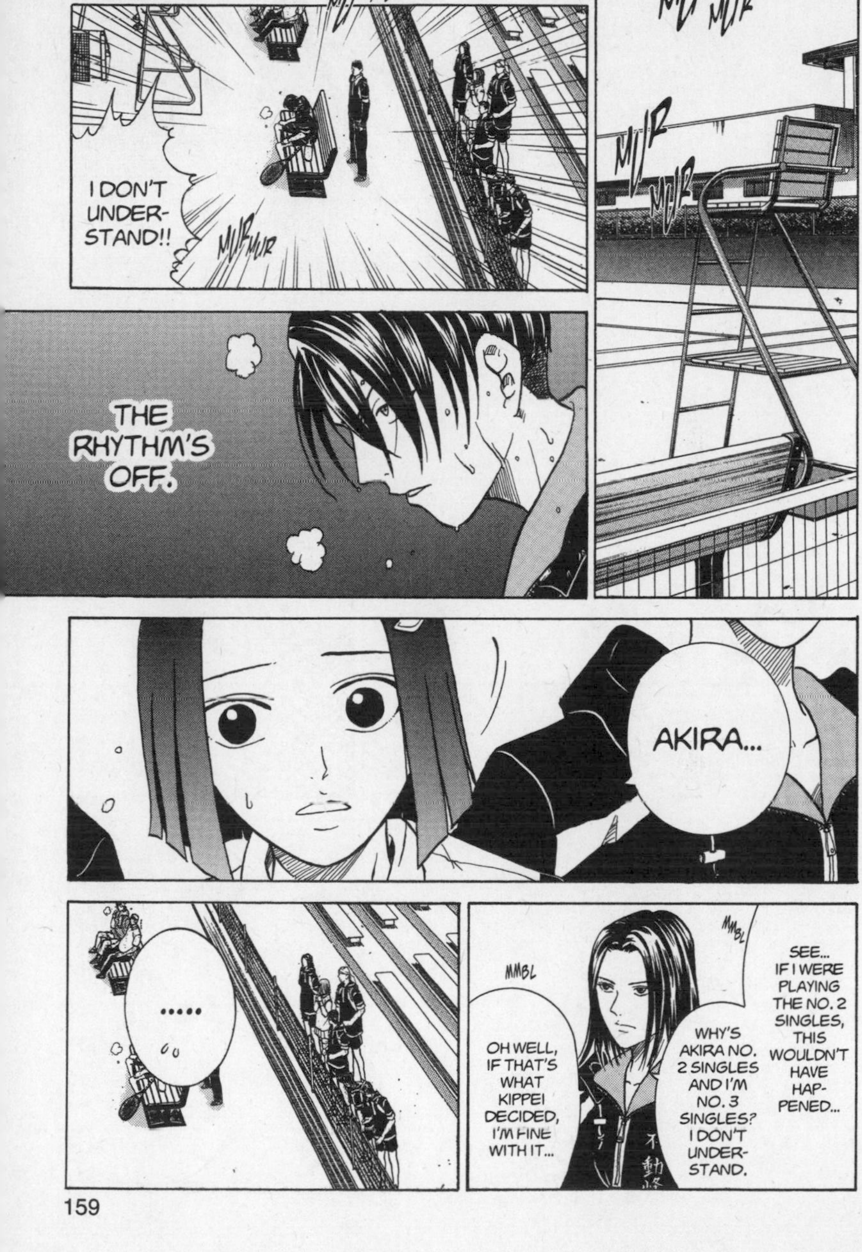
MUR MUR
MUR MUR
MUR MUR
I DON'T UNDER-STAND!!
MUR MUR
THE RHYTHM'S OFF.
AKIRA...
SEE... IF I WERE PLAYING THE NO. 2 SINGLES, THIS WOULDN'T HAVE HAP-PENED...
MMBL
WHY'S AKIRA NO. 2 SINGLES AND I'M NO. 3 SINGLES? I DON'T UNDER-STAND.
MMBL
OH WELL, IF THAT'S WHAT KIPPEI DECIDED, I'M FINE WITH IT...
.....

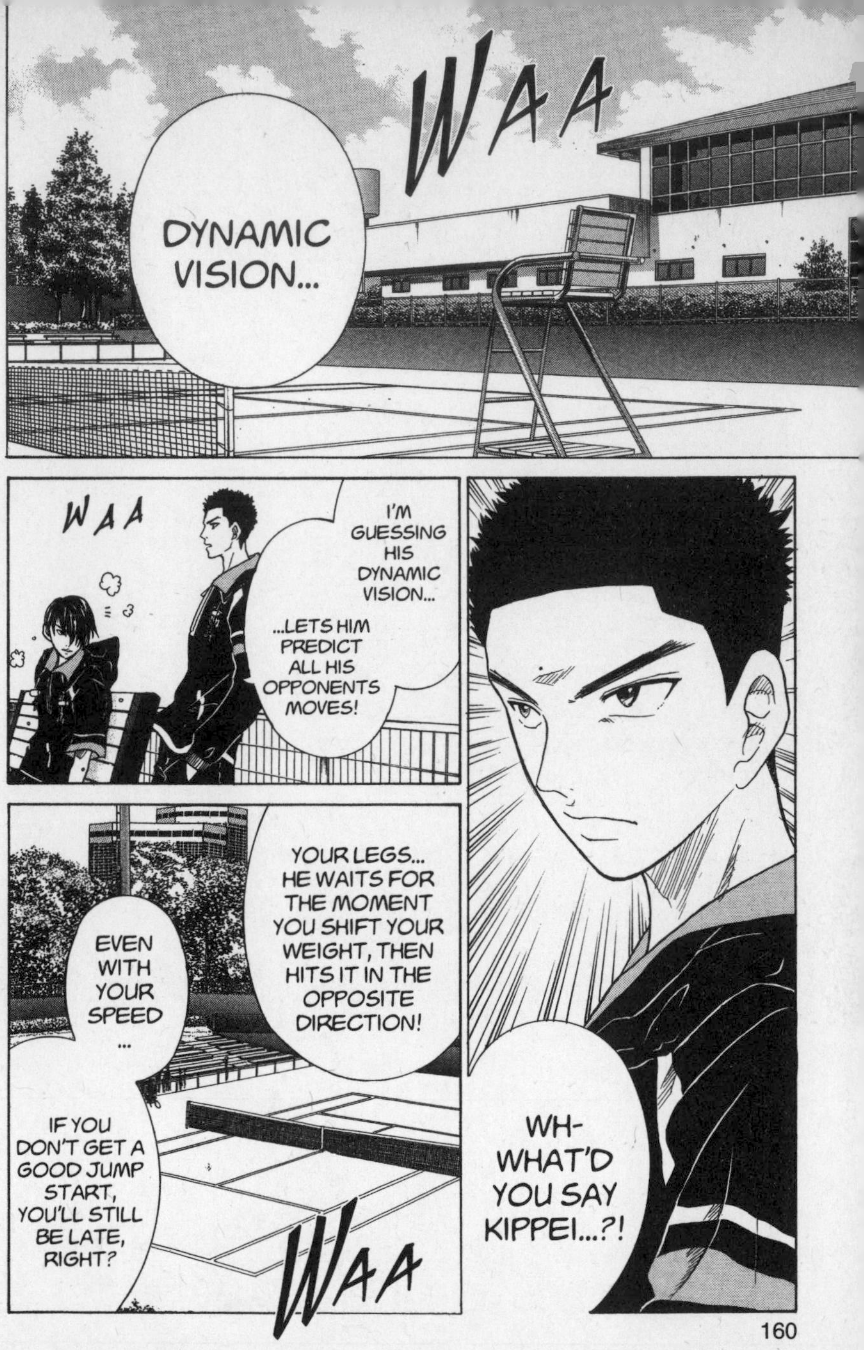
DYNAMIC VISION...
WAA
I'M GUESSING HIS DYNAMIC VISION...
...LETS HIM PREDICT ALL HIS OPPONENTS MOVES!
WAA
YOUR LEGS... HE WAITS FOR THE MOMENT YOU SHIFT YOUR WEIGHT, THEN HITS IT IN THE OPPOSITE DIRECTION!
EVEN WITH YOUR SPEED ...
IF YOU DON'T GET A GOOD JUMP START, YOU'LL STILL BE LATE, RIGHT?
WAA
WH- WHAT'D YOU SAY KIPPEI...?!

READ THIS WAY

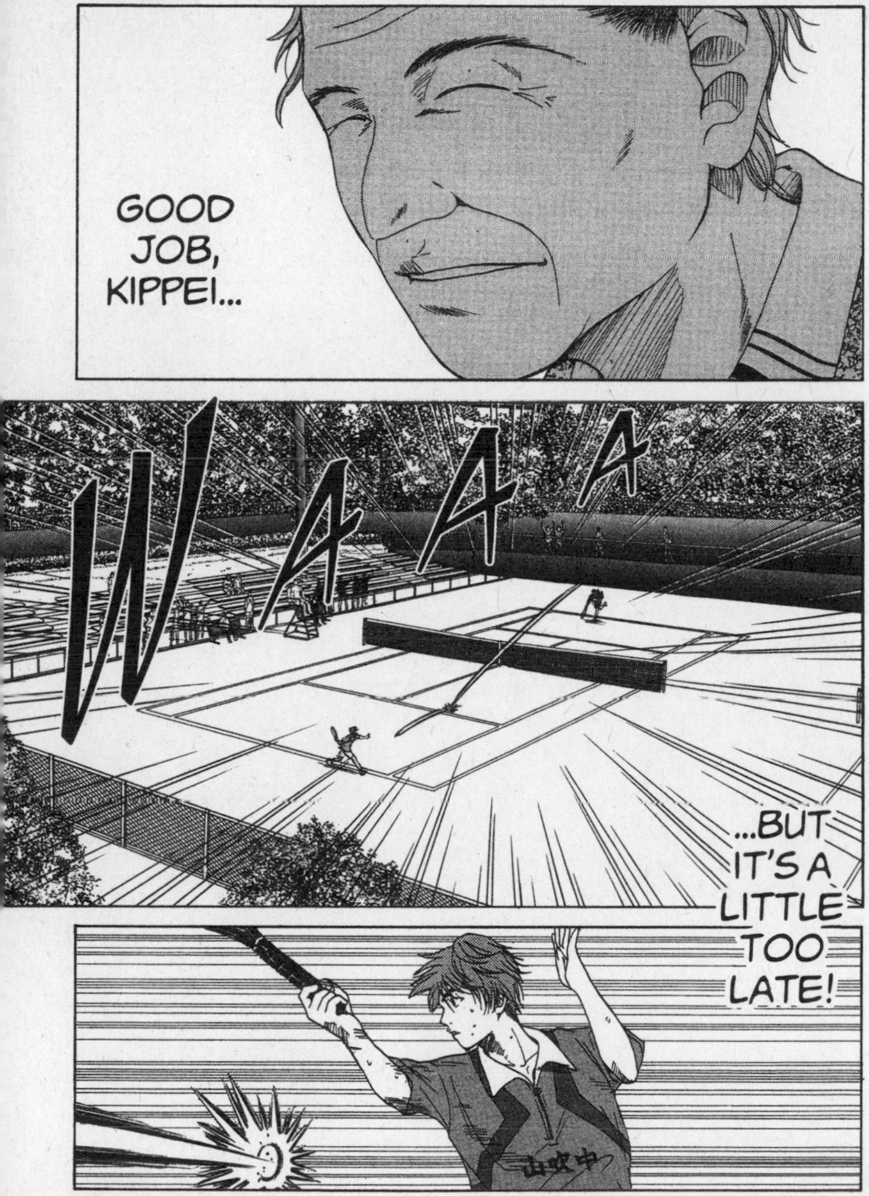
GOOD JOB, KIPPEI...
WAAA
...BUT IT'S A LITTLE TOO LATE!
山吹中

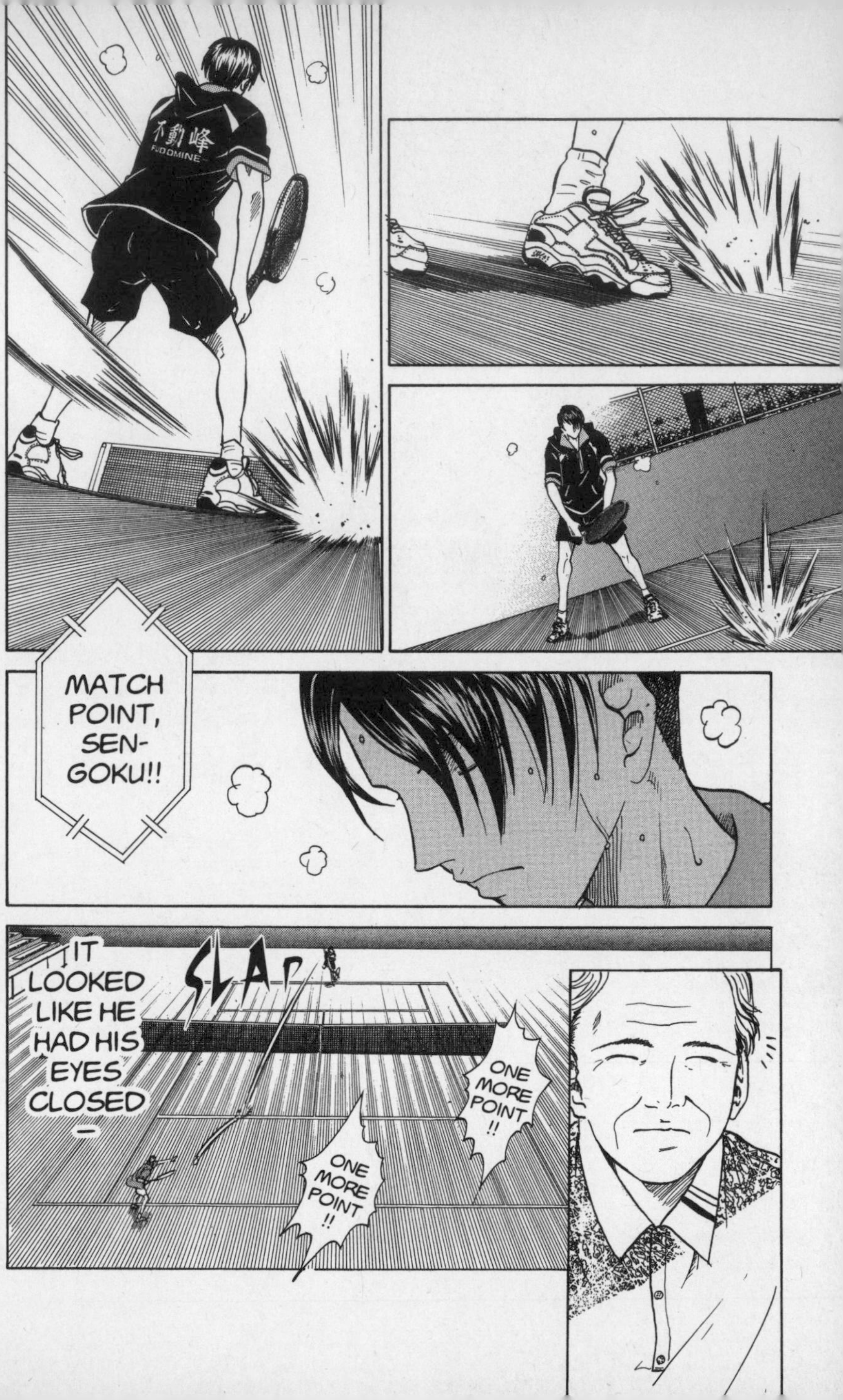
不動峰
FUDOMINE
MATCH POINT, SEN-GOKU!!
IT LOOKED LIKE HE HAD HIS EYES CLOSED –
SLAP
ONE MORE POINT!!
ONE MORE POINT!!

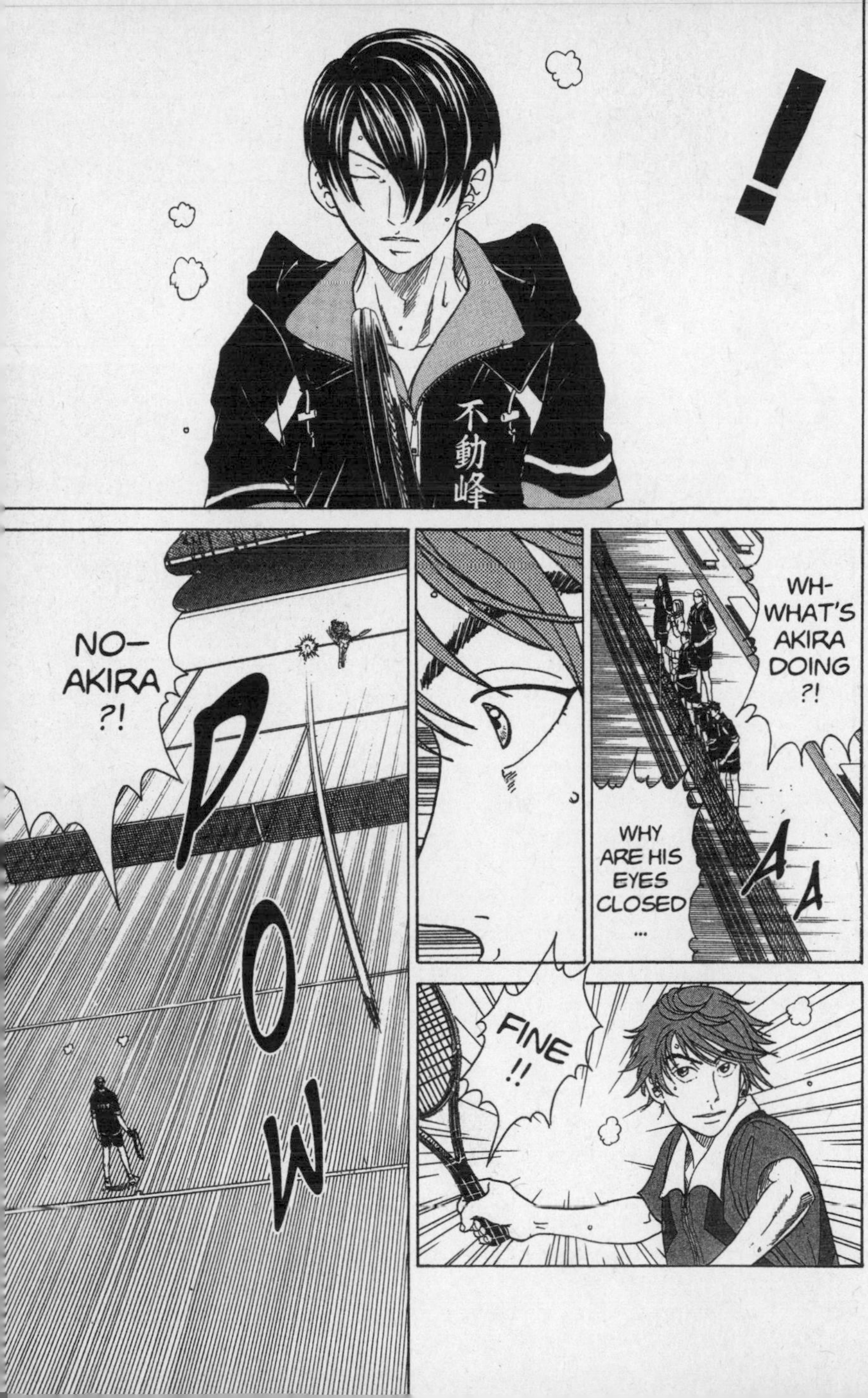
!
不動峰
WH-WHAT'S AKIRA DOING ?!
WHY ARE HIS EYES CLOSED ...
AA
FINE !!
NO—AKIRA ?!
POW

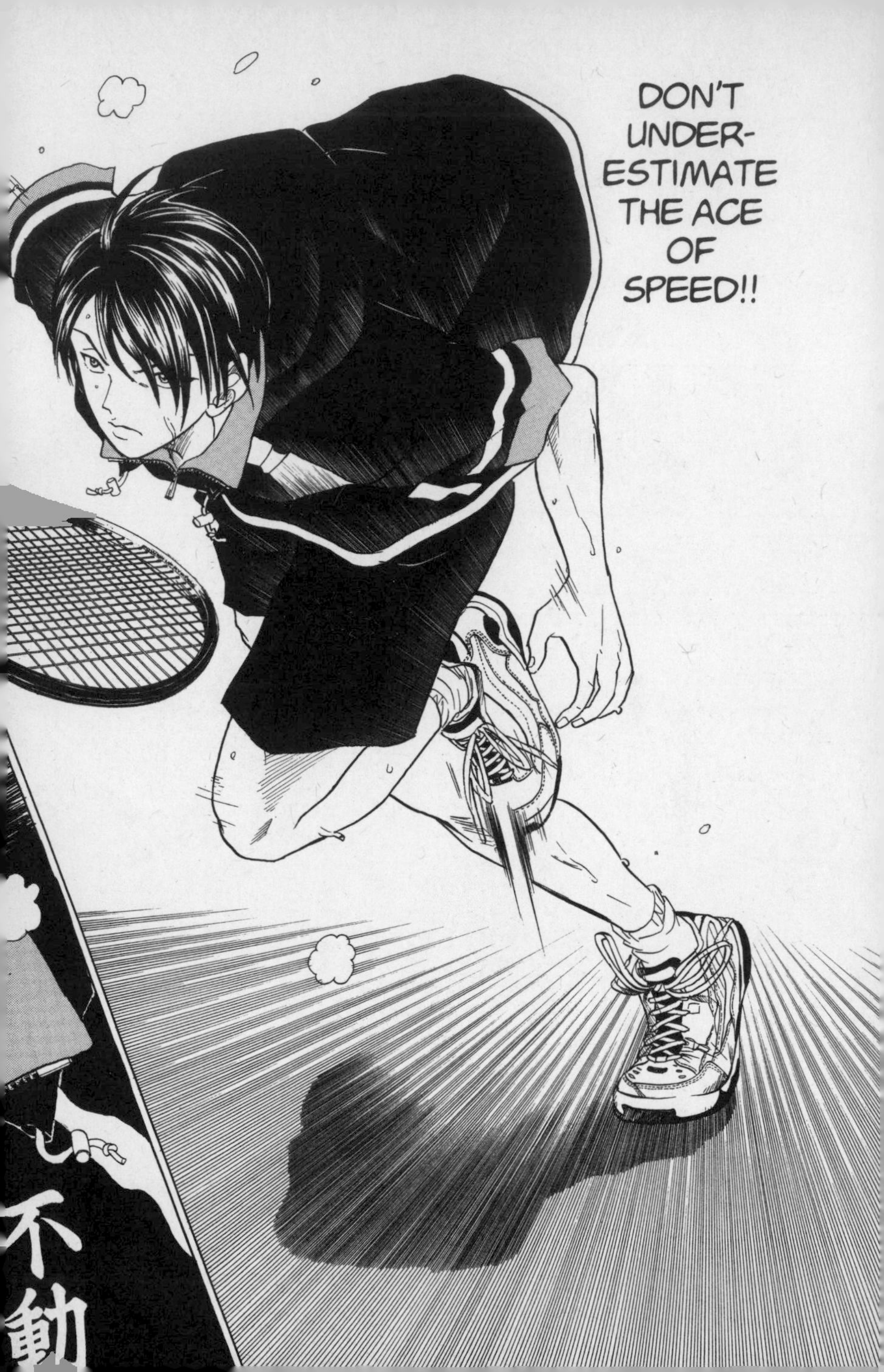
DON'T UNDER-ESTIMATE THE ACE OF SPEED!!
不動

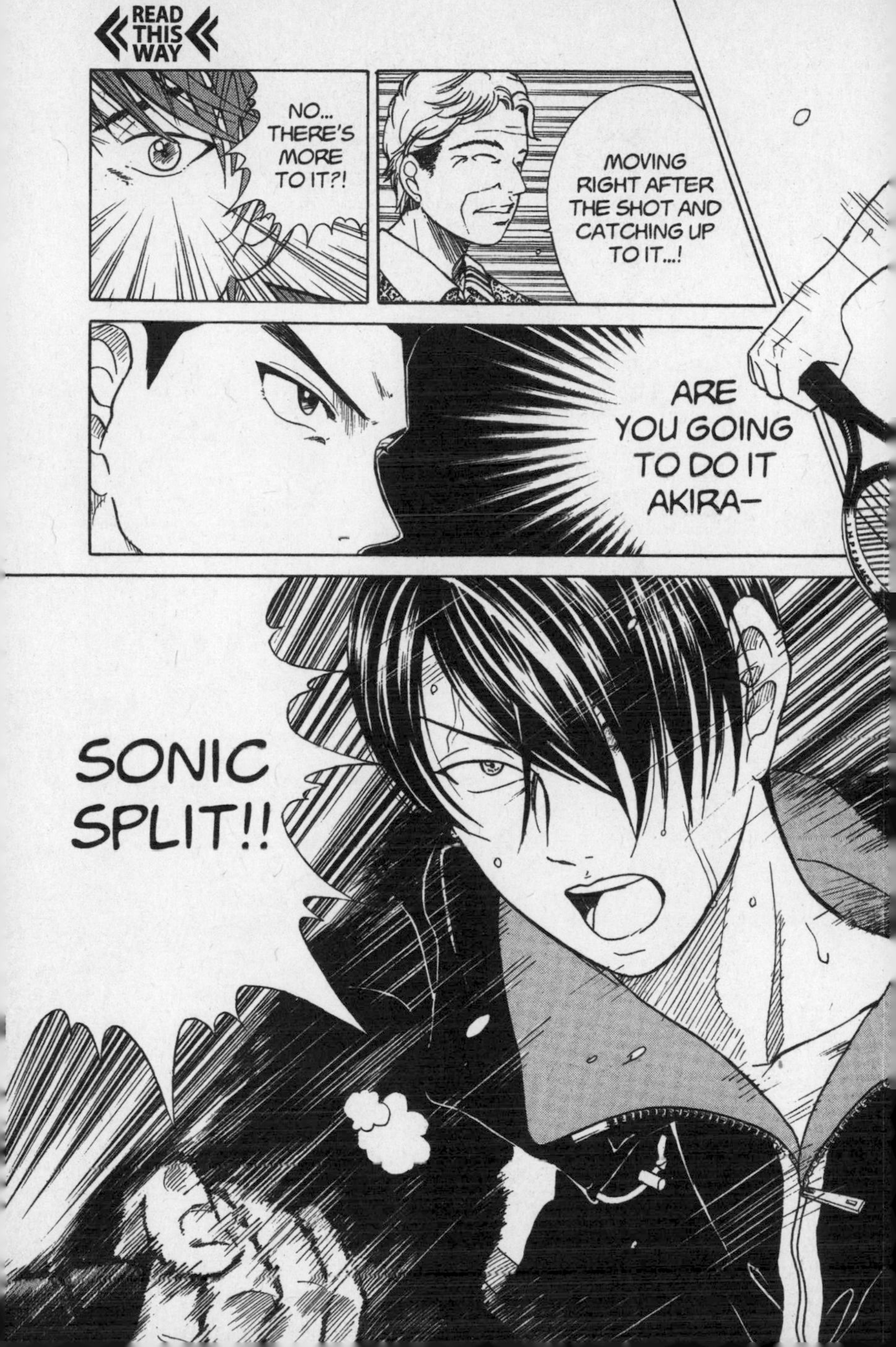
READ THIS WAY
MOVING RIGHT AFTER THE SHOT AND CATCHING UP TO IT...!
NO... THERE'S MORE TO IT?!
ARE YOU GOING TO DO IT AKIRA–
SONIC SPLIT!!

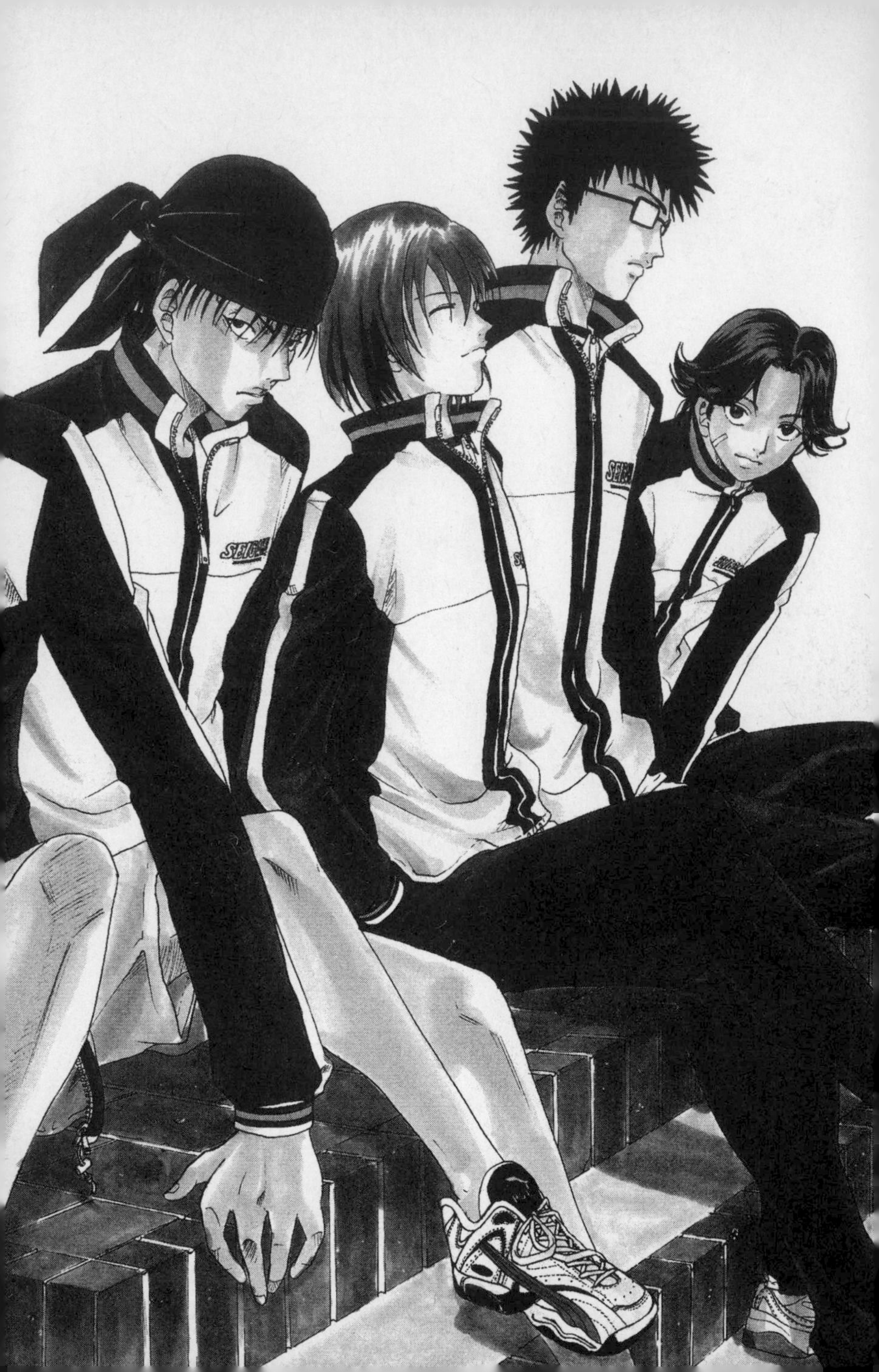

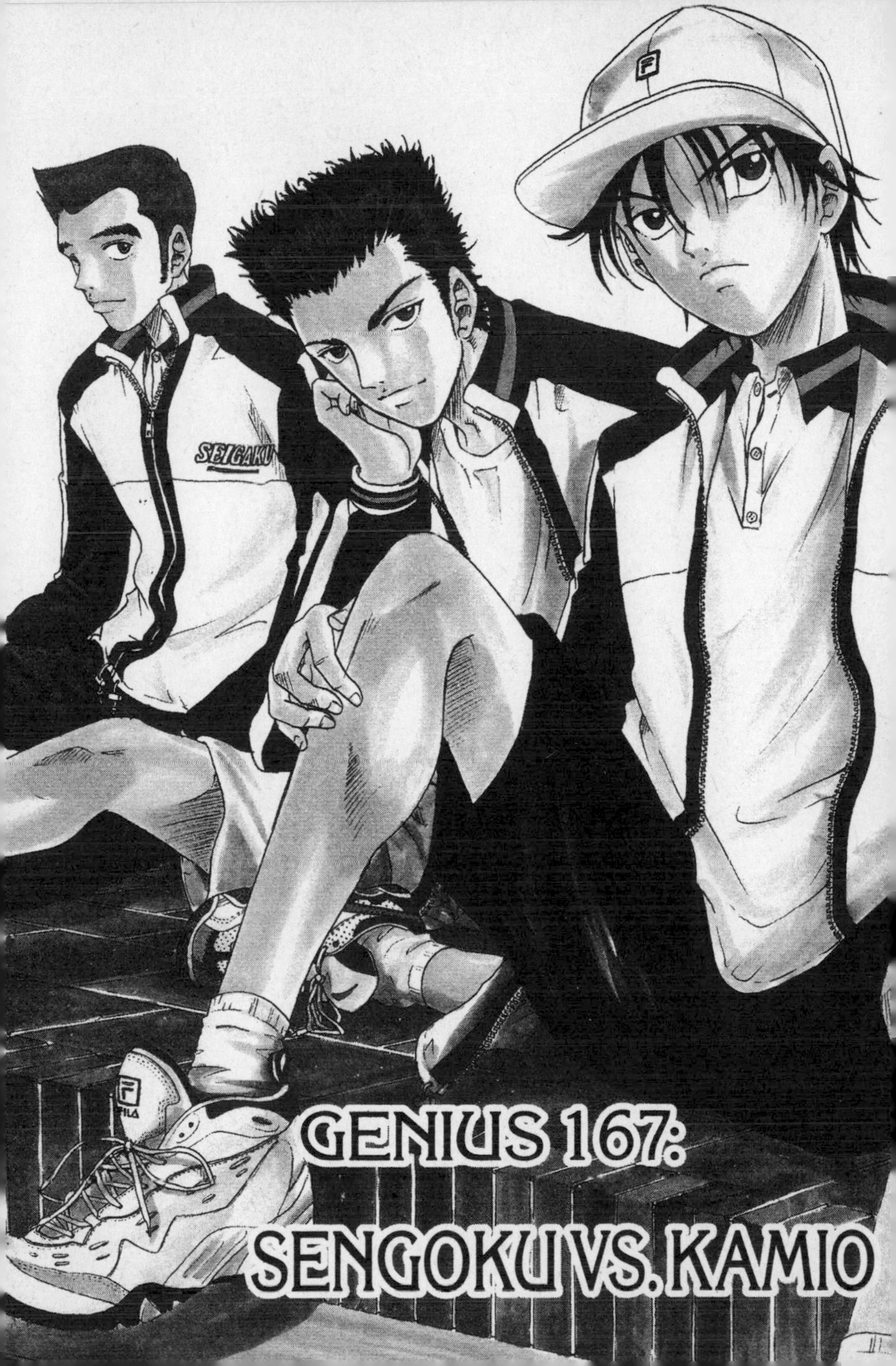
SEIGAKU
GENIUS 167:
SENGOKU VS. KAMIO

テニスの王子様

THE PRINCE OF TENNIS™

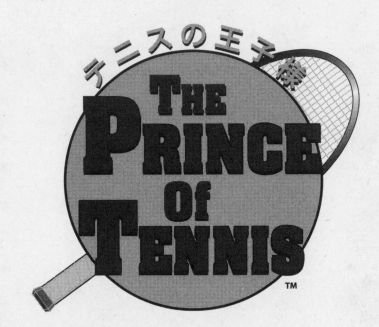

READ THIS WAY

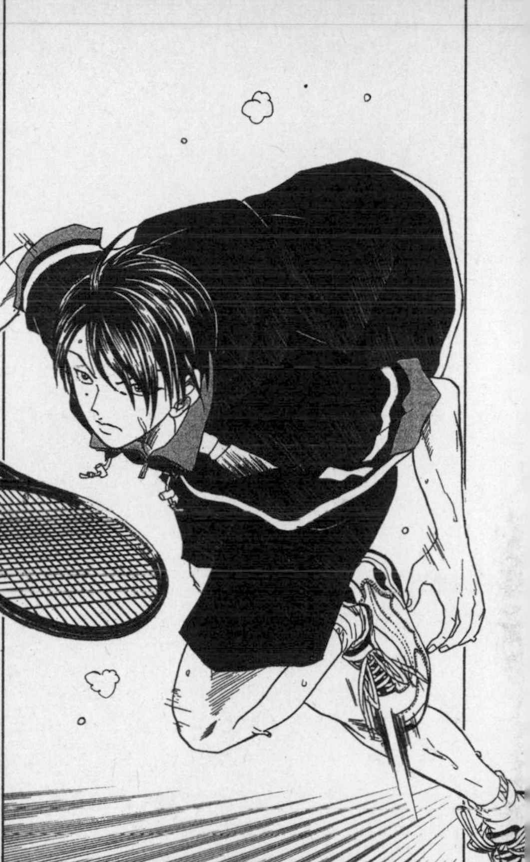
BECAUSE OF OUR ACCIDENT, WE EMBAR-RASSED KIPPEI AT THE DISTRICT PRELIM'S SEMI-FINALS.
I'M GONNA REPAY KIPPEI FOR LEADING US THIS FAR WITH MY OWN HANDS!!

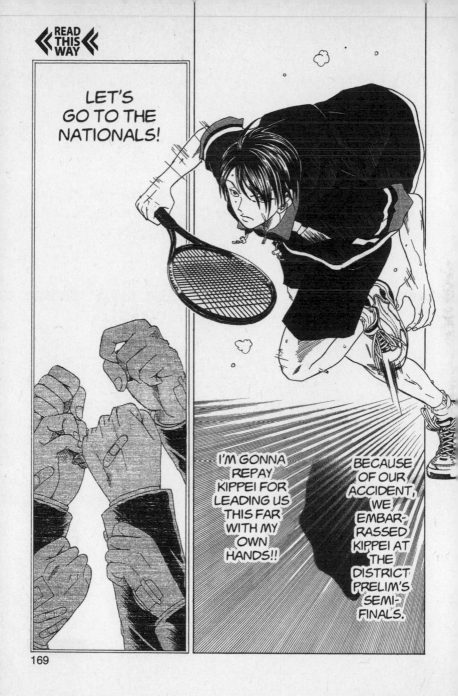

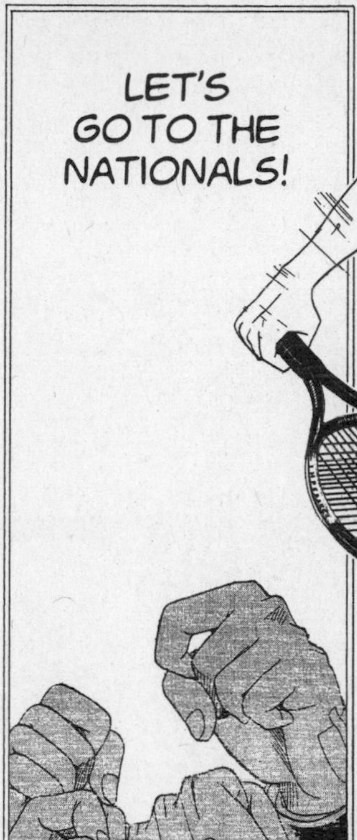
LET'S GO TO THE NATIONALS!

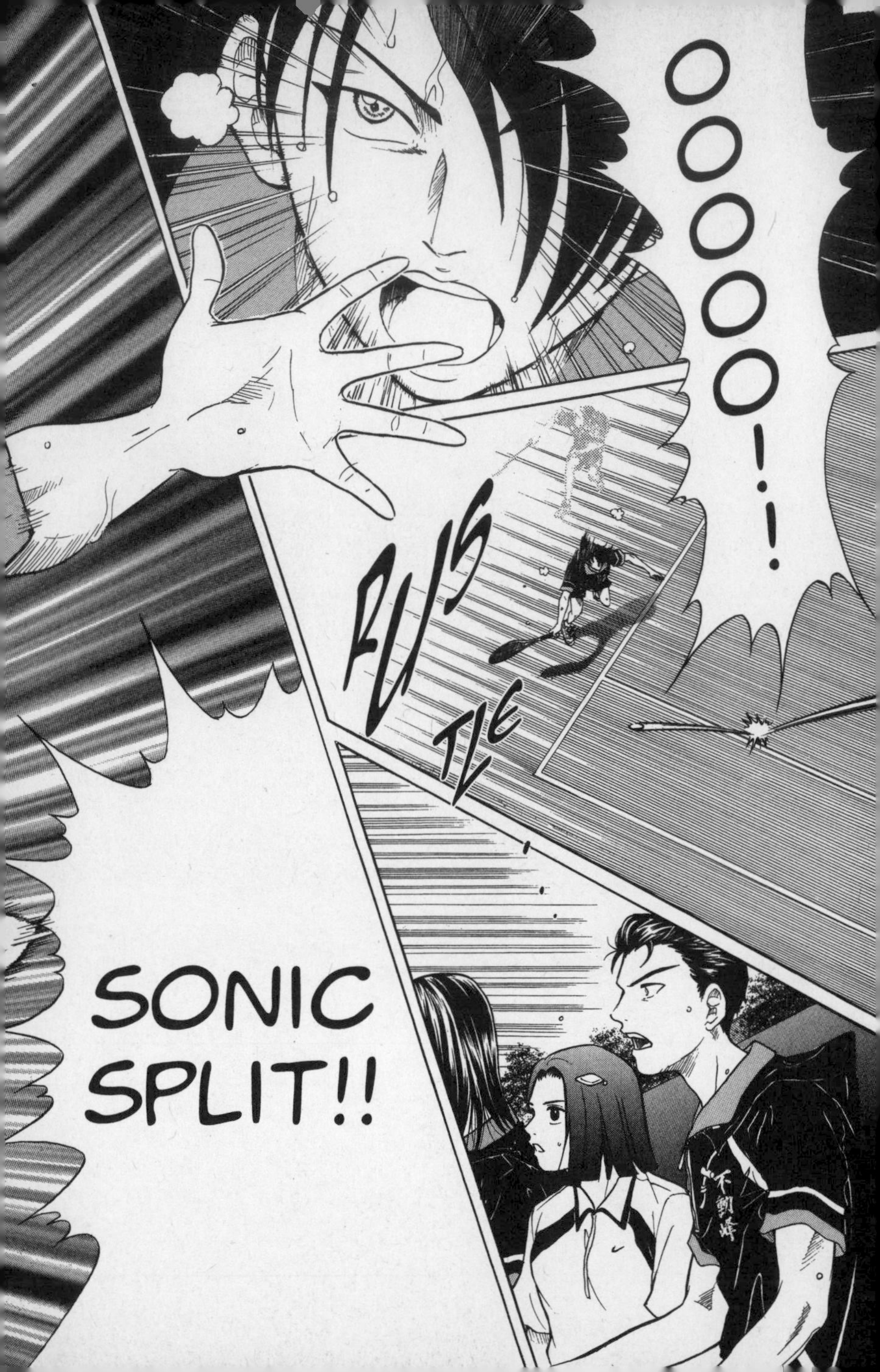

OOOOOO!!
RUSTLE
SONIC SPLIT!!
不動峰

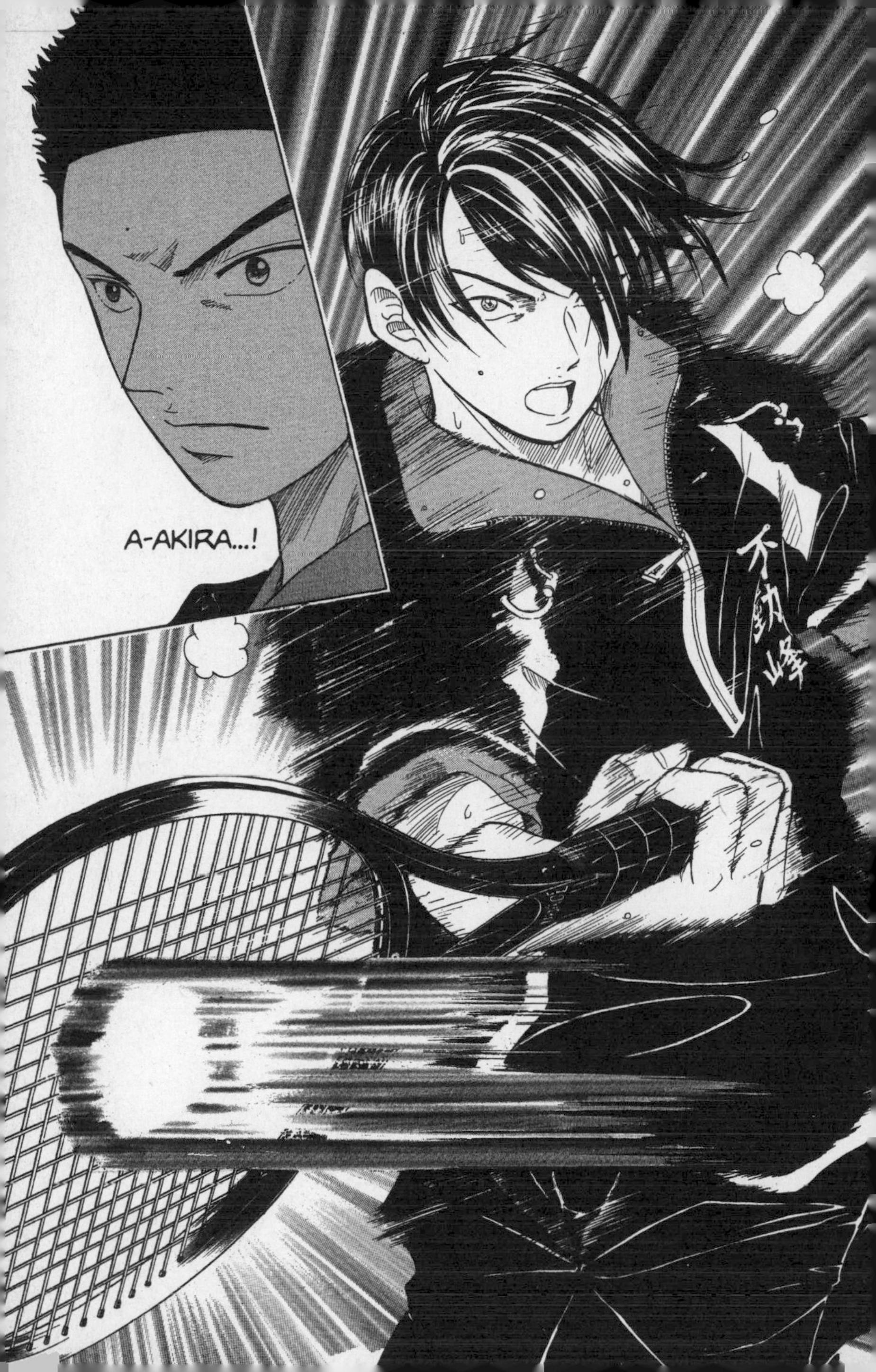
不動峰
A-AKIRA...!

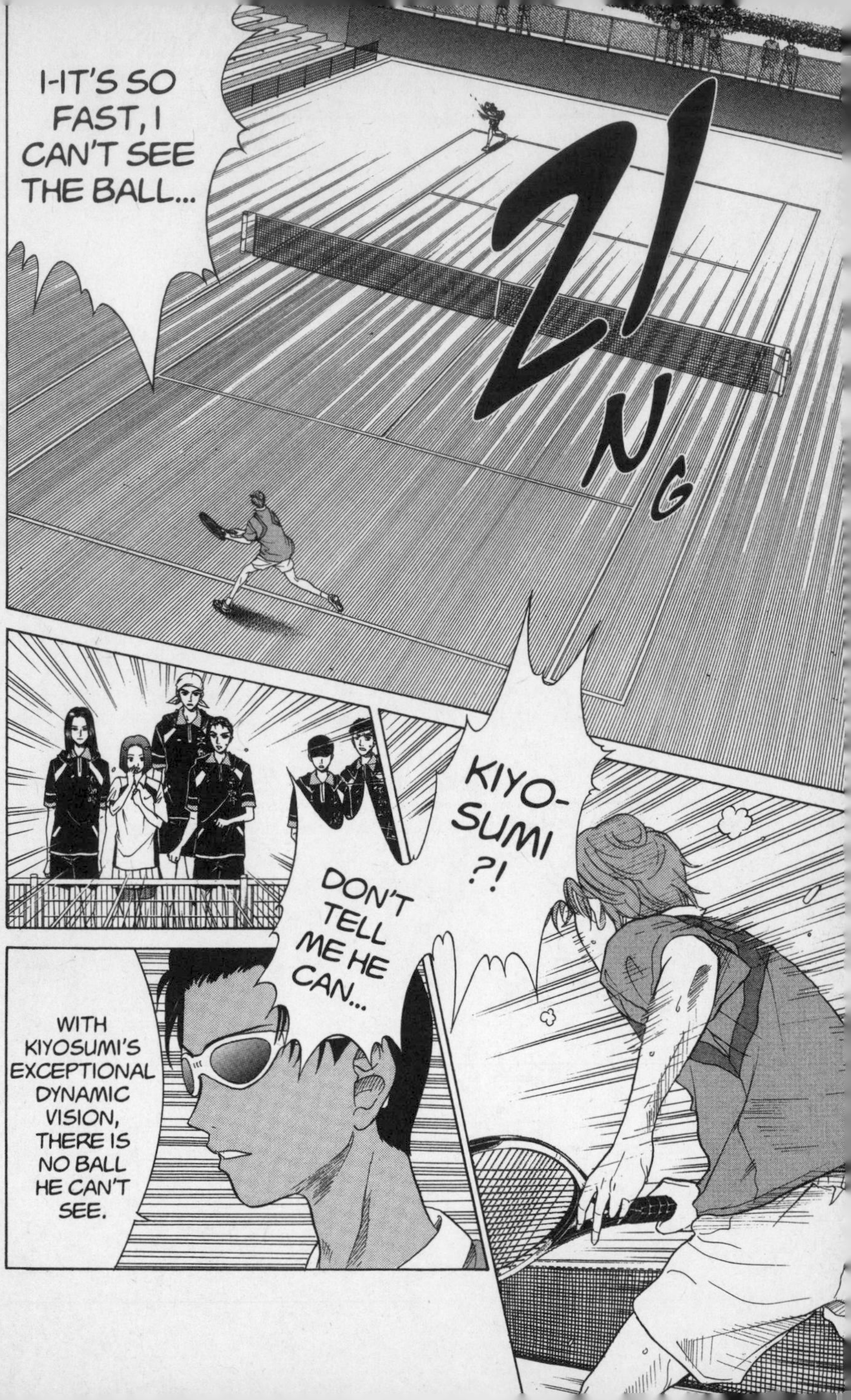
I-IT'S SO FAST, I CAN'T SEE THE BALL...
ZING
KIYO-SUMI?!
DON'T TELL ME HE CAN...
WITH KIYOSUMI'S EXCEPTIONAL DYNAMIC VISION, THERE IS NO BALL HE CAN'T SEE.

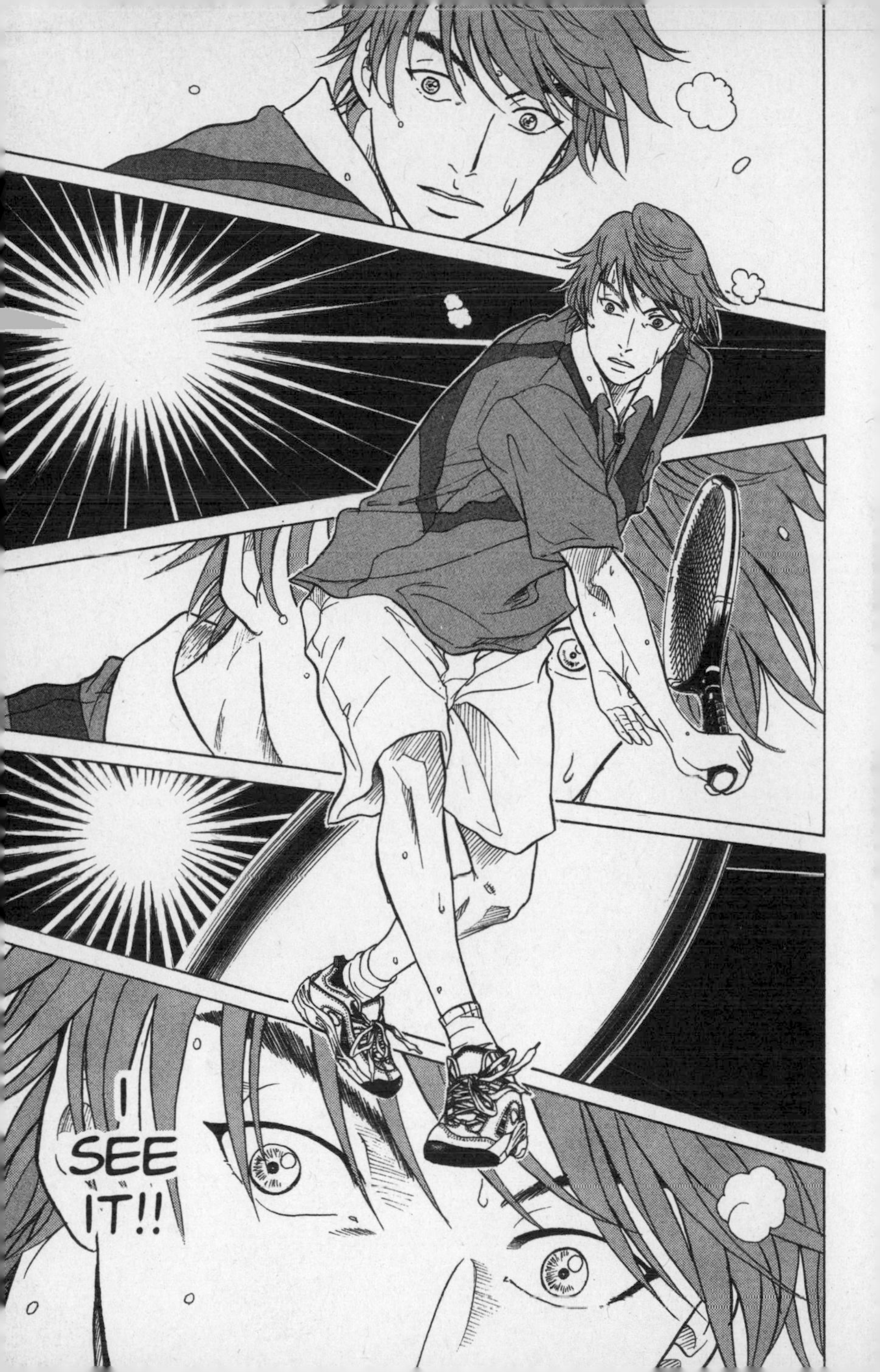
I SEE IT!!

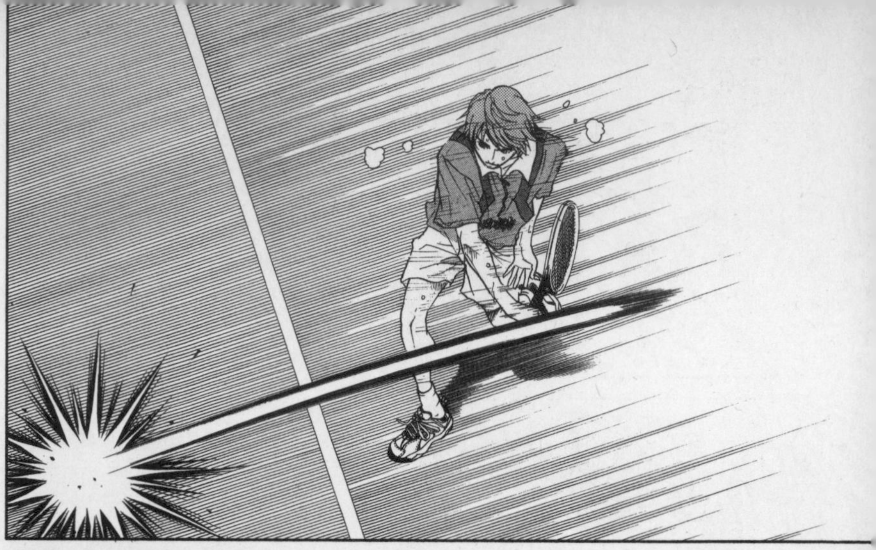

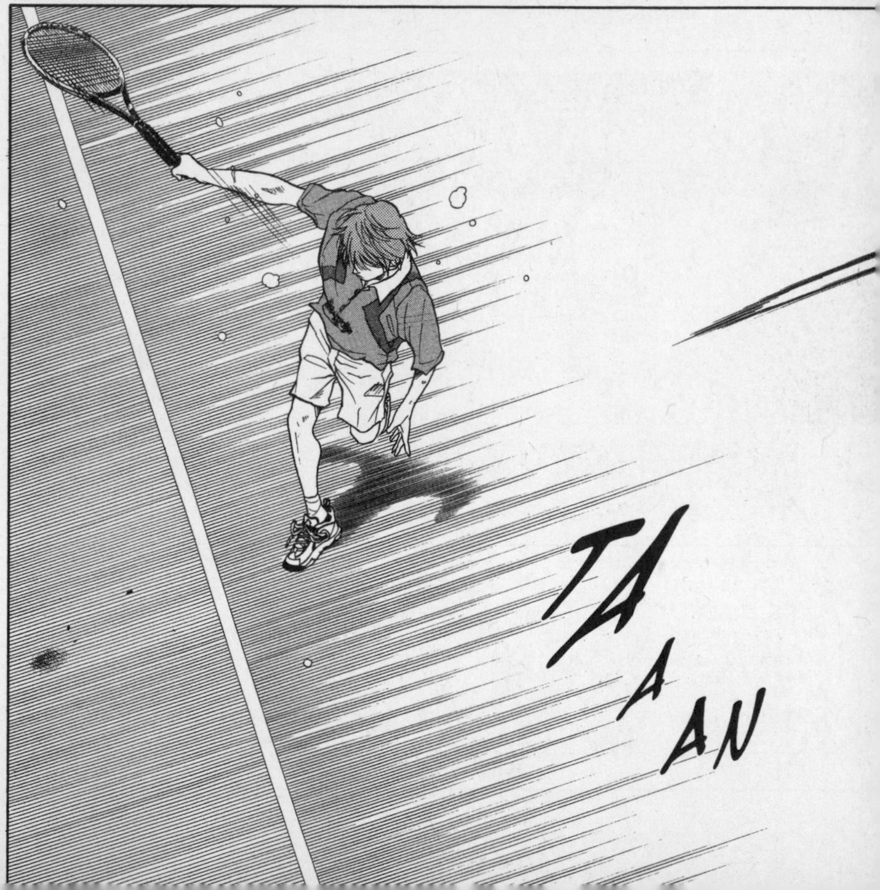
TAAAN

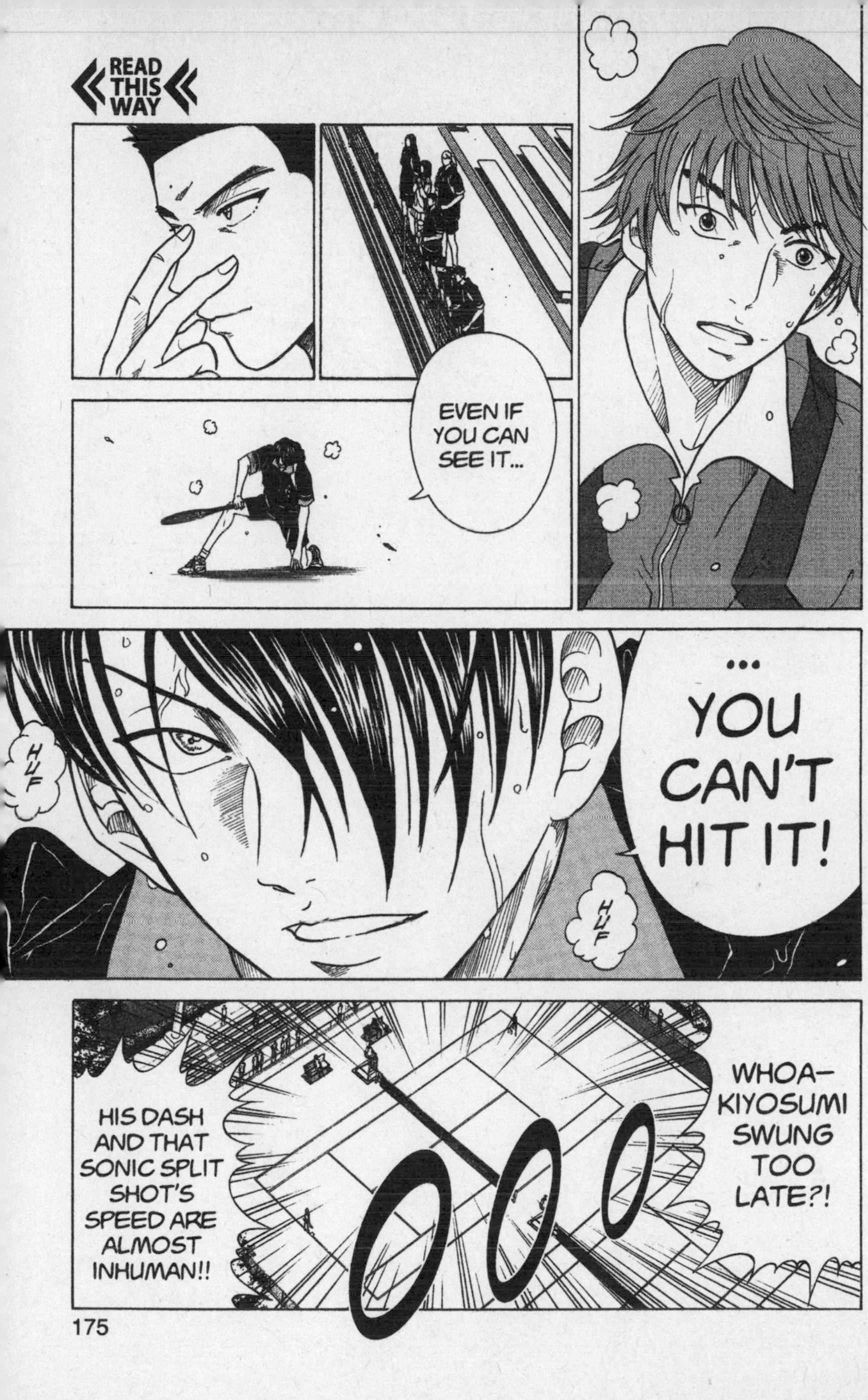
READ THIS WAY
EVEN IF YOU CAN SEE IT...
...YOU CAN'T HIT IT!
HUF
HUF
WHOA- KIYOSUMI SWUNG TOO LATE?!
HIS DASH AND THAT SONIC SPLIT SHOT'S SPEED ARE ALMOST INHUMAN!!

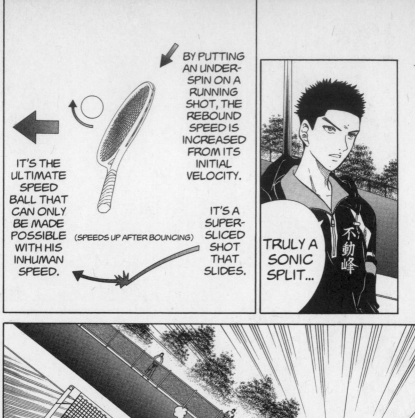

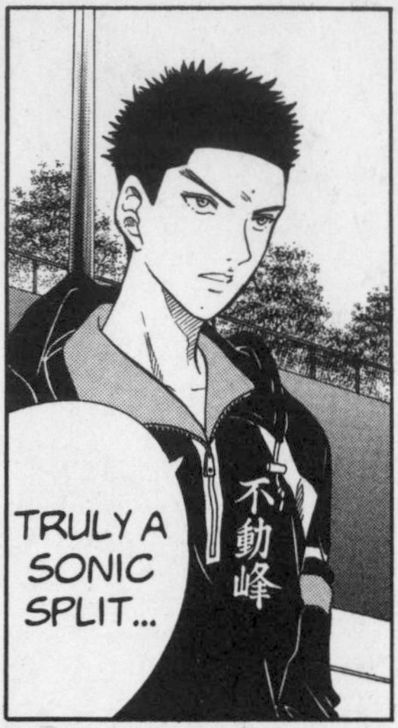
TRULY A SONIC SPLIT...
不動峰
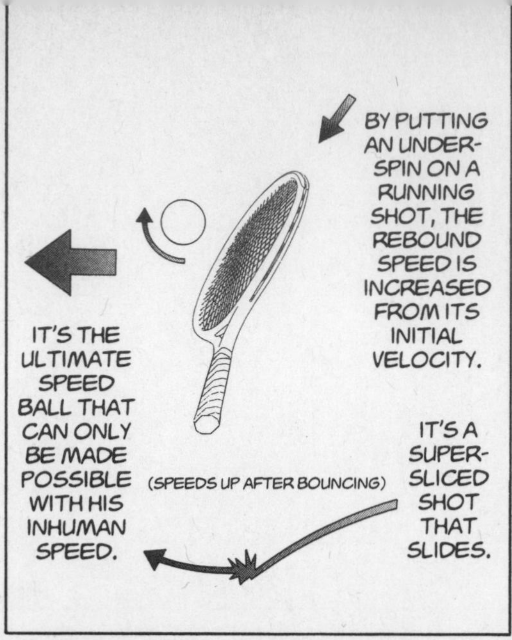
BY PUTTING AN UNDER-SPIN ON A RUNNING SHOT, THE REBOUND SPEED IS INCREASED FROM ITS INITIAL VELOCITY.
IT'S A SUPER-SLICED SHOT THAT SLIDES.
(SPEEDS UP AFTER BOUNCING)
IT'S THE ULTIMATE SPEED BALL THAT CAN ONLY BE MADE POSSIBLE WITH HIS INHUMAN SPEED.
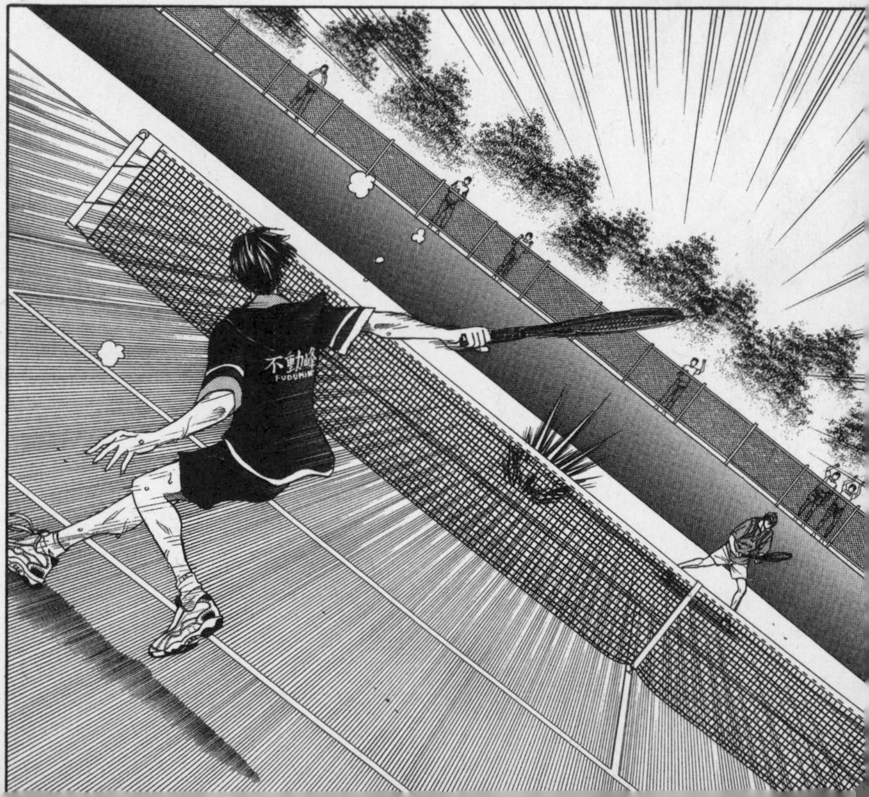
不動峰

READ THIS WAY

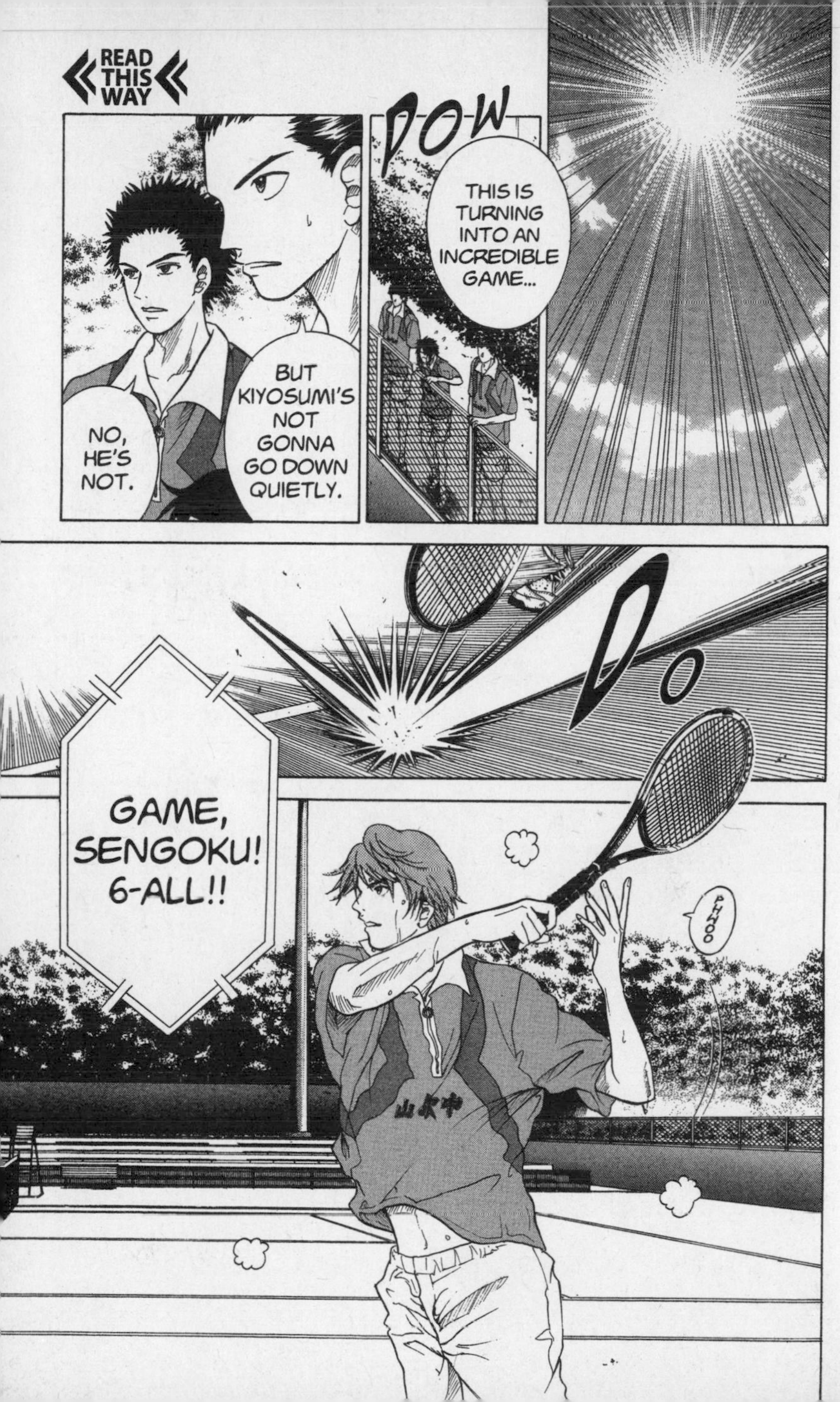
POW
THIS IS TURNING INTO AN INCREDIBLE GAME...
BUT KIYOSUMI'S NOT GONNA GO DOWN QUIETLY.
NO, HE'S NOT.
DO
GAME, SENGOKU! 6-ALL!!
PHWOO

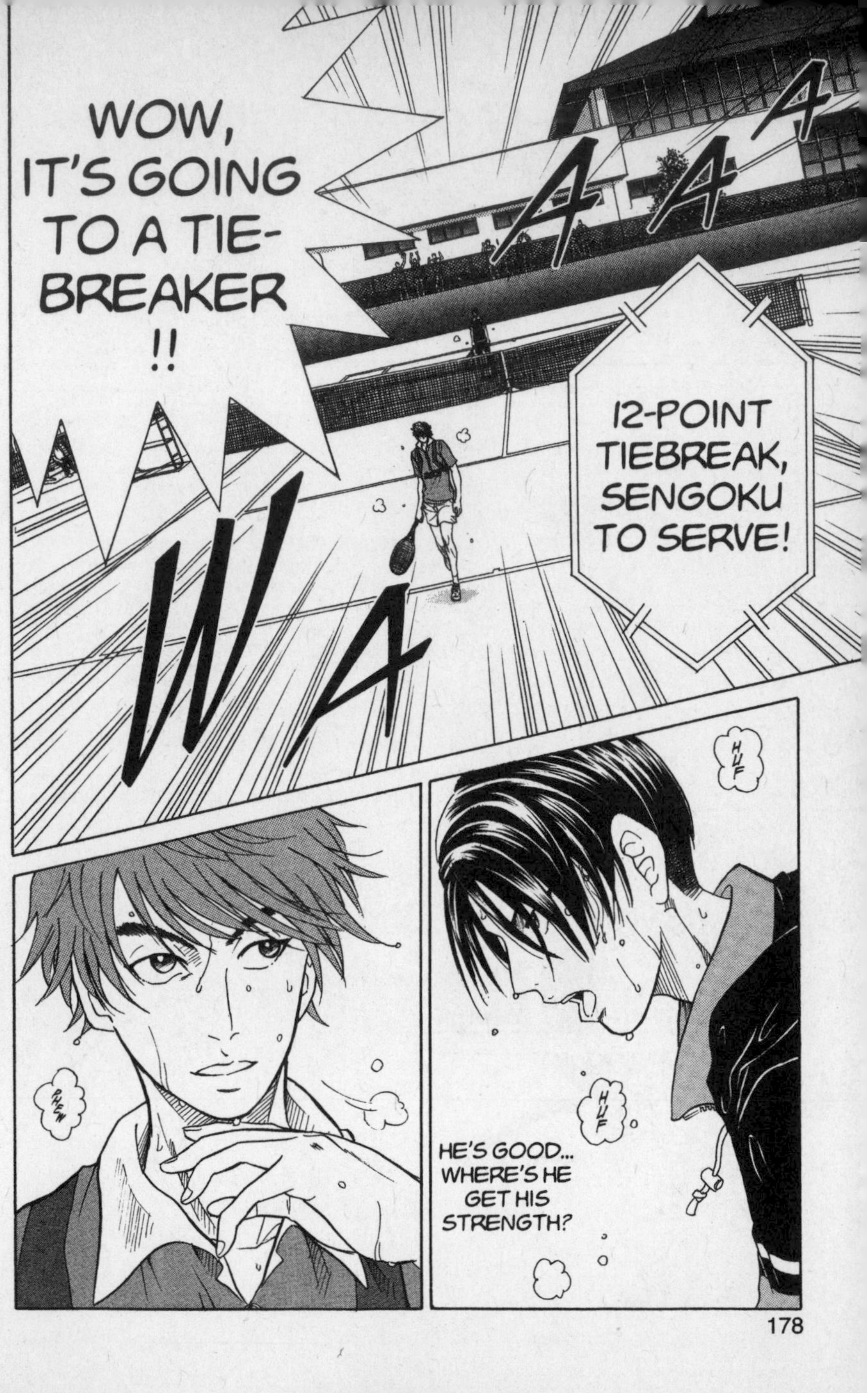
WOW, IT'S GOING TO A TIE-BREAKER!!
12-POINT TIEBREAK, SENGOKU TO SERVE!
WAAAA
HUF
HUF
HE'S GOOD... WHERE'S HE GET HIS STRENGTH?
PHEW

READ THIS WAY

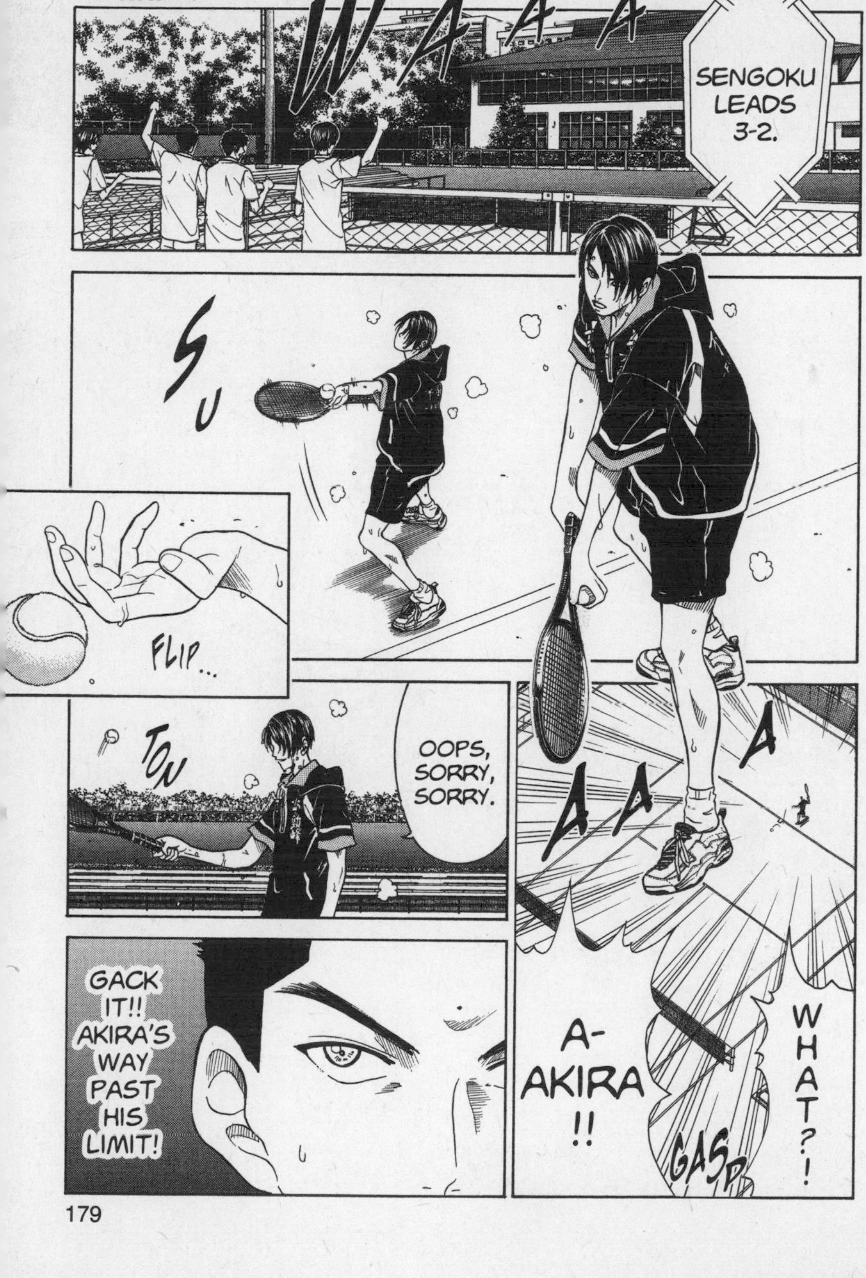
WAAAA
SENGOKU LEADS 3-2.
SU
FLIP...
AAA
OOPS, SORRY, SORRY.
TON
WHAT?!
A-AKIRA!!
GASP
GACK IT!! AKIRA'S WAY PAST HIS LIMIT!

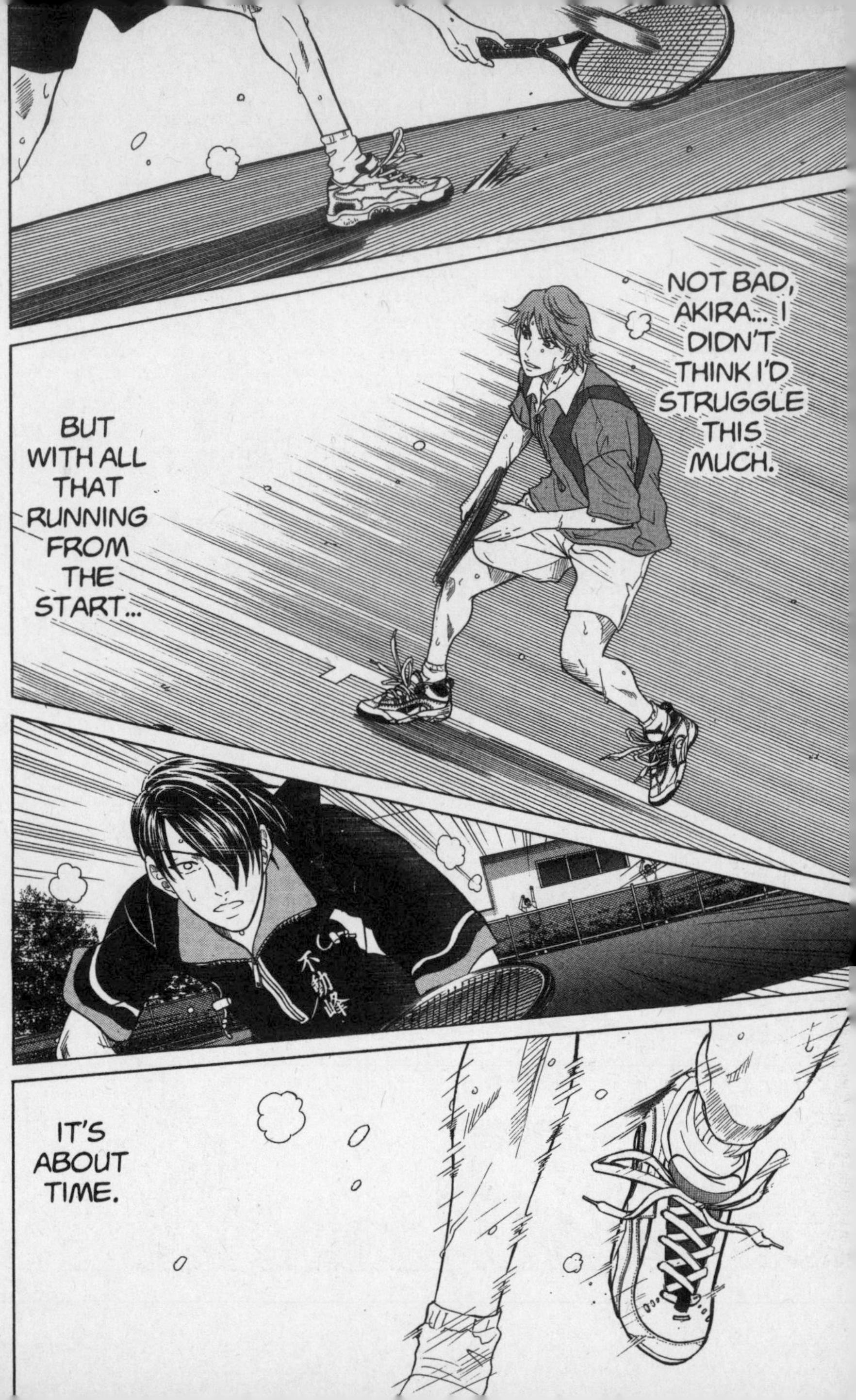
NOT BAD, AKIRA... I DIDN'T THINK I'D STRUGGLE THIS MUCH.
BUT WITH ALL THAT RUNNING FROM THE START...
不動峰
IT'S ABOUT TIME.

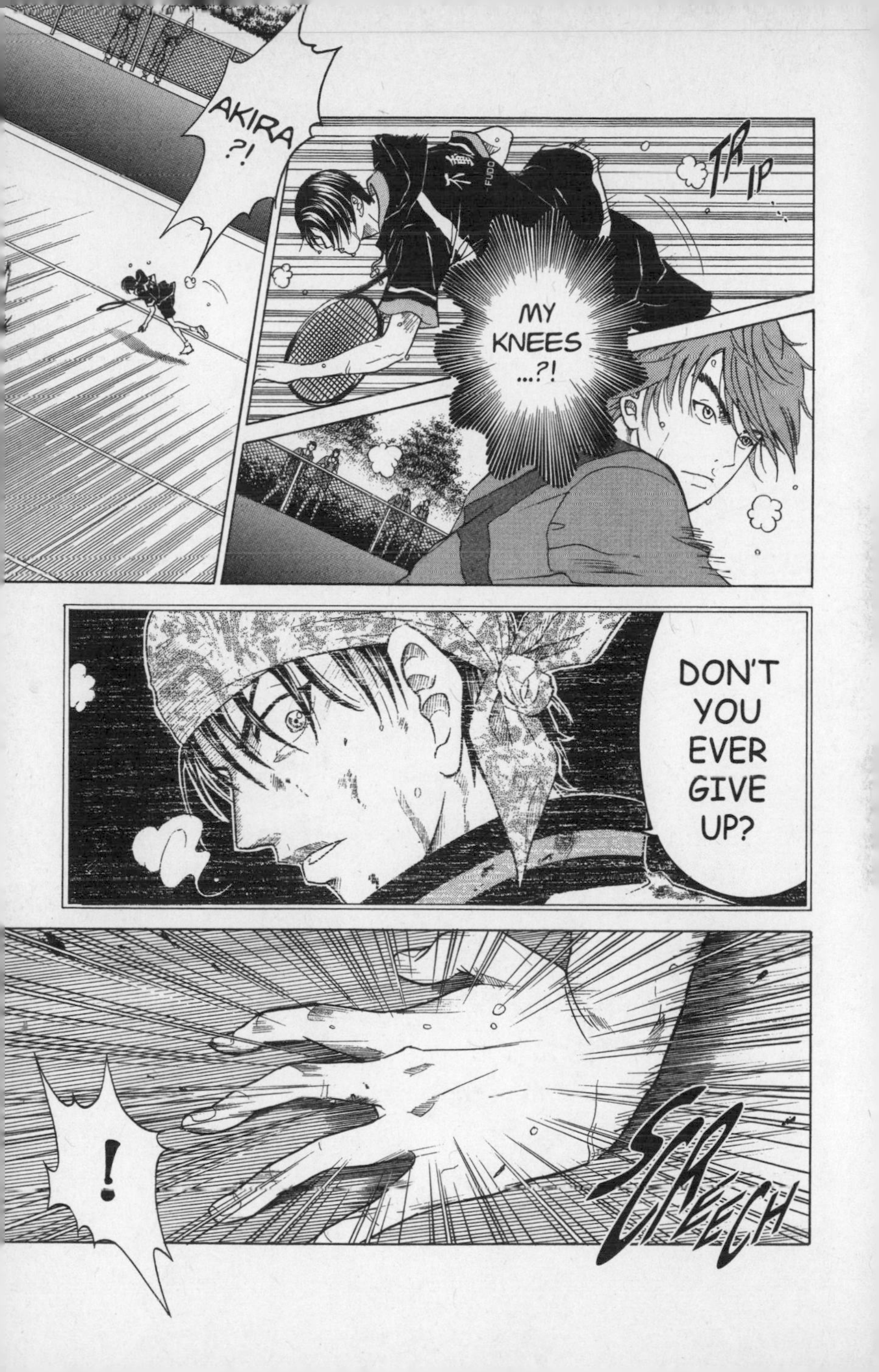
TRIP
MY KNEES ...?!
AKIRA ?!
DON'T YOU EVER GIVE UP?
SCREECH
!

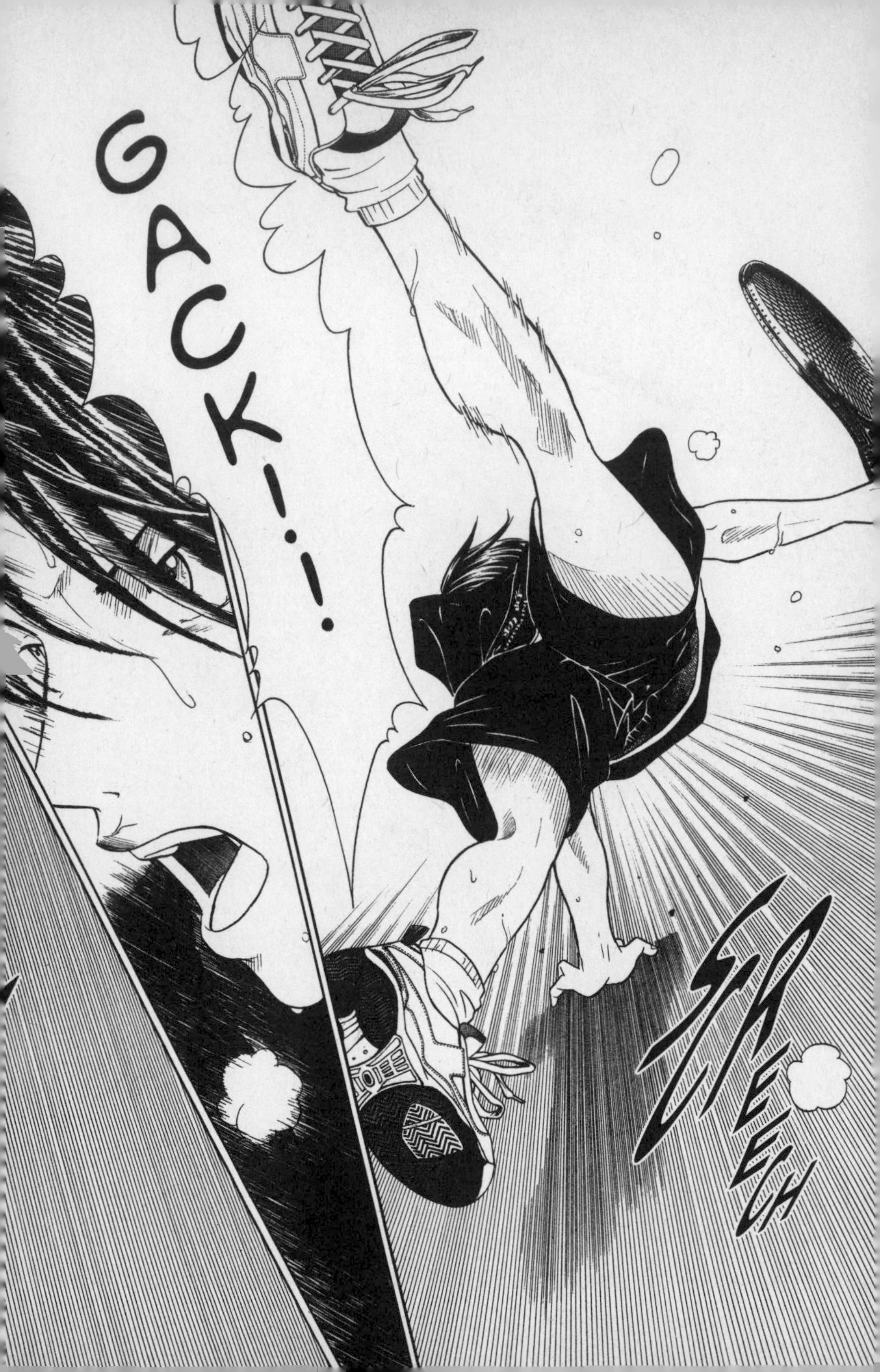
GACK!!
SKREEECH

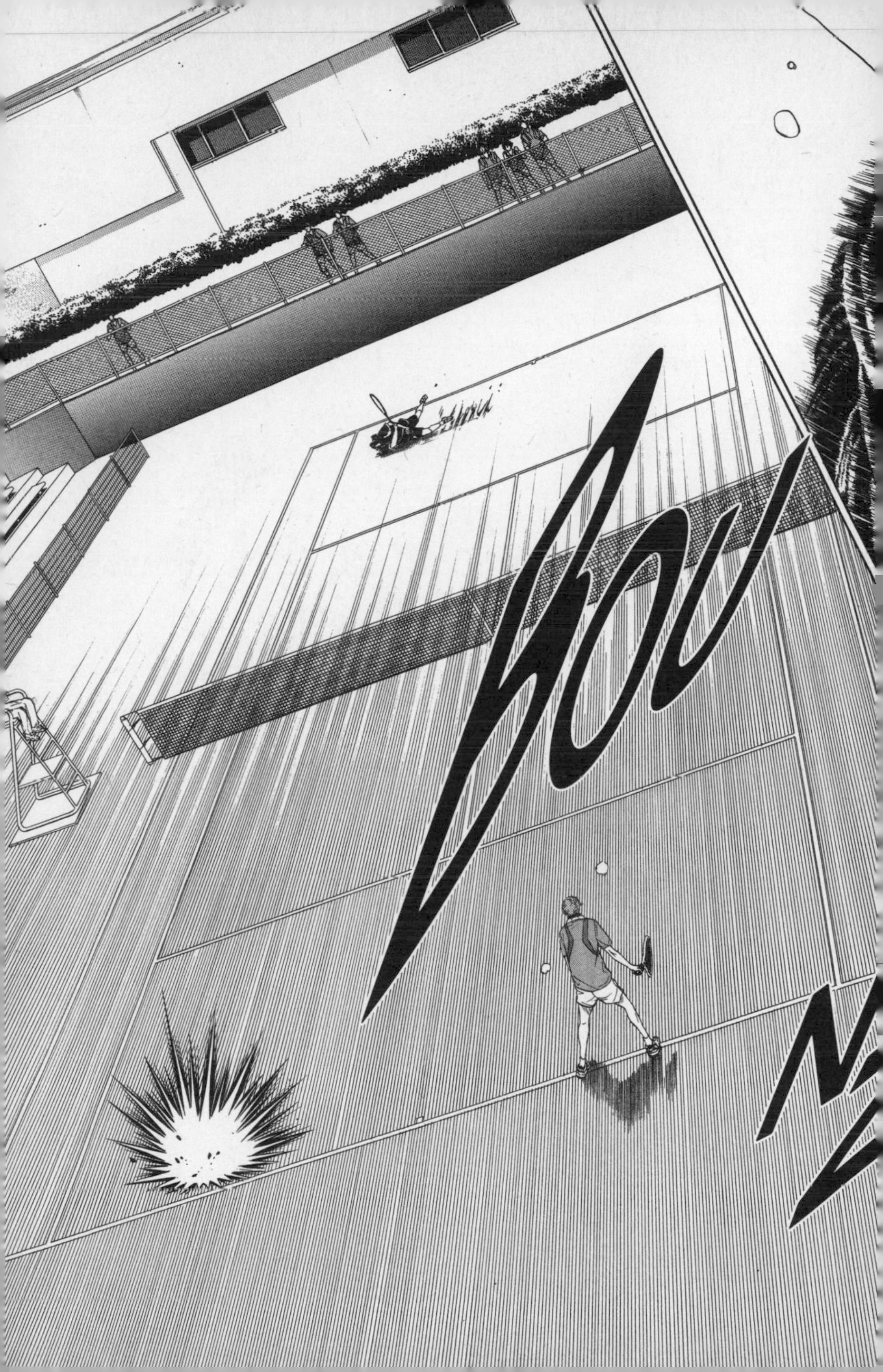

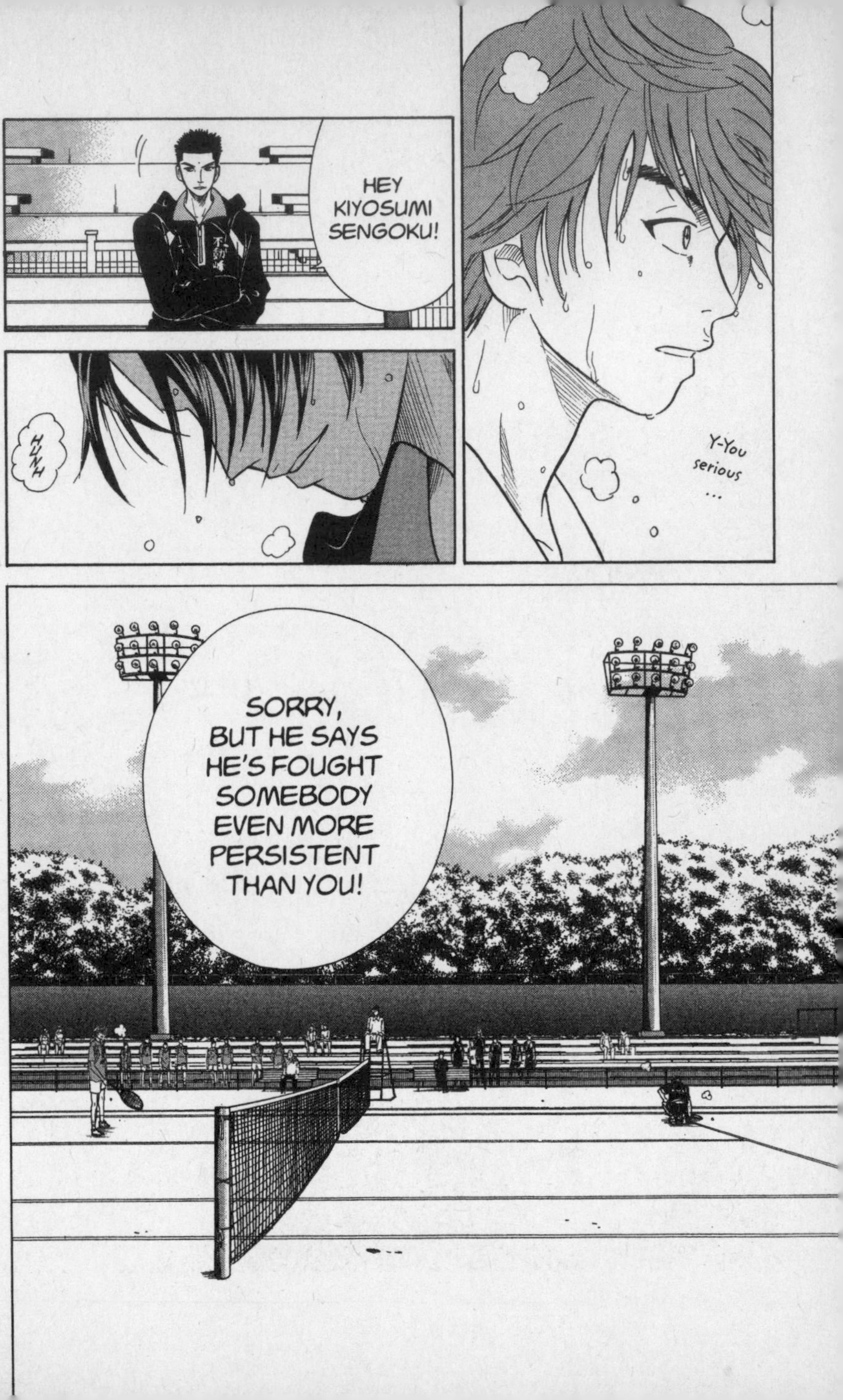
Y-You serious ...
HEY KIYOSUMI SENGOKU!
HUNH
SORRY, BUT HE SAYS HE'S FOUGHT SOMEBODY EVEN MORE PERSISTENT THAN YOU!

READ THIS WAY

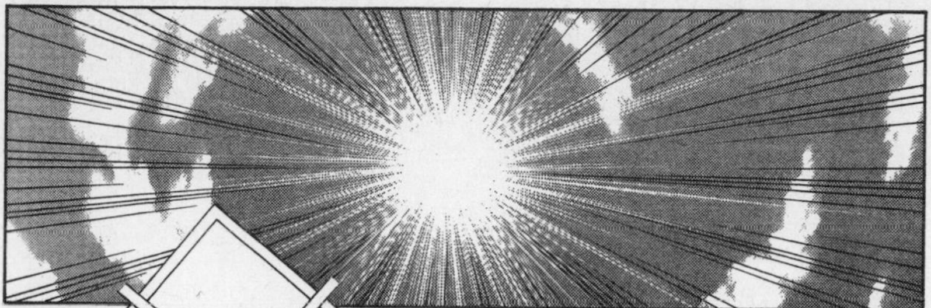

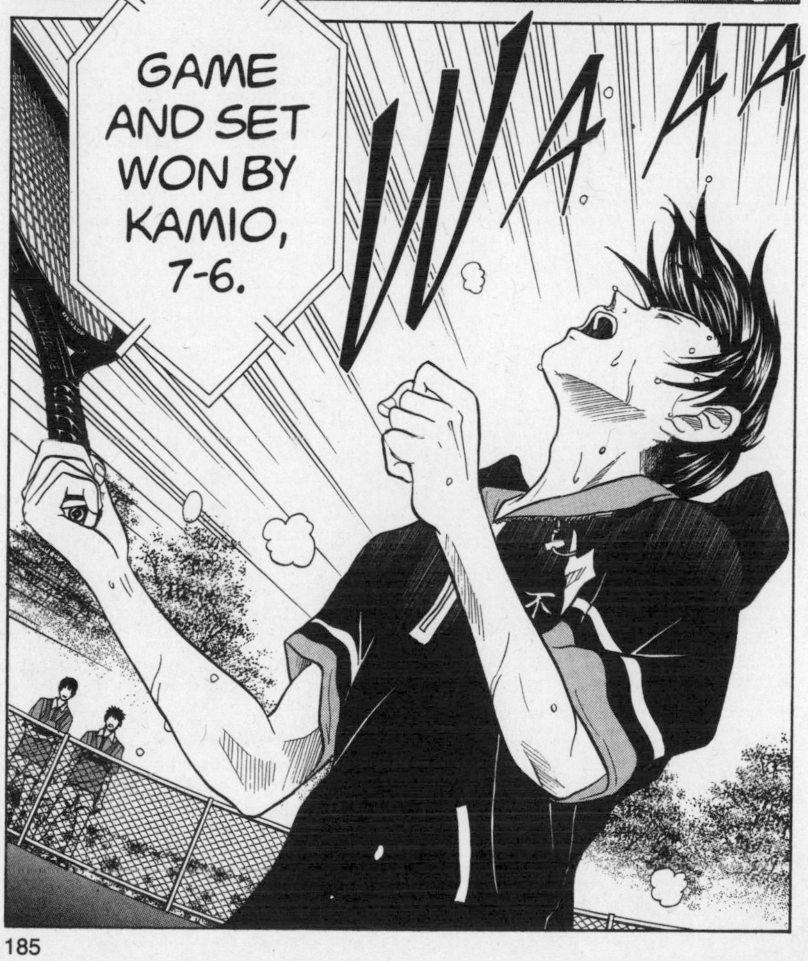
WAAA
GAME AND SET WON BY KAMIO, 7-6.

In the Next Volume...

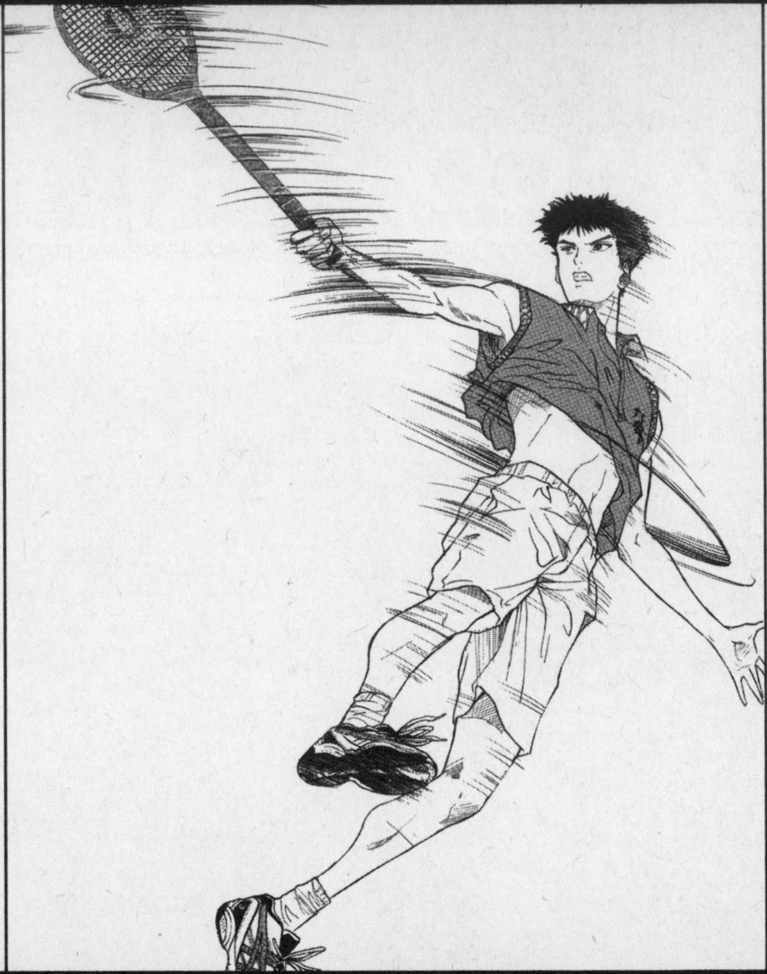

Seishun vs. Rokkaku

It's the Kanto Tournament semi-finals! And Shusuke's not playing his best—meaning the advantage may once again go to last year's winner, Rokkaku!

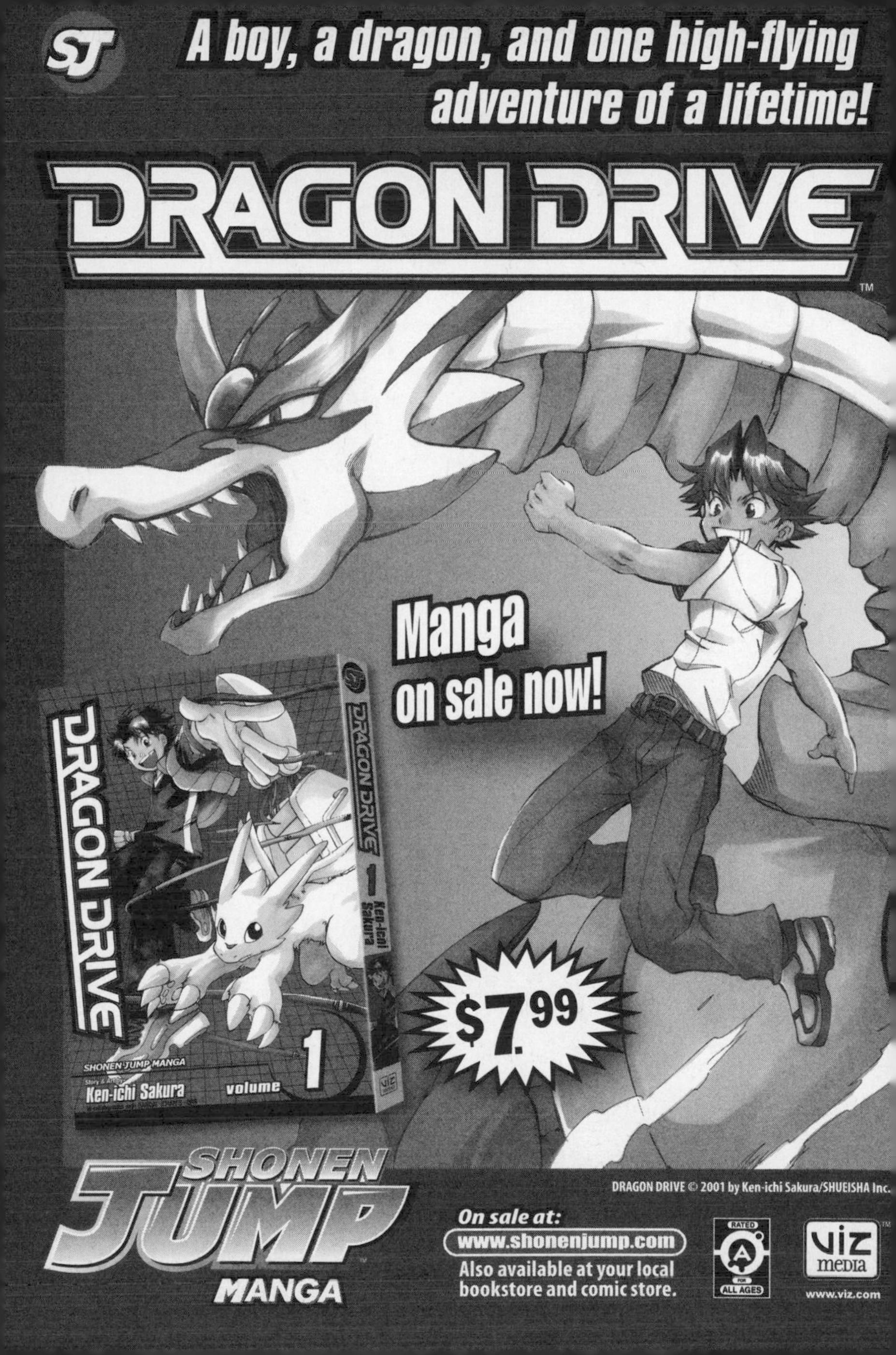
SJ
A boy, a dragon, and one high-flying adventure of a lifetime!
DRAGON DRIVE™
Manga on sale now!
DRAGON DRIVE
SHONEN JUMP MANGA
Ken-ichi Sakura
volume 1
DRAGON DRIVE 1 Ken-ichi Sakura
$7.99
SHONEN JUMP MANGA
DRAGON DRIVE © 2001 by Ken-ichi Sakura/SHUEISHA Inc.
On sale at:
www.shonenjump.com
Also available at your local bookstore and comic store.
RATED A FOR ALL AGES
VIZ MEDIA
www.viz.com

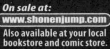

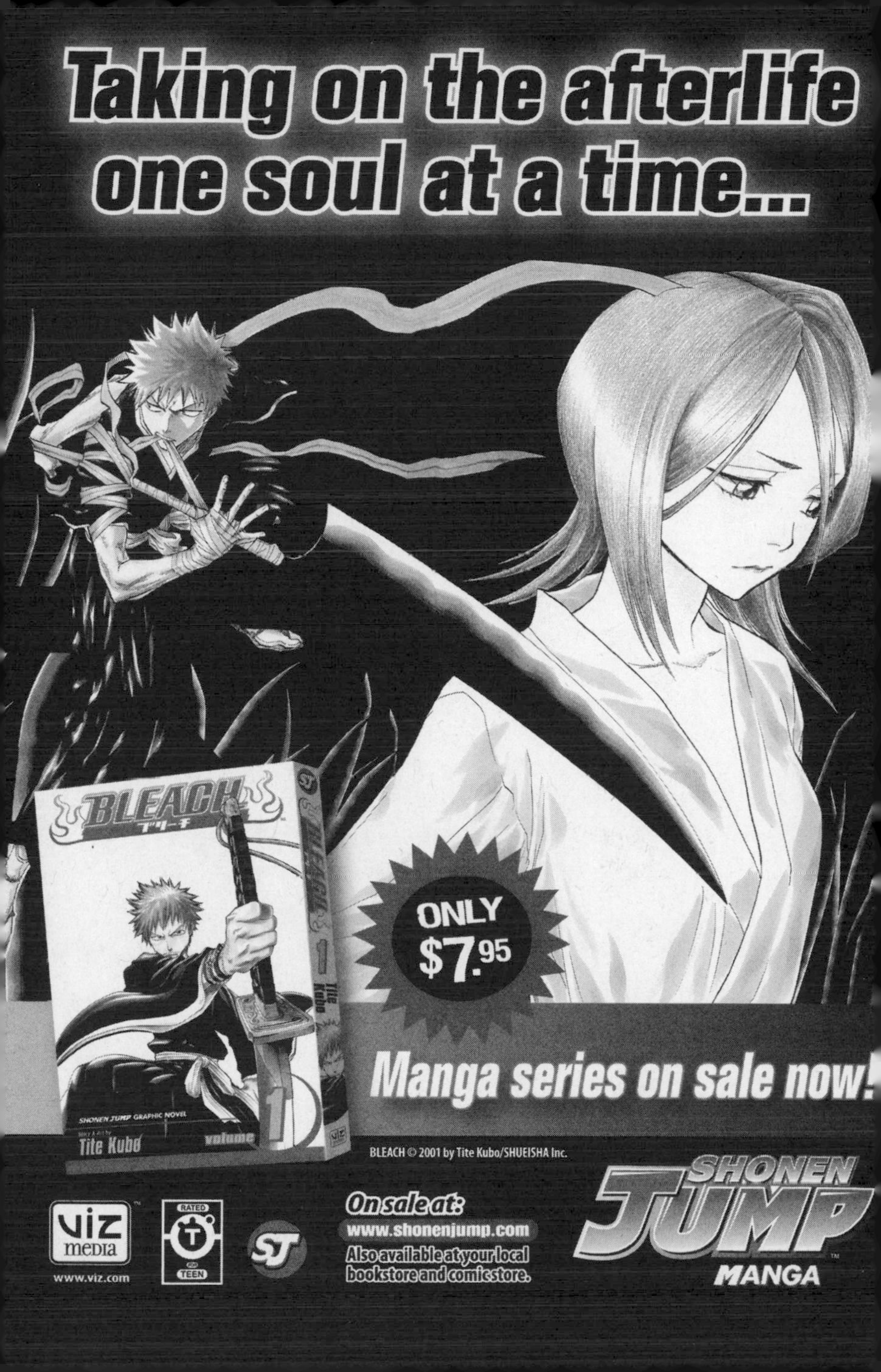

Taking on the afterlife one soul at a time...
BLEACH
ブリーチ
SHONEN JUMP GRAPHIC NOVEL
Story & Art by
Tite Kubo
volume 1
ONLY $7.95
Manga series on sale now!
BLEACH © 2001 by Tite Kubo/SHUEISHA Inc.
viz media
www.viz.com
RATED T FOR TEEN
SJ
On sale at:
www.shonenjump.com
Also available at your local bookstore and comic store.
SHONEN JUMP MANGA

Tell us what you think about SHONEN JUMP manga!

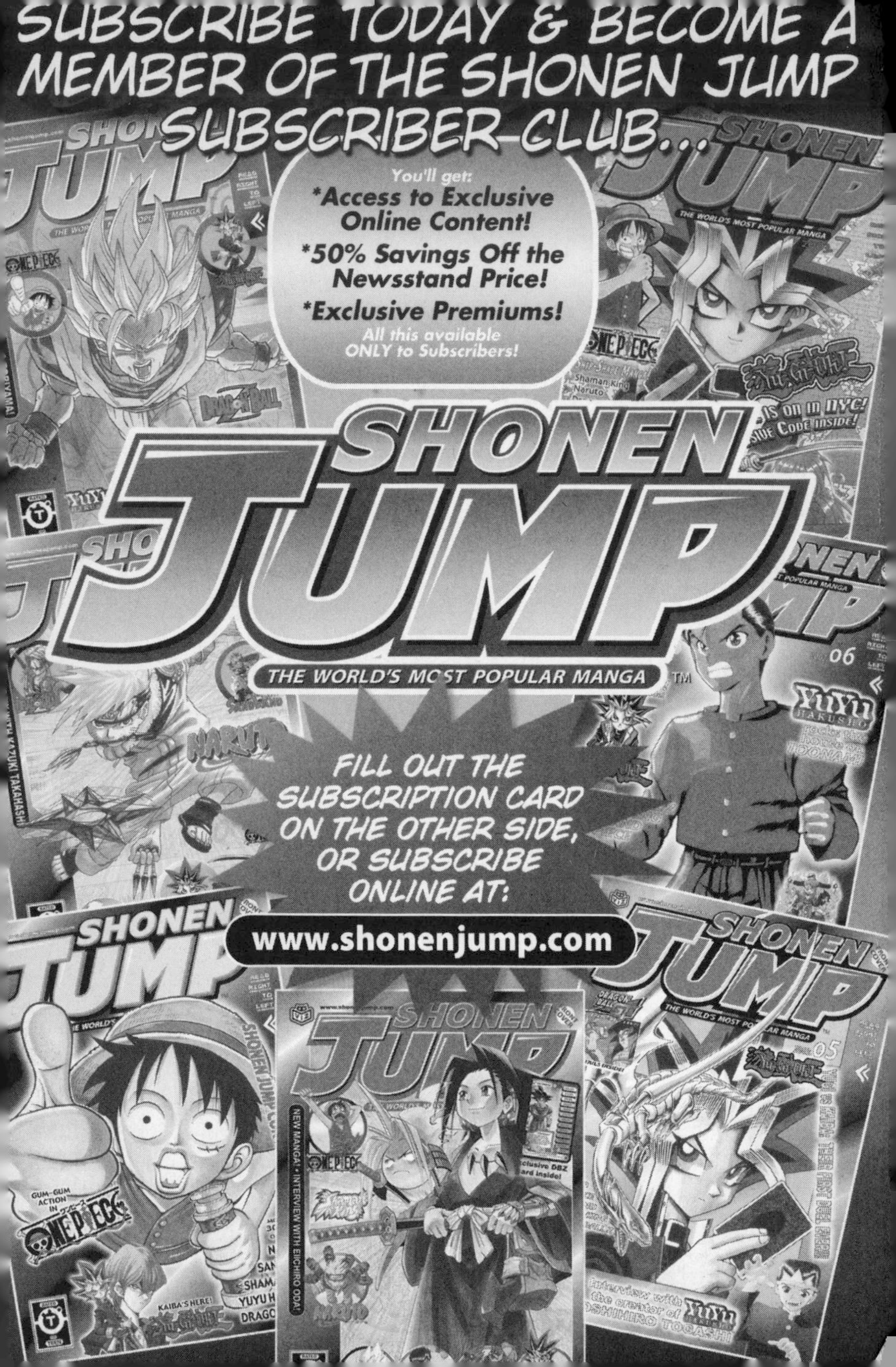
SUBSCRIBE TODAY & BECOME A MEMBER OF THE SHONEN JUMP SUBSCRIBER CLUB...
You'll get:
*Access to Exclusive Online Content!
*50% Savings Off the Newsstand Price!
*Exclusive Premiums!
All this available ONLY to Subscribers!
SHONEN JUMP
THE WORLD'S MOST POPULAR MANGA™
FILL OUT THE SUBSCRIPTION CARD ON THE OTHER SIDE, OR SUBSCRIBE ONLINE AT:
www.shonenjump.com